Children, Youth and Adults with Asperger Syndrome

Integrating Multiple Perspectives

Edited by Kevin P. Stoddart

Jessica Kingsley Publishers
London and Philadelphia

Diagnostic criteria for Asperger's Disorder (p.16) reprinted with permission from the Diagnostic and Statistical Manual of Mental Disorders, Fourth Edition, Text Revision, Copyright 2000. American Psychiatric Association.
Diagnostic criteria for Tourette Syndrome (p.74) reprinted with permission from the Diagnostic and Statistical Manual of Mental Disorders, Third Edition – Revised, Copyright 1987. American Psychiatric Association.

First published in 2005
by Jessica Kingsley Publishers
116 Pentonville Road
London N1 9JB, UK
and
400 Market Street, Suite 400
Philadelphia, PA 19106, USA

www.jkp.com

Copyright © Jessica Kingsley Publishers 2005
Reprinted twice in 2005

Library of Congress Cataloging in Publication Data
Children, youth and adults with Asperger Syndrome : integrating multiple perspectives / edited by Kevin P. Stoddart.— 1st American ed.
p. cm.
Includes bibliographical references and index.
ISBN 1-84310-268-4 (hardback) — ISBN 1-84310-319-2 (pbk.) 1. Asperger's syndrome. I. Stoddart, Kevin P., 1962-
RC553.A88C456 2005
616.85'88—dc22
2004021987

British Library Cataloguing in Publication Data
A CIP catalogue record for this book is available from the British Library

ISBN-13: 978 1 84310 319 6 (pbk)
ISBN-10: 1 84310 319 2 (pbk)

ISBN-13: 978 1 84310 268 7
ISBN-10: 1 84310 268 4

Printed and Bound in Great Britain by
Athenaeum Press, Gateshead, Tyne and Wear

Contents

Part II: Discipline-based Perspectives

Part III: Theoretical and Research Perspectives

Part IV: Parent and Personal Perspectives

List of figures and tables

Preface

In the decade since Asperger Syndrome (AS) was included in the *DSM-IV*, we have learned a great deal. We have gained more experience with this presentation of symptoms, and the resulting needs of children, adults, and their families. At the same time, we have discovered more about the diverse, rich, and varied ways in which the world is perceived. We have been reminded of how "difference" can put our fellow citizens at risk of marginalization, discrimination, and isolation, resulting in problems simply surviving from day to day. We again have seen the high price that society places on conformity and its discomfort with diversity.

Despite recent interest in this cluster of symptoms, AS characteristics are nothing new. Undoubtedly, there have been people who have been affected by similar traits throughout history. We have only recently come to identify them. It is often said that many of the features associated with AS easily meld into our perception of what are "normal" human traits.

In many ways, we are more comfortable in dealing with obvious differences. In such cases, we have a better idea of what we are dealing with, and are able to make accommodations or adaptations to the environment as necessary. For example, people with physical challenges may struggle less because accommodations related to entering and moving through public buildings are now legislated.

Unfortunately, the deceiving invisibility of AS has put those affected by this syndrome at a disadvantage. Not surprisingly, I hear from both those with AS and their family members that they would be better off if they were more severely affected by autism. Ironically, the subtlety of AS is also sometimes its curse. Societal response, or lack of it, to individuals with AS can be more disabling than the "disability" itself.

In an already overwhelmed social service and medical system, there is concern among care providers about whether they can accommodate the needs of the ever-growing group of individuals diagnosed with AS. Misdiagnosis of AS or inability to recognize traits of AS is common in the mental health, medical, and social services fields despite the valiant attempts of those affected by AS to advocate on their own behalf. In looking for services, people with AS commonly have doors closed to them. Many professionals and service providers, though experienced in child and adult mental health or developmental disabilities, feel clinically unprepared and fiscally unable to address the needs of individuals with AS.

There is therefore a great need for those of us who have had experience with AS, to share our practice knowledge. Specialists in AS have been flooded with requests for help in the past several years. In Canada, we have seen staggering increases in the recognition of AS.

As professionals, we recognize that we cannot effectively help affected children and adults without the support of colleagues in our discipline, and that we need the expertise of our colleagues in other disciplines. If ever there were a collection of symptoms that required multidisciplinary assessment and intervention, AS is it. It is hoped that this book continues the process of bringing together the interdisciplinary perspective and discourse needed to promote improved recognition and support of individuals with AS.

AS affects adults as well as children. I have worked with those who, in later life, have been diagnosed with AS. The lifelong angst that they report of "not fitting in", or feeling as if they were "an outsider" because they did not have a diagnosis, needs to be avoided in future generations at all costs. So, as far as possible, the contributors to this book have attempted to address issues relevant to adulthood, as well as those seen in childhood. We hope that future volumes will provide greater practice insights into the needs of adults at various life stages.

In the current environment emphasizing evidence-based practice, we are counselled to look to empirical research for proof of the efficacy of our interventions. This continues to be an important endeavour, especially in a field that has been plagued by "treatments" and theories that have not been empirically validated. However, we also need to be reminded of the value of narrative descriptions in informing our work. Fortunately, the autism and Asperger community has a well-established history of embracing the stories of affected children and adults and those of their parents. Adults with AS have articulated not only their experience of their condition, but of the services and treatments they have received. Their accounts provide strong voice to the experience of the broader social and cultural barriers facing people with an "invisible" disability.

For these reasons, the accounts of adults with AS and their parents are included in this book. The experiences identified in their stories echo in other chapters of the book. Peter Jansen, Fern Lee Quint, Donna Moon, Margot Nelles, and Chris Dakin are to be commended for articulating their views so honestly and poignantly. These are the true experts. It is our task to continue to incorporate their and others' personal perspectives into our practice.

One of the great benefits of editing a book such as this is having the privilege to work with such a distinguished group of colleagues. Many of the contributors to this work have worked in the field of autism spectrum disorders in Canada for decades. In their chapters, they offer their clinical, research, and theoretical insights to enable practitioners of all disciplines to meet the complex needs of this group better. Their contributions to the lives of people living with autism spectrum disorders and AS have been outstanding. Thank you for your enthusiastic support of this project.

Finally, I would like to express my gratitude to Jessica Kingsley, Lyndsey Martin, Ruth Ballantyne, and the staff at Jessica Kingsley Publishers. Your guidance and support in this process have made this a truly enjoyable undertaking. My appreciation also goes to Margot Nelles, Kathy Avrich-Johnson, Pam Prideaux, Paul Harbridge, Robert Bancroft, Cheryl Stoddart, and Charmaine Williams for their comments on the content of this book, reviews of portions of the manuscript, and their much-valued personal support.

Kevin P. Stoddart
Toronto, Canada

Introduction to Asperger Syndrome:
A developmental-lifespan perspective

Kevin P. Stoddart

He was reported to be a very difficult toddler, paying heed to neither his indulgent mother nor his strict father. He was said to be unable to cope with the ordinary demands of everyday life. The mother believed that it was because of his clumsiness and impracticality that he had more difficulties than other children. For instance, it was still necessary to dress him, since, by himself, he would dawdle endlessly and also make a lot of mistakes. He had learnt to eat by himself only recently and was still a messy eater… Before he entered school everyone was convinced that he would learn particularly well, since he was always making clever remarks and original observations. Moreover, he had by himself learned to count to twenty as well as picking up the names of various letters. At school however, he failed miserably. (Asperger 1944/1991, p.59)

This was Hans Asperger's description of Ernst, a 7½-year-old boy seen in his clinic in Vienna. In his 1944 paper, Asperger reported on Ernst and other children who suffered from "autistic psychopathy". His descriptions and analysis provide us with one of the first views of these children, their intriguing profile of skills, and puzzling deficits.

In terms of expressive characteristics, Asperger observed the abnormal eye gaze and "paucity of facial and gestural expression". Just as he noted the limiting relational aspects of a fleeting gaze, Asperger felt the language of these children also impaired their ability to communicate nuance and relate to others. He characterized their language as feeling "unnatural" and being spoken "as if into empty space". He termed the pragmatic deficits in communication, "contact-creating expressive functions".

In his discussion, Asperger detailed his observations of what he termed "autistic intelligence". This, he characterized as having a strength for original thought, yet an opposing difficulty in assimilating and learning "adult knowledge". An example was the use of language, in that they expressed their experiences in "linguistically original form", atypical of peers their age.

Asperger argued the "fundamental disorder of autistic individuals is the limitation of their social relationships". He felt that this problem was evident from the smallest social group, the family, to larger groups such as peers at school. Even within the family, the children were isolated. An observer of one of the children in Asperger's clinic poignantly noted: "He dwells among people as if a stranger." These children were "tormented and rejected by their classmates" as their language and behavioural oddities "cries out to be ridiculed".

Asperger saw stereotypic activity in these children such as movements or interaction with a toy. In contrast to their tenuous connections to peers, relations to objects were abnormally intense. Attachment to objects was so extreme that removal of the object often resulted in tantrums. Some of these interests or fixations would turn into chronic and maladaptive preoccupations, such as the boy with a serious eating problem who fixated on the specks of fat that were floating on the surface of his soup.

Recent descriptions of Asperger Syndrome

Interest in Asperger Syndrome (AS) grew throughout the 1980s, following Lorna Wing's discussion of children and adults seen during her epidemiological research of childhood psychosis in London and of children referred to her for diagnosis (Wing 1981). On most points, she agreed with the description of these children provided by Asperger in 1944. However, she added that the child may show specific signs of AS during the first year of life: "there is a lack of the intense urge to communicate in babble, gesture, movement, smiles, laughter and eventually speech that characterizes the normal baby and toddler" (Wing 1981, p.73). Wing observed that imaginative pretend play does not occur in some children, but that when it does, it is limited to a few themes, is enacted repetitively, and does not involve other children except when peers are willing to follow the routine prescribed by the child with AS.

Wing differed from Asperger on a few issues. In response to Asperger's suggestion that speech developed before walking in these children, Wing asserted that half of her cases walked at the usual age and were slow to talk, and the other half talked normally but were slow to walk. She pointed out that although the children's speech was impressive because of good grammatical skills and vocabulary, the content of speech was impoverished since much of it was learned by rote. Asperger felt that people with these traits could be capable and original in their field of work; Wing remarked that this showed their unique thought process and chain of reasoning, which resulted in new insights.

In Canada, Peter Szatmari and colleagues compared gender- and age-matched children and adolescents with traits of AS to children and youth who were "isolated and odd" (Szatmari, Bremner, and Nagy 1989). Following comparison of the clinical features of these groups, their criteria for the diagnosis of AS included: (1) solitariness; (2) impaired social interaction; (3) impaired nonverbal communication; (4) odd speech and (5) does not meet criteria for autistic disorder.

Uta Frith (1991) provided a translation of Asperger's original paper, which raised awareness of the syndrome in English-speaking countries. In the 1994 edition of the *Diagnostic and Statistical Manual* (*DSM-IV*: APA 1994) criteria for Asperger Disorder[1] were first included in the category of Pervasive Developmental Disorders (PDDs). The current text revision of the *DSM-IV* (APA 2000) criteria for AS is seen in Figure 1.1. According to these criteria, there are two characteristics used to distinguish autism and AS: (1) delayed language development in autism and not in AS, and (2) at least average/near-average intellectual abilities necessary in AS. Other PDDs include Autistic Disorder, Rett's Disorder, Childhood Disintegrative Disorder, and Pervasive Developmental Disorder – Not Otherwise Specified.

Although the formal inclusion of the diagnostic criteria of AS in the *DSM-IV* (APA 1994) gives the impression that consensus has been reached about the diagnostic criteria for AS, there remains considerable debate about the set of characteristics which define AS (Gillberg 1998; Frith 2004). Central to this deliberation is the question of whether AS is qualitatively different from high-functioning autism (HFA) (Mayes, Calhoun, and Crites 2001). In their review of studies published by 2002 comparing AS to HFA, Macintosh and Dissanayake (2004) suggest there is insufficient evidence to prove that AS is distinct from HFA. However, a meta-analysis of ten studies examining cognitive and adaptive behaviour reported significant differences in these groups (McLaughlin-Cheng 1998). Most researchers and clinicians do agree however, that AS is a part of the spectrum of autistic presentations, commonly known as autism spectrum disorders (ASDs).

In an attempt to further refine diagnostic criteria, and to differentiate HFA from AS, studies in the last decade have focussed on variables such as

---

1   Throughout this book, the more common term "Asperger Syndrome" (AS) will be
         used as opposed to "Asperger Disorder".

A. Qualitative impairment in social interaction, as manifested by at least two of the following:

   1. Marked impairment in the use of multiple nonverbal behaviours such as eye-to-eye gaze, facial expression, body postures, and gestures to regulate social interaction

   2. Failure to develop peer relationships appropriate to developmental level

   3. A lack of spontaneous seeking to share enjoyment, interests, or achievements with other people (e.g. by a lack of showing, bringing, or pointing out objects of interest to other people)

   4. Lack of social or emotional reciprocity

B. Restricted repetitive and stereotyped patterns of behaviour, interests, and activities, as manifested by at least one of the following:

   1. Encompassing preoccupation with one or more stereotyped and restricted patterns of interest that is abnormal either in intensity or focus

   2. Apparently inflexible adherence to specific, non-functional routines or rituals

   3. Stereotyped and repetitive motor mannerisms (e.g. hand or finger flapping or twisting, or complex whole body movements)

   4. Persistent preoccupation with parts of objects

C. The disturbance causes clinically significant impairment in social, occupational, or other important areas of functioning

D. There is no clinically significant general delay in language (e.g. single words used by age 2 years, communicative phrases used by age 3 years)

E. There is no clinically significant delay in cognitive development or in the development of age-appropriate self-help skills, adaptive behaviour (other than in social interaction), and curiosity about the environment in childhood

F. Criteria are not met for another specific Pervasive Developmental Disorder or Schizophrenia

Figure 1.1 DSM-IV-TR (2000) diagnostic criteria for 299.80 Asperger Disorder. Reprinted with permission from the Diagnostic and Statistical Manual of Mental Disorders, Fourth Edition, Text Revision, Copyright 2000, American Psychiatric Association.

clumsiness/motor performance (e.g. Ghaziuddin *et al.* 1994; Manjiviona and Prior 1995), neuropsychological traits (i.e. language development, motor skills, visual–spatial abilities, and executive function; e.g. Miller and Ozonoff 2000), and pedantic speaking style (e.g. Ghazuiddin and Gerstein 1996). Cluster analysis of groups of children with mild presentations of ASDs have been carried out to discover if they cluster according to characteristics based on current diagnostic groupings (e.g. Prior *et al.* 1998).

Although refining of the diagnosis of AS is required through continuing empirical study, clearly the emergence of the label has led to increasing use by clinicians and individuals affected by the disorder. Clinical practice has not waited for the extensive study that clarification of criteria involves. It will be important to continue to uncover the clinical value of differentiating AS from autism.

What is the prevalence of autism spectrum disorders? Is the incidence increasing?

These questions were the subject of epidemiological inquiry in the 1990s that continues to be of considerable debate (e.g. Wing and Potter 2002; Fombonne 2003; Tidmarsh and Volkmar 2003). Clinical experience suggests that a diagnosis of an ASD, including AS, is now more frequently given. Social service, medical, and educational systems involved with children and adults with ASDs are burdened beyond what could have been predicted a decade ago. Many influences have brought this issue to the forefront of autism research, such as the overwhelming increase of children with ASDs seeking services in parts of the United States (e.g. Croen *et al.* 2002).

For AS, the diagnosis is more commonly known, in part because of the inclusion of the diagnosis in the *DSM-IV* (APA 1994). AS and other mild ASDs are frequently discussed in the media (e.g. Harmon 2004; Vallis 2004) and in popular books (Haddon 2002). Diagnosticians are recognizing that the breadth of ASDs is much wider than once thought. Although practice experience provides a compelling case for the increasing incidence of ASDs, what does the epidemiological literature indicate?

Various methodological issues are relevant in studies of the epidemiology of ASDs. These include changes in diagnostic classification, diagnostic precision, differing types of screening, the size of the population screened, and the relative rarity of some of the ASDs. There has been improved case finding in recent studies (Fombonne 2003), which may prove deceptive. It is therefore premature to conclude that the incidence of autism and other ASDs has risen (Wing and Potter 2002; Fombonne 2003; Tidmarsh and Volkmar 2003).

An early screening of children for AS in Göteborg, Sweden between the ages of seven and 16, suggested a minimum prevalence rate for AS of 3.6 per 1000 and a male to female ratio of 4:1. When "suspected" and "possible" cases were included, the prevalence rose to 7.1 per 1000 children and the male to female ratio dropped to 2.3:1 (Ehlers and Gillberg 1993). Fombonne and Tidmarsh (2003) have noted several weaknesses in the methodology of this study, however.

Fombonne (2003) has reviewed 32 epidemiological surveys of PDDs published between 1966 and 2001. He suggests that for all PDDs, the prevalence rate is from 30 per 10,000 to 60 per 10,000 and that a conservative rate for AS is 2.5 per 10,000. This figure, based on rates of AS identified in six recent studies of all ASDs, must be interpreted with caution. Fombonne (2003) estimates the rate of AS is one-quarter that of autism.

Aetiology

The search for cause(s) of AS is intimately linked to the search for cause(s) of other ASDs. A central theory at this time is genetic. Evidence suggests the genetics of ASDs is complex, with at least several genes acting in unison (IMGSAC 1998; 2001). Traits of AS are often recognized in family members either by the individuals themselves or by clinicians. A genetic aetiology does not preclude the potential role of biological/environmental variables. However, recent concern over the use of the MMR vaccine contributing to autism has not found empirical evidence (Taylor *et al.* 1999; Fombonne and Cook 2003).

Although there has been no conclusive aetiological evidence to distinguish individuals with AS from others on the spectrum (Szatmari 2003), there have been observations that have suggested the cause of AS specifically. For example, Ellis and Gunter (1999) have proposed that AS is reflective of a right-hemisphere dysfunction.

A developmental-lifespan perspective

In the introduction to his seminal discussion of these children, Asperger (1944/1991) noted that they presented "a common fundamental disturbance which manifests itself in their physical appearance, expressive functions and, indeed, their whole behaviour" (p.37). The first feature that he noted was that the "autistic personality" demonstrated "persistence over time":

> From the second year of life we find already the characteristic features that remain unmistakable and constant throughout the whole life-span... In early childhood there are the difficulties in learning simple practical skills and in social adaptation. These difficulties arise out of the same disturbance which at

school age cause learning and conduct problems, in adolescence job and performance problems, and in adulthood, social and marital conflicts. (pp.67–8)

A *lifespan perspective* has been considered in the study of autism (e.g. Marcus, Kunce, and Schopler 1997) and in the literature on AS (Bauer 1996; Stoddart 2003). Typically, in these discussions, greater attention is given to the issues in childhood and early adulthood, with little information on middle and late adulthood.

In a *developmental paradigm*, the task of meeting individual or family developmental milestones is seen as intrinsic to preparing successfully for future developmental tasks and navigating through the next life stage. Family therapists have long recognized that developmental transitions for individuals and their families are stressful for any family. Such stress increases when families and individuals are "stuck" and unable to proceed to the next stage (Haley 1973; McGoldrick and Carter 1982). Although a developmental perspective can also be considered for the family (i.e. family stages: McGoldrick and Carter 1982), individual developmental issues are the focus here. It is evident, though, that the developmental tasks of family members are closely connected to the progression of a family as a whole through developmental stages (McGoldrick and Carter 1982).

A common occurrence in clinical practice is that many children or adults diagnosed with AS are identified in response to a developmental crisis. They are not able to fulfill the social or developmental expectations of various life stages because of a lack of internal or external resources and because of specific challenges related to the syndrome. A frequent cause of distress for individuals with AS is their realization that they are lagging developmentally behind their peers in key transitional tasks. For example, the adolescent with AS is often aware that she is behind her peers in developing intimate relationships. Difficulty in accomplishing this task is a continuing source of distress for many young adults. Parents are also keenly aware of this. It is helpful to consider individual characteristics in the context of broader social and developmental tasks and obstacles that are encountered across the lifespan, since the characteristic skills and deficits of AS are reflected in this context.

Infancy and early childhood (0–four years)

In a survey of parents of children with AS, most frequently parents reported that they first had concerns about language development, social development and play, and general behaviour problems (e.g. toileting, eating, and tantrums) (Howlin and Asgharian 1999). Often, young children will exhibit unusual language development. Parents may report that much of their child's language is related to his particular interests. Children with AS may learn and use language in rote ways, such as continually repeating a movie dialogue verbatim. If there is interaction with other children, it may be parallel in nature and play may involve the child with AS directing the other child in his own interests. Even at this age, toddlers may engage in repetitive types of play or demonstrate limited imaginative play. Problems with changes and transitions may be seen. Sensory sensitivities may be observed as well, but not realized as such; for example, when a child refuses to wear certain clothing, responds unusually to a sound or touch, or interacts in unusual sensory ways with objects in the environment. All of these developmental issues can lead to behavioural difficulties. Without diagnosis, they may be mistakenly understood as related to other antecedents such as inadequate parenting.

Early identification of children with AS needs much more attention. Often, recommendations by professional and policy groups (Filipek *et al.* 2000; NIASA 2003) include recommendations for early detection and intervention of ASDs, but the issues may be different for children at the mild end of the spectrum. Howlin and Asgharian (1999) reported that a diagnosis of AS is rarely given to children below five years of age. Barriers to diagnosis identified in the UK include "failure to recognise symptoms; denial of problem; failure to get a referral; waiting time for appointment; inadequately trained staff for diagnosis; and separate waiting lists for each professional group" (NIASA 2003, p.25). As well as these causes, concerns about labelling or inappropriate diagnosis can be problematic (Filipek *et al.* 2000). The mild presentation of autistic symptoms may delay the diagnosis of AS (Howlin and Asgharian 1999; NIASA 2003) since the diagnostician may be unfamiliar with the entire range of functioning in this spectrum of disorders and characteristics of AS may be less obvious in early years (Wing 1981). Unfortunately, well-meaning physicians sometimes tell parents the child will grow out of their difficulties (Szatmari 1995; Howlin and Asgharian 1999). Delayed early identification leads to delays in interventions; early intervention is recognized by most as essential in remediation of the ASDs (Szatmari 1995; Bryson, Rogers, and Fombonne 2003).

Screening tests for ASDs in toddlers have been developed, but children with AS may not always be identified with these tools. Further development of screening tools for children with mild presentations of ASDs is therefore needed (Filipek *et al.* 2000). One such tool is under development for children between the ages of four and 11 years (Childhood Asperger Syndrome Test: Scott *et al.* 2002).

It is helpful to ensure that a preschooler suspected of or identified as having AS is involved with normally developing peers. This may involve participation in a preschool program with help from a developmental specialist. Participation in a playgroup can begin early to teach co-operative play and pragmatic language skills in a supportive setting. Other services such speech-language assessment can begin as early as the preschool years. At this early stage, it is critical that parents begin to understand the implications of the diagnosis in term of behaviour, management, and planning.

Childhood (five–11 years)

Although increasing numbers of children are being recognized as having AS in early childhood, many are still overlooked until they reach elementary school (NIASA 2003). In fact, a group of children with AS received a diagnosis of AS at an average age of 11 years, even though their parents began to have concerns about their children as early as 30 months of age (Howlin and Asgharian 1999). Before entering school, they may have been perceived as "shy", "loners", or "little professors", and family members may have seen that they had unusual interests and engaged in activities atypically. Good language skills may lead caregivers to believe the child is precocious.

At this developmental stage, the child with AS may begin struggling with the social demands of the school milieu. She may demonstrate a lack of awareness of the norms in the classroom, and may be easily overwhelmed by stimuli such as those occurring at transitional periods at school – times before and after school, lunchtime, and recess. In the environment of the classroom, play may be seen as restricted, or rote, compared to other children. Co-operative play and interaction may be difficult. Of the undiagnosed child, educational personnel may voice suspicions of "mild autism".

Comorbid symptoms may be observed during this developmental period. A subgroup of children with AS present with heightened anxiety, for example. In the author's practice, some children at a young age have shown extreme fear of getting sick, being alone in parts of the house, and falling victim to terrorist attacks. Usually, anxieties and resulting behaviour difficulties can be effectively treated with behaviour management approaches and direct child intervention; in some cases, however, these concerns may have to be addressed with medication (Towbin 2003).

The focus of assessment and intervention at this time in the child's life is often related to the child's performance in the educational setting and may best include naturalistic observation in the classroom, as well as child assessment and interviews with parents. Finding a suitable school and classroom for the school-aged child with AS is sometimes difficult for parents, especially as their children reach the second or third grades. The child with AS needs to be identified as an exceptional student and teachers may have to familiarize themselves with how this exceptionality is reflected in the student's education plan. Children with AS have been described as "perfect targets" for bullying

(Heinrichs 2003), a problem that needs careful monitoring by parents and school personnel.

Adolescence (12–18 years)

One of the major developmental tasks of adolescence is individuation. Establishing close ties with peers, identifying with adolescent culture, and relying less on parental direction and nurturing is integral to this process (McGoldrick and Carter 1982). While the majority of adolescents have interests that are largely dictated by their peers, the adolescent with AS may have unusual preoccupations. Adolescents with AS may have gravitated to interests that are solitary in nature, thus perpetuating their social isolation. The tendency for the adolescent with AS to display mental health problems, such as depression, may be aggravated by the adolescent's awareness that he is different from his peers.

Individuals with AS often receive their first diagnosis in adolescence. In fact, they may self-identify (Stoddart 1999). Fortunately, entire books have been published to address the issues of adolescence (e.g. Bolick 2001; Myles and Adreon 2001). By the teenage years the main characteristics of AS, such as a restricted range of interests and poor social skills, have been clearly seen, but may not be recognized as symptomatic of an ASD. The adolescent's uneven skill profile can be puzzling to parents or clinicians. Differential diagnosis of adolescents may present as a "diagnostic dilemma" to clinicians (Fitzgerald 1999).

It is known that AS and other ASDs coexist with other disorders (Gillberg and Billstedt 2000). Adolescents who are referred for the assessment of possible AS may have previously received diagnoses including Attention Deficit Disorder (ADD), Tourette Syndrome, anxiety, depression, or Nonverbal Learning Disability (NVLD). Proper identification of comorbid conditions can be helpful.

Unfortunately, the social and academic demands of school can mean great difficulties for the adolescent with AS. Here, they face an increasing academic workload, greater organizational demands, and the stress of unstructured social and transition times (e.g. between classes). The pressure of these demands may be experienced as overwhelming without the mediating influence of adequate supports and understanding. School pressures often precipitate depression and anxiety.

With medication to address mental health or behavioural symptoms, individual counselling can be helpful for the adolescent as it gives him the opportunity to discuss their diagnosis and social experiences (Stoddart 1998, 1999). Although parents may fear having to tell their child the diagnosis of AS, such knowledge sometimes comes as a relief to the adolescent. Understandably, deciding when and how to tell children about their diagnosis is a difficult decision and parents may need to seek professional support. Family intervention is also useful during this developmental transition. Social skills groups can teach these adolescents how to interact appropriately with their peers but, more significantly, such groups give them an opportunity to meet others who are similarly affected.

Early adulthood (19–30 years)

Young adults face decisions about employment, involvement in post-secondary education, and independent living arrangements. The emotional and developmental tasks of the developmentally typical "unattached young adult" include the "differentiation of self in relation to family of origin", "development of intimate peer relationships", and the "development of self in work" (McGoldrick and Carter 1982, p.176).

Parents, and often the young adult with AS, pursue an assessment in response to the realization that the young adult is not prepared for the tasks of this developmental period. His problems may increase as he tries to adapt to adult life without the necessary understanding, accommodations, or supports. While their peers are leaving home, dating, going to college or university, or finding gainful employment, some young adults with AS describe a feeling that they have "been left behind", and a grief-like response may be experienced. Their struggle with mental health problems, social isolation, and lack of functional life skills may further motivate them or their families to search for the origins of these difficulties.

Unfortunately, the ramifications of not having a diagnosis until early adulthood can be profound. A recent study in the UK suggested that mental health problems are more common in those young adults with ASDs who have gone without a diagnosis until after the age of 30 (Barnard et al. 2001). The author's clinical experience suggests that mental health problems (particularly depression and anxiety), low self-esteem, addictions, and related psychosocial problems can take firm root in situations where an instructive diagnostic opinion is absent.

With the increased information available to the public on AS in adulthood, many young adults with AS find out about the symptoms through the Internet or the media. Since AS is typically first detected in childhood, diagnostic criteria and assessment approaches that have emerged are based on the presentation of AS in children rather than adults. Clinicians may therefore not recognize symptoms of AS in adults. Diagnostic screening tools for adults with AS are in the development stage (e.g. Stoddart and Burke 2002). Service providers in the developmental or mental health systems may not feel as confident in giving a diagnosis of AS when they do recognize that it may be present. Some adults with AS and other

ASDs may be initially misdiagnosed with other psychiatric or developmental disorders (Perlman 2000; Stoddart, Burke, and Temple 2002).

Most young adults are faced with the choice between either finding employment or entering post-secondary education. Such a decision may be difficult for the young adult and parents express concern about their children's ability to be successful in either of these settings. Most often supports are needed in college and university, at least at the onset of these academic pursuits. For those young adults with some employment experience the transition to full-time employment is often less problematic. In other situations, employment services may need to aid the young adult with AS to find and keep a job. Regular involvement in structured activities is critical for the continued development of life skills and self-esteem, and as a possible deterrent to worsening mental health problems.

An added problem for young adults with AS, once they have been diagnosed, is finding treatment and supports. Unfortunately, services for children often end at the age of 18 and there is little assistance transitioning to the adult services sector. The lack of transitional assistance is especially problematic given that young adults with AS often have great difficulty making the shift to an independent adult lifestyle. Another pressing concern is the gap often found between mental health and developmental services. Policy-makers and administrators are faced with a unique developmental delay in that it is not associated with severe cognitive delays. Often, supports that are associated with other developmental delays or mental health problems are not suitable. Parents and other advocates for this group have much to do in ensuring the creation and maintenance of supports for this group. Fortunately, this work has already begun in some parts of the world (Powell 2002).

Middle adulthood (31–50 years)

The developmental tasks of the mid-adulthood stage of life are usually thought to be increasing independence from the family of origin, mating, and procreation. Many individuals with AS have difficulty moving to these tasks given their core social deficits. Adults who have succeeded in keeping employment may be found in vocations that rely on a circumscribed area of knowledge. An adult who receives a diagnosis at this stage in life is, most often, relieved finally to have an explanation for his puzzling characteristics. Such information is helpful to family members or spouses in understanding their relative's behaviours or poor abilities to function in relationships.

Some adults with AS, whether diagnosed or not, do find a mate. Fortunately, we are finding out more about the experience of partnership with a spouse with AS (Attwood 2000; National Autistic Society 2004). In the author's clinical practice, it is common to see divorcing and separating couples in which a partner has AS or traits of AS. Many of the relationships may have been supported by a clinician who was aware of their traits related to AS. Family and marital therapists are beginning to see adults with ASDs in their practices and a literature is evolving that describes the experience of having intimate relationships with somebody with AS, and the possible professional tasks for facilitating such relationships (Slater-Walker and Slater-Walker 2002; Aston 2003; McCabe, McCabe and McCabe 2002).

At times, parents, and most often fathers, recognize AS symptoms in themselves after their child has been diagnosed with an ASD such as autism or AS (e.g. Willey 1999; Spicer 2004). It has been stated by one father with autism that parenting is "an intensely social activity" (Spicer 2004, p.46); therefore, the parenting process may be more difficult for those with an ASD. In these instances, careful determination of the support needs of partners of those with AS is warranted, as they learn to understand the similar and dissimilar needs of their partner with AS and their child with AS. Future research and practice literature needs to address the complexities of parenting with an ASD. Clearly, many parents with AS have great empathy for their child with AS (Willey 1999).

Late adulthood (51 years and over)

Clearly, the social, psychiatric, and medical needs of ageing adults with developmental disabilities requires greater attention, as increasing numbers of individuals with developmental disabilities are reaching older ages (Holland 2000; WHO 2000). The specific disability of mild autism and AS experienced by older people has received little attention (Gold and Whelan 1992).

Case examples of older people with AS or autistic features have been reported, often in the context of family studies (e.g. Gillberg 1991; Ritvo et al. 1994). Ritvo and colleagues (1994) reported on a series of 14 parents of patients with ASDs that they saw in their clinic. The clinicians suspected that these parents had mild traits of autism; their suspicions were based on observations made by the spouses of these parents during the assessment of their children. Ten of the 14 parents had more than one child with autism. The parents were subsequently assessed and found to meet diagnostic criteria for autism. At the year of publication, their ages ranged from 37 to 77 years, with six of the 14 being over 50 years.

It is possible that some of those in the ageing population who have exhibited lifelong problems in social functioning, experienced mental health problems, or displayed a restricted range of interests have AS that has gone unrecognized. As is the case for children with AS, older adults may have been diagnosed with comorbid psychiatric disorders, such as anxiety or depression, which serve as an explanation, though incomplete, for their difficulties. An older man described by Burke and Stoddart (submitted) spent many decades unsuccessfully participating in community psychiatric programs until his eventual diagnosis at 63 years of age. Clinical practice in Canada suggests that increasingly, ageing individuals with suspected AS are coming to the attention of clinicians, often through self-recognition of the symptoms of AS, by spouses, or by other family members.

One group of older individuals with AS may be parents, aunts, uncles, or grandparents of individuals who have been diagnosed with an ASD. They are sometimes recognized as "loners", "eccentric", or "socially odd" by family members, yet there is no explanation for these characteristics until their relative's diagnosis. Realization that an older family member may have traits of AS can lead to a better understanding of the individual's behaviour or what was previously thought to be their "personality".

Many questions remain about the social, psychiatric, and relationship history of ageing adults with AS. It is important to discover the negative effect of diagnosis that only comes late in life. A late diagnosis based on clinical experience has brought relief to many who have struggled with their rigid ways, restricted interests, social deficits, and mental health issues (Burke and Stoddart 2004). Sometimes, we have seen that the emotional costs of going a lifetime without an explanation for these traits has been devastating. Many ageing individuals with AS may have had no long-term relationships nor ever been married; when they have, the relationship with their partner may have been conflictual or of a caretaking nature. Bolte and Bosch (2004) describe the outcome of a 69-year-old man who had been first assessed when he was 22 years old. Although he displayed a good outcome, his wife characterized the marriage as "not having taken place, and that she just overtook a mother role" (p.12). Retirement is also an issue for these individuals. With retirement often come less structure and more social isolation. Many older people with AS have relied on the structure and routine of their work life. With few interests and friends, retirement may be an unwelcome life stage for ageing individuals with AS.

With ageing comes the requirement to access health services, which the older adult with AS may not be able or willing to do. We currently know little about the health needs of older adults with ASDs (Gold and Whelan 1992) and this is in need of research. Exploration of specific later-life needs of adults with AS and ASDs has begun, including their health needs and problems with social isolation (Lennox 2002). We have little understanding of the life expectancy of individuals with AS. Currently there is no indication that it may be shorter than average. However, it is vital to consider the possible effects of co-existing medical conditions, poor medical attention, inadequate diet, infrequent exercise, and social isolation. It is known that Fragile X can contribute to some ASDs, though a small proportion. Among the ageing population with Fragile X, mitral valve prolapse, musculoskeletal disorders, early menopause, epilepsy and vision problems are common (WHO 2000).

Much needs to be accomplished to meet the service needs of ageing adults with AS. Day programs and residential services for the elderly have shown some interest in accommodating persons with developmental disabilities, but acknowledge that they need training and community resources to serve this group appropriately (Sparks *et al.* 2000; WHO 2000). The collaboration of service providers from various service sectors will be essential if the needs of this under-recognized group are to be met.

Future considerations

Unquestionably, we have made great strides in recognizing AS and in establishing suitable supports and treatment in the past decade. While much of our attention has been focussed on refining diagnostic criteria, establishing assessment protocols, and providing professional and public education, the major task of the next decade will be to develop a greater breadth of services for individuals with AS across the lifespan. Comprehensive service models and practice guidelines from the preschool years (Filipek *et al.* 2000; NIASA 2003) to adulthood (Powell 2002) require further refinement. Considering the widespread use of the label "Asperger Syndrome", despite controversy about its external validity, practice parameters need to be articulated that are specific to this group.

The recognition that AS displays "persistence over time" (Asperger 1944/1991) will, we hope, lead to greater acknowledgement of a developmental-lifespan approach. This will enable greater understanding of the challenges of AS at transitional periods, and greater recognition of symptoms of AS at all ages, including wider discourse about the commonalities and differences between specific developmental periods. This progress will require the collaborative efforts of clinicians, parents, researchers, individuals with AS, administrators, and all levels of government. Although daunting, this task is essential in ensuring societal acceptance, protection of the rights of individuals with AS, and the provision of opportunities to be the valued contributors that they can be to their local and global communities.

References

APA (American Psychiatric Association) (1994) *Diagnostic and Statistical Manual of Mental Disorders, Fourth Edition.* Washington, DC: APA.

APA (American Psychiatric Association) (2000) *Diagnostic and Statistical Manual of Mental Disorders, Fourth Edition, Text Revision.* Washington, DC: APA.

Asperger, H. (1944/1991) "Autistic psychopathy" in childhood. In U. Frith (ed.) *Autism and Asperger Syndrome.* Cambridge, UK: Cambridge University Press.

Aston, M.C. (2003) *Aspergers in Love: Couple Relationships and Family Affairs.* London, UK: Jessica Kingsley Publishers.

Attwood, T. (2000) Workshop for partners of people with Asperger's syndrome. Retrieved from the World Wide Web: www.nas.org.uk/

Barnard, J., Harvey, V., Potter, D., and Prior, A. (2001) *Ignored or Ineligible: The Reality for Adults with Autism Spectrum Disorders.* London, UK: The National Autistic Society.

Bauer, S. (1996) Asperger syndrome. Retrieved April 11 2004 from the World Wide Web: www.udel.edu/bkirby/asperger/as_thru_yers.html.

Bolick, T. (2001) *Asperger Syndrome and Adolescence: Helping Preteens and Teens Get Ready for the Real World.* Gloucester, MA: Fair Winds Press.

Bolte, S., and Bosch, G. (2004) Bosch's cases: A 40 years follow-up of patients with infantile autism and Asperger Syndrome. *The German Journal of Psychiatry, 7,* 10–13.

Bryson, S., Rogers, S.J., and Fombonne, E. (2003) Autism spectrum disorders: Early detection, intervention, education, and psychopharmacological management. *Canadian Journal of Psychiatry, 48,* 8, 506–16.

Burke, L., and Stoddart, K.P. (submitted) The older adult with an autism spectrum disorder. Submitted to *Canadian Journal on Aging.*

Croen, L.A., Grether, J.K., Hoogstrate, J., and Selvin, S. (2002) The changing prevalence of autism in California. *Journal of Autism and Developmental Disorders, 32,* 3, 207.

Ehlers, S., and Gillberg, C. (1993) The epidemiology of Asperger syndrome: A total population study. *Journal of Child Psychology and Psychiatry, 34,* 8, 1327–50.

Ellis, H.D., and Gunter, H.G. (1999) Asperger syndrome: A simple matter of white matter? *Trends in Cognitive Sciences, 3,* 5, 192–200.

Filipek, P.A., Accardo, P.J. Ashwal, S., Baranek, G.T., Cook, Jr E.H., Dawson, G., *et al.* (2000) Practice Parameter: Screening and Diagnosis of Autism. *Neurology, 55,* 468–79.

Fitzgerald, M. (1999) Differential diagnosis of adolescent and adult pervasive developmental disorders/autism spectrum disorders (PDD/ASD): A not uncommon diagnostic dilemma. *Irish Journal of Psychological Medicine, 16,* 4, 145–8.

Fombonne, E. (2003) Epidemiological surveys of autism and other pervasive developmental disorders. *Journal of Autism and Developmental Disorders, 33,* 4, 365–82.

Fombonne, E., and Cook, E. (2003) MMR and autism: Consistent epidemiological failure to support the putative association. *Molecular Psychiatry, 8,* 133–4.

Fombonne, E., and Tidmarsh, L. (2003) Epidemiologic data on Asperger disorder. *Child and Adolescent Psychiatric Clinics of North America, 12,* 15–21.

Frith, U. (ed.) (1991) *Autism and Asperger Syndrome.* Cambridge, UK: Cambridge University Press.

Frith, U. (2004) Emanuel Miller lecture: Confusions and controversies about Asperger Syndrome. *Journal of Child Psychology and Psychiatry, 45,* 4, 672–86.

Ghaziuddin, M., Butler, E., Tsai, L., and Ghaziuddin, N. (1994) Is clumsiness a marker for Asperger syndrome? *Journal of Intellectual Disability Research, 38,* 519–27.

Ghaziuddin, M., and Gerstein, L. (1996) Pedantic speaking style differentiates Asperger syndrome from high-functioning autism. *Journal of Autism and Developmental Disorders, 26,* 6, 585–95.

Gillberg, C. (1991) Clinical and neurobiological aspects of Asperger syndrome in six family studies. In U. Frith (ed.) *Autism and Asperger Syndrome.* Cambridge, UK: Cambridge University Press.

Gillberg, C. (1998) Asperger syndrome and high-functioning autism. *The British Journal of Psychiatry, 172,* 3, 200–209.

Gillberg, C., and Billstedt, E. (2000) Autism and Asperger syndrome: Co-existence with other clinical disorders. *Acta Psychiatrica Scandinavica, 102,* 321–30.

Gold, N., and Whelan, M. (1992) Elderly people with autism: Defining a social work agenda for research and practice. In F.J. Turner (ed.) *Mental Health and the Elderly: A Social Work Perspective.* New York, NY: The Free Press.

Haddon, M. (2002) *The Curious Incident of the Dog in the Night-time.* Toronto, ON: Doubleday Canada.

Haley, J. (1973) *Uncommon Therapy: The Psychiatric Techniques of Milton J. Erickson.* New York, NY: Norton.

Harmon, A. (2004) Neurodiversity forever: The disability movement turns to brains. *The New York Times,* 9 May, 1 and 7.

Heinrichs, R. (2003) *Perfect Targets: Asperger Syndrome and Bullying.* Shawnee Mission, KS: Autism Asperger Publishing.

Holland, A.J. (2000) Ageing and learning disability. *British Journal of Psychiatry, 176,* 26–31.

Howlin, P., and Asgharian, A. (1999) The diagnosis of autism and Asperger syndrome: Findings from a survey of 770 families. *Developmental Medicine and Child Neurology, 41,* 834–9.

IMGSAC (International Molecular Genetics Study of Autism Consortium) (1998) A full genome screen for autism with evidence for linkage to a region on chromosome 7q. *Human Molecular Genetics, 7,* 571–8.

IMGSAC (International Molecular Genetics Study of Autism Consortium) (2001) A genome wide screen for autism: Strong evidence for linkage to chromosomes 2q, 7q, and 16p. *American Journal of Human Genetics, 69,* 570–81.

Lennox, N. (2002) Health promotion and disease prevention. In V.E. Prasher and M.P. Janicki (eds) *Physical Health of Adults with Intellectual Disabilities.* Oxford, UK: Blackwell Publishing.

Macintosh, K.E., and Dissanayake, C. (2004) Annotation: The similarities and differences between autistic disorder and Asperger's disorder: A review of the empirical evidence. *Journal of Child Psychology and Psychiatry, 45,* 3, 421–34.

Manjiviona, J., and Prior, M. (1995) Comparison of Asperger syndrome and high-functioning autistic children on a test of motor impairment. *Journal of Autism and Developmental Disorders, 25,* 23–39.

Marcus, L.M., Kunce, L.J., and Schopler, E. (1997) Working with families. In D.J. Cohen and F.R. Volkmar (eds) *Handbook of Autism and Pervasive Developmental Disorders.* New York, NY: John Wiley and Sons.

Mayes, S.D., Calhoun, S.L., and Crites, D.L. (2001) Does DSM IV Asperger's exist? *Journal of Abnormal Child Psychology, 29,* 263–71.

McCabe, P., McCabe, E., and McCabe, J. (2002) *Living and Loving with Asperger Syndrome.* London, UK: Jessica Kingsley Publishers.

McGoldrick, M., and Carter, E.A. (1982) The family life cycle. *Normal Family Processes.* New York, NY: Guilford Press.

McLaughlin-Cheng, E. (1998) Asperger syndrome and autism: A literature review and meta-analysis. *Focus on Autism and Other Developmental Disorders, 13,* 4, 234–45.

Miller, J.N., and Ozonoff, S. (2000) The external validity of Asperger disorder: Lack of evidence from the domain of neuropsychology. *Journal of Abnormal Psychology, 109,* 2, 227–38.

Myles, B.S, and Adreon, D. (2001) *Asperger Syndrome and Adolescence: Practical Solutions for School Success.* Shawnee Mission, KS: Autism Asperger Publishing Company.

National Autistic Society (2004) Issues for partners of people with Asperger syndrome. NAS. Retrieved June 8 2004 from the World Wide Web: www.nas.org.uk

NIASA (National Initiative for Autism: Screening and Assessment) (2003) *National Autism Plan for Children (NAPC).* London, UK: National Autistic Society.

Perlman, L. (2000) Adults with Asperger disorder misdiagnosed as schizophrenic. *Professional Psychology: Research and Practice, 31,* 2, 221–5.

Powell, A. (2002) *Taking Responsibility: Good Practice Guidelines for Services – Adults with Asperger Syndrome.* London, UK: The National Autistic Society.

Prior, M., Eisenmajer, R., Leekman, S., Wing, L., Gould, J., Ong, B., and Dowe, D. (1998) Are there sub-groups within the autistic spectrum? A cluster analysis of a group of children with autistic spectrum disorders. *Journal of Child Psychology and Psychiatry, 39,* 6, 893–902.

Ritvo, E.R., Ritvo, R., Freeman, B.J., and Mason-Brothers, A. (1994) Clinical characteristics of mild autism in adults. *Comprehensive Psychiatry, 35,* 2, 149–56.

Scott, F.J., Baron-Cohen, S., Bolton, P., and Brayne, C. (2002) The CAST (Childhood Asperger Syndrome Test): Preliminary development of a UK screen for mainstream primary-school-age children. *Autism: The International Journal of Research and Practice, 6,* 1, 9–31.

Slater-Walker, G., and Slater-Walker, C. (2002) *An Asperger Marriage.* London, UK: Jessica Kingsley Publishers.

Sparks, B., Temple, V., Springer, M., and Stoddart, K.P. (2000) Service provision to older adults with developmental disabilities: A survey of service providers. *Canadian Journal on Aging, 19,* 2, 210–22.

Spicer, D. (2004) Parents on the autism spectrum. *Autism–Asperger's Digest,* January/February, 46–7.

Stoddart, K.P. (1998) The treatment of high-functioning pervasive developmental disorder and Asperger's disorder: Defining the social work role. *Focus on Autism and Other Developmental Disabilities, 13,* 1, 45–52.

Stoddart, K.P. (1999) Adolescents with Asperger syndrome: Three case studies of individual and family therapy. *Autism: The International Journal of Research and Practice, 3,* 3, 255–71.

Stoddart, K.P. (2003) The diagnosis and treatment of Asperger syndrome. In I. Brown and M. Percy (eds) *Developmental Disabilities in Ontario, Second Edition.* Toronto, ON: Ontario Association on Developmental Disabilities.

Stoddart, K.P., and Burke, L. (2002) Asperger Screening Questionnaire for Adults (ASQ-A). Unpublished.

Stoddart, K.P., Burke, L., and Temple, V. (2002) A re-examination of the characteristics and clinical needs of adults with pervasive developmental disorders: A summary of 100 cases. Paper presented at the State of the HART, Sponsored by UBC and BC Association for Mental Health in Developmental Disability, Vancouver, BC.

Szatmari, P. (1995) Identification and early intervention in pervasive developmental disorders. *Recent Advances in Pediatrics, 13,* 123.

Szatmari, P. (2003) The causes of autism spectrum disorders. *British Medical Journal, 326,* 173–4.

Szatmari, P., Bremner, R., and Nagy, J. (1989) Asperger's syndrome: A review of clinical features. *Canadian Journal of Psychiatry, 34,* 6, 554–60.

Taylor, B., Miller, E., Farrington, C.P., Petropoulos, M.C., Favot-Mayaud, I., Li, J., and Waight, P.A. (1999) Autism and measles, mumps, and rubella vaccine: No epidemiological evidence for a casual association. *The Lancet, 353,* 2026–9.

Tidmarsh, L., and Volkmar, F.R. (2003) Diagnosis and epidemiology of autism spectrum disorders. *Canadian Journal of Psychiatry, 48,* 8, 517–25.

Towbin, K.E. (2003) Strategies for pharmacologic treatment of high functioning autism and Asperger syndrome. *Child and Adolescent Psychiatric Clinics of North America, 12,* 23–45.

Vallis, M. (2004) Michelangelo joins Who's Who of Asperger's syndrome. *National Post, 6,* June 2, A1–15.

WHO (World Health Organization) (2000) *Ageing and Intellectual Disabilities – Improving Longevity and Promoting Healthy Aging: Summative Report.* Geneva, Switzerland: World Health Organization.

Willey, L.H. (1999) *Pretending to be Normal: Living with Asperger's Syndrome.* London, UK: Jessica Kingsley Publishers.

Wing, L. (1981) Asperger's syndrome: A clinical account. *Psychological Medicine, 11,* 115–29.

Wing, L., and Potter, D. (2002) The epidemiology of autistic spectrum disorders: Is the prevalence rising? *Mental Retardation and Developmental Disabilities Research Reviews, 8,* 151–61.

Part I

Clinical and Service Perspectives

CHAPTER 1

Clinical assessment of children and adolescents with Asperger Syndrome

Rosina G. Schnurr

As Asperger Syndrome (AS) becomes more widely known to the public, greater numbers of children with suspected or diagnosed AS are coming to the attention of professionals. Clinicians are asked to assist with clinical and behavioural issues, and with providing a diagnosis to procure services for the child. There is often urgency to the request as many referrals are precipitated by a crisis. For clinicians new to the field of AS, assessing a child for AS is a challenge as considerable clinical experience with this group is sometimes required to recognize significant symptoms.

The purpose of this chapter is to provide an introduction to assessment of the child or adolescent with AS. This discussion is based on the author's experience as a clinical psychologist in assessing and diagnosing children with AS. Introductory issues in assessment will be reviewed and followed by a discussion of the interview of the child or youth with suspected AS. Then, 11 areas for exploration in the parent interview are summarized.

Introduction to assessment

The most comprehensive assessment of the child or adolescent suspected of having AS includes reviewing past evaluations of the child, observing the child in the home and school settings, evaluating language and motor skills, and using a battery of instruments designed to measure traits of AS. These measures assess the extent of autistic symptoms, emotional maturity, academic abilities, achievement, and learning difficulties. In addition, the use of personality assessment instruments and those designed to evaluate emotional difficulties (e.g. anxiety and depression) may be necessary. Obtaining ratings and reports from others involved with the child complement the clinician's direct assessment. A clinician with limited time is not able to undertake as thorough an assessment. Nevertheless, a good clinical assessment can be completed in approximately an hour.

Several questionnaires have been developed that specifically assess symptoms of AS or other autism spectrum disorders (ASDs). O'Brien *et al.* (2001), Goodlin-Jones and Solomon (2003) and Howlin (2000) have reviewed available instruments. While these are useful, they should only be considered as adjuncts to the clinical interview and not as diagnostic. These assessment instruments are neither comprehensive nor conclusive, nor do these tools address the question of differential diagnosis. Parents, who are informants for these measures, are very familiar with the child's behaviour, and may inadvertently minimize symptoms. Nevertheless, some assessment instruments are useful when explaining a diagnosis to parents as visual cut-off scores and graphs help to make clinical findings more concrete.

It is important to remember that each child who has AS is unique. It is a mistake to assume that a child with AS will fit exactly into the syndrome description with well-defined symptoms that do not vary from child to child. The exclusive use of the diagnostic criteria in the *DSM-IV* (APA 1994) or the *ICD-10* (WHO 1992) is not likely to be helpful. Some of these criteria are still being clarified and modified. For example, some would argue that a speech delay is present in some children with AS (Attwood 1998). Some commonly seen aspects of AS, such as motor impairment, are not mentioned in these diagnostic criteria. Characteristics discussed in the research literature tend to be more comprehensive (e.g. Gillberg and Gillberg 1989; Szatmari, Bremner, and Nagy 1989).

The child/adolescent interview

The following guidelines for the clinical interview of the child or adolescent suspected of having AS are modified from Schnurr (2004).

As you, the examiner, gain experience assessing children and adolescents for AS, you will more readily notice small signs and symptoms of the syndrome which become apparent in the interview with the child or adolescent. The following traits to observe and note during an interview may not be part of any standardized assessment protocol. These features include eye contact, speech, voice (i.e. tone, pitch, volume), understanding of words, ability to follow and contribute to a conversation appropriately, perception of social cues and boundaries, mannerisms, and degree of emotional maturity.

Children with AS may present in the clinical interview in one of three ways. The *quiet child*, who is not sure why he is seeing the clinician, is often placid and becomes upset when a question is asked that he cannot answer. The *defensive and unwilling child* may experience the interview as again being called to account for some difficulty he has been having. The child may have his own version of events precipitating the interview and be prepared to defend them. With these children, it is important to spend time establishing rapport and a non-threatening atmosphere. Failure to do this can result in the child walking out of the room and becoming entrenched in an uncooperative or resistant attitude. The *little adult* often knows your name and pronounces it correctly. He is often "in your space", crosses social boundaries, and may be prepared to take over the interview, correcting parents and directing conversation. He may ask personal and intrusive questions. With this child, it is important to establish structure in the session and maintain control.

A good setting for the assessment interview is a quiet room with standard play items that are out of the child's reach. These could include soft toys that can be manipulated, puzzles with *all* the pieces, simple games, drawing materials, a playhouse with human figures, puppets, and toy cars or trains. Books of maps, animals, birds, and dinosaurs are also helpful items. A child will often bring his own amusement, such as a toy or a book that relates to his particular interest. However, if the child is exclusively involved with these favourite toys in the interview, social interaction or the gathering of important information may be hindered. Sometimes, clues to a child's special interest can be observed by noting something that he is wearing (e.g. a picture on his shirt).

Beginning the interview with familiar questions is a non-threatening approach to take with the child. These questions may concern his age, grade in school, and who is in his family, including any pets. His answers may be given in rote, formal, or overly elaborated manner. Once it is established who is in the family, you can ask more about the individual members of it. This gives you information about the child's ability to describe personality characteristics. Inquiring about parents' work may produce a concrete and literal answer. A question about why the child has come to the interview to see you might prove difficult, even if the purpose of the visit has been discussed ahead of time.

Questions about school and friends are often answered vaguely. Here, the examiner is looking for the child's descriptive abilities and, in particular, his ability to talk about the emotional features of a situation. A child's description also can be lacking important information, which is necessary to the understanding of the uninformed listener.

The child's verbal and emotional expressiveness can be assessed using a sentence completion task (e.g. "Something that makes me feel happy is…"). This is typically a difficult task as it is unstructured and there is no objective or "right" answer. The sentence completions may be repetitive, as the child will repeat what he thinks is an acceptable answer.

Gaining a sense of the child's understanding of and ability to use facial expression is an important part of the assessment. Games related to making facial expressions are therefore useful assessment activities. A child can often recognize and make expressions of being happy, sad, angry, and surprised. However, the expressions may look similar, be exaggerated, or use few facial muscles. More subtle expressions, such as trying to pass on a message using the eyes or demonstrating "I know a secret", are harder. You can also have the child try to recognize your expressions. Another way to assess emotional expressions and recognition is to tell a story and to ask the child to insert the expressions of the characters involved.

Having a child do three simple drawings of a house, tree, and person gives good information about fine motor co-ordination and the child's perception of himself and his surroundings. Some children do not want to draw, as this has been an unsuccessful area of endeavour for them. The examiner should not persevere in these situations. A child may also be asked to draw something related to his special interest. This usually animates the child and can produce quite a different response.

It is helpful to have younger children complete a play assessment. Here, the examiner is looking for the child's social interaction and communication skills, spontaneous creativity, and the emotional content of the play. Using human figures with other toys, the child can be asked to make up a scenario that can be played with the examiner. Playing a board game with a child will give valuable information about how the child plays, his ability to take turns, and his adherence to rules. Having toys available that are related to a child's special interest can facilitate identification of many traits of AS.

The interview with the child or adolescent can be ended positively by talking with him about his special interest. This can show the depth and detail of his interest. At this time, his demeanour is likely to become more animated and spontaneous. However, switching topics can be difficult once engaged in such discussions.

The parent interview

The parent interview can give important details that you may not obtain with the child or adolescent present. However, it is essential to observe the child in the presence of the parents, even for a short period. Eleven areas of content should be addressed in the parent interview: (1) transitions and changes, (2) friends, (3) social behaviour, (4) sensory sensitivities, (5) routines, (6) special interests and exceptional skills, (7) school, (8) communication skills, (9) early developmental history, (10) motor skills and sports, and (11) family history. The first eight areas represent symptoms that may be the most prevalent and troublesome. The final three topics give necessary background information. The examiner also needs to ask about the child's general health and any other interventions. Finally, questions to determine possible comorbidity should also be asked.

Transitions and changes

The ability to be flexible and adaptable during periods of transitions and changes is a key feature to assess. A child with AS is likely to demonstrate more rigidity and need for sameness than would an unaffected child. Questions can be asked about the amount of change required to produce an adverse reaction, and if preparing the child ahead of time is helpful. Even small changes may need preparation and produce reactions that are out of proportion to the degree of change. Enquiring about situations such as having a replacement teacher, moving homes, and a change in clothing suitable to the season may jog a parent's memory about an event.

Friends

When asking about friends, it is important to assess three issues: (1) the importance of friends to a child, (2) the child's concept of friendship, and (3) the child's friendship skills. Younger children may not be interested in having friends, as they are happy with their own activities. As the child matures, friends become more important and the child may start to experience more of the negative aspects of peer relationships. This is especially true when the child realizes that he or she is different. Often, a child with AS does not have a good friend, although he may tell the examiner that he has one. Clarifying this with the parent often reveals that the friend is an acquaintance or someone the child knew at another time in his life. Children with AS may prefer to play with either younger or older children rather than with same-age peers.

It is valuable to ask if the child conforms to peer standards. For example, is the child more interested in his own ideas than those of his peers? Would he rather wear comfortable clothes than fashionable ones? Alternatively, adolescents who want to fit in with their peer group can be obsessive about their appearance and clothing. A child or adolescent may find acceptance in the opposite sex peer group and follow the norms of this group. For example, a girl might present as a tomboy and dress much like her male peers.

When asking about play, it is helpful to determine the child's skills in this area. For example, is the child able and willing to arrange a play date, or is this done by his parents? How the child plays is also important. Usually, the child with AS wants to play according to his wishes; play periods are often short because of disagreements, lack of interest, or the child with AS becoming over-whelmed and needing to retreat.

Asking about recess and birthday parties can give good information about a child's social acceptance. Recess is usually a solitary time with the child not fitting in socially and they may not be invited to birthday parties. When they are included, they may have difficulty participating in these activities and may display inappropriate social behaviour. It is always vital to ask about bullying and victimization by others. Usually, bullying and teasing are not isolated events, but happen over quite some time and involve different schools and social situations. Peers easily take advantage of a child with AS without the child even being aware. A child with AS can be seen as a bully in his pursuit of his activities and interests. For example, the child may take from others whatever toys he wishes to play with, or may push another child off a swing if he wants to use it.

Social behaviour

A child with AS shows many behavioural characteristics that affect his social functioning. It is important to ask if the child is a loner, with whom he socializes, and in what manner. It is useful to note whether the child has a strongly developed sense of fairness. This behaviour is usually related to siblings and peers, and in adolescents can include broader issues such as politics and marketing principles. A question to ask parents is whether the child acts as the "house police".

You should also ask the parents whether the child often "misses the point", "does not get it", or is lacking in common sense. This will likely lead to a discussion of inappropriate social behaviour, such as when the child asks embarrassing questions in public, is unusually naïve, tells family secrets, or invades others' personal space.

Other features of social behaviour to enquire about include the child's understanding of manners and the extent to which he demonstrates them rotely or with diminished feeling. These can often be observed in the interview. The child's ability to empathize is often compromised and should be asked about directly. A parent may report that the child helped another child but, when questioned further, may reveal that empathy was not shown. For example, a child with AS might bring a bandage to a child with a cut but show more interest in the blood than in offering sentiments of comfort to the injured child.

Another key area of social behaviour is the child's ability to recognize and understand subtle nonverbal communication such as facial expressions. Parents may state that strong emotional expressions are understood, so it is important to ask about subtle expressions. For example, does the child know when the parents or others are politely annoyed or bored?

Children with AS often laugh at inappropriate times. They may laugh at their own jokes that others do not understand. A subtle and witty sense of humour is often described by parents and may be observed during the interview. When asking about a sense of humour, you can also ask if a child can tell a joke effectively and if he understands practical jokes.

Sensory sensitivities

The child with AS is likely to be excessively sensitive to everyday stimuli. To discover the child's sensitivities, one can pose questions about each sense. In terms of taste, children with AS often prefer bland food. You could ask them about any dislike of mixing foods or of foods touching others on the plate, about toothpaste that may be too strong, and about dislikes of certain textures of food. Loud repetitive noises such as lawn mowers or the school fire alarm are often difficult for the child with AS to tolerate. The sensitivity to noise is likely to have been present from a young age. A child may report the sun hurts his eyes if he is visually sensitive. He may report smelling offensive odours that others cannot smell. Tactile sensitivity is important and can be assessed if you ask questions about clothes. Often, the tags in clothing, the seams in socks, and any clothing that fits tightly will be irritating. It is not unusual for an AS child to not want others to touch them. A hug may be interpreted as a "squeeze" as opposed to an affectionate gesture (Attwood 2003).

The child's reaction to pain might be heightened or diminished. Some parents report significant physical injuries that did not upset their child. Alternatively, some children overreact to small injuries and are terrified of medical procedures.

Routines

An important area to explore with respect to routines is whether they are non-functional. Perhaps the child insists on always eating in a certain way, getting dressed in a particular manner or order, and following particular bathroom and bedtime routines. An aspect of this is the degree of rigidity and perfectionism (e.g. reworking homework or ordering items in their room) a child demonstrates. Rules and routines are often learned and followed precisely and rigidly. An example of this might be if a teacher outlines the steps by which homework is to be completed and the child is not able to skip any steps although he may not need to follow them. Other examples of routines may be related to household chores (e.g. the child likes to organize the food cupboard).

Special interests and exceptional skills

One of the hallmarks of AS is a restricted range of interests, behaviours, or activities (APA 1994). Asking parents if the word "obsessed" applies to the child's interest will indicate the time spent on the interest and the depth of the interest. Usually the parents remark on the detail in which the child knows a topic and his incessant talk about it. Interests can change over time and be varied. Common topics of interest are the weather, maps, trains, Pokémon, an animal species, or something mechanical.

Special skills can be related to interests but may stand out on their own. These include an excellent memory for detail that is present at an early age. The child may remember what everyone was wearing at a family gathering but not remember the emotional aspects of the celebration. Sometimes, children with AS possess a strong visual memory. Other skills include good ability for mathematics and mechanical and technical interests. Parents may be amazed at the skill with which the child was able to work technical equipment in the home at an early age. They might also report the child's ability to remember telephone numbers and licence plates, or to perform some other difficult memory task. When asking about the child's interest in computers, it is useful to distinguish between playing games and actual computer knowledge. The child may be obsessed with and skilled at computer games, but not be as knowledgeable about computers in general. This distinction can be helpful when making recommendations for the child. Artistic skills in music and drawing may also be present. Drawings might include detailed patterns, pictures, or cartoons, or be related to the child's particular interest.

School

School is a major part of any child's life and involves both academic and social demands. Children with AS must work equally hard in both areas and school is often difficult and, at times, overwhelming. Some children with AS do not come to the attention of professionals until they enter the complex world of school. You should ask the parents about the early years of schooling. How did the child separate from the parents? How did he adapt to the classroom? It is not unusual for a child to show little reaction when separating from parents and to adhere to his own agenda in the classroom. Children may also display social difficulties (e.g. aggressive behaviour) when they are not allowed to finish a task. Other problematic social behaviours may be observed during unstructured times such as recess and lunch period. Teachers may report unusual behaviour during these times. It is important to determine whether the child has been formally identified within the school system as a special student and what assistance the child is receiving.

When assessing an older child, the examiner can ask about the child's learning style, which may be more visual than auditory. Children with AS also show an unevenness of skills, performing well in some subjects and not in others. Mathematical abilities may be very good or may represent a learning difficulty. The child may be able to read at a level above his comprehension level. Verbal expressiveness and the ability to think outside boundaries may be poor.

Communication skills

Communication is a key feature to assess in children and adolescents suspected of having AS. Expressive and receptive language is assessed in many domains. These domains include early speech development; the quality of voice; the use of big words, invented words and phrases; and pedantic expression. When and how the child communicates is also important information. Conversations are often one-sided with the child preferring to talk only about his own interest. Children with AS may have difficulty knowing how and when to start and stop a conversation. They often do not pick suitable times for conversations, and talk incessantly about their interest. The child usually prefers to speak with adults.

Sometimes the child has difficulty understanding and answering questions. For instance, when asked to relate an event, the child with AS will give an explanation with many gaps and pieces of information missing. AS affects other characteristics of communication as well: having difficulty considering the needs of the listener, taking words and expressions literally, and being able to talk about facts more easily than feelings.

Early developmental history

Questions about pregnancy and birth are for general information rather than diagnosis. It is more important to ask about the child's *nature* at an early age, such as what kind of a baby he was. If the reply is a "good baby", then specifics can be asked to discover if the child was undemanding and able to play for long periods on his own. A "cuddly baby" may be one that clings to Mom more for protection than for affection. Alternatively, a demanding child may be one who is overwhelmed by his environment and cannot cope, may have rage episodes, and may be inconsolable for long periods of time. You can enquire about coping behaviours and any stereotypic or repetitive movements. A question should always be posed about transitions, changes in routine, and new situations. For example, discussion of the processes of giving up the bottle and toilet training is useful, as it gives information about a child's early ability to be flexible and adaptable.

You should ask about milestones and note anything unusual, especially in terms of the acquisition of language and motor skills. Language development may be precocious and motor skills may have been lacking. The *DSM-IV* (APA 1994) places emphasis on children being developmentally able and having no language delay. It should be clarified that, while no language delay may be apparent, it is the *use* of language (pragmatics) that may be poor. Early speech often occurs in "chunks" rather than in single words; for example, the child reciting an entire cartoon script.

Early social behaviour is also an important trait to explore. This includes enquiring about eye contact at an early age. Questions can be asked about the child spontaneously bringing things to show parents, being "in a world of his own", lacking interactive and pretend play, having imaginary friends; about how the child participates in a group, his ability to wave "bye-bye" appropriately, and what happens when the parents left the child with a sitter.

It is also helpful to ask about specific interests and behaviours in early development. Children with AS often display a good memory; they may be interested in parts of objects, or may be fascinated by lining up toys according to colour or some other attribute. It is sometimes informative to ask what was the child's first word as this could be related to a particular interest. The ability to remember dialogues of television shows or movies perfectly is a significant indicator. In this instance, the child is learning about talking by how he hears and perceives it from the television and by then repeating it.

Motor skills and sports

Both fine and gross motor skills may be compromised in the child with AS. Asking about when and how a child learned to tie shoelaces and to ride a bike will provide useful information. Sometimes the parents will also note that their child has an odd gait when walking and running. Participation in group sports is usually reported as a failure for the child. It is important to ask about why the child could not function as a team member. This is likely to be because the child has difficulty understanding group dynamics and following the rules of the game, which sometimes change according to specific circumstances. Parents report much more success in individual and non-competitive sports such as swimming.

Family history

It is important to find out if there are any significant mental disorders within the family history. Checking for similar traits in extended family members is important as research shows a probable genetic aetiology (Szatmari and Jones 1998). You need to attend to disorders of learning, attention deficit, anxiety, depression, Obsessive Compulsive Disorder and Thought Disorder. Sometimes ASDs or significant developmental delays will be reported. It is better to ask about the symptoms as opposed to the names of the disorders. This is particularly true when asking about ASDs, as the terms that are now used to diagnose these disorders were not used in past generations. Typical areas include asking if there is anyone in the family who could be described as socially inept, eccentric, or odd; as having a specific obsessional interest or talent; as talking a lot about one topic; or as brilliant but having difficulty holding a job.

General health

It is always helpful to check for chronic health problems or current medical treatments and about the child's sensitivity to medication. Sometimes children with AS experience more side effects than is usually the case and the side effects can be severe enough to terminate a medication. If the child has had a strep infection or high fevers, it is important to ask if there were any residual effects (e.g. the child's behaviour may have changed for the worse). Sometimes personal hygiene is lacking in children with AS. A parent might report a struggle related to getting the child to wash and to brush his teeth. It can also be useful to ask about any unusual visits to the Emergency Department of a hospital. A child might have done something odd (e.g. put an object in his ear). Also, the child might not have realized the danger in a situation and been injured. Further, with diminished pain sensitivity, an injury or infection may not have been detected until it was serious.

Interventions

Information about previous or current interventions can be collected before an interview or briefly asked about in the interview. Generally, it is important to know if a school evaluation has been done and when. Also, find out which professionals have been involved with the child and over what period of time. It can be informative to enquire about other interventions such as special diets, vitamins, herbal remedies, and any other therapeutic treatments that may have been attempted.

Comorbidity

It is not unusual for comorbid disorders to be present in children with AS (Gillberg and Billstedt 2000; Ghaziuddin 2002). It is often useful to diagnose them separately, particularly when they are outside of the realm of AS by virtue of the nature and severity of the symptoms.

Learning disorders may be described in many different ways, varying from a specific difficulty to a more general one. The terms "Nonverbal Learning Disorder" (NVLD) and "Semantic-Pragmatic Disorder" are sometimes used. These disorders are similar to AS (Rourke and Tsatsanis 2000).

Children with AS have often been previously diagnosed with Attention Deficit Disorder (ADD). However, parents may state that medication for ADD did not help and the child experienced severe side effects. While a child with AS might have ADD, there are some distinguishing features. It is important to check if the child's reported distractibility and inability to focus is more related to the child being in "his own world" or if the child is genuinely distractible and has difficulty focussing. Similarly, a child with AS can be very active. The activity level can be greater than that which is usually associated with ADD. It might also be directed towards an interest and learning about the child's favourite topic.

Tourette Syndrome can be ruled out by asking about tics and involuntary blurting. If present, these might be observed during the interview.

Anxiety is often comorbid with AS (Kim *et al.* 2000). The source of the anxiety is a major distinguishing factor. For children with AS, anxiety is more related to transitions, new situations, emotional immaturity, dependence on parents for help rather than emotional needs, and negative social experiences. Further, social and performance anxiety may or may not exist. Measuring anxiety using standard measures might not give a clear or accurate picture. Some of the questions may be taken literally and others misunderstood. It is sometimes difficult for the child to be attuned to an inner state of anxiety, so he or she may not report the anxiety in a traditional or usual way.

Depressive symptoms need to be assessed according to the age of the child. It is not unusual for depression to be present, particularly in adolescents with AS. Again, adolescents may not truly represent their mental state on a standard instrument. Direct questioning is often more useful. The presence of vegetative signs is a good indicator of depression. At all ages, unhappiness is expressed through behaviour. Often, these are outbursts of anger and frustration. It is important to look for environmental influences when these behaviours occur. A child or adolescent's depressive symptoms are frequently a reaction to a current situation. The child may use depressive language (e.g. threats of harm to self or others), but not realize the impact of these statements.

AS can be distinguished from Obsessive Compulsive Disorder (OCD) by looking at the types of thoughts and behaviours. While an AS child may think obsessively about a special interest, the thoughts of a child with OCD may revolve around a specific fear. The behaviour of a child with OCD is usually directed towards preventing an act or is a routine or ritual that is non-functional. The behaviour of a child with AS may be related to the child's special interest or to sensitivities. For example, an OCD child may save everything while a child with AS will only collect items related to his particular interest. It should be noted, however, that OCD traits are seen in children with AS.

Thought Disorder can usually be determined by the type and extent of symptoms present. However, caution must be exercised in assessing the areas of suspiciousness and fantasy. Suspiciousness is often more specific than general and can be based in reality. The child may genuinely feel that someone is out to harm him. Further discussion may reveal bullying. A child's fantasy life might involve the child talking to herself or to imaginary friends or invented cartoon characters that others do not see or hear. This represents the child's involvement in his own fantasy world that she knows is not real. Absorption in games such as "Dungeons and Dragons", drama, or the writing of bizarre stories does not necessarily reflect a thought disorder.

Conclusion

Diagnosing AS is not as difficult as might be initially perceived. The main elements for a clinician to remember are process and content. Attention to process involves being flexible, going with the flow, and never assuming anything about the child. Content areas can be explored in many different ways through the interactions with the child or adolescent and the parents. The clinical assessment of the child with AS is always interesting and what initially seems like a challenging task can actually become one of the most rewarding types of assessments for a clinician.

References

APA (American Psychiatric Association) (1994) *Diagnostic and Statistical Manual of Mental Disorders, Fourth Edition.* Washington, DC: APA.

Attwood, T. (1998) *Asperger's Syndrome: A Guide for Professionals and Parents.* London, UK: Jessica Kingsley Publishers.

Attwood, T. (2003) Assessment, diagnosis and intervention for individuals with Asperger's Syndrome. Conference sponsored by the Miriam Foundation, September 2003. Montreal, Quebec.

Ghaziuddin, M. (2002) Asperger Syndrome: Associated psychiatric and medical conditions. *Focus on Autism and Other Developmental Disabilities, 17,* 3, 138–44.

Gillberg, C., and Billstedt, E. (2000) Autism and Asperger Syndrome: Co-existence with other clinical disorders. *Acta Psychiatrica Scandinavica,* 102, 321–30.

Gillberg, I.C., and Gillberg, C. (1989) Asperger syndrome – some epidemiological considerations: A research note. *Journal of Child Psychology and Psychiatry, 30*, 4, 631–38.

Goodlin-Jones, B.L., and Solomon, M. (2003) Contributions of psychology. In S. Ozonoff, S.J. Rogers, and R.L. Hendren (eds) *Autism Spectrum Disorders: A Research Review for Practitioners.* Washington, DC: American Psychiatric Publishing.

Howlin, P. (2000) Assessment instruments for Asperger Syndrome. *Child Psychology and Psychiatry Review, 5*, 3, 120–9.

Kim, J.A., Szatmari, P., Bryson, S.E., Streiner, D.L., and Wilson, F.J. (2000) The prevalence of anxiety and mood problems among children with autism and Asperger Syndrome. *Autism: The International Journal of Research and Practice, 4*, 2, 117–32.

O'Brien, G., Pearson, J., Berney, T., and Barnard, L. (2001) Measuring behaviour in developmental disability: A review of existing schedules. Section 1: Schedules for the detection, diagnosis, and assessment of autistic spectrum disorder. *Developmental Medicine and Child Neurology*, Supplemental, 87, 5–18.

Rourke, B.P., and Tsatsanis, K.D. (2000) Nonverbal learning disabilities and Asperger Syndrome. In A. Klin, F.R. Volkmar, and S.S. Sparrow (eds) *Asperger Syndrome.* New York, NY: Guilford Press.

Schnurr, R.G. (2004) *Schnurr Interview Guidelines for Asperger's Disorder in Children and Adolescents (SIGADCA).* Ottawa, ON: Anisor Publishing.

Szatmari, P., Bremner, R., and Nagy, J. (1989) Asperger's Syndrome: A review of clinical features. *Canadian Journal of Psychiatry, 34*, 6, 554–60.

Szatmari, P., and Jones, M.B. (1998) Genetic epidemiology of autism and other pervasive developmental disorders. In F.R. Volkmar (ed.) *Autism and Pervasive Developmental Disorders.* New York, NY: Cambridge University Press.

WHO (World Health Organization) (1992) *The International Statistical Classification of Diseases and Related Health Problems, Tenth Edition.* Geneva: WHO.

CHAPTER 2

Anxiety and depression in children and adolescents with Asperger Syndrome

M. Mary Konstantareas

It has been well documented that many individuals with Asperger Syndrome (AS) suffer from anxiety and depression. Whether AS is distinct from high-functioning autistic disorder (AD) continues to be debated. Although some have opted against differentiating between the two, others have not (e.g. Schopler, Mesibov, and Kunce 1998). Regardless of this, evidence exists for the presence of anxiety and depression across all autism spectrum disorders (ASDs) and not only AS.

The aim of this chapter is to provide a summary of select findings that support the contention that anxiety and mood disorders are frequently seen in children and adolescents with AS. Factors likely to be related to anxiety and depression will then be discussed. Subsequently, findings from a recent study from our laboratory on the presence of anxiety and mood difficulties in a sample of children and adolescents with AS will be presented. The author will draw from her clinical work and research to elaborate further upon relevant issues. Information on likely aetiological factors will then be presented. The chapter will conclude with the implications of the findings and suggestions on how to assist children and youth with AS to combat their anxiety and depression.

Anxiety and mood disorders in those with Asperger Syndrome: Existing evidence

Since the first systematic attempts to delineate the characteristics of Early Childhood Psychosis, as AD was referred to at the time, Creak (1961) and the British working party emphasized the presence of anxiety. Criterion six of ten was worded as follows: "frequent, acute, excessive, and seemingly illogical anxiety". To this day, the precise relationship between ASDs and anxiety or depression remains unclear. Anxiety is included as a criterion in some key diagnostic scales such as the Childhood Autism Rating Scale (CARS) (Schopler, Reichler, and Renner 1986) and the Autistic Disorder Checklist (Krug, Arick and Almond 1980). However, it is not included in the *DSM-IV* (APA 1994) or key scales for AS such as the Australian Scale for Asperger's Syndrome (Attwood 1998) and the Gilliam Asperger Disorder Scale (Gilliam 2001). Furthermore, a number of volumes on the subject of both AD and AS make only passing or no reference to either anxiety or depression (e.g. Matson 1994; Klin, Volkmar, and Sparrow 2000). Recent literature does provide evidence, particularly for depression (e.g. Clarke *et al.* 1999; Kim *et al.* 2000). Considering the high comorbidity between anxiety and depression, it is somewhat surprising that most studies have concentrated on depression and have ignored the relevance of anxiety for those with AS. There are exceptions to this however.

Kim *et al.* (2000) studied both low mood and anxiety in children with high-functioning AD and with AS, and compared them to a sample of 1751 typical children. The combined ASDs group showed higher levels of depression and anxiety than controls. Interestingly, both anxiety and depression were positively correlated with disruptive behaviour. Gillott, Furniss, and Walter (2001) examined anxiety in three groups of children: AS, Specific Developmental Language Disorder, and typical. The group with AS were significantly more anxious than the other two groups. Green and colleagues (2000) compared a group of 20 children with AS to a group of 20 with Conduct Disorder (CD). Those with AS displayed significantly higher levels of anxiety. The issue remains, however, as to whether anxiety and mood disorders are comorbid in those with ASDs, and to what degree. It is also unclear whether one or both are part of the symptomatology of the ASDs, much as is the case for other associated symptoms, rather than being coexisting distinct disorders. The prediction of who is likely to develop symptoms of anxiety and depression also remains obscure since not all individuals with AS have them. Both genetic vulnerability and contextual factors appear to play a role, although once again the evidence is quite limited. It was because of the limited systematic work concurrently examining a variety of potentially relevant factors for their relationship to the presence of anxiety and depression, that we undertook a study on the topic.

Factors likely to be related to anxiety and mood difficulties

Intellectual and communication ability

There is a wide range of cognitive competence, ranging from low normal to superior in those with ASDs. Intellectual ability is bound to influence every aspect of an individual's functioning. In our clinical work, we have assessed a number of children with AS whose IQ was in the superior range, particularly in the verbal domain. Although we did not test these aspects specifically, we observed that their environmental awareness, theory of mind, executive function and other capacities tended to be higher than of those with lower cognitive ability, despite weaknesses in the social and pragmatics domains. Thus, a six-year-old boy who met full criteria for AS and obtained a full-scale IQ at the 98th percentile, was particularly anxious to succeed during testing and kept asking whether he did better than all other children we had tested. He also demonstrated excellent theory of mind in his attempts to sneak glances at the stimulus items behind the examiner's back. Moreover, he was fully aware of his differences from others and commented that he was the smartest in his class. Interestingly, the mother of this child, a highly competent individual herself, told us that she also has AS.

To what extent is higher cognitive ability a predictor of depression and anxiety? Studies on this issue have yielded conflicting results. In a study antedating the inclusion of AS in the *DSM*, Gillberg (1984) reported that brighter adolescents with AD were more likely to suffer from depression, as they became aware of their differences from other children. Consistent with this, Ghaziuddin and Greden (1998) found that their depressed patients with AD had a higher full-scale IQ than a non-depressed group. In contrast to these findings, in their review of 14 case reports of individuals with AD or AS and depression, Lainhart and Folstein (1994) noted that the incidence of mental retardation was quite high, and that a large number were female, who are well known to be lower functioning than males (Konstantareas, Homatidis, and Busch 1989). Yet, in the study by Kim *et al.* (2000) no relationship was found between measures of nonverbal and verbal IQ and depression. It can therefore be seen that, although some writers report that higher-functioning individuals with AD or AS show greater depression, contradictory results have also been reached.

Related to intellect is communication ability. It is intuitively evident that higher communication competence is more likely to be related to the ability to share information as to one's unhappiness or anxiety. Of course, we infer anxiety in low-functioning children with AD from their nonverbal behaviour, frequently at the risk of being wrong. We base such inferences on crying, agitation, or withdrawal. In the one study that addressed the issue, no relationship was found between depression/anxiety and verbal IQ, which can be used as a proxy for communication ability (Kim *et al.* 2000).

Problems with social competencies and friendships

There is considerable evidence that children and adults with AS are interested in forming friendships but have difficulties starting and maintaining them. In a recent consultation, for example, the parents of a ten-year-old boy with AS reported to us that he was eager to have peers join him at home but, as soon as they arrived, he imitated what they did so precisely that the peers were "spooked" by his mimicry. When they demanded that he stop, he claimed that he could not control himself. This resulted in the peers shunning him and refusing to attend his birthday party. An 11-year-old gifted girl I saw a few years ago had a comparable problem. She would invite her friends over and when they arrived, would proceed to insensitively correct their grammar and diction, to their obvious embarrassment and anger. She would also get bored and depart for her room, leaving the peers on their own.

Is it possible that lack of friendships is responsible for the AS children's anxiety and depression? Bolton *et al.* (1998) have concluded that poor social skills could act as a risk factor for depression. Their assumption is that close friendships play a buffering role against depression. However, in the Kim *et al.* (2000) study, early problems in social interaction in AS and AD were unrelated to level of depression six years later. Green *et al.* (2000) replicated this.

Awareness of the disability

Higher cognitive ability does not imply greater awareness of disability. In the study by Green *et al.* (2000), children with AS were significantly less likely than those with CD to report a disability or difference from others. Further, only 35% of the AS group could give an accurate description of their disability. The authors concluded that there appears to be no clear relationship between awareness of disability and psychological distress in individuals with AS. However, these workers suggest that this issue should be further researched.

In the author's clinical caseload, there have been a number of young adults who were fully aware of the nature of their disability and had read a great deal about it. Based on their awareness, some reported being unhappy while others did not. A 14-year-old male, in particular, was paradoxically looking for physical stigmata to substantiate his difference from others. A 12-year-old girl who attended a psychiatric day treatment program identified with those children who attended her school and were, as she called them, "my group of people", suggesting that the group allowed her to identify with others like her and to belong. However, there was also sadness in her statement. Clinical evidence thus suggests that there appears to be considerable variability to both the degree of awareness of differences and the degree of dysphoria in belonging to the AS group. A 25-year-old with AS who was a graduate student in computer science identified himself to me as "one of the geeks", something I have heard from others as well. There is both pride and embarrassment in such statements.

Systematic research is thus needed to determine when awareness of differences emerges, and how it is handled by the child and significant others, such as parents and teachers. The ultimate aim of this research should be to ensure that children with AS arrive at a positive self-identity and one that emphasizes their gifts and competencies rather than their challenges and problematic behaviours.

The impact of bullying

At the first conference of the Aspergers Society of Ontario, held in Toronto in 2001, parents unanimously declared bullying to be one of the most stressful experiences for their children. The literature on the topic leaves few margins: children with AS are being bullied on an ongoing basis. Little (2001) mailed out surveys on peer shunning and victimization to 411 mothers of children with AS or Nonverbal Learning Disorders (NVLD). She found that 75% of the children had been bullied, with children with AS being at greater risk than those with NVLD. Mishna and Muskat (1998) also noted that many of the children with AS who participated in their clinical practice were shunned in group therapy because other children could not tolerate their strange interests and behaviours.

In the author's practice, bullying is practically a universal complaint of all those with AS, primarily because many typical peers find them easy targets for overt or covert aggression. Parenthetically, in a recent study, Craven-Thuss and Konstantareas (in preparation) found that parents of children with ASDs were more likely to engage in reactive (responding to provocation) rather than proactive (planned) aggression. Thus, when bullied some are likely to react and, because of their bullying peers' greater "theory of mind" skills, are more likely to be seen as the aggressors, to the amusement and reinforcement of the bully's behaviour. Unfortunately, some school principals and administrators do not distinguish between proactive and reactive aggression, resorting to repeated suspensions of children with AS. That bullying could result in anxiety and depression in children with AS is therefore self-evident.

The relevance of temperament

Temperament has only recently been given its due in research and theorizing on psychopathology. Defined by some as "individual differences in reactivity and self-regulation", temperament is thought to be biologically based but also to be modifiable by experience. Over the last ten years, considerable evidence for the relevance to social and emotional functioning of such temperament dimensions as fearfulness, approach, flexibility, and positive mood, among others, has been obtained (Rothbart *et al.* 2001). Windle and Lerner (1986) specifically found that temperamental attributes such as approach, flexibility, and positive mood were negatively related to depression in typical adolescents. There is little research on temperament in those with ASDs. Konstantareas and Stewart (in press), using the Children's Behaviour Questionnaire (Goldsmith and Rothbart 1991), found that children with ASDs showed higher fear and anxiety, lower inhibitory control, and poorer attentional focussing and shifting than typical children. These characteristics have direct relevance to negative mood in these children.

Findings from our study on anxiety and depression in Asperger Syndrome

Bethany Butzer, an honours thesis student, and I obtained data from 22 children and adolescents with AS. Participants were 13 males and nine females, with an average age of 11.3 years, and a range of six to 19 years. The factors outlined earlier (namely social skills, bullying, degree of symptomatology, awareness of disability, communication ability, intellectual ability, temperament) and also life events were considered for their relevance to anxiety and depression. We based the presence of anxiety and depression on the following three instruments: (1) the "anxious/depressed" sub-scale of the Child Behaviour Checklist (CBCL: Achenbach 1988) that addresses anxiety over the past six months; (2) scores on the "mood" sub-scale of the Dimensions of Temperament Scale (DOTS: Windle and Lerner 1986) which consists of seven items that measure a child's general quality of mood; (3) for those participants who could self-report we employed the Children's Depression Inventory (CDI: Kovacs 1992), a 27-item multiple- choice questionnaire. The CDI is well standardized and asks children to rate themselves on how they have felt in the past two weeks.

As we had anticipated, findings revealed that a lower level of social skills was associated with a higher level of depression and a lower level of "mood", on the DOTS. A positive relationship was also found between how well the child got along with others and t-scores on both the anxiety/depression sub-scale of the CBCL and the CDI, with better ability being related to a lower level of depression on both instruments. Finally, a higher number of close friends was related to a higher level of "mood" on the DOTS.

Turning to bullying, 100% of the parents reported that the child had been victimized by his/her peers. The victimization was on average 1.25 times per week, with as many as 23% of the parents reporting that their child was victimized between two and three times per week. In addition, 81% of parents indicated that their child understood the nature of the victimization. However, when we attempted to examine the relationship between bullying and each of the measures of depression and anxiety, none emerged. A significant correlation was found between degree of symptomatology and quality of mood as measured by the DOTS, with more severe symptomatology being related to a lower quality of mood. Of course, we cannot say with certainty that the direction of effects is from symptoms to mood because of the correlational nature of the findings.

We had anticipated that awareness of disability would have been related to greater anxiety and depression. First, as to percentages of awareness, 69% of the parents reported their child to be somewhat or very aware of his/her difference from others while 50% indicated that he/she understood that he/she had a developmental disorder. A higher total awareness furthermore was related to higher-level anxiety and depression, a result consistent with the findings of some studies but not of others. As for communication ability, a significant relationship emerged between communication ability and anhedonia (weak awareness of pain). As we had anticipated, better communication ability related to a lower level of anhedonia and better quality of mood. As to intellectual ability, contrary to our hypotheses, and consistent with other studies, no relationship was found between IQ scores and any of our measures of depression/anxiety.

As we had expected, the children in our sample were rated as having a lower quality of mood than a sample of 975 typical adolescents reported by Windle (1992). They were also rated as having lower levels of attempts at initiating any form of contact or activity, of flexibility, and of general activity level than Windle's sample. Finally, our sample had a higher level of eating rhythmicity (a pattern of eating certain foods at certain times of the day/week) than Windle's sample, consistent with the fact that they insist on the same foods. An unexpected and highly significant relationship emerged between eating rhythmicity and CDI scores, with higher eating rhythmicity being associated to lower anxiety and depression scores on the CDI. Was this because they felt more comfortable by the consistency of their food intake? This needs further examination. Interestingly, no relationship was found between life events (e.g. moving, parental unemployment, etc.) and depression/anxiety.

Of particular interest was congruence between parental and child self-reports of depression. We found that while 10% of the parents rated their children as being at the borderline clinical level of depression/anxiety on the CBCL and 25% within the clinical range (i.e. a total of 35%), the children's own self-reports of depression on the CDI were different. They rated themselves as being comparable to typical children, with only two of the 15 who completed the CDI reporting an above-average level. Thus, the parents rated their children as significantly more depressed than the children themselves. Our analyses showed that, contrary to other populations of children and adolescents, our group of children with AS did not differ in depression depending on their gender.

The present findings are offered tentatively for their heuristic value rather than constituting the final word on the subject. We have since added another 20 children, and are in the process of re-analysing the data to determine if these findings will be replicated with a larger sample.

Possible aetiologic mechanisms

Anxiety and mood disorders in the family background

There is considerable evidence for the presence of anxiety and depression in the relatives of children with AS and those with AD. Some authors have argued that this is more likely to be true for those with AS than those with high-functioning AD (Szatmari, Bartolucci, and Bremner 1989). DeLong and Dwyer (1988) found higher rates of bipolar depression in the families of children with high-functioning AD, with the highest expression in those with AS. Our early research concurs with these findings since in a comparison of children with AD, Mental Retardation, and typical controls, we found no differences in either the language or the cognitive abilities of the relatives but did find evidence that the group with AD had relatives with a greater number of psychiatric difficulties. These consisted mainly of affective and anxiety disorders, along with what the parents described to us as "eccentric behaviour" in members of the extended family (Konstantareas and Homatidis, unpublished). The heritability of mood and anxiety disorders in AS may relate to the more general fact that ASD is genetically transmitted, with a heritability of 93% (Bailey, Phillips, and Rutter 1996).

Neurobiological findings

In their examination of the neurofunctional models of AD and AS, Schultz, Romanski, and Tsatsanis (2000) offer evidence on the possible brain mechanisms responsible for anxiety and mood disregulation. They attribute it to malfunctioning of the amygdala and the orbital-medial prefrontal cortex. The connections of the amygdala with these structures and the temporal and occipital structures of the neocortex, as well as the limbic system and the prefrontal subcortical regions of the thalamus and the basal ganglia, are responsible for regulating the processing of emotional stimuli. According to Schultz et al. (2000), in both humans and in nonhuman primates the orbital-medial prefrontal cortex, which is linked to the amygdala and the limbic system, is responsible for integrating information on rewards and punishments necessary for the organism's future functioning. The authors review a study by Morgan, Romanski, and LeDoux (1993), who demonstrated that when lesions in the medial prefrontal cortex were made just before fear conditioning to an auditory stimulus, animals showed normal learning of emotional behaviour. That is, they showed freezing to the auditory stimulus that was paired with shock. However, when shock no longer followed the auditory stimulus, the animals continued to display freezing behaviour since their lesioned medial prefrontal cortex no longer sent the signal to the amygdala to turn off the freezing. Schultz *et al.* (2000) conclude by arguing that the high levels of arousal that many individuals with AS and AD experience, and the avoidance of eye contact, are related to malfunctioning of the amygdala–medial prefrontal circuit.

Environmental factors

Even though the aetiology of mood and anxiety difficulties is likely to be biological, this does not preclude the relevance of contextual factors. There is considerable evidence for the presence of stress in families with a member with AD, some from our own research (Konstantareas 1991). Some of the children who were included in this early research were not, of course, identified as having AS. However, in retrospect, they quite likely met criteria for what we now consider to be AS or, at least, high-functioning autism. More recently, support for the presence of stress has been obtained by a number of people (Stoddart 2003). Having a child with the symptomatology of AS clearly stresses the parents, as our own clinical work thus far suggests. In one of the cases, the child's many presenting characteristics have impacted negatively on the marital relationship, which in turn has acted to exacerbate the child's own difficulties since children are adversely affected by parental and family conflict on an ongoing basis.

Comparable problems may emerge at school, particularly when teachers are poorly aware of the special needs and characteristics of the child's behaviour and assume that he/she purposefully misbehaves. The frequent suspensions of children with AS who are aware of their characteristics and of the negative ramification of suspensions, despite the short-term relief of being out of school, are also adding to the stress and hence may trigger anxiety and depression. Thus, difficulties in the key settings of the child's life may be responsible for either triggering anxiety and depression or exacerbating these problems if they exist.

Implications of existing evidence for intervention

Although space prevents full coverage of the topic of intervention, some suggestions will be offered based on the relevant literature and clinical work. First, if children with AS in our study did not report feeling depressed, were they truly not depressed or were they defending against accepting that they suffer from low mood? Alternatively, were they less aware of how they compare to typical children in this respect? This requires further investigation. Second, assuming the presence of low mood and moderate or high anxiety, as many of the parents of some of the children reported, what can we do to reduce these difficulties? We saw that the presence of friendships was negatively related to reports of depression and anxiety. Clearly this suggests that training in how to relate to other children and how to "mind read" and accommodate to their peers' needs, should be a priority for children with AS. Some workers in the area have argued that social skills training in the context of other children with AS may not always be the best approach in this respect (Kunce and Mesibov 1998). In my experience, there are substantial differences in the presenting profiles and needs of children and youth with AS which may need to be accommodated through individual counselling and not group counselling alone.

Another issue is bullying. There is considerable work on this for typical children but little for children with AS. We need to systematically examine the natural history of bullying in children with AS. There has been increased awareness of the importance of maintaining zero tolerance for unsafe school environments. Unfortunately, as indicated earlier, reactive aggression on the part of children with AS is sometimes seen as part of CD by some school personnel who are unaware of these children's special characteristics, and their response to these behaviours is punishment. We need to educate them and the larger community about the characteristics and special needs of children with AS. Rather than suspension, these children require support during recess or other times of excessive confusion and noise.

To assist with specific difficulties in managing transitions and change in routine, children with AS may require visual schedules and maps, or other means, to be made aware of special assignments, school events, etc. Communication books between school and home are necessary. In addition, it may be necessary for children with AS to forego participation in things that are not of interest to them. Thus, flexibility in academic and extracurricular activities needs to be given special consideration to reduce anxiety and negative mood in these children. This may take various forms. For example, the anxiety of a 13-year-old was reduced considerably when I met with his teachers and persuaded them to allow him to leave assignments on the teacher's desk rather than hand them in personally – a source of major anxiety to him. The same was the case for allowing him extra time for tests and changing the assignments from being handwritten to being typewritten.

The use of social stories and comic strips (Gray 1998) may also assist with transitions and issues of empathy, managing frustration, and becoming aware of others' needs. Exposure of parents and teachers to the principles of behaviour modification is also necessary, since many children with AS exacerbate their difficulties by resorting to inappropriate verbal comments, or behaviours that may create difficulties for them and their social context. These and other modifications may go a long way towards reducing environmentally induced anxiety. For difficulties that are more serious, parental counselling or medication may be indicated. A number of volumes addressed to parents and teachers of children with AS have appeared and need to be consulted for more comprehensive accounts of how to ensure that a given child's needs are best served (e.g. Attwood 1998; Howlin 1998).

Conclusion

In conclusion, it appears that anxiety and depression are aspects of functioning of children with AS that need to be systematically examined and addressed through intervention in the home and school. Further research on the issues outlined in this chapter may help clarify the best practices approach to their special needs.

References

Achenbach, T.M. (1988) *Child Behavior Checklist for Ages 4–16*. Burlington, VT: University of Vermont.

APA (American Psychiatric Association) (1994) *Diagnostic and Statistical Manual of Mental Disorders, Fourth Edition*. Washington, DC: APA.

Attwood, T. (1998) *Asperger's Syndrome: A Guide for Parents and Professionals*. London, UK: Jessica Kingsley Publishers.

Bailey, A., Phillips, W., and Rutter, M. (1996) Autism: Towards an integration of clinical, genetic and neurobiological perspectives. *Journal of Child Psychology and Psychiatry, 37*, 89–126.

Bolton, P.F., Pickles, A., Murphy, M., and Rutter, M. (1998) Autism, affective and other psychiatric disorders: Patterns of familial aggregation. *Psychological Medicine, 28*, 385–95.

Clarke, D., Baxter, M., Perry, D., and Prasher, V. (1999) Affective and psychotic disorders in adults with autism: Seven case reports. *Autism: The International Journal of Research and Practice, 3*, 149–64.

Craven-Thuss, B., and Konstantareas, M.M. (in preparation) Proactive and reactive aggression in children with autism spectrum disorder. University of Guelph, Guelph, ON.

Creak, M. (1961) Schizophrenia syndrome in childhood: Progress report of a working party. *Cerebral Palsy Bulletin, 3*, 530–5.

DeLong, R., and Dwyer, J.T. (1988) Correlation of family history with specific autistic subgroups: Asperger's syndrome and bipolar affective disease. *Journal of Autism and Developmental Disorders, 18*, 593–600.

Ghaziuddin, M., and Greden, J. (1998) Depression in children with autism/pervasive developmental disorders. *Journal of Autism and Developmental Disorders, 25*, 495–502.

Gillberg, C. (1984) Autistic children growing up: Problems during puberty and adolescence. *Developmental Medicine and Child Neurology, 26*, 122–9.

Gilliam, J.E. (2001) *Gilliam Asperger's Disorder Scale*. Austin, TX: PRO-ED Inc.

Gillott, A., Furniss, F., and Walter, A. (2001) Anxiety in high-functioning children with autism. *Autism: The International Journal of Research and Practice, 5*, 227–86.

Goldsmith, H.H., and Rothbart, M.K. (1991) Contemporary instruments for assessing early temperament by questionnaire and in the laboratory. In J. Strelau and A. Angleitner (eds) *Explorations in Temperament*. New York, NY: Plenum.

Gray, C.A. (1998) Social stories and comic strip conversations with students with Asperger Syndrome and high functioning autism. In E. Schopler, G.B. Mesibov, and L.J. Kunce (eds) *Asperger's Syndrome or High Functioning Autism?* New York, NY: Plenum.

Green, J., Gilchrist, A., Burton, D., and Cox, A. (2000) Social and psychiatric functioning in adolescents with Asperger syndrome compared with conduct disorder. *Journal of Autism and Developmental Disorders, 30*, 279–93.

Howlin, P. (1998) *Children with Autism and Asperger Syndrome: A Guide for Practitioners and Carers.* Chichester, UK: John Wiley and Sons.

Kim, J.A., Szatmari, P., Bryson, S.E., Streiner, D.L., and Wilson, F.J. (2000) The prevalence of anxiety and mood problems among children with autism and Asperger syndrome. *Autism: The International Journal of Research and Practice, 4*, 117–32.

Klin, A., Volkmar, F.R., and Sparrow, S.S. (eds) (2000) *Asperger Syndrome.* New York, NY: Guilford.

Konstantareas, M.M. (1991) Autistic, learning disabled and delayed children's impact on their parents. *Canadian Journal of Behaviour Science, 23*, 358–75.

Konstantareas, M.M., and Homatidis, S. (unpublished) The hereditary backgrounds of children with autistic disorder, mental retardation and normal controls. Unpublished manuscript. Clarke Institute of Psychiatry, Toronto, Ontario.

Konstantareas, M.M., Homatidis, S., and Busch, J. (1989) Cognitive, communication, and social differences between autistic boys and girls. *Journal of Applied Developmental Psychology, 10*, 411–24.

Konstantareas, M.M., and Stewart, K. (in press) Affect regulation and temperament in children with autism spectrum disorder. *Journal of Autism and Developmental Disorders.*

Kovacs, M. (1992) *The Children's Depression Inventory* (CDI). Toronto, ON: Multi-Health Systems.

Krug, D.A., Arick, J., and Almond, P. (1980) Behavior checklist for identifying severely handicapped individuals with high levels of autistic behavior. *Journal of Child Psychology and Psychiatry, 21*, 221–9.

Kunce, L., and Mesibov, G.B. (1998) Educational approaches. In E. Schopler, G.B. Mesibov, and L.J. Kunce (eds) *Asperger's Syndrome or High Functioning Autism?* New York, NY: Plenum.

Lainhart, J., and Folstein, S.E. (1994) Affective disorders in people with autism: A review of published cases. *Journal of Autism and Developmental Disorders, 24*, 587–601.

Little, L. (2001) Peer victimization of children with Asperger spectrum disorders. *Journal of the American Academy of Child and Adolescent Psychiatry, 40*, 995–6.

Matson, J.L. (1994) *Autism in Children and Adults: Etiology, Assessment and Intervention.* Pacific Grove, CA: Brooks/Cole.

Mishna, F., and Muskat, B. (1998) Group therapy for boys with features of Asperger syndrome and concurrent learning disabilities: Finding a peer group. *Journal of Child and Adolescent Group Therapy, 8*, 97–114.

Morgan, M.A., Romanski, L.M., and LeDoux, J.E. (1993) Extinction of emotional learning: Contribution of medial prefrontal cortex. *Neuroscience Letters, 163*, 109–113.

Rothbart, M.K., Ahadi, S.A., Hershey, K.L., and Fisher, P. (2001) Investigations of temperament at 3–7 years: The children's behavior questionnaire. *Child Development, 72*, 5, 1401–08.

Schopler, E., Mesibov, G.B., and Kunce, L.J. (1998) *Asperger's Syndrome or High Functioning Autism?* New York, NY: Plenum.

Schopler, E., Reichler, R.J., and Renner, B.R. (1986) *The Childhood Autism Rating Scale.* Los Angeles, CA: Western Psychological Services.

Schultz, R.T., Romanski, L.M., and Tsatsanis, D. (2000) Neurofunctional models of autistic disorder and Asperger's Syndrome: Clues from neuroimaging. In A. Klin, F.R. Volkmar, and S.S. Sparrow (eds) *Asperger Syndrome.* New York, NY: Guilford.

Stoddart, K.P. (2003) Reported stress, personality and mental health in parents of children with Pervasive Developmental Disorders. Doctoral dissertation, University of Toronto.

Szatmari, P., Bartolucci, G., and Bremner, R. (1989) Asperger's syndrome and Autism: Comparison of early history and outcome. *Developmental Medicine and Child Neurology, 31,* 709–720.

Windle, M. (1992) Revised dimensions of temperament survey (DOTS-R): Simultaneous group confirmatory factor analysis for adolescent gender groups. *Psychological Assessment, 4,* 228–34.

Windle, M., and Lerner, R.M. (1986) Reassessing the dimensions of temperamental individuality across the life span: The revised dimensions of temperament survey (DOTS-R). *Journal of Adolescent Research, 1,* 213–30.

CHAPTER 3

Enhancing academic, social, emotional, and behavioural functioning in children with Asperger Syndrome and Nonverbal Learning Disability

Barbara Muskat

Authors such as Klin and Volkmar (2000) contend that children with Asperger Syndrome (AS) may be diagnosed with a number of disorders. Many, if not most children with AS struggle at school, and hence are often diagnosed with a learning disability. The diagnosis of a learning disability can enable students with AS to benefit from support in special education programs in the educational setting. It is possible for students with AS to receive a diagnosis of a particular type of learning disability, Nonverbal Learning Disability (NVLD). Even without this diagnosis, some of the theoretical underpinnings of NVLD can be helpful in understanding the problems which children with AS experience.

This chapter will present an overview of NVLD. Features common to NVLD and AS will be highlighted. Specifically, the academic, social, emotional, and behavioural difficulties that are features of both NVLD and AS will be reviewed. Individual and group strategies that can be implemented in home, school, or community settings to address these concerns will be presented. While many of these strategies are presented in the context of a discussion of individuals with NVLD, their applicability for those with AS and other Pervasive Developmental Disorders are evident.

Asperger Syndrome and Nonverbal Learning Disabilities

DSM-IV (APA 1994) diagnostic criteria for AS include: (1) qualitative impairment in social interaction evidenced by impairments in the use of nonverbal cues, failure to develop peer relationships, lack of spontaneous sharing of enjoyment, or lack of social or emotional reciprocity; (2) restricted repetitive and stereotyped patterns of behaviour, interests, and activities; and (3) impairment in social, occupational, or other important areas of functioning. Individuals with AS have no clinically significant general delays in language, cognitive development, or in the development of age-appropriate self-help skills, adaptive behaviour, and curiosity about the environment. Some authors report current debate about whether AS is different from high-functioning autism (Mayes, Calhoun, and Crites 2001; Volkmar *et al.* 2000).

There is no universally agreed-upon definition of "learning disabilities" (Kavale and Forness 1998) and the definition of learning disabilities has been revised many times. However, there is agreement on several key elements. These include the presence of average cognitive abilities, unexplained learning failure, and specific problems in the psychological processes related to learning (Kavale and Forness 1998). The most common learning disabilities are those in the areas of reading, writing, and spoken language.

In recent years, awareness of another type of learning disability has been growing. The term "Nonverbal Learning Disabilities" (NVLD) has been increasingly applied to children who struggle with visual-spatial organization; adapting to change; nonverbal problem solving; social language usage; mathematics; visual-motor co-ordination; and social perception, judgement and interaction. Some of the features of NVLD are strikingly similar to those of AS (Rourke and Tsatsanis 2000).

Dr Byron Rourke, a Canadian neuropsychologist, was one of the first to describe the "Syndrome of Nonverbal Learning Disabilities". The term "Nonverbal Learning Disability" can be misleading. When many hear the term, they believe that it means that an individual has a learning disability that impairs speaking (thus the person is nonverbal). However, the "nonverbal" description relates to the learning disability, not to the individual. Thus, the term "Nonverbal Learning Disability" means the learning disability is not in the verbal domain. Rourke (1995) describes the following difficulties associated with NVLD:

- bilateral tactile perception; sensing and responding to stimuli on either side of the body

- bilateral psychomotor co-ordination; co-ordination during activity, particularly when skills are complex

- visual-spatial perception; this includes interpreting visual cues from the environment
- interpreting and organizing visual-spatial information into meaningful patterns, such as discriminating foreground from background
- adapting to change or novel situations
- time concepts; difficulties estimating amount of time spent during activities
- math (relative to reading)
- memory when presented with complex verbal material
- organization (breaking tasks into component parts and combining parts to make a whole)
- nonverbal problem solving, particularly dealing with cause–effect relationships, appreciating incongruities, receiving and incorporating feedback on new situations and understanding nonverbal aspects of communication
- social use of language and modifying language to fit various social situations; overuse of repetitive, rote language
- social perception, social judgement, and social interaction.

These difficulties are found alongside normally developed rote verbal capacities and verbal memory skills. Not every individual diagnosed with NVLD has all the features described above. However, many of the features have the capacity to seriously affect the quality of life of those who struggle with NVLD. Indeed, Rourke (1995) was concerned about the high risk of mood disorders, particularly depression, in this population.

Research on the causes of NVLD is in its infancy. However, Rourke and Tsatsanis (2000) posit that NVLD originates from dysfunctional white matter of the brain. Based on research carried out by Rourke, NVLD is also seen as involving dysfunctions in the right hemisphere of the brain. These dysfunctions may manifest in individuals with NVLD in that they cannot create mental representations of the world, cannot code and represent novel situations, and cannot create or apply solutions to novel situations. There have not been any epidemiological studies of the prevalence of NVLD; however, some authors feel that as awareness of this category of learning disability has grown over the past ten to 15 years, so has prevalence (Roman 1998). Roman describes the lack of consensus on a suitable test battery for NVLD. There is no formal consensus on the number or severity of symptoms necessary to make the diagnosis.

A comprehensive study comparing the neuropsychological profiles of individuals with AS and high-functioning autism (Klin *et al.* 1995) gave evidence of a relationship between AS and NVLD. The two diagnostic categories shared the following: problems in fine motor skills, visual-motor integration, visual-spatial perception, nonverbal concept formation, gross motor skills, and visual memory. Klin *et al.* (1995) subsequently proposed that the concepts of AS and NVLD may offer different perspectives on overlapping groups of individuals. However, a study by Barnhill and colleagues (2000) found no significant difference between the verbal IQ scores and the performance IQ scores of a sample of children and adolescents with AS. Their sample did not represent the cognitive profile consistent with NVLD.

Thus, it appears that some individuals with AS have a cognitive profile similar to those with NVLD while others clearly do not. In addition, some individuals with NVLD have some of the idiosyncratic interests of those with AS. Figure 3.1 depicts the possible relationship between the two syndromes. While there is no definitive answer about whether all individuals with AS also have NVLD, there is much to be gained for each group by studying the theory and approaches used by both.

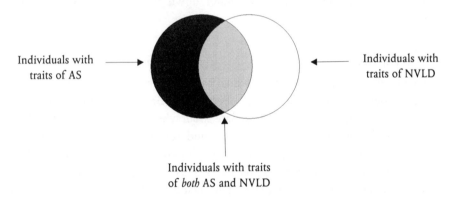

Figure 3.1 Possible overlap between Nonverbal Learning Disability and Asperger Syndrome

Cognitive theories

Some authors have described three major theories that guide understanding of the social cognitive difficulties of individuals with NVLD and AS. These are: (1) central coherence theory, (2) executive dysfunction theory, and (3) theory of mind.

Central coherence theory

"Central coherence" is the ability to construct higher meanings from a set of details. Individuals with NVLD often have difficulty relating parts to a whole. They have trouble seeing how a whole can be broken into parts and have trouble seeing how a series of parts can be made into a whole. They also have difficulty connecting details of what they know through interpretation and analysis. They struggle with drawing together diverse information to construct higher meaning in context, and have difficulty using context to understand information, and particularly social information (Frith and Happé 1995).

Executive functioning

Executive functioning is the skills needed to prepare for and execute complex behaviour. This includes planning, mental flexibility, and the mental representation of tasks and goals (Ozonoff and Griffith 2000). This also involves the ability to shift attention between tasks, allowing one to carry out multiple activities at a time. Individuals with NVLD have difficulty creating organizational structures that would allow them to be flexible, plan, and prioritize activities and goals. They have difficulty planning, breaking down information into steps, and managing time.

Theory of mind

"Theory of mind" describes an individual's ability to think about and act on information about one's own and others' mental states (Baron-Cohen 1995; Ozonoff and Griffith 2000). There is some debate about whether individuals with NVLD (and AS) actually struggle with theory of mind. It may be observed in some individuals with NVLD that they have difficulty thinking about and acting on beliefs, desires, and intentions. They may have problems tracking what others know and using it in interpersonal interactions. This includes difficulty understanding and monitoring their own responses when in an interaction and not understanding that others do not know what they are thinking.

Academic implications of NVLD

Motor difficulties

Many individuals with NVLD struggle with fine and gross motor co-ordination. This can translate into difficulty holding a pen or pencil or controlling the mouse on a computer. Problems with integrating visual information and motor movements negatively affect activities such as copying material from a blackboard and participation in sports activities requiring hand–eye co-ordination. NVLD also influences co-ordination and balance, thus speed of motor movement is often slow. For example, when one considers the skills required for a sport such as baseball, struggling with hand–eye co-ordination (e.g. aiming a throw, positioning a bat), co-ordination and balance problems (e.g. throwing, catching, and hitting), and speed (e.g. base running) would seriously affect one's ability to play the game.

Individuals with NVLD also have difficulty with grasping and manipulating spatial relationships. This leads to problems understanding the position of oneself in space and directional orientation. Individuals with NVLD often find themselves getting lost in new situations and struggling to make sense of directions presented in maps or offered verbally by others.

Written expressive problems

As well as the struggle with visual-motor aspects of writing, individuals with NVLD may also experience problems with the organizational requirements of the writing process. They may produce a large quantity of words that lack proper sequencing, a flow from beginning to end, and a coherence of content. Despite their relative strength in rote language skills, some individuals with NVLD produce words, thoughts, and ideas that require significant organization before they become coherent stories and essays.

Mathematics (reasoning and calculation) problems

Individuals with NVLD often struggle with understanding concepts related to time, space, depth, volume, or area. Organizational and sequencing difficulties lead to problems following mathematical steps. Visual processing deficits in individuals with NVLD may affect the correct copying of numbers, remembering to add in carried numbers, and accurately observing operational signs (e.g. differentiating an addition (+) sign from a multiplication (x) sign). Individuals with NVLD have particular difficulty in high school math. For example, difficulties in organization and sequencing will affect their ability to follow the order of operations in algebra; problems in understanding visual-spatial relationships will influence their ability to understand and solve problems in geometry.

Social implications of NVLD

Human beings live in a world where interaction with others is an integral part of the human experience. Humans prefer connectedness to loneliness. Person-to-person communication is a basic need. Therefore, developing the ability to be a socially competent individual is a protective factor for mental health and well-being. There is an association between poor peer relations and psychosocial problems (Boivin, Hymel, and Bukowski 1995). Social competence is particularly important for students with cognitive, academic, attentional, and emotional or behavioural problems. Feeling competent enables individuals to try their best, feel optimistic, and, in turn, do their best.

Individuals with NVLD often default to their areas of strength, one of which is producing rote language. Therefore, they often speak too much, using language that is verbose, repetitive, and lacking variations and emphasis in intonation. They do not understand the needs of the listener so they fail to modify their language to fit their audience. They do not understand the rules of discourse, the purpose or intent of social language, and how language is adapted to fit different situations. Social difficulties are often one of the earlier manifestations of NVLD.

Individuals with NVLD often do not understand the complexity of the social world, which is normally accomplished through development of social cognition. An understanding of the social world is based on observing others' behaviours, determining which behaviours are fitting for given situations, and reading the environmental contexts and the nonverbal cues of others. All these tasks are difficult for individuals with NVLD. Social understanding also requires the ability to correctly perceive the needs of others. Individuals with NVLD cannot easily sense the needs of others as they have difficulties interpreting and understanding information that is not conveyed directly through words (i.e. through facial expressions, body language, tone of voice, nuance, humour, sarcasm, metaphor, and imagery).

Most individuals learn social skills automatically by observing and copying the skills of those they live and interact with. Individuals with NVLD, who struggle with visual perception and social interaction, do not seem to learn these skills from their family and peers. While these skills may be explicitly taught, those with NVLD who are taught social skills often perform them in a rote, scripted manner. They may also lack opportunities for social practice because of social isolation. They frequently do not know when to apply them at acceptable levels. They often worry about failure. Some individuals with NVLD have difficulty regulating emotions and adjusting social performance to fit a situation. Anxiety, depression, withdrawal, aggression, and impulsivity can interfere with the ability to form relationships.

"Self-esteem" is the feelings and thoughts we have about ourselves, developed through experiences of relating to others, completing tasks competently, and self-direction. It includes our optimism about success. Self-esteem has been compared to the immune system of the mind, soul, and heart (Brooks and Goldstein 2001). It protects and buffers our inner self from potential damage brought on by failure or blocked attempts at success. Self-esteem allows us to continue taking risks in our lives. The social difficulties, academic difficulties, and experiences of failure experienced by individuals with NVLD have the potential to affect their self-esteem negatively. It is important for individuals with NVLD to work on developing positive views of themselves.

General strategies used with Nonverbal Learning Disability and Asperger Syndrome

Self-talk

Given the relative verbal strengths of individuals with NVLD, it can be helpful to translate nonverbal information into words. Individuals with NVLD can benefit from developing an internal dialogue, to help them in talking through difficult situations. They need others to model "self-talk". This can be accomplished by talking aloud through activities that rely on nonverbal cues, visual-spatial-organizational abilities or social perception. Feelings and emotions can be labelled aloud, as they occur. Patterns can be pointed out and made explicit. This can also aid individuals with NVLD with memorizing routines and detecting errors.

Breaking tasks into steps

Individuals with NVLD have difficulty with central coherence or parts-to-whole relationships. Therefore, it can be helpful for individuals with NVLD to break tasks into steps. If the steps are repeated verbally, written on a list, rehearsed, and practised, they can become part of the individual's daily routine. For example, the task of getting ready for school can be broken into: (1) Get out of bed. (2) Make bed. (3) Take shower, wash hair, body and face. (4) Get dressed, comb hair. (5) Eat breakfast.

Adapting to change

Change is difficult for individuals with NVLD. Parents or teachers can work with individuals with NVLD to develop strategies to assist in adapting to change. These include: planning events ahead of time; reviewing new situations in advance; discussing what might happen in a new setting; reviewing a series of questions to ask in case of confusion; planning appropriate responses to potential dilemmas or problems; and practising or rehearsing responses using role play.

Socialization

Most individuals with NVLD are not loners by choice. In adolescence, there is a tendency for these individuals to become despondent, negative, and clinically depressed. Increased awareness of social difficulties and repeated experiences of failure to make and/or maintain relationships may lead to depression.

In general, individuals with NVLD cannot learn about socialization in the midst of large, complex social situations. Therefore, it can be helpful to avoid over-stimulating group environments. Smaller, calm, controlled group settings offer a greater chance for safety and success. Feelings of belonging and acceptance are most likely to develop among individuals who share interests or talents. Individuals with NVLD need to learn to recognize situations that are potentially problematic and develop strategies to deal with them, such as recognizing that large groups are too stimulating, and requesting permission to be in a smaller group.

While individuals with NVLD need tolerance and acceptance from others, they also need to recognize and understand when they have behaved inappropriately. Therefore, others should not ignore or explain away inappropriate behaviours. It is best not only to say that something is wrong, but also to explain what was wrong and why it was wrong, using plain language, and offering alternatives for the next time. This should extend to the use of blunt language by individuals with NLVD, which sometimes presents as "rudeness". Individuals with NVLD also need help in developing rules for language suitable to the presence of adults and different rules for language to be used among peers. Being blunt and failing to modify language to specific situations are part of the disorder and require explicit, direct assistance.

Because of problems developing theory of mind, individuals with NVLD often need help to understand why it is important to consider the needs and feelings of other people. They need direct help to learn how to observe and notice others. Garcia-Winner's (2002) program has many helpful suggestions to assist individuals with NVLD to develop social perspective-taking skills. Her programs begin with helping individuals to learn why it is important to care about the views of others and illustrate the elements that go into being social, including knowing that an individual's behaviour has an impact on others, that others see things differently, and that behaviour needs to match specific situations. As well, individuals with NVLD need to be aware of the importance of watching others' behaviour, reading the reactions of the audience or listener, and adjusting reactions to the audience or listener.

Once an individual understands the importance of considering the needs of others, it then becomes important for that person to work on making a positive impression on others. For individuals with NVLD, making impressions needs to be taught explicitly. This would include information on how to dress, personal hygiene, what one says, how one says it, monitoring amount of information given, adjusting tone of voice and body language, and monitoring facial expressions. This also may include learning to show interest in what others are saying, regardless of how one may feel about it! Individuals with NVLD need to learn explicitly about appropriate social distance. Several authors describe programs to assist in learning and practising these skills (Duke, Nowicki, and Martin 1996; Stewart 2002).

Parents of children with NVLD are encouraged to help in practising the elements of making impressions to increase the accuracy and fluency of performance. This can be supplemented by organized play dates, where parents invite other children who may share the child's interests or can be positive role models for supervised play. Organized and supervised play with peers can increase the child's exposure to prosocial models, allow for practice, and reinforce successful performance of skills.

Children with NVLD are often prone to having anxiety and difficulties with emotional regulation. Strategies that are based on cognitive-behavioural programs can be useful (Kendall and Braswell 1993). Children with NVLD can benefit from techniques to help them learn to calm down, to relax and breathe, to stop and think, to make connections between their thoughts, feelings, and actions, and to become more "in tune" with their bodies.

Building self-esteem

Building positive self-esteem is important for individuals with NVLD. This begins with acknowledging and validating these individuals' feelings, particularly the difficult ones. This allows them to feel heard and understood. Parents and teachers need to provide environments that tolerate and accept differences while providing structure, consistency, appropriate expectations, support, and reassurance.

Performance expectations for individuals with NVLD should be appropriate to what they can do. They should not be measured by what others believe they ought to be able to do. Children need to develop an accurate self-concept that is realistic yet does not discourage them from trying to reach the upper limits of their potential. The adults in a child's life need to value what a child can do and consider the amount of effort that goes into accomplishments. This should include giving positive, genuine, and meaningful feedback as well as providing opportunities to feel valued.

Children with NVLD can be assisted in building self-esteem through participating in activities that interest them. They can be given responsibilities, such as taking care of a pet, assisting a senior citizen, or volunteering in the community.

They should be provided with opportunities to make choices and solve problems. Self-esteem can be enhanced through opportunities to help others.

Group approaches

Group approaches can be supportive for individuals with NVLD. Traditionally, groups for children with learning disabilities have had a social skills focus, placing an emphasis on the overt and explicit teaching of social skills. The benefits for a child of participating in a group for children with learning disabilities include the opportunity to be with a group of peers who are struggling with similar problems and concerns, and the chance to talk about having a learning disability and its impact. Difficulties can be addressed as they occur, in an environment adapted to members' cognitive difficulties and strengths (Mishna 1996a, 1996b; Mishna and Muskat 2004).

It is important that physical and emotional safety is maintained in groups for children with NVLD. The group experience should not replicate the negative experiences these students often have with peers. Groups provide a place to meet peers and play together in a supervised environment. Group members can be assisted to give one another feedback on problematic behaviour. They can also help one another to feel more acceptable to peers. Group members can practise skills while playing, including expressing affect, taking turns, sharing, initiating activities, resolving conflict, and making choices.

Creation of supportive environments

Intervention with individuals with NVLD is found to be most effective when the individual, family, school, and clinic are working on the same issues. Generalization is best achieved when the same issues are being addressed and similar approaches are being used in all settings of the individual's life. Goals for change should be developed and monitored jointly with the individual. Evaluation of progress can occur in a manner that strengthens self-esteem. Garcia-Winner makes an important point: "...these treatment strategies remain 'under construction' for all of us who specialize in this field. Virtually no longitudinal studies have been completed to look at the long-term effects of embedding this treatment approach in with others" (Garcia-Winner 2002, p.xii).

Expectations for growth and change in individuals with NVLD should be kept positive yet realistic. Science has not yet figured out how to remediate the difficulties associated with NVLD. The suggestions offered in this chapter represent ideas that may be supportive. What is most important to keep in mind is that we need to accentuate the best of individuals with NVLD in environments that are tolerant, encouraging, and growth enhancing.

References

APA (American Psychiatric Association) (1994) *Diagnostic and Statistical Manual of Mental Disorders, Fourth Edition.* Washington, DC: APA.

Barnhill, G, Hagiwara, T., Myles, B.S., and Simpson, R.L. (2000) Asperger Syndrome: A study of the cognitive profiles of 37 children and adolescents. *Focus on Autism and Other Developmental Disorders, 15,* 3, 146–53.

Baron-Cohen, S. (1995) *Mindblindness: An Essay on Autism and Theory of Mind.* Boston, MA: MIT Press/Bradford Books.

Boivin, M., Hymel, S., and Bukowski, W.M. (1995) The roles of social withdrawal, peer rejection, and victimization by peers in predicting loneliness and depressed mood in childhood. *Development and Psychopathology, 7,* 765–85.

Brooks, R., and Goldstein, S. (2001) *Raising Resilient Children.* Chicago, IL: Contemporary Books.

Duke, M., Nowicki, S., and Martin, E. (1996) *Teaching Your Child the Language of Social Success.* Atlanta, GA: Peachtree Publishers.

Frith, U., and Happé, F. (1995) Autism: Beyond "theory of mind." In J. Mehler and S. Franck (eds) *Cognition on Cognition, Cognition Special Series.* Cambridge, MA: The MIT Press.

Garcia-Winner, M. (2002) *Thinking About You Thinking About Me.* East Moline, IL: LinguiSystems, Inc.

Kavale, K.A., and Forness, S.R. (1998) The politics of learning disabilities. *Learning Disabilities Quarterly, 21,* 245–73.

Kendall, P.C., and Braswell, L. (1993) *Cognitive-behavioural Therapy for Impulsive Children, Second Edition.* New York, NY: Guilford Press.

Klin, A., and Volkmar, F.R. (2000) Treatment and intervention guidelines for individuals with Asperger Syndrome. In A. Klin, F.R. Volkmar, and S.S. Sparrow (eds) *Asperger Syndrome.* New York, NY: Guilford Press.

Klin, A., Volkmar, F.R., Sparrow, S.S., Cicchetti, D.V., and Rourke, B.P. (1995) Validity and neuropsychological characteristics of Asperger Syndrome: Convergence with Nonverbal Learning Disabilities Syndrome. *Child Psychology and Psychiatry and Allied Disciplines, 36,* 7, 1127–40.

Mayes, S.D., Calhoun, S.L., and Crites, D.L. (2001) Does DSM-IV Asperger's Disorder exist? *Journal of Abnormal Child Psychology, 29,* 3, 263–71.

Mishna, F. (1996a) Finding their voice: Group therapy for adolescents with learning disabilities. *Learning Disabilities Research and Practice, 11,* 249–58.

Mishna, F. (1996b) In their own words: Therapeutic factors for adolescents who have learning disabilities. *International Journal of Group Psychotherapy, 46,* 265–73.

Mishna, F., and Muskat, B. (2004) "I'm not the only one!" Group therapy with older children and adolescents who have learning disabilities. *International Journal of Group Psychotherapy, 54,* 4, 455–476.

Ozonoff, S., and Griffith, E.M. (2000) Neuropsychological function and the external validity of Asperger Syndrome. In A. Klin, F.R. Volkmar, and S.S. Sparrow (eds) *Asperger Syndrome.* New York, NY: Guilford Press.

Roman, M.A. (1998) The syndrome of Nonverbal Learning Disabilities: Clinical description and applied aspects. *Current Issues in Education, 1,* 1.

Rourke, B.P. (1995) *Syndrome of Nonverbal Learning Disabilities: Neurodevelopmental Manifestations.* New York, NY: Guilford Press.

Rourke, B.P., and Tsatsanis, K.D. (2000) Nonverbal Learning Disabilities and Asperger Syndrome. In A. Klin, F.R. Volkmar, and S.S. Sparrow (eds) *Asperger Syndrome.* New York, NY: Guilford Press.

Stewart, K. (2002) *Helping a Child with Nonverbal Learning Disorder or Asperger's Syndrome.* Oakland, CA: New Harbinger Publications.

Volkmar, F.R., Klin, A., Schultz, R.T., Rubin, E., and Bronen, R. (2000) Asperger's disorder. *American Journal of Psychiatry, 157,* 2, 262–7.

CHAPTER 4

Tourette Syndrome and Asperger Syndrome: Overlapping symptoms and treatment implications

Trina Epstein and Jennifer Saltzman-Benaiah

Tourette Syndrome (TS) has been classified as part of a larger group of developmental neuropsychiatric disorders, a term reflecting the growing recognition of the neurobiological underpinnings of behaviours previously viewed as psychogenic. It is therefore not surprising that much of the current research on TS has focussed on neurological mechanisms of tics and the other prominent symptoms that are associated with this condition. Autism spectrum disorders (ASDs) such as Asperger Syndrome (AS) have also been viewed as developmental neuropsychiatric disorders. Moreover, there is speculation about the relationship and overlap between ASDs and tic disorders.

The purpose of this chapter is to provide a discussion of TS that alerts readers to important and potentially challenging issues that can arise when considering the overlap of TS and AS symptomatology. The first section will provide a brief overview of the commonly associated features of TS, including some similarities and differences from the presentation of AS. Some of the suspected neuropathological mechanisms of TS are then briefly reviewed; this may help in understanding the intriguing relationship between many seemingly unrelated symptoms. Focusing on one of the similarities in symptom presentation (i.e. inflexibility), the second section of this chapter will provide an example of an effective behavioural management approach for TS and AS. The final section highlights key issues through a case illustration.

Tourette Syndrome: An overview

Diagnostic criteria and main features

TS is one of several related tic disorders characterized by non-rhythmic, repetitive movements known as tics. The criteria for diagnosing TS are set out in the *Diagnostic and Statistical Manual*. Although the most recent version of these criteria is provided in the fourth edition of the *DSM* (APA 1994), concerns about these criteria have led some experts to propose the use of alternate criteria for both clinical and research purposes.

First, it has been argued that the *DSM-IV* (APA 1994) criteria, which require there be some impairment based on the presence of the tics, is inappropriate since many individuals experience tics that are not intrusive or impairing to their daily functioning (Freeman, Fast, and Kent 1995). Notably, the criterion for significant impairment of functioning is not required for stereotypic movement disorder, developmental co-ordination disorder, or neuroleptic-induced tardive dys-kinesia. Although many individuals with less impairing forms of tic disorders do not require medical treatment (and therefore do not require the diagnosis), failing to give a diagnosis in these cases may have other ramifications, such as reducing the likelihood that such a person would receive appropriate genetic counselling (Sandor 2004).

Second, *DSM-IV* (APA 1994) states that, for a diagnosis of TS, there should not be any tic-free period for more than three consecutive months, a criterion which is considered arbitrary and not scientifically meaningful. Given that retro-spective parental report of tic behaviour in children can be unreliable or imprecise, it could be difficult to be certain that tics had not been present for a specific period. Thus, in the Tourette Syndrome Neurodevelopmental (TSN) Clinic in Toronto where we practice, the previous *DSM-III-R* (APA 1987) criteria are considered more suitable for making the TS diagnosis (see Figure 4.1).

Like AS, TS is a disorder with a childhood onset and is more commonly diagnosed in males. The estimated male to female ratio is 4:1 (Freeman *et al.* 2000). The overall prevalence of TS is estimated to be around 1% to 2%. The median age for the onset of tics is around seven years of age. Tic symptoms can multiply and worsen during the school-aged years, but may then lessen later in adolescence and into adulthood. (For a detailed review of the natural history of TS, see Leckman and Cohen 1999.) Tics themselves can have a fluctuating course that is referred to as "waxing and waning", meaning the tics can come and go and can change in presentation over time. A history of multiple motor tics and at least one vocal tic is required for a diagnosis of TS, whereas children who present with either motor or vocal tics may receive a diagnosis of Chronic Motor or Vocal Tic Disorder. Examples of motor tics include eye blinking, facial grimacing, shoulder shrugging, neck stretching, stomach or buttock tensing, tapping, and twirling.

A.   Both multiple motor and one or more vocal tics have been present at some time during the illness, although not necessarily concurrently.

B.   The tics occur many times a day (usually in bouts), nearly every day or intermittently throughout a period of more than one year.

C.   The anatomic location, number, frequency, complexity, and severity of the tics change over time.

D.   Onset before age 21.

E.   Occurrence not exclusively during Psychoactive Substance Intoxication or known central nervous system disease, such as Huntington's chorea and postviral encephalitis.

Figure 4.1 DSM-III-R (APA 1987) diagnostic criteria for Tourette Syndrome. Reprinted from the Diagnostic and Statistical Manual of Mental Disorders, Third Edition – Revised, Copyright 1987, American Psychiatric Association.

Vocal tics can appear as noises such as sniffing, coughing, throat clearing, humming, barking, and screaming. Some children with TS repeat words or phrases said by others (i.e. echolalia) or themselves (i.e. palilalia). A small proportion of the TS population (10% to 15%: Freeman *et al.* 2000) exhibits tics in the form of swearing, saying rude words, or inappropriate gesturing (i.e. coprolalia).

Overlap of Asperger Syndrome and Tourette Syndrome features

At the TSN Clinic, children who are referred to query the diagnosis of TS, frequently also meet the criteria for AS. In an ongoing research project, the authors of this chapter have been seeking to identify the rate at which children referred as possibly having TS also receive a diagnosis of AS. Preliminary results suggest there may be an increased likelihood of seeing children with both diagnoses in this kind of clinical setting. In one clinical setting, it was found that 9% of TS patients also met criteria for AS (Berthier, Bayes, and Tolosa 1993). In general, there is limited information about the specific overlap between AS and TS, although there is some documentation about the rate of occurrence of tics in those with ASDs, and the rate of occurrence of ASDs in children with tics. Baron-Cohen and his colleagues (1999) reported the presence of a tic disorder in 6% to 8% of their sample with ASDs. It has been suggested that the rate of occurrence of ASDs in children diagnosed with TS may be as high as 4.5% (Freeman *et al.* 2000).

When individuals present with symptoms of both AS and TS, the process of discriminating between behaviours that represent tics and those that are autistic stereotypies can be challenging, since both are repetitive movements that can wax and wane. Recognizing the differences between tics and stereotypies can be an important aspect of treatment planning, since certain medications may be helpful in reducing tic-like behaviours but are not necessarily effective in changing the presentation of stereotypies.

Rapin (2001) highlighted some of the other similarities and differences that can be helpful when making this distinction. Both tics and stereotypies can appear as simple or complex movements. Both are suppressible for a time, and may be preceded by a premonitory urge (i.e. an urge to perform the movement). Tics and stereotypies both tend to be exacerbated by anxiety but may disappear when an individual is concentrating or engaged in activity. Interestingly, there have been cases reported in the media of professionals (e.g. a surgeon) who have been diagnosed with TS, but do not experience tics when they are focussed on work activities.

Despite these similarities, Rapin (2001) points to some differences that can be noted both in the presentation and the pattern of tics compared to stereotypies. While tics often first appear during the school-aged years, stereotypies are often present at a younger age. As part of the waxing and waning pattern, tics can remit for months at a time, while stereotypies tend to be more persistent. Tics can change in presentation over time, while stereotypies are less variable, but may become miniaturized with age. Tics tend to be brief, sudden, non-rhythmic movements that are not necessarily symmetrical. Stereotypies may present for a longer duration, and often appear to be both rhythmic and symmetrical. Interestingly, tics can occur during sleep, while this is uncommon for stereotyped behaviours.

Based on clinical experience, it can also be helpful to consider these repetitive behaviours in the larger context, taking into account when behaviours tend to occur and any environmental triggers. An example of confusion between stereotypies and tics can be seen in the following case of a child who was seen in the TSN Clinic. This boy had been previously diagnosed with TS based on several repetitive behaviours including hand-flapping movements and "whooping" noises. The referral was made because of ongoing behavioural difficulties and a concern that the tics were not being managed effectively by his current medication regimen. Detailed questioning revealed that some of the "tics" occurred exclusively when the child was engaging in a particular ritual (e.g. flicking a light switch off and on) but at no other times. Given the developmental history and profile of other features that were consistent with AS (e.g. long-standing social difficulties, inflexible thinking), it was determined that these behaviours were more likely to be representative of stereotypies and not tics. Some of the other repetitive behaviours that were reported (e.g. eye blinking, neck stretching) were consistent with the original TS diagnosis. This case example demonstrates the importance of considering not only that AS and TS may be comorbid, but that features of AS may resemble those of TS, and *vice versa*.

Associated features and comorbid conditions

The two most common comorbid conditions associated with TS are Attention Deficit Hyperactivity Disorder (ADHD) and Obsessive Compulsive Disorder (OCD), which can be present together or separately in upwards of 50% of individuals diagnosed with TS (Leckman and Cohen 1999). Inattentive and/or hyperactive behaviours that meet criteria for a diagnosis of ADHD are often present from a young age, and usually pre-date the emergence of tic symptoms (Leckman and Cohen 1999). Impulsivity can be a prominent feature of many individuals diagnosed with TS and ADHD. Impulsive interrupting or acting out can contribute to problems in school and peer relationships. Thus, reports of academic difficulties and social problems are common in children diagnosed with TS and ADHD, even though the child's profile is not consistent with an ASD.

Although many individuals with TS receive a comorbid diagnosis of OCD, others present with a sub-clinical level of Obsessive Compulsive Behaviour (OCB) that does not meet the criteria for a full OCD diagnosis. Children with OCB in the context of TS often do not present with the more obvious symptoms of OCD, such as fear of germs and hand washing. Instead, research has documented that individuals with TS display more issues with symmetry and evening things out. They may also report tapping, touching, or counting rituals (Leckman and Cohen 1999). Rather than expressing strong feelings of anxiety in connection with the compulsive behaviours, many individuals with TS will describe a need for something to feel "just right".

Both ADHD and OCD can also be associated with AS. When these symptoms are present in an individual for whom AS is also queried, one must carefully consider the overlapping impact of each disorder (Attwood 1998). For example, many children with AS appear to be inattentive to tasks that are not within the realm of their special interest, yet it is possible for a child to appropriately receive all three diagnoses (TS, AS, and ADHD). Obsessive-compulsive features such as those present in TS can resemble the need for routine in individuals with AS. Discriminating between tics, compulsions, and stereotypies can be a challenging task for a clinician.

Another feature that is common in both TS and AS is heightened sensory sensitivity. Children with TS often report sensitivities to different types of sensory stimulation, including tactile (e.g. tags in shirts), visual (e.g. bright lights), and auditory inputs (e.g. loud noises).

Rage behaviour is a characteristic that is sometimes associated with TS. Parents describe temper tantrums that can be explosive, aggressive, or simply argumentative. Triggers for these behaviours include being told "no" or encountering unexpected changes in plans. Parents' descriptions often reflect a child who is easily frustrated and has a tendency to get "stuck" on certain ideas or ways of acting. In such cases, children are often characterized as "oppositional" despite later showing remorse for their behaviour. In the moment, the child appears to have little control over behaviour or rational thinking and attempts to reprimand the child can escalate behaviour rather than calm it. Clinical accounts of children with AS include descriptions of argumentativeness, difficulty adjusting to new situations, and the same inflexibility and/or tendency to get "stuck" as is seen in some children with TS.

In some cases it may be important to understand the underlying aetiology of a behaviour (i.e., is it part of the TS or the AS?), although clinicians may find that available options are the same regardless of this determination. This may be true for many pharmacological and/or behavioural interventions targeting specific symptoms that are present in the context of AS or TS. An example of this approach is discussed in the second section of this chapter.

Cognitive and social features

Social interaction difficulties are the hallmark of AS and include significant impairments in understanding emotions and cognitions relevant to social situations (Attwood 1998). Children with TS do not, overall, experience social difficulties of this sort, but can experience problems in peer interactions for several reasons. Sometimes, children may be teased because of prominent tics. Difficulties with impulsiveness and aggression also make children unpopular with their peers. Thus, the presence of significant misunderstandings and poor social judgement in a child with TS warrants further investigation into the possibility of AS, and should not be considered to be subsumed within the diagnosis of TS alone.

Academic difficulties can be reported in children with TS, particularly if another comorbid condition such as ADHD is present. There is no consistent profile associated with TS on neuropsychological testing, but clinical experience suggests that written output is an area of frequent concern, including poor handwriting, slow writing speed, and poor composition skills. This area may merit further investigation. In AS, uneven cognitive profiles are frequent (Myles *et al.* 2001), but research in this area is limited.

Neurobiological mechanisms and genetics

An exhaustive review of the neurobiological mechanisms of TS is beyond the scope of this chapter. Much of the current research in TS focusses on mechanisms related to the cortico-striato-thalamo-cortical pathways (CSTC), a series of circuits which form loops to connect subcortical regions (e.g. basal ganglia) and cortical regions (e.g. prefrontal cortex). Some researchers have hypothesized that tics may be related to reductions in the normal inhibitory projections from the striatum to the globus pallidus externa (GPe), resulting in the reduced inhibition of GPe inhibitory projection neurons to the subthalamic nucleus (STN), globus pallidus interna (GPi), and substantia nigra pars reticulata (SNr). This in turn, decreases activity in thalamo-cortical excitatory neurons. This decreased activity in the thalamo-cortical neurons then causes the initiation of a movement, which in TS manifests as a tic (Leckman and Cohen 1999).

Although it may be difficult to see why symptoms of hyperactivity, obsessionality, and repetitive movements would co-occur with such frequency, this becomes clearer when one recognizes the involvement of CSTC in each of these conditions. In particular, regions of the basal ganglia and/or prefrontal cortex have been implicated in structural and/or functional imaging studies of TS, OCD, and ADHD (Leckman and Cohen 1999). Preliminary findings have suggested that many of these same circuits may be implicated in AS (McAlonan *et al.* 2002). Berthier and colleagues (2003) described a case example of an adolescent male with a positive family history of tics and OCD, who developed symptoms consistent with AS and TS following a discrete hypoxic-ischemic necrosis of the midbrain, infrathalamic and thalamic nuclei, and striatum. The authors suggested that increased involvement of midbrain and related components of basal ganglia-thalamocortical circuits in individuals predisposed to TS might contribute to developing AS symptomatology.

It is generally recognized that there are significant genetic contributions to the presentation of TS, although it is also acknowledged that being genetically predisposed to TS does not mean that symptoms will be expressed in the same way. Evidence suggests that OCD may be a variant expression of the same genes involved in TS (Eapen, Pauls, and Robertson 1993). Future research into the neurobiological mechanisms as well as the genetic underpinnings of these neuro-psychiatric conditions may lead to greater insight into the comorbidity of TS and AS.

An approach for parenting inflexible children

Considering the number of overlapping features seen in TS and AS, it is more helpful to conceptualize these children in terms of their prominent difficulties (such as their inflexibility) than to focus only on their diagnoses. For the purpose of guiding treatment intervention, there are several reasons why it is more important to understand these children's unique symptom profiles than to know what diagnostic categories they fit into. Given the breadth of possible symptomatology, two children, each meeting criteria for both disorders, may present differently and with unique treatment priorities. Further, an overlap in features means that a child may meet the full diagnostic criteria for one of the two disorders, but remain sub-clinical for the other disorder. If the clinician is concentrating on symptoms instead of diagnoses, this valuable sub-clinical information will not be overlooked.

An approach to treatment that has been helpful with the AS/TS population of children is one that has been developed by Dr. Ross Greene, a psychologist at Massachusetts General Hospital (Greene 1998). Greene's approach, called Collaborative Problem Solving (CPS), was not designed for the AS and TS populations *per se*, but rather more broadly for "inflexible/explosive" children. However, CPS fits well with the types of difficulties faced by these children, as described in the previous section of this chapter.

While CPS has a direct impact on the child, the focus of the intervention is on the parents and/or teachers who are managing the child's behaviour. CPS offers an alternative to traditional behaviour management approaches that are based primarily on rewards and punishments. The CPS approach stresses understanding the underlying reasons, or "pathways", for a child's inflexibility or explosion. For instance, a child may experience frustration because of a deficit in his language pathway that impairs his communication. Anxiety or obsessiveness may contribute to frustration, as may low mood. Executive dysfunction, such as planning or shifting set, can contribute to explosiveness. Weaknesses in understanding social cues can lead to misinterpretations of interactions that can, in turn, result in frustration and explosive behaviour.

By definition, children with AS are impaired in their social pathway. Children with AS are also typically rigid and obsessive, as are children with TS. Of course, many weaknesses along many pathways can contribute to explosiveness, and although knowing a child's diagnosis can give us some clues about the pathways that are implicated, diagnosis does not provide all the answers.

Regardless of the pathway(s) affecting a given child, Greene argues that children who display inflexible or explosive behaviour are impaired in the domain of frustration tolerance for which the behavioural manifestation may be internalized (e.g. crying) or externalized (e.g. yelling). It is proposed that a deficit in frustration tolerance is no different from any other skill deficit, such as a weakness in reading or math. In this way, impairment in frustration tolerance can be thought of as a learning disability. In much the way that rewards and punishments are unhelpful in remediating a reading disability, it is argued that these approaches are equally unhelpful in ameliorating an underlying deficit in frustration tolerance. Thus, although a child's problems might be demonstrated in behavioural ways (e.g. hitting), these behaviours are merely an outward manifestation of the underlying cognitive deficit in frustration tolerance. Simply dispensing consequences for disruptive behaviour or offering rewards for the absence of behaviour is not helpful and will not teach the child the requisite skills that are lacking.

For instance, a child who has difficulty changing from one activity to another (i.e. shifting set) may throw a tantrum when his parent asks that he stop a favourite activity and come to dinner. If we believe the tantrum is because of a difficulty shifting set and managing the frustration that comes with this weakness, then punishing the child will not have an impact on her future behaviour. Punishment does not accomplish the goal of teaching the child to shift set more easily. Similarly, offering the child a reward for coming to dinner when asked will prove equally ineffective because the child does not have the shifting set skill required to comply. Parents with children with this difficulty often report frequent utilization of rewards and consequences without any demonstrable learning. Parents of children with AS and/or TS may find this example familiar. It is important to recognize that the reason little learning occurs is that, in developmental neuropsychiatric disorders, cognitive difficulties have a neurological basis. Of course, this does not mean that children are incapable of learning, but it does mean that they require explicit instruction and repetition to do so.

Parents trained in the CPS model are reminded that rewards and punishments work well at increasing motivation when the child already possesses the underlying set of required skills. Such strategies also work well when teaching a simple skill. Few would agree that skills such as shifting set and managing emotions in the face of frustration are "simple" and that they can be taught merely by using rewards and consequences.

Accepting the CPS model involves making a philosophical shift from "my child is having a tantrum to be manipulative" to "my child is having a tantrum because he cannot cope in the face of frustration". This philosophical shift is sometimes difficult for parents to make since the deficit presents as behavioural. Greene reiterates that the deficits are cognitive but are expressed in behavioural ways. He suggests the mantra "Children do well if they can" as a replacement to the preconceived mantra that parents often uphold: "Children do well if they want to." That is, he takes as the starting point the fact that typically children are already motivated to do well since the meltdowns are as destabilizing for the child as they are for the family.

Once parents come to believe that their children are not exploding as a means of getting their own way, but rather are behaving inflexibly because they lack the requisite skills to problem solve in the face of frustration, parents are encouraged to use preventive approaches to keep the child from experiencing frustration. CPS advocates a proactive rather than a reactive approach.

At the same time that parents are working preventively with their children, they are also attempting to teach the lacking skills (for instance, by direct instruction and modelling). Depending on the implicated pathways, sometimes parental coaching is insufficient. For instance, a child whose quick frustration and explosiveness is related to underlying problems with depression may benefit from a pharmacological and/or a cognitive-behavioural intervention to address the mood issue. Similarly, a medication intervention is often helpful for an underlying attentional problem since this is an area that does not respond well to teaching. Children with specific weaknesses in the social pathway may benefit from participating in a social skills group.

Keeping in mind that both TS and AS are genetic disorders, it is important to remember that children with specific pathway difficulties might come from families who struggle with similar issues. In these cases, parents might benefit themselves from consultation with a therapist. Greene reminds us: "It takes two to tango." Although CPS does not uphold that "bad behaviour" in children is the result of "bad parenting", he discusses a transactional model wherein the types of deficits existing in the child may be poorly matched with the management style of the parents (Greene, Ablon, and Goring 2002).

Given what we know about the helpfulness of the CPS approach, the TSN Clinic has undertaken the development of a treatment model to serve children with TS who may or may not have AS symptoms as well. One component of the treatment model is directed at parents only, and involves a series of workshops that teach the CPS approach. The sessions utilize a combination of video, didactic lecture, role play, and discussion to teach the CPS principles. Parents are given homework assignments (such as mapping their children's pathways and practising specific preventive approaches to meltdowns) between sessions and these are reviewed with an emphasis on troubleshooting. Parents are given many opportunities to practise the CPS skills both in and out of workshop sessions.

For families requiring further assistance, the TSN Clinic offers psychoeducational groups for children and parents. Children with TS/AS attend weekly sessions to learn some of the skills they are lacking, with a particular focus on the social pathway, the rigid/obsessive pathway, and the executive functioning pathway. At the same time they learn more about TS and AS and have an opportunity to meet other children who may be experiencing similar struggles. Parents attend a group that occurs concurrently in which they receive booster input regarding the CPS approach, learn more about TS and AS, receive psychoeducation about medication, and brainstorm other key topics such as how to interface effectively with schools. Research to evaluate the effectiveness of this approach is continuing; however, feedback from families has been positive.

Case example: Sam

Sam was referred to the TSN Clinic due to concerns about his repetitive behaviours and received a diagnosis of TS. Attentional concerns and hyperactivity led to a diagnosis of ADHD. Obsessive-compulsive features were also present, although it was felt that these symptoms were sub-clinical. Consistent with a diagnosis of TS, he also experienced numerous sensory sensitivities, emotional lability, and behavioural outbursts.

During follow-up appointments, Sam's mother raised specific concerns about his lack of social and emotional reciprocity. Despite his mother having invested much time in directly instructing Sam in friendship-making skills, he had few friends and continued to appear confused in social interactions. Another concern was Sam's tendency to focus on areas of special interest (e.g. trains) and his rigid adherence to routines, so that even small changes were challenging for him. Based on this information as well as a detailed developmental history gained through an interdisciplinary assessment, a diagnosis of AS was given.

Because of the behavioural concerns, Sam's mother was encouraged to attend a parent workshop on the CPS treatment model. She was able to identify the key pathways that typically led to Sam's escalating frustration and therefore she began to problem solve innovative ways to intervene proactively with Sam before he became frustrated. For instance, Sam often showed resistance to showering. Although his mother might have initially interpreted this as oppositionality, an understanding of his sensory sensitivities revealed that Sam was bothered by the sound of the shower. This understanding modified her emotional response to the situation and provided the basis for developing alternative strategies.

Conclusions

As a developmental neuropsychiatric disorder, TS presents with many key and associated features that can appear similar to or overlap with the symptoms of AS. Careful clinical investigation is essential for the diagnostic process and must be guided by an awareness of the overlap between TS and AS. Treatment approaches, such as CPS, which focus on pathways of difficulty rather than diagnostic categories, can be effective for children with TS and/or AS when children share similar symptoms.

References

APA (American Psychiatric Association) (1987) *Diagnostic and Statistical Manual of Mental Disorders, Third Edition, Revised.* Washington, DC: APA.

APA (American Psychiatric Association) (1994) *Diagnostic and Statistical Manual of Mental Disorders, Fourth Edition.* Washington, DC: APA.

Attwood, T. (1998) *Asperger's Syndrome: A Guide for Parents and Professionals.* London, UK: Jessica Kingsley Publishers.

Baron-Cohen, S., Scahill, V.L., Izaguirre, J., Hornsey, H., and Robertson, M.M. (1999) The prevalence of Gilles de la Tourette syndrome in children and adolescents with autism: A large scale study. *Psychological Medicine, 29*, 5, 1151–9.

Berthier, M.L., Bayes, A., and Tolosa, E. (1993) Magnetic resonance imaging in patients with concurrent Tourette's disorder and Asperger's Syndrome. *Journal of the American Academy of Child and Adolescent Psychiatry, 32*, 3, 633–639.

Berthier, M.L., Kulisevsky, J., Asenjo, B., Aparicio, J., and Lara, D. (2003) Comorbid Asperger and Tourette syndromes with localized mesencephalic infrathalamic, thalamic, and striatal damage. *Developmental Medicine and Child Neurology, 45*, 3, 207–12.

Eapen, V., Pauls, D.L., and Robertson, M.M. (1993) Evidence for autosomal dominant transmission in Tourette's syndrome. *British Journal of Psychiatry, 162*, 593–6.

Freeman, R.D., Fast, D.K., Burd, L., Kerbeshian, J., Robertson, M.M., and Sandor, P. (2000) An international perspective on Tourette syndrome: Selected findings from 3,500 individuals in 22 countries. *Developmental Medicine and Child Neurology, 42*, 7, 436–47.

Freeman, R.D., Fast, D.K., and Kent, M. (1995) DSM-IV criteria for Tourette's. *Child and Adolescent Psychiatry, 34*, 4, 400–401.

Greene, R.W. (1998) *The Explosive Child.* New York, NY: HarperCollins.

Greene, R.W., Ablon, J.S., and Goring, J.C. (2002) A transactional model of oppositional behavior. Underpinnings of the Collaborative Problem Solving approach. *Journal of Psychosomatic Research, 55*, 67–75.

Leckman, J.F., and Cohen, D.J. (eds) (1999) *Tourette's Syndrome.* New York, NY: John Wiley and Sons, Inc.

McAlonan, G.M., Daly, E., Kumari, V., Critchley, H.D., van Amelsvoort, T., Suckling, J., *et al.* (2002) Brain anatomy and sensorimotor gating in Asperger's syndrome. *Brain, 125*, 7, 1594–606.

Myles, B.S., Barnhill, G.P., Hagiwara, T., Griswold, D.E., and Simpson, R.L. (2001) A synthesis of studies on the intellectual academic social/emotional and sensory characteristics of children and youth with Asperger Syndrome. *Education and Training in Mental Retardation and Developmental Disabilities, 36*, 3, 304–11.

Rapin, I. (2001) Autism spectrum disorders: Relevance to Tourette Syndrome. *Advances in Neurology, 85*, 89–101.

Sandor, P. (2004) Personal communication.

CHAPTER 5

Young adults with Asperger Syndrome: Psychosocial issues and interventions

Kevin P. Stoddart

Young adults with Asperger Syndrome (AS) and their families find themselves at the intersection of various potentially stressful developmental transitions and life decisions. The need to make necessary accommodations in this period may lead them to seek counselling or other types of clinical support. Unfortunately, "The majority of adults with Asperger syndrome receive no assistance from outside agencies; they feel isolated and singled out as people whose disability is deemed unworthy of assistance" (Powell 2002, p.7). Comprehensive community supports for this group are severely lacking, although there are interventions and support models that are now being reported or recommended (Macleod 1999; Powell 2002). The fact that many early case descriptions of AS are of young adults (Wolff and Chick 1980; Wing 1981) is easily overlooked. Fortunately, increased recognition of the psychosocial needs of adults with AS started to occur in the 1990s (Simblett and Wilson 1993; Hare 1997; Bankier *et al.* 1999; Engstrom, Ekstrom, and Emilsson 2003). Similarly, there are descriptions of psychosocial adjustment and mental health issues in this age group in personal accounts, such as those in this volume.

The aim of this chapter is to describe some of the presenting issues that clinicians may see in a young adult with AS. Specifically, transitional concerns and comorbid problems will be reviewed. Following this, interventions will be summarized and illustrated with a case example. In this chapter, the term "young adult" refers to those between roughly 18 and 30 years old. Although the specific diagnostic category of AS is the focus of this chapter, those with high-functioning autism (HFA) or mild Pervasive Developmental Disorders (PDDs) may also experience similar psychosocial issues at this juncture in their life and require comparable supports. This chapter is based on the author's clinical experience with this group over the past decade and the available literature. Young adults who have not yet become involved in long-term intimate relationships are the focus of this discussion and compose the majority of young adults seen in the writer's practice. A review of outcome in adults with AS is beyond the scope of this chapter. For this, readers can refer to recent discussions (e.g. Howlin 2000).

Young adults with AS present with a range of clinical and psychosocial problems, some with all of the issues discussed below, and others with few. It is probable that clinicians only see the "tip of the iceberg" of young adults; that is, those who are functioning poorly, those who require ongoing supports, or those who have been diagnosed. Therefore, the clinical description depicted here may not be representative of all young adults with AS, whether they are or are not suitably diagnosed, and may not be illustrative of those young adults who do not seek clinical support.

Transitional issues

Typically, individuals with AS have difficulty with transitions. Life transitions involve shifting focus, addressing anxiety, experiencing new sensory and spatial challenges, and performing in unique social situations. In a study by Barnard and colleagues (2001), parents stated that where a transition plan had been established for their young adult with an autism spectrum disorder (ASD) it was helpful, but one existed only 53% of the time. Transitional planning from late adolescence to young adulthood is essential in preparing for the individual's greater independence from parents, and a successful transition to post-secondary education or employment and adult services.

The transition to independence from parents

The developmental progression of a typically developing youth from adolescence to young adulthood can create major struggles for any family. The tensions in redefining parent–child boundaries and potentially competing roles of the parent and young adult can be confusing and challenging. Negotiating the "rules" of this period for young adults with AS is even more difficult because of the youth's exceptional needs and the lack of a clear understanding about how to address them. The "shades of grey" involved in the highly abstract and social transition to independence are difficult for the individual with AS to decipher. Such confusion for parents, for the young adult, and in community supports may be seen in disagreements about living arrangements, use of financial aid, post-secondary education and career planning, management of mental health, motivation to accomplish goals, making friends, and responses to the young adult's restricted range of interests.

In clinical work, both the young adult and his parents express concern about the degree of parental involvement, usually with the young adult feeling that his parents continue to be excessively involved. In the parents' view, he may not have a realistic understanding of his limitations, or the support that he requires; nor may he possess the organizational skills necessary to be more independent. The lack of clear roles, as well as the under- or over-involvement of parents, may delay development of the life skills that lead to greater independence and other supportive relationships. Under-involvement of family members may lead to the development of risky relationships or situations. A clear discussion of family and individual roles and responsibilities may need to be facilitated by a professional in these situations.

The transition to post-secondary education

Young adults with AS might find the transition from high school to post-secondary education problematic, especially if the high school experience has been troubled and psychosocial and mental health issues have not been addressed in adolescence. Stoddart (1999) noted adolescents might experience anxiety, depression, repetitive thoughts and behaviours, poor academic performance, and social isolation; they might also be misunderstood by teachers and peers. On the other hand, as Myles and Simpson (1998) argue, if "persons with AS have received appropriate educational and social strategies and adequate interpersonal support throughout their academic lives, there is no reason to doubt that prognosis for a successful adult life is good" (p. 98). Nevertheless, they note that these students do not always receive the aid with post-secondary and vocational planning that they need.

The process of finding a supportive post-secondary setting which is suitable for the young adult with AS can be difficult. Academic performance may have been poor during high school, putting the young adult at a disadvantage in the post-secondary admission process. Admission interviews that require good social skills may be stressful, especially in conjunction with the other demands in the admission process, such as organizing applications and reference letters. Unfortunately, many post-secondary institutions are not yet familiar with AS and therefore need education about how best to support these students. Ideally, this education should be provided by professional supports who are already familiar with the individual's specific educational, social, and emotional needs in light of his or her diagnosis, but this task is unfortunately often left to the student or their family.

If they are to be successful in their education after acceptance to a college or university, young adults with AS often benefit from being clearly identified as having exceptional needs. Young adults vary widely in their willingness to disclose their diagnosis of AS to post-secondary institutions. Some prefer to label their symptoms as a "social disability" or "learning disability" while others opt to not disclose any label, and therefore do not receive accommodations or support. Most colleges and universities now have resources, practices, and policies in effect to encourage the inclusion of individuals with learning disabilities. These practices provide options such as offering the student longer periods in which to complete assignments and exams, tutoring, or a modified curriculum. In the author's experience, those students who do not take advantage of these accommodations may find the college or university experience unduly stressful. This in turn may precipitate new emotional issues or worsen existing mental health problems, thus making the program of study difficult to complete.

To ensure successful adaptation to the college or university setting, at the beginning of the academic year an individual on the college or university campus should be identified to whom the student can go for support and advice on various academic and social issues. This individual may be a peer, a professor, or a special needs support person. Ideally, meetings can be scheduled regularly with this support person to address proactively any potential problems and reduce the anxieties of the student and his parents. Young adults with AS may need help with this, as it cannot be taken for granted that they will initiate this novel social behaviour. In understanding any school-related problems, it is important that the interaction of social difficulties (e.g. initiating a conversation with a professor), emotional problems (e.g. anxiety), and learning and organizational differences (e.g. the need to process assignments visually) be carefully addressed. A determination needs to be made about the relative contribution of each of these variables in confronting academic problems.

The transition to employment

As with the issue of a transition to post-secondary education, it is best if there is the perception of a seamless transition into paid employment. Often, young adults with disabilities leaving high school may not have enough work skills or job search skills. It has been suggested that several factors contribute to the successful employment of young adults with various disabilities, including: "employment in the community before leaving school, participation in vocational or educational instruction designed to provide pragmatic skills for living independently in the community, exposure to career or vocational guidance programs, and proper coordination of program planning and delivery systems" (Fabian, Lent, and Willis 1998, p.311).

There is little employment outcome literature specific to youths diagnosed with AS. In the author's experience, young adults with AS feel emotionally prepared and are successful in finding employment if: (1) they have participated in co-op placements in high school, (2) there has been recognition by themselves and others of their individual strengths, interests, and learning weaknesses, and (3) they have been provided opportunities for increasing degrees of responsibility and task demands in summer employment. Jobs in which the individual has to switch tasks rapidly and work with the public requiring good social skills are difficult for this group. Some young adults may perform well in these situations if the task is closely related to their interests or if they receive comprehensive employee training. Some entry-level jobs with large retail companies involve training programs and manuals including "social scripts", such as how to deal with a "difficult" customer, how to help an undecided customer, what the dress code is, etc. If the adolescent or young adult is struggling with behavioural or emotional/mental health issues, he cannot be expected to perform adequately in a paid work situation. In these instances, actively treating these symptoms first and volunteering part-time may be a successful approach.

The transition to adult services

Although most would readily admit specialized services for children with AS are difficult to find, the problem for adults with AS is even more discouraging. Pre-existing feelings of isolation can be reinforced by the absence of specialized services for these young adults. Problems finding competent professionals in the adult services sector may exacerbate pre-existing mental health and other psychosocial problems. For example, in the city where the author practises, children's services typically end when the individual reaches the age of 18. Young adults are then forced to make the transition to the adult service sector. Unfortunately, this change occurs when a working knowledge of the individual and his condition is crucial in delivering a continuum of integrated supports.

Furthermore, the artificial divide between mental health and developmental services that often exists in the adult services sector perpetuates the lack of continuity in care. As Simblett and Wilson (1993) have perceptively noted, adults with AS are: "(1) not autistic enough for autistic services; (2) not ill enough for psychiatric services; and (3) not learning disabled enough for mental handicap services" (p. 93).

Co-existing issues

Mental health symptoms

The psychiatric needs of adults with AS have long been recognized as a significant issue in treatment (Wolff and Chick 1980; Wing 1981) and continue to be discussed in recent case accounts (Simblett and Wilson 1993; Hare 1997; Bankier *et al.* 1999). Nylander and Gillberg (2001) discovered that out of 1323 adult psychiatric outpatients, a minimum of 1.4% met diagnostic criteria for AS. Raja and Azzoni (2001) reported a 0.2% prevalence rate of first diagnosis of AS in nearly 2500 patients admitted to a psychiatric crisis unit. These diagnoses were made for the first time despite the patients having a long history in psychiatric services.

Although there have been some case reports of psychotic disorders in individuals with autism or AS, it is most likely rare. Based on clinical experience and larger studies, symptoms of depression or anxiety are the primary psychiatric concerns in this group (Howlin 1997). Specific anxieties/phobias are sometimes seen (e.g. performance demands, social situations, contamination, simple medical procedures, agoraphobia), but more often anxiety is generalized. The clinical experience of this author also suggests an inclination to abuse substances such as alcohol and marijuana and, in rare instances, sedating preparations such as cold remedies. At times, this represents an attempt to "self-medicate" without suitable pharmacological intervention. Unfortunately, addictions can be difficult to remediate even after proper medical attention.

Typically, individuals with AS function optimally when their schedule is routine and structured. An unsuccessful transition to post-secondary education or work and the resulting lack of structure in their lives aggravates a tendency to psychiatric symptomatology. As well, there may be a grief reaction at the end of high school, frustration with the inflexibility of social systems, and the perception that siblings have successfully progressed to greater independence while they have not (Gilson and Levitas 1987).

For example, the mental health of one young AS adult has been exacerbated by the lack of structure and routine in his life. Feelings of boredom, depression, and obsessive thoughts about drug and alcohol abuse are heightened during these periods and he has made several suicide attempts. Another young adult has cleverly devised a regular schedule of going for long walks downtown and visiting the local library to read history books, in order to address his need for structure and routine.

Social skills, rejection, and isolation

Many young adults with AS seen in clinical work are painfully aware of their social isolation from their peers. This realization most often appears to be a continuation of the experience of trying to navigate through the complex social demands of adolescence. Social isolation is aggravated because these young adults can no longer rely on the structure and social interaction with others that high school brought. Often, young adults need to recount the difficulties of being misunderstood and rejected by others and, frequently, the trauma inflicted by peers during grade school and high school (Mishna and Muskat 1998; Tantum 2000).

The literature on normally developing children points out that victims of bullying often exhibit "internalizing problems" such as anxiety, depression, and withdrawal, the effects of which continue to be seen later in life (Craig, Peters, and Konarski 1998). For children with AS, these powerful childhood experiences magnify characteristic pre-existing anxiety in social situations (sometimes based on the self-realization of deficient social skills), leading to the belief that lack of success in social situations is a given. Sadly, many young adults with AS feel that social situations are too emotionally strenuous, or even threatening, to provide any enjoyment. The fear of being taken advantage of by peers is a problem that lingers into the young adulthood of this group (Stoddart submitted).

Bullying of adults in the general population, particularly in the workplace, has received recent attention in the literature (Smith 1997; Cowie *et al.* 2002) and is a phenomenon that young adults with AS may be at risk of experiencing. For example, one young man with AS who is supported by the author was "dared" by employees to grab the buttocks of a co-worker in a warehouse setting. He did so, and subsequently was fired on the grounds of sexual harassment.

Despite a history of difficulties in making friends, young adults with AS begin to feel more pressure to enter dating relationships, with an increasing recognition that they are developmentally behind their peers. Some males are teased or thought to be homosexual by their peers because they do not have a girlfriend. In the context of supportive counselling, dating and sexuality may need to be discussed as individuals with AS, despite their intelligence, sometimes have a surprisingly naïve or shallow understanding of these topics.

Life skills

Often, the life skills of young adults with AS are surprisingly poor. They may have been trained in and shown the skills in the past, but they cannot carry out the necessary activities. This may be due to depression, organizational problems, sensory issues, or a lack of motivation. Problems generalizing skills previously learned in one setting may interfere with the use of these skills in another. Such problems present as a point of conflict between parents and their child or the individual and his or her housemates. The clinician might not get an accurate depiction of the quality of his or her living conditions if the individual is seen in the clinic setting exclusively; sometimes home visits can provide invaluable information. Parents and other visiting community workers can also provide useful information in planning intervention.

Powell (2002) summarizes 11 life skill areas in which individuals with AS need varying degrees of assistance. They are (1) financial; (2) morning routines; (3) organization and reminder systems; (4) food hygiene; (5) diet; (6) avoiding loss of personal possessions; (7) home safety; (8) home skills and maintenance; (9) personal care; (10) community skills; and (11) understanding and applying for welfare benefits (p.31). Not included in this list, but also relevant, is the development of leisure skills.

Interventions

Individual intervention

There continues to be a concerning lack of accounts describing individual psychotherapy for youth or adults with AS in the literature. Case examples include discussion of the efficacy of psychotherapy for children and adolescents with AS and their families (Stoddart 1999) and a description of the use of a cognitive-behavioural intervention with a 26-year-old with AS (Hare 1997). Cognitive behaviour therapy is gaining recognition with this group (Beebe and Risi 2003). Although increasing numbers of clinicians recognize that a structured psychotherapy approach can be useful (Wing 1981; Klin and Volkmar 2000; Tantum 2000), others have suggested that psychotherapy is not necessarily indicated in treating AS (Gillberg 1998).

In counselling sessions with the young adult, many of the issues raised in this chapter can be addressed. Young adults may have had negative experiences with service providers in the past and sometimes are reluctant to accept further help. Such concerns can be raised through supportive therapy. The benefits of a long-term therapy relationship can be enormous for the young adult; however, broader systemic changes in the individual's life (such as those discussed in this chapter) are also needed to reinforce needed changes explored in therapy. For example, although the young adult may benefit from and appreciate the support of the therapist, and may even subjectively experience the therapist as a "friend", the goal of therapy must be for the young adult to find and engage in other social contacts in his or her life.

Family intervention

Simblett and Wilson (1993) make the case for intervention at the systemic family level, but note that the lack of such an approach for many years and the presence of unrealistic expectations may mean this is difficult. The clinician must strike a careful balance between addressing the agenda of both the young adult, and those of his family members. The tendency is for the family and the clinician to deem it necessary for the young adult to have private sessions with the clinician for counselling, and the family may express relief that somebody can "be there" for their child. It is seen as developmentally appropriate for the young adult to have this privacy and to begin to seek supports and resources outside the family system. However, the experiences and insights of family members must not be overlooked.

Similarly, many parents find it helpful to meet with the clinician on their own to address concerns about the future and assist in the degree of direction that they give their child. Other parents need help to address their own guilt and disillusionment with professionals in cases of a late diagnosis. They may also express concern about their child's future needs and the burden of care that may be left to unaffected siblings. Further, parents need a safe environment in which to address their own mental health or AS traits, and their own needs at their stage in life.

Meetings of the entire family, including unaffected siblings, help in the transition of roles, discussion of information on AS, and exploration of future responsibilities.

Group intervention

At this time, there are few clinical reports of groups for young adults specifically with AS, although there are reports of groups for children and youth (e.g. Marriage, Gordon, and Brand 1995; Mishna and Muskat 1998). Stoddart (submitted) has discussed a short-term group therapy format for young adults with AS. Although the goals of provision of mutual support, reduction of isolation, and education were met, the practising of new, more adaptive social behaviours in sessions and of making contact with members outside the clinic setting did not occur. The latter goals are best addressed in long-term community-based informal activity groups.

Powell (2002) reports that informal social groups can be of great benefit given that such activities provide a place to go in the community, the participants can feel they are with others with similar needs, and they provide the opportunity to develop social relationships. In a similar way we have found locally, that the group for young adults with AS facilitated by the Aspergers Society of Ontario has been valuable in providing developmentally suitable *in situ* learning experiences for some young adults who often are extremely isolated, yet crave social interaction with peers.

Support for parents can also be provided in a group format. Many parents of young adults with AS report that they have never talked to other parents with similar struggles. Group support need not be explicitly defined as a "support group" or "therapeutic group". The author currently provides professional support for a local committee of parents of young adults with AS who are concerned about the future housing needs of their children. Although the focus of discussion is on the issue of housing and independent living supports, added benefits are sharing experiences, sharing knowledge of resources and interventions, and sharing fears about the future needs of their children.

Pharmacological intervention

Most of the adolescents and young adults with AS in the author's practice are prescribed medication(s) to address mental health and/or behaviour problems. It is of note that 55% of subjects were reported to be using psychotropic medication in the study by Martin and colleagues (Martin et al. 1999). Although it is reassuring for parents of young adults with AS to know the efficacy of psychotropic medication is better established in adults than in children, it may also be premature to assume that adults with ASDs have a comparable symptom profile and treatment response to that seen in children with ASDs (Martin et al. 1999).

Adults with AS do benefit from short-term pharmacological intervention but more often as an augmentation to other interventions over the long term. In the author's experience, Selective Serotonin Reuptake Inhibitors (SSRIs) are successfully used in reducing symptoms such as anxiety, depression, and obsessive thoughts. Insomnia is commonly found in adults with AS, and can present in association with anxiety and depression (Tani et al. 2003). Feelings about the use of psychotropic medication need to be regularly and sensitively discussed with the young adult and his or her family in the context of a therapeutic framework established over time (Towbin 2003).

Unfortunately, a trial and error approach is necessary in ascertaining the most effective medication, and the pool of physicians experienced in prescribing medication to this group is limited. Common problems faced during medication use tend to be in helping the patients organize themselves to ensure that they are taking medication regularly and at the recommended times, dealing with side effects at the beginning of treatment (sometimes due to a starting dose that is too high), and addressing patient discomfort with experiences of flattened affect, weight gain, somnolence, increased anxiety, or impaired cognitive and sexual functioning.

When using medication, it is helpful to use a brief standardized measure of anxiety and depression that is sensitive to pharmacological treatment gains. Regular administration of a brief symptom checklist at the beginning of therapy sessions or medical appointments can also give the individual with AS comfort in knowing what symptoms to discuss with the physician or therapist. Over the long term, such data can be graphed to give a visual depiction. Long-term tracking of changes in anxiety and depression can give the clinician, young adult, and family insights into the influences of interventions such as changes in medication or of the influence of temporal variables (e.g. winter months, vacation, college examinations) that accompany the waxing or waning of mental health symptoms.

Case example: David

David, a 17-year-old, was referred by his parents regarding his transition from child services to adult services. He was diagnosed with AS at the age of 15 after a long and difficult attempt to understand his clinical presentation. David was an avid writer and his increasing fixation on his writing led to more isolation. He had few friends at his high school despite having attended the same school for several years. His parents were becoming increasingly concerned about David's future and overall presentation. Although he had received brief treatment with an SSRI in the past, it was discontinued because of excessive sedation. He was again presenting with heightened anxiety and notable lethargy, which his parents saw as symptomatic of a recurring depressive episode.

An assessment was conducted with David and his family. This was carried out with the use of individual interviews, whole family interviews, and parent interviews. As well, measures of depression, anxiety, adaptive behaviours, and sensory problems were used. It was found that David was struggling with heightened levels of anxiety. Much of the anxiety related to social situations. He was suspicious of people and demonstrated fear in groups as he felt socially inept and did not like people accidentally brushing against him. More often than not, he was compelled to leave social occasions. Exams at school were distressing for him. David also struggled with depression, but less so. He expressed concerns about his future. He felt that high school had left him depleted of energy and he did not want to enter post-secondary education, as his parents wished. Despite having intense crushes on young women at school, David also expressed frustration that he had not yet had a date, and that he was lonely.

In family sessions, there was considerable tension between David and his parents. David wanted to continue to develop his writing skills and pursue a career in creative writing. His parents, however, felt this was an alternative that would not lead to paid employment and eventual self-sufficiency. As was revealed in the measure of adaptive functioning, David displayed exceptional skills in some areas of his life, but was severely lacking in demonstrated skills in other areas. On a recent occasion, for example, David's parents went away for the weekend. When they called him in the evening, they found that David had not eaten for the entire day or walked the dog. Instead, he had spent the entire day writing at his computer. Situations such as this raised questions about what David would do when they were no longer able to support him. David voiced that when he turned 18 in a few months, he was "officially an adult" and, therefore, his parents "couldn't tell him what to do any more".

After the assessment, recommendations were made to David and his parents about future involvement with the therapist and other supports. One of the major interventions included introducing Paxil to reduce anxiety and depression, which was prescribed by the family doctor. This resulted in noticeable improvement in David's anxiety. Individual and family therapy sessions also occurred. Because the Paxil resulted in an overall reduction in his anxiety, David was more able to negotiate about his future. He decided to go to school part-time, which resulted from a session of negotiating in family therapy. He was referred to a local employment service to assess his work skills. He wanted to work in a bookstore when he was not attending school. Sensory issues that were raised in the assessment were attended to as potential antecedents to David's feelings of being overwhelmed in both settings. Further areas were identified that David and parents needed to discuss in the future such as the increasing responsibility that they wanted him to take around the house, and in managing his finances. Occasional sessions were offered to David's parents to allay their fears about the future for their son, and discuss reasonable short-term expectations for him. David was seen for continuing individual therapy to address his self-perception, anxiety, and social isolation. He was referred to the local community group for young adults with AS.

Conclusion

With suitable supports, young adults with AS can have satisfying relationships and productive lives. The lack of understanding of appropriate services for the needs of this group may be more "disabling" than the actual symptoms associated with AS. Further research is required to address early contributors to good outcomes in this group, along with the effectiveness of various interventions in early adulthood. It is imperative that interventions addressing these transitional challenges be further discussed in practice descriptions as clinical experience suggests that an increasingly larger cohort of adolescents diagnosed with AS are entering this age group. In addition, many more young adults are receiving their first diagnosis of AS in their late adolescence or early 20s, this being precipitated by mental health symptoms or psychosocial crises.

References

Bankier, B., Lenz, G., Gutierrez, K., Bach, M., and Katschnig, H. (1999) A case of Asperger's Syndrome first diagnosed in adulthood. *Psychopathology, 32,* 43–6.

Barnard, J., Harvey, V., Potter, D., and Prior, A. (2001) *Ignored or Ineligible? The Reality for Adults with Autism Spectrum Disorders.* London, UK: The National Autistic Society.

Beebe, D.W., and Risi, S. (2003) Treatment of adolescents and young adults with high-functioning autism or Asperger syndrome. In M.A. Reinecke, F.M. Dattilio, and A. Freeman (eds) *Cognitive Therapy with Children and Adolescents: A Casebook for Clinical Practice, Second Edition.* New York, NY: Guilford Press.

Cowie, H., Naylor, P., Rivers, I., Smith, P.K., and Pereira, B. (2002) Measuring workplace bullying. *Aggression and Violent Behaviour, 7,* 33–51.

Craig, W.M., Peters, R.D., and Konarski, R. (1998) *Bullying and Victimization Among Canadian School Children.* Hull, Quebec: Applied Research Branch Strategic Policy, Human Resources Development Canada.

Engstrom, I., Ekstrom, L., and Emilsson, B. (2003) Psychosocial functioning in a group of Swedish adults with Asperger syndrome or high-functioning autism. *Autism: The International Journal of Research and Practice, 7,* 1, 99–110.

Fabian, E.S., Lent, R.W., and Willis, S.P. (1998) Predicting work transition outcomes for students with disabilities: Implications for counselors. *Journal of Counseling and Development, 76,* 311–16.

Gillberg, C. (1998) Asperger Syndrome and high-functioning autism. *The British Journal of Psychiatry, 172,* 3, 200–209.

Gilson, S.F., and Levitas, A.S. (1987) Psychosocial crises in the lives of mentally retarded people. *Psychiatric Aspects of Mental Retardation Reviews, 6,* 6, 27–31.

Hare, D.J. (1997) The use of cognitive-behavioural therapy with people with Asperger Syndrome. *Autism: The International Journal of Research and Practice, 1,* 2, 215–25.

Howlin, P. (1997) *Autism: Preparing for Adulthood.* London, UK: Routledge.

Howlin, P. (2000) Outcome in adult life for more able individuals with autism or Asperger syndrome. *Autism: The International Journal of Research and Practice, 4,* 1, 63–83.

Klin, A., and Volkmar, F.R. (2000) Treatment and intervention guidelines for individuals with Asperger Syndrome. In A. Klin, F.R. Volkmar, and S.S. Sparrow (eds) *Asperger Syndrome.* New York, NY: Guilford Press.

Macleod, A. (1999) The Birmingham community support scheme for adults with Asperger syndrome. *Autism: The International Journal of Research and Practice, 3,* 2, 177–92.

Marriage, K.J., Gordon, V., and Brand, L. (1995) A social skills group for boys with Asperger's Syndrome. *Australian and New Zealand Journal of Psychiatry, 29,* 58–62.

Martin, A., Scahill, L., Klin, A., and Volkmar, F.R. (1999) Higher-functioning Pervasive Developmental Disorders: Rates and patterns of psychotropic drug use. *Journal of the American Academy of Child and Adolescent Psychiatry, 38,* 7, 923–31.

Mishna, F., and Muskat, B. (1998) Group therapy for boys with features of Asperger Syndrome and concurrent learning disabilities: Finding a peer group. *Journal of Child and Adolescent Group Therapy, 8,* 3, 97–114.

Myles, B.S., and Simpson, R. (1998) *Aspergers Syndrome: A Guide for Educators and Parents.* Austin, TX: Pro-Ed.

Nylander, L., and Gillberg, C. (2001) Screening for autism spectrum disorders in adult psychiatric out-patients: A preliminary report. *Acta Psychiatrica Scandinavica, 103*, 6, 428–34.

Powell, A. (2002) *Taking Responsibility: Good Practice Guidelines for Services – Adults with Asperger Syndrome.* London, UK: The National Autistic Society.

Raja, M., and Azzoni, A. (2001) Asperger's disorder in the emergency psychiatric setting. *General Hospital Psychiatry, 23*, 285–93.

Simblett, G.J., and Wilson, D.N. (1993) Asperger's syndrome: Three cases and a discussion. *Journal of Intellectual Disability Research, 37*, 1, 85–94.

Smith, P.K. (1997) Bullying in life-span perspective: What can studies of school bullying and workplace bullying learn from each other? *Journal of Community and Applied Social Psychology, 7*, 249–55.

Stoddart, K.P. (1999) Adolescents with Asperger syndrome: Three case studies of individual and family therapy. *Autism: The International Journal of Research and Practice, 3*, 3, 255–71.

Stoddart, K.P. (submitted) Group therapy for young adults with Asperger Syndrome. *Focus on Autism and Other Developmental Disabilities.*

Tani, P., Lindberg, N., Nieminen-von Wendt, T., von Wendt, L., Alanko, L., Appleberg, B., and Porkka-Heiskanen, T. (2003) Insomnia is a frequent finding in adults with Asperger syndrome. *BMC Psychiatry, 3*, 12.

Tantum, D. (2000) Adolescence and adulthood of individuals with Asperger Syndrome. In A. Klin, F.R. Volkmar, and S.S. Sparrow (eds) *Asperger Syndrome.* New York, NY: Guilford Press.

Towbin, K.E. (2003) Strategies for pharmacologic treatment of high-functioning autism and Asperger syndrome. *Child and Adolescent Psychiatric Clinics of North America, 12*, 23–45.

Wing, L. (1981) Asperger's Syndrome: A clinical account. *Psychological Medicine, 11*, 115–29.

Wolff, S., and Chick, J. (1980) Schizoid personality in childhood: A controlled follow-up study. *Psychological Medicine, 10*, 85–100.

CHAPTER 6

Getting to work: Helping the adolescent with Asperger Syndrome transition to employment

Gail Hawkins

Despite having higher intellectual levels and the potential to work, few people with Asperger Syndrome (AS) are in regular employment (Goode, Rutter, and Howlin 1994). Furthermore, even those with formal qualifications are often underemployed and it is common for jobs to end prematurely. Pre-vocational life skills training, combined with good planning and support, is crucial for a successful work experience for people with AS. When introduced at an early age, these factors dramatically increase the chances for meaningful, long-term employment.

The successful transition from school to work begins long before graduation and requires comprehensive planning. Wehman, Kregel, and Barcus (1985), who have written on the overall importance of transitional planning for individuals with autism, contend that a transitional plan from school to work supersedes the potential significance of all other aspects of transitional services.

The skills that will help an individual with AS maintain employment are learned in childhood, and further develop as the child enters grade school, high school, and post-secondary education. The student with AS needs additional understanding and support to help him or her acquire suitable skills. The knowledge that professionals have about AS, how it manifests, and how people with AS learn and process information, will have a considerable impact on what teaching strategies and support systems they use. Often this professional support lays the groundwork for accomplishment in the workplace.

The purpose of this chapter is to discuss some of the common challenges young people with AS face when trying to obtain and keep work. This chapter will address how they might position themselves better for employment success.

This discussion is based on the author's experience in developing and running employment programs for people with AS and other autism spectrum disorders (ASDs) over the past two decades.

The role of the vocational counsellor and other professionals in supporting employment

The road to employment for many people with AS is a long and hilly one. Along the way, the individual is likely to run into various roadblocks and barriers. These need not stop him or her from moving forward. It is part of the journey to learn how to navigate over and around obstacles. As with any life journey, there will be times when support from others will be helpful. Individuals with AS and their families will benefit from exploring which professionals in the community have the skills and connections to support them at various junctures along the way. Educational, medical, social service, and employment professionals are the most likely to play a role in helping people with high-functioning autism and AS prepare for and gain employment. These professionals will include, but are not limited to, teachers, guidance counsellors, social workers, therapists, psychologists, psychiatrists, career counsellors, and employment specialists. Each professional offers a unique and valuable contribution in the process.

Educational professionals play a significant role in helping students prepare for employment through skill development. Co-operative education teachers help students find suitable work experiences, which help the student gain valuable insight into the working world. Guidance counsellors in post-secondary schools help students evaluate their abilities, interests, talents, and personality characteristics to develop realistic academic and career goals.

Medical and social service professionals play a role by diagnosing individuals so they may seek the proper supports within the community. They are also the professionals who prescribe medication that may help individuals with AS address some of the issues that can affect their performance on the job. Issues such as high anxiety, lack of focus, and depression often impede the individual from reaching full potential. These professionals are often called on to help verify diagnosis so people with AS can receive the needed financial support from government programs. It is often through these programs and services that people with AS access the support that helps them find and keep a job.

Employment professionals help the person with AS identify what challenges he or she must address to be prepared for competitive employment. They also play a key role in identifying the appropriate career direction and outlining the steps to achieve employment goals. Once placed in a job, it is the employment professional, often a job coach, who assists the new employee in transitioning into the job. For the transition to be most effective, employment professionals must have a clear understanding of AS. This will allow them to support the individual properly and effectively, setting him or her up for success.

Transitioning to paid employment takes effort and a willingness to take responsibility for one's strengths and challenges. People generally do not enjoy looking at their challenges; however, it is the honest examination of one's difficulties that leads to growth and success. By identifying the problematic areas, one can be focussed in addressing the issues that create barriers. By identifying strengths, new ideas are revealed and doors are opened.

Eight vocational and life skills

Every employer will have their own criteria for hiring staff. These criteria will differ depending on the employer, the job, and the labour market. There are several skills, however, which employers agree affect their hiring decisions. Perhaps surprisingly, employers attend to "soft skills", which encompass communication, social, and interpersonal skills. Employers want people working for them who can communicate, work in a team environment, take initiative, and represent the company positively. Many of the soft skills that employers demand are difficult for people with AS to deliver without training and support.

At a young age, individuals with AS can begin learning some of the valuable skills employers desire of their employees. Learning these skills early paves the way for greater vocational success and allows the individual to further develop these and other abilities in the late teen and young adult years.

There are many soft skills that employers value; however, the eight listed here create an excellent foundation of basic abilities to support the learning that comes later in life. If these skills are taught to a child and cultivated throughout adolescence, it is likely that the chances of successfully finding and maintaining paid employment as an adult increase. Hawkins (2004) outlines other effective strategies.

Personal presentation

Very few employers will argue that the first impression in an interview is unimportant. When attending the interview for a job, how one presents in the first few seconds can mean the difference between getting a job offer or a rejection letter. Proper hygiene and grooming are skills that will repeatedly serve an individual well. Employers are often willing to make accommodations for people with disabilities but they are rarely willing to make accommodations in the area of personal presentation. Employees represent the company image and there are no exceptions for individuals with AS.

At an early age, it is vital to teach the child with AS proper grooming and hygiene practices. This can often be supported with a morning and evening routine. This should include bathing, dental hygiene, combing of hair, shaving (in teen years), and dressing. If an individual has difficulty choosing appropriate clothing, it can be helpful to purchase clothes that colour match regardless of the combination. This will result in a good choice of attire every day, supporting self-esteem and confidence.

Manners

Good manners may not be noticed but poor manners or a lack of manners will be! This includes table manners, something often not associated with employment skills. Employees may need to attend luncheons, coffee breaks, or meetings where food is served. An employee is alienated if there is food on his face or clothes when eating with others.

Basic manners, such as saying "please", "thank you", and "excuse me", are also essential. Holding a door for someone as he walks through, rather than letting the door slam on him, is a kind gesture. Although poor manners may not be reason for dismissal, they can isolate or alienate the employee from co-workers. When helping a person with AS prepare for employment, it is important to do everything possible to help that individual fit in.

Boundaries

People need boundaries for them to learn. In fact, boundaries help people feel safe because they set limits around what is and is not acceptable; and what is and is not good. Boundaries teach self-discipline, emotional stability, positive values, a focussed and perceptive mind, and self-esteem. People with AS who are accustomed to boundaries will do better, both socially and in their work performance. They will understand that "no means no", they will "get it" when the manager sets a deadline, and they will be in a position to adhere to social rules.

The goal in boundary setting for children is to help them grow into independent, well-balanced adults. These adults will do better in the workplace and in life in general. It is harder to set boundaries with people who are not used to having boundaries set. If an adult was not brought up in an environment where boundaries were present, then he or she will have greater difficulty adapting to the workplace where boundaries are not only present, but expected to be honoured.

A large company called the author to consult about a problem they were having with an employee who had been diagnosed with AS. This employee was making racial slurs and swearing at people in the office. The manager wanted to know what could be done to accommodate him and, at the same time, how she could go about addressing this behaviour. It was clear that the employee had not been brought up in an environment where these boundaries had been either set or enforced. This situation could have been avoided if the employee had known from an early age that name-calling and racism are not acceptable. As an adult, he needed extremely clear and firm boundaries placed on him that were enforced by meaningful, consistent consequences. Unfortunately, at this point, these consequences may include dismissal.

Setting, teaching, and upholding consequences in children with AS will set them up for success in the workplace. There are times when every adult is worn down by a child's behaviour. By remaining dedicated to setting and maintaining boundaries, it is helpful to know that each time they are enforced it gets a little easier. The long-term gain is worth the effort.

Flexibility

People with AS can be rigid (Ehlers, Gillberg, and Wing 1999; Myles, Bock, and Simpson 2001) and therefore they may struggle to shift from one assignment to another. However, employers usually require flexibility in employees. They want employees who can move from one task to another to accommodate fluctuating priorities. Although many people with AS have difficulty with quick changes, they are capable of coping, particularly when they have been brought up to accept that things change.

Teaching children with AS to cope with change is vital to their acceptance of it later in life. Creating even small changes in routines and supporting the child through the process of "going with the flow" will have large dividends when that adult is required to switch tasks at her job because a big shipment of a new product just came in.

Awareness

Awareness can be divided into two sub-categories: inner awareness and outer awareness. "Inner awareness" is the awareness of oneself; for example, of one's emotions, thoughts, and feelings. "Outer awareness" is the awareness of what is going on around one; for example, what other people might be thinking or feeling, personal space, the environment etc. Both types of awareness are important in the workplace as they offer valuable information and insight into situations and thus help an individual understand what is expected of him or her.

Both inner and outer awareness can be challenging for people who have AS. They often have difficulty identifying what emotions they are experiencing and can have trouble communicating thoughts. Conversely, they frequently struggle to empathize with what others are potentially feeling or thinking. This difficulty relating to the thoughts and feelings of others (Baron-Cohen, Leslie, and Frith 1985; Barnhill 2001) is often referred to as "theory of mind". This, too, complicates communication because people with AS may not be able to predict a reaction, situation or outcome. This poor ability to read others and to express themselves fully can strain working relationships, unless co-workers and management have some understanding.

Although challenged in this area, it is possible for people with AS to develop skills that will help them address this obstacle, and therefore blend more easily into a work environment. Supporting a child with AS to identify emotions as they are experienced is a good practice. By helping the child be more "in tune" with him- or herself, the child will be in a better position to communicate this to others. Working with the child to identify physical signals of emotional reactions will also help develop his or her inner awareness.

When an adult has a reaction or emotion, this can be an excellent opportunity to teach outer awareness to the child with AS. Taking the time to demonstrate or discuss which facial expressions and postures go with different emotions and feelings, better equips the child to read others. These are very helpful skills to have as the child matures and enters stages where reading nonverbal cues is crucial to developing communication skills.

Eye contact

In Western culture, eye contact is an important part of communication and social interaction. The better an employee with AS is at eye contact, the easier he or she will find it to blend in at work. A lack of eye contact sends nonverbal messages that can alienate the employee with AS from his or her peers. Lack of eye contact during an interview, without the interviewer having any background understanding of AS, can be detrimental to the job-finding process. Teaching children with AS the importance of eye contact and helping them to become more comfortable with making at least *some* contact will help them considerably in their adult life and in making the transition to work.

Decision making

Decision making can be a difficult skill for many people with AS to learn because it involves judgement and common sense, two things that AS makes challenging (Myles and Simpson 1998). Employers will expect employees to have at least some basic decision-making skills.

The process of decision making can be introduced to children with AS by helping them determine the pros and cons of situations that arise. As they grow, they will learn that they are faced with many choices in life. Teaching them how to weigh and measure the potential outcome of a given decision helps them experience, and thus understand, the outcome. Often people with AS require support to make wise decisions. However, if they learn the process at an early age, they will increase the chances of making good decisions independently as adults. If they are unsure of a decision, they should be encouraged to ask for advice or support. In the workplace, this will serve them well.

Responsibility

Employers want employees to act responsibly. This includes taking responsibility for one's performance and actions. This is referred to as "self-responsibility". Self-responsibility is an attitude and it must come from within the individual. It cannot be given to someone, just as self-esteem cannot. The opposite of self-responsibility is *blame*. In other words, it is everyone else's fault that the situation is as it is. This is not to allude that one should take responsibility that is not one's own; however, it is important that people learn early that they play a role in what happens to them in life. In the workplace, if employees do not take responsibility for their actions they may suffer harsh consequences, including reprimands and dismissals. To be successful, they need to realize that their life is the way it is because of the choices they make, including how they choose to behave.

Learning self-responsibility is perhaps more difficult for people with AS because they have trouble relating their behaviour to a consequence or become confused with the inconsistency of social rules (Myles and Simpson 2001). They need support to learn and absorb the lesson. Self-responsibility is usually learned best when it is modelled in childhood; however, it is also possible to learn it as an adult although it may take a more determined effort. When self-responsibility is *required* of an individual, he or she grows up learning to be responsible.

People with AS need expectations outlined clearly. They need to know what is required of them beforehand. They also need consequences outlined as well as the connection drawn between the behaviour and the consequence. This process is an effective way of teaching self-responsibility.

Building work experience and choosing career direction

A common dilemma that many people face when entering the job market is that employers want experienced employees, but a new employee needs to work to get the experience the employer desires. People with AS face this dilemma along with everyone else, and it is frustrating.

So, how does someone build work experience if employers are not willing to hire him or her? Employers want experience, but the experience does not have to come from a paid position. One way around this problem is to work for an employer at no charge. This can be done through two avenues: co-operative education placements and volunteer placements. Either way, the payoff in terms of experience for the person with AS seeking a career is significant and the opportunity can be very rewarding. Not only does this allow the person with AS to build a résumé, but also it offers that individual a realistic view of what employment is.

Co-operative and volunteer work experiences, along with part-time and summer jobs, help the young person with AS build experience. They also help to develop realistic expectations. Indeed, these early work experiences help the entire family understand and support realistic, viable career goals for their loved one with AS.

One of the major benefits for people with AS of having early work experiences is the introduction these offer to how the working world works. Young people with AS will begin to understand that today's competitive employment market and its employers demand employees who are skilled and possess *at least* basic social and communication skills. It is a valuable lesson that, despite the interest employers may have in hiring employees who are disabled, they still require them to do the job. Gaining this realization early and then focussing on developing a foundation of social and communication skills and a well-chosen career path is central to a successful long-term work experience. Assessing challenges and developing effective strategies to address those challenges will support the transition into the workplace and, ultimately, support the ability to maintain a job.

Developing a career or employment path is a process that takes time and nurturing and this is important for individuals with AS and their families to understand. In today's employment market, the first job an individual gets is unlikely to be the one he or she retires from in 50 years' time. The current generation can expect between five and seven career shifts over the span of their lives. Knowing this and being prepared to work into a career helps the individual understand that beginning in an entry-level position does not necessarily mean staying in one forever. There will be some people who wish to remain at the entry level or have difficulty, for various reasons, moving past the entry level in a job. Not everyone is meant to climb the "corporate ladder". Employers need, indeed highly value, good entry-level employees who are committed and reliable.

For others, the goal will be to move toward middle- or even high-level jobs. For these individuals, it will be sensible to expect a progression into these positions. These employees may have to move from one job to another in strategically planned steps to build a career. Regardless of the career goal or level, the major obstacles employees with AS will face along the way will continue to relate back to social, communication, and interpersonal skills. If part of his or her performance relies on the ability to interact with others, accommodation may be required to help the employee meet the demands of the job. Early work experiences will help the employee with AS identify issues and can offer the opportunity to address them. If the issues cannot be addressed or accommodated, these experiences can help direct the individual toward a more fitting job match.

Continued education and training

Should a person with AS decide on further education or training, it is important that he or she chooses proper avenues after secondary school. General post-secondary education, for example a Bachelor of Arts degree (BA), is often less useful than specific skill-based training, such as a diploma in book-keeping. General education still needs to be applied and developed after graduation if that individual is to perform effectively in a job. This application of general knowledge is often a challenge for people with AS. Job-specific training, often found at the community college level or in apprenticeship programs, gives the individual a particular skill set – as an electrician, veterinary technician or computer programmer, for example. Keeping this in mind and planning appropriately will direct the individual with AS into a career where his or her potential can be tapped more successfully.

Ensuring success in work placements

Many high schools have co-operative education programs that offer students credits for work experience. This is a wonderful opportunity for a youth with AS to get out into the working world and try it out. Young adults who do not have the opportunity to participate in co-operative work placements through school can seek out volunteer experiences in areas of interest. Summer and part-time after-school jobs provide valuable experience and are often paid.

Whether paid or not, work placements are only positive experiences if they are set up with some forethought. How a placement is set up for a person with AS can make the difference between a terrific experience and a disastrous one for all involved.

There are several steps to setting up a positive work experience. First and foremost, the key to a successful job placement for a person with AS is in the matching of the job to the individual. Using the person's strengths, interests, and abilities and balancing them with his or her challenges to come up with a suitable job match is crucial. With the right match, the stage is set for a successful experience.

Once placed, another important factor in a successful placement is educating the employer and key staff members about AS and how they can work effectively with an employee who has it. This can occur either formally through a presentation or informally in a meeting. Either way, education is fundamental to setting the stage for success and should be done before the employee's first day. The best person to play this role is usually the employment professional.

Clearly defining job responsibilities is another variable in establishing a positive work experience. It is vital to establish beforehand that the duties of the position are within the new employee's scope of ability. Beware of any responsibilities that require multitasking, strong interpersonal skills, and considerable judgement. Although not impossible for the employee with AS to perform, jobs that require these skills tend to be significantly more challenging for a person with AS. When these skills are required, it will be necessary to coach the employee and plan strategies that will assist her in performing the job.

As with any new job, establishing natural supports helps a new employee grow and blend into the workplace. The employee with AS may need help to create the necessary relationships to be successful in his job. Identifying one main contact and two secondary contacts for the employee helps him problem solve and perform when having difficulty. Once a comfort level is established, the new employee often blossoms and then may independently expand his circle of contacts.

A job coach (a professional who supports the employee at the work site) is helpful in establishing all the components mentioned earlier. In addition, the job coach becomes a valuable resource and support to both the employer and the employee should concerns arise over the course of the placement. A study conducted on a supported employment scheme for people with AS (Howlin and Mawhood 1996) found that this support was a key factor in ensuring a successful job placement. Furthermore, the study concluded that satisfaction was high amongst supported employees, line managers, and senior staff. Long-term support was also determined to be the most important reason for success in TEACCH, a supported employment program for people with autism (Keel, Mesibov, and Woods 1997).

Future issues

The transition from school to work for many people with AS is only one piece in the employment puzzle for this population. Once in a job or on a career path, they will encounter challenges where they will require further or ongoing support. Mission Possible, an employment service established by the author and based in Toronto for people with AS, has demonstrated the effectiveness of follow-up support. In 2003, they had a 94% placement rate and 90% of the people placed remained in their jobs for longer than six months. Mission Possible credits this success rate to the long-term follow-up services they provide to both the employee with AS and the employer. TEACCH's supported employment program in the United States attributes its 89% retention rate to the long-term support services they provide to individuals with autism. This support is expensive and usually requires funding. Lobbying for government support to these service will be a critical step in helping people with AS be successful in the workplace. Over time, the support required for each individual decreases, which affects the funding required.

There are few employment services for people with AS. Limited specialized services mean there are few organizations that understand the unique challenges and needs of people with AS. This makes pre-vocational life skills training, developed specifically for this population, less accessible. Family members, teachers, social workers, and employment counsellors may have to research effective strategies and assessment methods to help support the employment process for people with AS.

The media has helped to increase public awareness of AS. Yet most people remain unaware of the syndrome. Public education plays a key role in promoting the strengths and assets employees with AS can bring to the workplace. With knowledge comes the shattering of misconceptions and fears about hiring people who are different. The more aware the public is of AS, the greater the chances of employment opportunities and the finding of understanding and compassionate employers.

References

Barnhill, G.P. (2001) Social attribution and depression in adolescents with Asperger Syndrome. *Focus on Autism and Other Developmental Disabilities, 16*, 46–53.

Baron-Cohen, S., Leslie, A.M., and Frith, U. (1985) Does the autistic child have a "theory of mind"? *Cognition, 21*, 37–46.

Ehlers, S., Gillberg, C., and Wing, L. (1999) A screening questionnaire for Asperger Syndrome and other high-functioning autism spectrum disorders in school age children. *Journal of Autism and Developmental Disorders, 29*, 129–41.

Goode, S., Rutter, M., and Howlin P. (1994) A twenty year follow-up of children with autism. Paper presented at the 13th Annual Biennial Meeting of the International Society for the Study of Behavioural Development, Amsterdam, The Netherlands.

Hawkins, G. (2004) *How to Find Work that Works for People with Asperger Syndrome.* London, UK: Jessica Kingsley Publishers.

Howlin, P., and Mawhood, L. (1996) *An Evaluation of a Pilot Two-Year Supported Employment Service for People with Autism.* London, UK: The National Autistic Society.

Keel, J.H., Mesibov, G.B., and Woods, A.V. (1997) TEACCH supported employment program. *Journal of Autism and Developmental Disorders, 27*, 3–10.

Myles, B.S., Bock, S.J., and Simpson, R.L. (2001) *Asperger's Syndrome Diagnostic Scale.* Austin, TX: Pro-Ed.

Myles, B.S., and Simpson, R.L. (1998) *Asperger Syndrome: A Guide for Educators and Parents.* Austin, TX: Pro-Ed.

Myles, B.S., and Simpson, R.L. (2001) Understanding the hidden curriculum: An essential social skill for children and youth with Asperger Syndrome. *Intervention in School and Clinic, 36*, 279–86.

Wehman, P., Kregel, J., and Barcus, M.J. (1985) From school to work: A vocational transition model for handicapped students. *Exceptional Children, 52*, 25–37.

CHAPTER 7

Sexuality and Asperger Syndrome: The need for socio-sexual education

Isabelle Hénault

Individuals living with high-functioning autism or Asperger Syndrome (AS) present with a specific sexual profile. They show the same interests and sexual needs as the general population but they differ from their peers in the manner in which they behave and manifest their interests. Their lack of social skills and their communication difficulties add to the obstacles that they encounter when they try to establish relationships (Hingsburger 1993; Griffiths 1999).

To date, research on sexuality and structured intervention programs adapted to the needs of the AS population are lacking. The purpose of this chapter is to summarize some of the sexual issues that individuals with AS may experience, and to discuss the application of a socio-sexual training program for individuals with AS. The structured educational approach employed in these groups address themes that respond to the unique socio-sexual profile presented by individuals with AS. This program also meets the growing needs of parents, therapists, and individuals. The goal in delivering this education is to allow participants to gain some independence while demonstrating the appropriate behaviours for acceptable social and sexual functioning.

An introduction to sexuality and Asperger Syndrome

Griffiths, Quinsey, and Hingsburger (1989) state that six factors influence the sexual development of individuals with developmental disorders: (1) lack of socio-sexual information, (2) sexual segregation, (3) restrictive environments, (4) intimacy, (5) medical status, and (6) developmental history including, where applicable, sexual abuse. Their lack of socio-sexual information is due to the discomfort that accompanies the subject of sexuality. Two tendencies are often observed in attitudes to these in individuals' sexuality: over-protection and asexualization. The former serves a protective function while the latter denies the existence of their sexuality. Such attitudes only serve to limit access to information and services which could be of benefit to individuals with AS.

Sexual segregation and restrictive environments do not foster sexual growth. Institutional policies and staff members are stricter about the sexuality of individuals with autism than of those with an intellectual deficit (Roy 1996). According to Griffiths (1999), teams working with these populations should create an environment that is open to dealing with issues of sexuality by preventing abuse, providing education tailored to their needs, and by recognizing their sexual needs and rights.

Recognizing the sexuality of individuals with AS implies a respect for intimacy. If opportunities are provided, individuals can learn to expand their social networks, establish better communication skills, and explore a range of emotions, all of which favour the development of interpersonal relationships.

Medical status and medication use can lead to problematic behaviours observed in individuals with AS. For example, various medications (e.g. antidepressants, antipsychotics) have significant sexual side effects. Those most commonly documented include priapism (i.e. prolonged erection), delayed or painful ejaculation, anorgasmia, and erectile dysfunction (Paradis and Lafond 1990; Alarie and Villeneuve 1992; Hénault 2004). As such, an individual with AS can develop an inappropriate sexual behaviour because of sexual side effects of medication. Erectile difficulties resulting from the use of antidepressants or antipsychotics can lead to "compulsive" or excessive masturbation if an individual tries to regain his erections through self-stimulation.

With respect to the sexual repertoire of individuals with autism or AS, several studies (Konstantareas and Lunsky 1997; Van Bourgondien, Reichle, and Palmer 1997; Haracopos and Pedersen 1999) confirm the presence of an active sexual life that includes masturbatory practices similar to those of the general population (see Masters and Johnson 1988 in Haracopos and Pedersen 1999). Individuals living with autism or AS frequently express their frustrations through inappropriate or aggressive sexual behaviours (Kempton 1993; Mortlock 1989 as cited in Roy 1996). They have difficulty interpreting emotions and the nuances of complex interpersonal relationships escape them. They try to imitate social behaviours but do not always succeed. These factors are compounded by their sexual history which may include possible sexual abuse. The American Academy of Pediatrics (1996) requested a study from the National Center on Child Abuse and Neglect who reported a mean of 36 cases of sexual abuse per 1000 among children with a developmental disorder. This rate is 1.7 times higher than that found in the general population. Their lack of sexual information, knowledge, and social skills can lead to a naïveté, which may influence their notion of consent.

Masturbation

Masturbation is the most common sexual behaviour reported by adolescents with AS. Discovery of one's body and the accompanying pleasant sensations is widespread. In and of itself, self-stimulation is not a problem, especially if expressed within given restrictions. However, behavioural problems related to masturbation are often observed in individuals with AS. Hellemans and Deboutte (2002) have found that public masturbation is the most frequent inappropriate behaviour expressed in autistic populations.

Masturbation can become a sexual compulsion or a source of distraction (just like any other activity). Some individuals achieve such pleasure that they constantly seek to reproduce it to distract themselves. They tend to engage in this behaviour when their level of general stimulation is not high enough (e.g. at school or work, or during free time). In general, teens masturbate one to five times per day. Several factors contribute to the frequency of self-stimulation. The high levels of sex hormones (testosterone and oestrogen) characteristic of adolescence cause an increase in sexual desire. Orgasm and the physical pleasure that accompanies masturbation also serve as powerful reinforcers.

Masturbation is usually discovered naturally, but individuals with AS sometimes need supplementary information, support, and intervention. Shyness, shame, or guilt can sometimes interfere with asking for information. Messages about masturbation can be contradictory: on one hand it can be considered "dirty" and unhealthy, and on the other, a natural and desirable way of discovering one's body. According to Hingsburger (1995), various behaviours or attitudes can lead to problematic masturbation: the individual masturbating incessantly; masturbation that does not end with ejaculation; the individual masturbating but believing that it is bad, dirty, immoral, dangerous, or disgusting; injury occurring from masturbation (due to overly intense stimulation); public masturbation; or the individual fearing masturbation.

Adolescents or adults with AS may display these behaviours or have difficulty forming their own opinion about the subject. Blum and Blum (1981) (as cited in Hingsburger 1995) suggest five learning objectives with respect to masturbation: (1) learning that masturbation is a normal and healthy behaviour; (2) learning the appropriate time and place in which to engage in the behaviour (private *versus* public places); (3) debunking myths and their effects; (4) introducing the notion that sexual fantasies can accompany masturbation; and (5) learning what kind of stimulation leads to pleasure. This education allows individuals with AS to express their emotions and any difficulties that they may have with self-stimulation. Providing clear and concrete information is critical.

The *Hand Made Love* guidebook and video (Hingsburger 1995) are interesting pedagogical tools for men. The guide presents information on sexual health, emotions, fears, and myths surrounding masturbation. The goals of the video are to provide pertinent information on male sexuality (on a behavioural level), create a welcoming and respectful atmosphere related to the expression of sexuality, offer information on physiology, and emphasize the private nature of masturbation. The young man in the *Hand Made Love* video explains and demonstrates the important steps of male masturbation (e.g. being alone in a private place, taking the necessary time, rhythm, touch, bodily sensations). This educational tool is not exhibitionist and was developed especially for adolescents and adults with developmental delays.

Some males are unable to ejaculate during masturbation. Lack of stimulation, tactile hyper- or hyposensitivity, or lack of skill can interfere with climax. Sexual arousal can reach the plateau phase and return to baseline without having reached orgasm. The sexual response cycle (Masters and Johnson 1968) shows the progression in arousal and is presented in the sexual education program. If ejaculation doesn't occur, testicular pain (epididimitis, or inflammation of the vas deferens, the canal that leads away from the epididimis), anxiety, or frustration can sometimes be experienced. Watching a video can sometimes help individuals learn the kinds of techniques that lead to successful stimulation. Any educational activity should emphasize self-respect and privacy. It is always possible to stop the video if individuals are uncomfortable.

The corresponding educational guidebook and video for women are entitled *Finger Tips* (Hingsburger and Haar 2000). The objectives are the same as those for men and the visual material is useful to demystify female masturbation. Female self-stimulation is rarely addressed due to the numerous taboos that surround it. According to Masters and Johnson (1988) (as cited in Haracopos and Pedersen 1999) 75% to 93% of women (including adolescents, young women, and adults) masturbate regularly. The rates drop to 40% to 80% of young autistic women. Prejudices such as unbridled sexuality, lack of self-control, and nymphomania are sometimes raised.

Social skills

"Social aptitude" can be defined as the ability to establish relationships, maintain contact, exchange conversation in a reciprocal manner, share emotions, and develop intimacy with others. Individuals with AS have difficulty with social skills. They experience considerable discomfort that interferes with their ability to develop relationships. Attwood (2003) lists several characteristics related to social impairment: lack of reciprocity and maturity in relationships, limited vocabulary to describe someone's personality, limited adaptation strategies, limited nonverbal expression, and poor management of emotions. Some individuals with AS have greater consideration for their circumscribed interest than for relationships. However, many show a strong interest in others. During adolescence they become attracted to other teens. Their desires multiply during adulthood to include meeting a partner, sharing life with someone, getting married, and starting a family. The image of the solitary, withdrawn adolescent or adult with AS is not accurate for everyone.

Individuals with AS who have the desire to establish relationships suffer the most from their limited social skills. Loneliness, depression, anxiety, and anger are most frequently associated with their distress. The goal of social skills training is to build and expand on the repertoire of adaptive behaviours of individuals with AS. There is a substantial relationship between interpersonal skills and sexuality. Except for self-stimulation, sexual behaviours are experienced and shared with other people. Verbal and nonverbal communication are important from the start to bring people together, express desires and feelings, and meet again. Before any of this can happen, some basic skills are necessary.

Sexual education for adolescents in the general population

During adolescence, several subjects need to be addressed that constitute the basis of sexual education. The following are examples (Sexuality Information and Education Council of the US 1991):

- sexual organs of both sexes: names, functions, and concrete descriptions
- bodily changes that accompany puberty
- self-esteem, self confidence, and body image
- nocturnal emissions and sexual cycle
- values and steps to decision making, choices, and maturity
- intimacy: private and public settings
- sexual health: behaviours and examination of sexual organs/gynaecological examinations
- communication about dating, love, intimacy, and friendship
- how alcohol and drug use influence decision making
- sexual intercourse and other sexual behaviours
- physical reactions, masturbation, and pleasure

- sexual orientation and identity
- birth control, menstruation, and hygiene
- condoms, contraception, and disease prevention
- emotions related to sexuality and interpersonal relationships.

A socio-sexual education program for individuals with Asperger Syndrome

The goal of a socio-sexual education program is to provide individuals with AS opportunities to learn suitable sexual behaviours as recommended by Hingsburger (1993), Kempton (1993), Hellemans (1996), and Griffiths (1999). A thorough review of the literature revealed that few sexual education programs are adapted to the AS population (Ouellet and L'Abbé 1986; Soyner and DesNoyers Hurley 1990; Kempton 1993; Lemay 1996; Durocher and Fortier 1999; Haracopos and Pedersen 1999). The author adapted and added to the content of Durocher and Fortier's (1999) sexual education program. The interventions were designed and implemented in such a way to meet the specific needs of autistic populations. This is the first known program of its kind created specifically for individuals with AS. The program's format, delivering the interventions in 12 consecutive weeks, is also a novel contribution.

According to Family Planning Queensland (2001) and the National Information Center for Children and Youth with Disabilities (1992), sexual education programs should provide information, develop values, encourage and develop interpersonal skills, and help individuals learn to be responsible. Sexuality should also be considered in its entirety and include notions of intimacy, desire, communication, love, deviance, and satisfaction (Haracopos and Pedersen 1999; Griffiths *et al.* 2002). Intervention programs should also discuss sexual and gender identity, needs, and sexual development. As suggested in the literature (Cornelius, Chipouras, and Makas 1982; Griffiths, Quinsey, and Hingsburger 1989; Hellemans 1996), a structured education program designed to meet the needs of the AS population must be part of the services offered and extended to them. The National Information Center for Children and Youth with Disabilities (1992), Kempton (1993), and Hingsburger (1993) state that the more individuals are informed about sexuality, the better able they are to make informed and autonomous choices. This not only decreases the risk of sexual abuse, but also allows individuals with AS access to a rewarding social and sexual life.

Several authors have recognized the need for sexual education for individuals with AS (e.g. Hingsburger 1993; Gray, Ruble, and Dalrymple 1996; Hellemans 1996; Haracopos and Pedersen 1992; Attwood, personal communication).

Several sexual education programs exist for individuals with intellectual disabilities (e.g. Kaeser and O'Neill 1987), but few address the specific needs of those with AS. One preliminary version of a program was proposed by Haracopos and Pedersen (1999). Kempton (1993), a pioneer in specialized sexual education, published a socio-sexual education program designed for individuals with a Pervasive Developmental Disorder (PDD). This program provides excellent information on social skills and other subjects, but topics related to sexuality are limited and the educational material is insufficiently concrete. The *Programme d'Éducation Sexuelle* (Durocher and Fortier 1999) appears to be the most promising given the sexual and cognitive profile of individuals with AS. Activities are concrete, use images, and require high levels of participation. The program was designed to be administered in a group format and focuses on interpersonal exchanges and social contacts. It has been used to help individuals with various behaviour disorders such as aggression, opposition, and hyperactivity. This program therefore constituted the foundation for the development of a socio-sexual education program for individuals with AS.

The socio-sexual education program developed by this author is divided into 12 topics related to sexuality. The program can be offered to individuals, but the section on social skills will require modification in such a case since the activities were designed to be administered in a group format. It was developed specifically to meet the needs of the AS population and to address their difficulties with social interactions. Numerous additions were made to the *Programme d'Éducation Sexuelle* (Durocher and Fortier 1999) such as including more concrete activities, increased visual support, and repeating exercises to allow participants to integrate the material better.

A variety of tools are also used in the program: the *Gaining Face* software (Team Asperger 2000), pictures from the *SexoTrousse* (Lemay 1996), social stories (Gray 2000), and specialized educational material (Hingsburger 1995; Hingsburger and Haar 2000; Baron-Cohen 2002). Activities can be adapted depending on the group (the members' age, special needs, receptivity, etc.). In general, groups should be created according to the participants' ages (from 16 to 20 years, 20 to 30 years, 30 to 40 years, etc.). Whenever possible, it is always preferable to include both genders in a group. Males are always curious to hear what females think, and *vice versa*.

Each workshop was developed to take place over a 90-minute period. A group leader could easily decide to divide it into two 45-minute workshops. Activities and exercises can also be repeated and extend over 20 workshops or more. The 12-session pedagogical formula described here can certainly be modified. However the results (from Hénault, Forget and Giroux 2003) described here are for the 12-session 90-minute format.

Each workshop consists of three to five activities. Various materials are used to meet the learning needs of individuals with AS. Each session is structured and has specific objectives. Instructions and the series of exercises are provided to facilitate and standardize the group leaders' tasks. The topics addressed in the 12 sessions of the program include:

1   *Assessment and introduction to the program*: The purpose of the first workshop is to complete the assessment forms and to introduce the participants to the socio-sexual education program and its procedures. Parents and partners are invited to attend the workshop. During the first part of the session, the group leader introduces the program and its accompanying materials (calendar, exercise sheets, videos, computer software, photographs and images, etc.). The consent form and the information sheet are then completed by the participants.

2   *Introduction to sexuality and communication*: The goal of this session is to have the participants share their feelings, improve their communication skills, and create an inviting environment within the group. "What is sexuality?" is the question for the warm-up exercise. After five minutes of brainstorming in small teams (words, phrases, images that come up), each team must count the number of words that were listed on a sheet of paper and share these with others in the group. At the end, participants are asked about how they found the exercise and where they learned these words (newspapers, radio, television, books, classes, etc.).

3   *Love and friendship*: This session serves as an introduction to the program. Interpersonal relationships for teenagers and adults are presented, and other questions are explored. Sharing on themes like sexuality, love, friendship and personal values stimulates discussion among participants. The "little ads" game completes this workshop.

4   *Physiological aspects and the sexual response cycle*: This theme allows the instructor to give information on the genitals (masculine and feminine) as well as their functions. Furthermore, the physical, psychological, and emotional changes that occur during adolescence and adulthood are identified. The objective is to define specific characteristics and to learn the appropriate words related to the sexuality of teenagers and adults.

5   *Sexual intercourse and other behaviours*: The aim of this theme is to inform and demystify sexual experiences on a physical and emotional level and to favour the expression of sexual needs. The presentation of a visual

document accompanies the activities. Finally, the sexual response cycle is presented to the group.

6   *Emotions*: This interactive workshop aims to teach the many emotions related to sexuality. The use of pictures and the *Gaining Face* software (Team Asperger 2000) are used. Following the learning phase, knowledge is evaluated by a quiz.

7   *STDs, HIV, and prevention*: This session includes information on contraception and STDs and HIV prevention. The objective is to sensitize individuals to the importance of contraception and make them more responsible for their sexual behaviour.

8   *Sexual orientation*: The goal of this activity is to sensitize teenagers and adults to different sexual orientations. They are invited to consider the person as a whole rather than judging her/him simply by her or his sexual orientation. The workshop aims at eliminating prejudices related to sexual orientation.

9   *Alcohol, drugs, and sexuality*: This session tries to inform individuals with AS about the effects of drugs and alcohol. Drugs and alcohol can be obstacles to safe and respectful sexual behaviour. The group creates a scenario based on healthy sexuality using collage or sketches.

10   *Sexual abuse and inappropriate behaviours*: The activities are aimed at sensitizing the group to sexism. Participants should learn to identify sexual stereotypes about gender roles in the media and in everyday life. Violence in relationships is also explored. Vignettes and questionnaires explore the notion of abuse.

11   *Sexism and violence*: This workshop teaches individuals with AS to consider what constitutes inadequate sexual behaviour. Participants learn to identify situations of possible abuse. Furthermore, they are helped to elaborate ways of protecting themselves and others when facing such situations. Illustrations and social circles are some of the activities presented to the group.

12   *Managing emotions, theory of mind, and intimacy*: Role-playing exercises teach the group members how to experiment and cope with different sexual situations that could happen in adult life. This last session is aimed at checking if participants generalize and apply the information presented in the preceding workshops to their own life.

The topics address the sexual reality of individuals with AS, as defined by Kempton (1993) and Haracopos and Pedersen (1999). Techniques such as role playing, rehearsal, and group sessions are used. These modifications have made it possible to offer an innovative program to adolescents and adults with AS. This program (Hénault 2004) has also been empirically validated (Hénault, Forget, and Giroux 2003). A summary of the results is presented below.

Evaluation of the socio-sexual education program

After attending the training program described above, the friendship and intimacy skills of the participants significantly increased whereas the frequency of inappropriate behaviours decreased. Skills such as introducing oneself, making conversation, and nonverbal communication improved over the course of the intervention. Helping and empathy behaviours were observed more frequently at the end of the program. The development of friendships among the participants is proof of closeness and openness to others manifested during the workshops. Attending the socio-sexual skills education program also decreased the frequency of inappropriate behaviours such as inappropriate masturbation, sexual obsessions, voyeurism, fetishism, and exhibitionism (Hénault, Forget, and Giroux 2003). In addition, behaviours of withdrawal and isolation were replaced by a greater reciprocity among group members. Impulsive behaviours such as self-mutilation and tantrums were not significantly represented. Generalization of treatment gains was shown at three months' follow-up. Finally, an increase in general sexual knowledge and a positive attitude towards sexuality were also observed in the participants.

The program's format is a significant strength. Since the intervention takes place over 12 consecutive weeks participants can associate with one another while developing friendships. This growth of friendships was especially noted during the last two sessions. Qualitative observations revealed that friendships developed among participants. For example, two participants discovered that they shared a common passion for wrestling. They exchanged magazines and began meeting one another outside the group context. In another group, three adults engaged in activities together weekly. One participant introduced her favourite activity (bowling) to the group. Two adults in one group discovered their common passion for computers, and an adolescent in another group introduced someone to drawing. Group activities made it easier for group members to become close. The need to socialize made it possible for friendships to develop and these increased the quality of relationships within the group.

Group participation also helped develop less self-centred and narcissistic attitudes. Social interaction enabled participants to become more open to the experiences of others, which decreased attitudes such as "I know everything", which was observed in some individuals. Peer reactions are very useful during the workshops. For example, after viewing a video on sexual abuse, the comments of some participants influenced those who tended towards sexual aggression. Similarly, a discussion and a short video on masturbation allowed an adolescent with high-functioning autism to make changes to his inappropriate behaviour, which his mother later confirmed. The change was still being maintained at the last follow-up three months post-treatment.

The use of visual materials (e.g. videos, photos, computer programs) and the group activities maintained the participants' interest and increased appropriate gazing behaviours. Staring behaviours need to be addressed in these populations as they are among one of the most frequently observed difficulties (Soyner and DesNoyers Hurley 1990; Bernier and Lamy 1998).

Other results showed that the group participants developed friendship and intimacy skills during the workshops (Hénault, Forget, and Giroux 2003). The targeted skills were selected based upon the diagnostic criteria for AS. Lack of reciprocity and difficulties related to communication, gaze, attachment, and empathy are among the observable manifestations of AS. Skills related to introducing oneself (joining the group, greeting others) increased considerably during the intervention. Interest shown towards group members favoured participation and exchange. General reciprocity increased over the course of the treatment. A tendency to isolate themselves and a lack of exchange between participants were observed during the first two weeks. The activities addressed in the following two sessions (physiology and sexual relations) provoked conversations among the group members. Therefore, despite the high language level of individuals with high-functioning autism and AS, it was possible to improve their communication skills.

Additional information was obtained on variables related to the personal history of participants. Despite their lack of experiences reported on the Derogatis Sexual Functioning Inventory (DSFI) (Derogatis and Melisaratos 1982), 19% of the participants were or had been in a relationship. The participants had all had certain interpersonal experiences (with their parents, friends, partners, colleagues, classmates, etc.) and manifested an interest in developing the skills necessary to forge friendships and intimate relationships with people in their environment. Their motivation and interest contributed to the success of the intervention. The rate of voluntary participation in the program was high at 82%; considerable, especially when we consider the 12-week time commitment and the active participation required (Hénault, Forget, and Giroux 2003).

Future services

Assessing the long-term generalization of treatment gains from participation in the socio-sexual education program should be a priority. All education and intervention programs for this population must address this issue. As mentioned by Griffiths, Quinsey, and Hingsburger (1989), generalization involves three aspects: therapist intervention, support networks, and community intervention. First, the therapist or educator works on interventions in the natural setting. That is, besides offering activities in the workshop context, *in vivo* training needs to take place to help the individual confront real situations. A second phase consists of creating a support network (family member, friend, counsellor, etc.) that helps to extend learning, provides social support, and maintains the link to the principal therapist. Finally, community interventions such as hobbies, support groups, and other services are offered. Future studies should include these phases of follow-up to ensure that gains are maintained over the long term. Support systems need to be established within pre-existing community services. The author's services were frequently requested for therapy and follow-up purposes. The intervention program described here therefore opens avenues to creating psychological and sexological services adapted to the specific needs of individuals living with AS.

References

Alarie, P., and Villeneuve, R. (1992) *L'impuissance: Évaluations et Solutions.* Montréal, Québec: Editions de l'Homme.

American Academy of Pediatrics (1996) Sexuality education of children and adolescents with Developmental Disabilities. *Pediatrics, 97,* 275–8.

Attwood, T. (2003) Autism and Asperger's Syndrome and children. Lecture at the Third International FAAAS Conference on May 9 2003, Boston, MA. Retrieved from www.faaas.org/ on May 18 2004.

Baron-Cohen, S., Golan, O., Wheelwright, S., and Hill, J.J. (2004) *Mind Reading: The Interactive Guide to Emotions.* Cambridge, UK: Human Emotions.

Bernier, S., and Lamy, M. (1998) *Programme d'Entraînement aux Habiletés Sociales Adapté pour une Clientèle Présentant un Trouble Envahissant du Développement.* Hôpital Rivière-des-Prairies: Clinique des Troubles Envahissants du Développement.

Cornelius, D.A., Chipouras, S., and Makas, E. (1982) *Who Cares? A Handbook on Sex Education and Counselling Services for Disabled People.* Baltimore, MD: University Park Press.

Derogatis, L.R., and Melisaratos, N. (1982) *Derogatis Sexual Functioning Inventory.* Towson, MD: Clinical Psychometric Research Inc. Available at: www.derogatis-tests.com/

Durocher, L., and Fortier, M. (1999) *Programme d'Éducation Sexuelle.* Montréal, Québec: Les Centres Jeunesse de Montréal et la Régie Régionale de la Santé et des Services Sociaux, Direction de la Santé Publique.

Family Planning Queensland (2001) *Sexual and Reproductive Health.* Family Planning Queensland, Brisbane: Australia.

Gray, C. (2000) *Writing Social Stories.* Arlington, TX: Future Horizons Inc.

Gray, S., Ruble, L., and Dalrymple, N. (1996) *Autism and Sexuality: A Guide for Instruction.* Bloomington, IN: Autism Society of Indiana.

Griffiths, D. (1999) La Sexualité des Personnes Présentant un Trouble Envahissant du Développement. Paper presented at Consortium de Services pour les Personnes ayant des Troubles Graves du Comportement. Montéeal, Québec, April.

Griffiths, D., Quinsey, V.L., and Hingsburger, D. (1989) *Changing Inappropriate Sexual Behavior.* Baltimore, MD: Paul H. Brookes.

Griffiths, D., Richards, D., Fedoroff, P., and Watson, S.L. (2002) *Ethical Dilemmas: Sexuality and Developmental Disability.* New York, NY: NADD Press.

Haracopos, D., and Pedersen, L. (1999) *Sexuality and Autism: The Danish Report.* Kettering, UK: Autism Independent UK. Available at www.autismuk.com

Hellemans, H. (1996) L'éducation sexuelle des adolescents autistes. Paper presented at Projet Caroline Conference, Brussels, March.

Hellemans, H., and Deboutte, D. (2002) Autism spectrum disorders and sexuality. Paper presented at Melbourne World Autism Congress, Melbourne, Australia, November.

Hénault, I. (2004) *Asperger's Syndrome and Sexuality: From Adolescence Through Adulthood.* London, UK: Jessica Kingsley Publishers.

Hénault, I., Forget, J., and Giroux, N. (2003) Le développement d'habiletés sexuelles adaptatives chez des individus atteints d'autism de haut niveau ou de syndrome d'Asperger. Doctoral Dissertation, Université du Québec à Montréal.

Hingsburger, D. (1993) *I Openers: Parents Ask Questions About Sexuality and Children with Developmental Disabilities.* Vancouver, BC: Family Support Institute Press.

Hingsburger, D. (1995) *Hand Made Love: A Guide for Teaching About Male Masturbation Through Understanding and Video.* Newmarket, ON: Diverse City Press. Available at www.diverse-city.com/video.htm

Hingsburger, D., and Haar, S. (2000) *Finger Tips: Teaching Women with Disabilities about Masturbation Through Understanding and Video.* Newmarket, ON: Diverse City Press. Available at www.diverse-city.com/video.htm

Kaeser, F., and O'Neill, J. (1987) Task analysed masturbation instruction for a profoundly mentally retarded adult male: A data based case study. *Sexuality and Disability, 8,* 17–24.

Kempton, W. (1993) *Socialization and Sexuality, A Comprehensive Guide.* Santa Barbara, CA: James Stanfield Company.

Konstantareas, M.M., and Lunsky, Y.J. (1997) Sociosexual knowledge, experience, attitudes, and interests of individuals with autistic disorder and developmental delay. *Journal of Autism and Developmental Disorders, 27,* 113–25.

Lemay, M. (1996) *La SexoTrousse.* Maniwaki: Pavillon du Parc.

Masters, W.H., and Johnson, V.E. (1968) *Les Réactions Sexuelles.* Paris: Robert Laffont.

National Information Center for Children and Youth with Disabilities (1992) Sexuality education for children and youth with disabilities. *NICHCY News Digest, 17,* 1–37.

Ouellet, R., and L'Abbé, Y. (1986) *Programme d'Entraînement aux Habiletés Sociales.* Eastman: Éditions Behaviora.

Paradis, A.F., and Lafond, J. (1990) *La Réponse Sexuelle et Ses Perturbations.* Boucherville: Les Editions G. Vermette.

Roy, J. (1996) Comparaison entre les attitudes des intervenants travaillant auprès d'adolescents autistes et ceux travaillant auprès d'adolescents déficients intellectuellement à l'égard des comportements sexuels de ces jeunes. In *Rapport d'Activités de Maîtrise en Sexologie.* Montréal, Québec: Département de sexologie, Université du Québec à Montréal.

Sexuality Information and Education Council of the US (1991) *Sexuality Education for People with Disabilities.* New York, NY: SIECUS.

Soyner, R., and DesNoyers Hurley, A. (1990) L'apprentissage des habiletés sociales. *Habilitative Mental Healthcare Newsletter, 9,* 1, 1–5.

Team Asperger (2000) *Gaining Face Software.* Appleton, WI: Team Asperger. Available at: www.ccoder.com/GainingFace/

Van Bourgondien, M., Reichle, N.C., and Palmer, A. (1997) Sexual behavior in adults with autism. *Journal of Autism and Developmental Disorders, 27,* 2, 113–25.

Part II

Discipline-based Perspectives

CHAPTER 8

Communication and Asperger Syndrome: The speech–language pathologist's role

Tracie Lindblad

Communication deficits are a central consideration in the diagnosis of autism spectrum disorders (ASDs). It is because of deficient or disordered communication (which includes nonverbal language, articulation, receptive and expressive language, the social use of language, and written language skills) that the speech–language pathologist (SLP) has become a fundamental member of the team supporting individuals with ASDs. In this role, the SLP assists with the diagnosis, and in the design and implementation of treatment.

When delineating the symptomatology necessary for the diagnosis of Asperger Syndrome (AS) however, the core communication deficits may not be readily apparent and may not be the primary cause for obtaining a diagnosis. If language impairment is a factor for these individuals, then what is the role of the SLP in diagnosis and treatment? The aim of this chapter is to describe the assessment and intervention process of the SLP in her work with children and adolescents with AS. First, the unique language and communication profile of individuals with AS will be reviewed.

The language and communication profile of individuals with Asperger Syndrome

According to the *DSM-IV* (APA 1994), AS is characterized by a triad of symptoms: (1) deficits in social interaction, (2) deficits in social communication, and (3) a restricted range of interests and behaviours. Individuals with AS demonstrate significant impairments in the social domain, namely in social skills and the social use of language. With respect to communication deficits, there is typically an absence of "clinically significant" language delay, but this should not be inter-preted as an absence of any unusual language features or qualities (Attwood 1998).

Therefore, in order to assist a multidisciplinary team with accurate and appropriate diagnosis, or with the development of appropriate treatment goals, the SLP can further investigate language and communication skills to pinpoint areas of weakness within these seemingly competent language users. The SLP may examine many areas which directly affect peer interaction skills, academic success, the ability to adapt to various environments (e.g. home, school, and community), and the ability to generalize information for use in novel ways.

Children with AS display a myriad of differences within their language skills. The broad diagnostic criteria lead to the definition of a heterogeneous grouping rather than a homogeneous sample, particularly when diagnosis is made before the age of six years. The language deficits can range from subtle difficulties with syntax and grammar skills, to significant weaknesses with understanding higher-level language constructs such as idioms, puns, and sarcasm. Szatmari *et al.* (2003) confirm this broad range of deficits within language skills in children with AS rather than a condensed set of difficulties; this is as one might expect because of their relatively "normal" language development in early childhood. Szatmari and colleagues found the features differentiating children with autism and AS were that the children with AS spoke before 36 months of age, there was no evidence of delayed echolalia, there was no pronoun reversal, and there was no evidence of neologisms (idiosyncratic words or standard words with idiosyncratic meanings).

"Language" is comprised of six major areas: speech and articulation skills (speech sound production), nonverbal language skills (gestures, facial expression, body language, tone of voice, rate of speech, pitch, etc.), receptive language skills (understanding), expressive language skills (output-augmentative, verbal and/or written), written language (spelling, decoding, reading, and writing), and pragmatic language skills (the social use of language). Upon examination of each area, deficits are often noted in individuals with AS. Each of these six areas will be reviewed below.

Speech and articulation skills

Within the area of speech sound production skills, significant differences or delays in articulation skills are not generally seen in this population. Articulation skills are age appropriate, if not advanced in development. At times, there can be overly precise articulation, or an "acquired" accent (Baron-Cohen and Staunton 1994), and difficulties with rate, loudness, prosody (flow) or pitch of speech, all of which can affect speech intelligibility.

Nonverbal language skills

"Nonverbal language skills" can be defined as the ability to send or receive a message without the use of verbal communication. Our nonverbal communication skills start in infancy and increase with age. Our earliest abilities to understand and use nonverbal skills can be observed when infants use eye gaze or pointing as a means of requesting objects. Other nonverbal skills, such as interpreting body language, natural gestures, facial expression, and emotional tone, develop with increasing age in typical toddlers. However, the individual with AS will demonstrate significant difficulties with the understanding and use of nonverbal communication skills at all ages. The difficulties with understanding and use of eye gaze, interpretation of body language, gestures, and facial expression lead to significant deficits in social communication skills that notably affect peer interactions and school success. Children with AS learn emotions cognitively rather than intuitively, thus gaining qualities such as being inflexible, moralistic, and naïve.

Receptive language skills

On the surface, comprehension skills can appear to be adequately developed in individuals with AS. However, receptive deficits are often seen. These deficits centre on the individual's ability to understand deeper meanings in words, phrases, and social situations (i.e. semantics). Comprehension of factual information and more "concrete" language skills (literal comprehension skills) remain intact, but higher-level language skills or abstract comprehension skills are problematic. The student may have difficulty with "reading between the lines", making inferences, predicting outcomes, or understanding humour – idioms, puns, and sarcasm – which involve multiple meanings or flexibility in language use. Problem-solving skills are often impaired with perspective-taking deficits (i.e. "theory of mind") at the core. Often, the person with AS displays difficulty in following the patterns in language and then applying these to novel contexts.

Expressive language skills

Expressive language skills can reveal subtle differences in individuals with AS. Typically, their expressive vocabulary development is above average. They can acquire high-level vocabulary quite easily and use it appropriately. However, they can lack true understanding of the vocabulary. At times it may be noted that they have word-retrieval deficits. Their syntax and grammar skills (sentence structure, verb tense, plurals, possession, etc.) can be highly developed. There is, however, often a reduction in figurative language, inflexibility in vocabulary, and a limitation in varied sentence formulation – observed in difficulties formulating novel ideas or in messages with a rigid grammatical form.

Written language

Written language skills typically mirror expressive language skills since writing is an "output" ability. Toddlers with AS are often thought to be "hyperlexic" with decoding of text beginning at an early age, often before three years of age. The spelling and decoding skills of individuals with AS are strong, with phonemic awareness (sound segmentation and blending) skills usually commensurate with receptive language skills. Reading comprehension may be compromised because of limitations with working memory, in understanding higher-level language, and in abstract thought. Understanding and generation of creative, narrative text (story reading and writing) may also be problematic, with a propensity for reading and writing based on expository works and factual information. In addition, fine motor deficits such as slow writing speed, difficulties in near- and far-point copying, and poor letter formation affects all areas of written language. Thus, written language may be depressed below the level of expressive language skills because of the added influence of fine motor and motor planning weaknesses.

Pragmatic language skills

Of all skill areas, pragmatic language skills remain the core deficit area of individuals with AS. Difficulties with nonverbal language skills coupled with a restricted range of repertoires and interests lead to significant deficits in social communication. Individuals with AS can be pedantic, speak in an overly formal style, and lack awareness of the need to modify the conversation and conversational style for the listener. Conversational difficulties are often myriad and may include weaknesses in topic initiation, understanding and use of nonverbal communication, topic maintenance, clarification, topic switching, and proper ending of the conversation. There is a lack of, or at best, an awkward, "back and forth" flow to the conversation.

The speech and language assessment

Speech and language assessments for individuals with AS are necessary for evaluating each person's specific language strengths and weaknesses. Specifically, an in-depth language assessment will assist in discovering the learning needs and learning style of the child or student with AS. It is imperative to determine each person's learning strengths as well as his or her weaknesses within language skills, in order to use specific approaches for teaching and programming that will promote development in receptive and expressive language, written communication, and social communication skills.

It is important to highlight that early speech and language development of a child with AS cannot be used to make a prognostic or definitive statement regarding future language abilities or overall success. Preliminary findings suggest that individuals diagnosed with AS have a better outcome than individuals diagnosed with autism, but these pathways can overlap and even cross in later childhood and adolescence. It also appears that early fluent language skills cannot solely predict a better outcome; rather, it may be the strength of the nonverbal language skills that holds the key as a better prognostic indicator of outcome (Szatmari et al. 2003).

Assessment can be thought of as an ongoing and multifaceted process that should lead to the design and implementation of particular strategies, interventions, and accommodations that address the learning needs of the student while supporting the strengths demonstrated. A multidisciplinary assessment, which examines all areas of functioning (i.e. play skills, self-help skills, verbal and nonverbal skills, social communication, academic skills, motor skills), provides the most accurate picture of the individual and highlights the interrelatedness of many areas of functioning.

Evaluation must be ongoing in nature. Individuals with AS may display significant behaviours that interfere with assessment: anxiety, difficulty in accepting new or unfamiliar materials or activities, unusual behavioural patterns of responding, difficulties with attention and on-task behaviour, and varying levels of interest or motivation. All of these responses serve to interact within the assessment process and skew the assessment results. Therefore, experience in assessing and working with this population is imperative in order to extract the most meaningful information. Thus, the "assessment" becomes a process where information must be gathered before the administration of standardized assessment tools and subsequently factored in during the interpretation of the assessment results.

The assessment process is comprised of multiple stages: (1) initial interview and collection of background information, (2) administration of standardized and/or informal assessment measures, (3) comparison and integration of assessment information with multidisciplinary team results, (4) design and implementation of services and supports, (5) evaluation of behaviours and responses over time, and (6) re-assessment.

The purpose of this chapter is to examine a sample of standardized assessment tools which can contribute information along only one phase in the multistep process. However, each phase must take place within a full assessment to provide the most complete picture of the individual's learning strengths and weaknesses. It is critical to obtain information from parents, teachers, therapists, and others involved in the individual's life on a day-to-day basis to get the most complete picture. It is this daily contact and observation of the individual in challenging environments or activities that will provide useful information. This information must then be integrated with the assessment results, as the latter are often acquired under ideal conditions and not reflective of skills exhibited in everyday contexts. This integration of the information from each phase is imperative to the appropriate design and implementation of services and supports.

Many speech and language assessment tools will yield useful information for this population. It is important to examine competency at the single word, sentence, paragraph, and conversational levels to determine the point at which breakdown or deficits occur.

Vocabulary and concept development

Acquisition of labels and the development of semantics (word meaning) at the single word level is crucial to the social and academic success of individuals with AS. Many standardized assessment tools allow the assessor the ability to compare comprehension *versus* use. Such tools include:

- Peabody Picture Vocabulary Test – III (Dunn and Dunn 1997)
- Expressive Vocabulary Test (Williams 1997)
- Test of Word Finding 2 (German 1989a)
- Test of Adolescent/Adult Word Finding (German 1989b).

Often, a pattern will emerge where receptive and expressive vocabulary skills are unevenly developed, although still within the average range for chronological age. The pattern of lexis acquisition in AS is not predictable. Expressive vocabulary may be found to be elevated in comparison to receptive vocabulary due to higher word use with weaker understanding of the words. Alternatively, expressive vocabulary skills may be depressed in comparison to receptive vocabulary because of significant word retrieval deficits or an inability to demonstrate flexibility in word usage (i.e. the ability to provide synonyms or multiple meanings for words). As well, rote information may be substantially elevated when compared to the development of relational or abstract concepts in young and early elementary-aged children. Evaluation of rote skills *versus* more relational concepts can be evaluated using the Bracken Basic Concept Scale – Revised (Bracken 1998).

Receptive and expressive language skills

Many language skills involving the understanding and use of lengthier utterances at the sentence and paragraph levels should also be examined. Various standardized assessment tools examine language constructs such as receptive and expressive syntax and morphology (word order and word endings), semantics and flexibility of language labels (synonyms, antonyms, associations, oral definitions, etc.), non-literal language (e.g. inferences, double meanings, idioms, metaphors, irony, sarcasm, and humour), following directions involving linguistic concepts, sentence comprehension, and listening comprehension skills. Such tools include:

- Structured Photographic Expressive Language Test 3 (Dawson, Stout, and Eyer 2003)
- Clinical Evaluation of Language Fundamentals – Fourth Edition (Semel, Wiig, and Secord 2003)
- Test of Language Development – Primary (Newcomer and Hammill 1997)
- Test of Language Development – Intermediate (Hammill and Newcomer 1997).

Language skills can be unevenly developed in the profile of an individual with AS. At times, grammar and syntax can be elevated with respect to chronological age and language comprehension skills. Basic language skills such as sentence construction and comprehension can also be age appropriate. However, the language skills examined within these test batteries are cursory in nature and further examination of higher-level language skills may be warranted. Often children and adolescents with AS achieve age-appropriate scores and demonstrate good abilities on these general language assessments that are not always evident in spontaneously occurring situations (Klin, Volkmar, and Sparrow 2000). Thus, further assessment of higher-level language, communication skills, and verbal problem-solving skills may be required. The following tests are particularly suited to this level of assessment.

- Test of Language Competence, Expanded Edition (Wiig and Secord 1989)
- Test of Problem Solving – Elementary (Zachman, Barrett, and Huisingh 1984)
- Test of Problem Solving – Adolescent (Zachman *et al.* 1991)

These tests focus on skills such as understanding ambiguity in messages, making inferences, determining cause and effect, predicting outcomes, determining solutions, understanding and use of "why" questions, understanding emotion and affect, and understanding and use of figurative language (idioms, jokes, puns, etc.).

Pragmatic language skills

Assessment of pragmatic language skills (i.e. the social understanding and use of language) and conversational skills, which include topic management (i.e. initiation of a topic, topic maintenance, appropriate topic switching, and topic closure), turn-taking skills, conversational repair strategies, and understanding of presupposition and perspective taking (i.e. understanding the background knowledge of the listener, the intention of the speaker, and being able to predict and share another's perspective) are a critical part of the assessment. Unfortunately, few standardized assessment tools exist which accurately measure each of these skill areas in isolation. A baseline measure can be obtained using the Test of Pragmatic Language (Phelps-Terasaki and Phelps-Gunn 1992).

Some students perform adequately on this test because they have stereotyped "learned" language skills and good memory skills. These same students can also perform adequately on other speech-language standardized tests such as the CELF-3. However, in various structured situations, significant difficulty with conversational speech remains evident. Therefore, in addition to administering a standardized measure of social communication competence, additional testing and observation of the individual must take place in various situations. This assists in determining the "cognitive" understanding and use of pragmatic language skills as compared to the "intuitive" understanding and use of those skills in spontaneous situations. The Social Skills Rating Scale (Gresham and Elliott 1990) can assist in this process.

Written language skills

Written language skills (i.e. decoding, spelling, reading comprehension, and writing) are the highest and most complex method of expression or "output" which develop subsequent to oral language. Within "written language" many interrelated sub-skills exist and operate both sequentially and simultaneously, often rendering the outcome difficult for those with AS. Several formal and informal measures are needed to assess these skill areas:

- Test of Auditory Analytic Skills (Rosner 1979)
- The Phonological Awareness Test (Robertson and Salter 1997)

- Dolch, Fry, or Brigance sight word lists (Dolch 1955; Brigance 1980; Fry 1980)

- Morrison–McCall Spelling Scale for Grades 2 to 8 (Morrison and McCall 1951)

- Spelling Performance Evaluation for Language and Literacy (Masterson, Apel, and Wasowicz 2002)

- Test of Reading Comprehension (Brown, Hammill, and Wiederholt 1995)

- Test of Written Language (Hammill and Larsen 1995)

- informal writing samples.

To show success within the area of written language the individual must have intact language skills (i.e. receptive and expressive), motivation for writing, organizational skills (verbal, visual, and spatial), decoding skills, spelling abilities, syntax and grammar knowledge, and the mechanics and conventions of writing (i.e. fine motor skills, motor memory skills, and knowledge of punctuation and capitalization rules). Many individuals with AS experience significant difficulties within one or multiple components of written language.

Often, rote skills such as decoding and spelling skills are relatively intact and may even be strength areas (i.e. visually based splinter skills). However, phonemic awareness skills – that is, sound segmentation and sound blending skills (foundation skills for phonics) – are often rotely learned in the early grades with poor application of this skill to novel or made-up words.

While decoding skills can be strength areas, reading comprehension and generative story-writing skills are often significantly weak. Higher-level language deficits in non-literal language skills, verbal problem-solving skills, and poor organizational skills contribute to the difficulties in reading comprehension of non-factual or narrative text. In comparison, expository or fact-based text is often better understood and more easily remembered for the individual with AS.

Assessment of written language skills should also be comparative in nature. That is, two samples of writing should be obtained: one written by hand, and one generated on the computer to bypass any fine motor weaknesses. Furthermore, two narratives (i.e. stories) should also be elicited from the student, one on a topic of their highest interest and one assigned as a general topic. It is the comparison between these samples that will often highlight the degree of difficulty dependent upon the task requirements and/or the motivation of the individual.

Assessment of children and adolescents with AS is most useful when multidisciplinary team members, family caregivers, and other professionals provide input on various traits to gain a complete picture of the "whole" learner.

This comprehensive picture of learner strengths and weaknesses can then be translated into the design and implementation of suitable services, supports, and strategies for the individual. Consequently, it follows that the evaluators or professionals that engage in assessment of individuals with AS provide beneficial information on programming, services, supports, and strategies that are individualized for that particular learner considering his or her unique profile. The goals or programming suggestions should be realistic in that caregivers, educators, and professionals must be able to implement them successfully within the context of the particular environment.

It is also important to be aware that the assessments may have limited usefulness due to the changing nature of children with AS and the various medical, behavioural, and developmental changes that are the hallmark of ASDs. Therefore, ongoing evaluation and reassessment of the student is imperative in recommending services and supports and in designing "individualized" programs and strategies.

Programming, treatment, and intervention

The functional application of the assessment process is the subsequent design and implementation of individualized programming, strategies, and supports. It is only the next phases in the process, comparison and integration of assessment information with multidisciplinary team results, which lead to the design and implementation of services and supports. This then leads to the evaluation of behaviours and responses over time. In other words, programming, strategies, and supports must also be assessed on an ongoing basis to determine treatment appropriateness and effectiveness. Thus, treatment goals need to be measurable to be evaluated (i.e. documentation of specific events, data collection, charting, and/or graphing).

Just as the profile of speech, language, communication, and learning abilities of individuals with AS are variable, so too are the interventions for these same individuals. Unfortunately, there is no single method or strategy that is suited for every individual with AS, nor any commercially available "cookbook" approach to treatment. Instead, treatment should be highly individualized and capitalize on strength areas while programming for specific areas of weakness. Many forms of intervention exist within the field of speech-language pathology:

- direct intervention: individual in a "pull-out" setting
- direct intervention: individual within a larger group setting such as a classroom
- direct intervention: small group in a "pull-out" setting

- direct intervention: small group within a classroom setting
- consultation regarding the development of the individual's educational program plan (IEP)
- consultation with the parents, caregivers, classroom teachers, and paraprofessionals (i.e. educational assistant, child and youth worker, communication disorder assistant)
- coaching or indirect intervention with the parents, caregivers, classroom teachers, and paraprofessionals.

Any one service may be delivered, or all may co-exist in the treatment plan for the individual with AS. However, in recommending and delivering suitable services for individuals with AS, current research findings must shape our intervention plans. That is: (1) intervention should be intense and begin as early as possible, (2) intervention should be functionally obvious, and (3) communication outcomes should demonstrate spontaneity and generalization (National Research Council 2001). If all recommendations and goal strategies reflect the principles of being intensive, functionally suitable, easily generalized, and measurable, then the individual with AS will receive a well-designed treatment plan.

Because of the sheer volume of treatment options available to address each of the deficit areas of speech, language, and communication as outlined previously, it is not possible to discuss here in detail the wide range of programs, strategies, and materials available within the field of speech, communication, and language therapy. However, the following programs, strategies, and treatment recommendations have been found useful when individually tailored to meet the unique needs of the individual with AS.

Articulation, speech, and prosody

Typical articulation therapy may be warranted in some children with AS. Generally, speech sound production errors should be corrected as early as possible because of the well-documented motor planning difficulties. It also appears that early correction of speech sound errors results in easier shaping of the new behaviour with better generalization of the new target sound. Developmental norms can be used as a treatment guide for beginning therapy. Often the sound error may be quite resistant to shaping and correction with little change in the speech patterns that were developed, reinforced, and maintained over a longer period of time.

Prosodic features (i.e. intonation, stress patterns, loudness variations, pausing, rhythm, pitch, loudness, and duration) are often disordered in the individual with AS. However, there has not been documented evidence to suggest that therapeutic techniques can remediate these differences in the person with AS. More research in this area is required as this often becomes one of the most notable features of the communication skills of the individual with AS.

Receptive and expressive language skills

Within treatment, the main language goals centre on comprehension and flexibility in language at the single word level, sentence, and paragraph/discourse level. In early childhood (i.e. developmental age of two to ten years), there are several areas to target: vocabulary development, word retrieval deficits, and concept development (i.e. the language of math, the language of time, and self- and social relationships). Many resources support skill development within these areas:

- DT Trainer Software (Smith 2000)
- Teach Me Language (Freeman and Dake 1997)
- Vocabulary Builder, Grade 3 to 6 (Essential Skills Software 2003e).

Written language skills

The main areas of focus within written language should follow the increasing hierarchy of skill acquisition: decoding, handwriting (cursive), and/or keyboarding skills, spelling, reading fluency, reading comprehension, sequencing and organization, written narratives, and expository writing.

A multidisciplinary assessment will guide the specific methodology to teach reading and writing for the individual with AS. The application and use of phonetic abilities, integrated with a sight- or visually-based approach, is demonstrated in individuals with AS to a much greater degree than with those with the other types of ASD. Many programs and software are available which capitalize on the motivation and interest of the individual with AS while providing direct instruction and intensity. Nevertheless, print or software programs must also be correlated with in-class curriculum content and activities to promote generalization of skill.

- Sight Words – Levels 1 and 2 (Essential Skills Software 2003c)
- Spelling Software (Essential Skills Software 2003d)
- Reading Comprehension – Levels 1, 2, and 3 (Essential Skills Software 2003b)
- Writing Fundamentals (Essential Skills Software 2003f)

- Kidspiration 2 and Inspiration (Inspiration Software)
- Creative Writing (Essential Skills Software 2003a).

Higher-level language skills and pragmatic language

The most effective way to improve higher-level language skills such as non-literal or figurative language, theory of mind, and verbal problem-solving skills (i.e. answering How? What if? Why? If...then? etc.) is intensive teaching with various materials and programs. To ensure generalization of skills, direct teaching must also occur within context. Modification of commercially available materials is usually needed to address the skill deficits for individuals with AS since many publications target the learning disabled (LD) population rather than the ASD population. For individuals with AS, however, the LD and Nonverbal Learning Disability (NVLD) resources appear better suited than some of the currently available ASD resources. Some aids include:

- *Social Star: General Interaction Skills (Book 1); Social Star: Peer Interaction Skills (Book 2); Social Star: Conflict Resolution and Community Interaction Skills (Book 3)* (Gajewski, Hirn, and Mayo 1993, 1994, and 1996)

- *Teaching Children with Autism to Mind-read: A Practical Guide for Teachers and Parents* (Baron-Cohen and Howlin 1998)

- *Navigating the Social World: A Curriculum for Individuals with Asperger's Syndrome, High Functioning Autism and Related Disorders* (McAfee 2001)

- *Social Skills Intervention Guide: Practical Strategies for Social Skills Training; Grades 3–High School* (Elliott and Gresham 1991)

- *Social Stories: Improving responses of students with autism with accurate social information* (Gray and Garand 1993)

- *Comic Strip Conversations* (Gray 1994).

Conclusion

The SLP has an integral role in the assessment and subsequent design and implementation of suitable programs, services, and supports for individuals with AS. Continued collection of assessment data, treatment methodologies, outcome data, and appropriate service delivery models for individuals with AS will lead to better evidence-based practice for this specific population. Assessment of speech, language, and communication must get to the root of the problem and ascertain whether the deficit is with skill acquisition, performance of the skill, or fluency in skill performance (i.e. consistent performance). Only then can specific skills be addressed at the level of the deficit, which will ultimately lead to generalization of the skill to all environments.

References

APA (American Psychiatric Association) (1994) *Diagnostic and Statistical Manual of Mental Disorders, Fourth Edition.* Washington, DC: APA.

Attwood, T. (1998) *Asperger's Syndrome: A Guide for Parents and Professionals.* London, UK: Jessica Kingsley Publishers.

Baron-Cohen, S., and Howlin, P. (1998) *Teaching Children with Autism to Mind-read: A Practical Guide for Teachers and Parents.* New York, NY: Wiley.

Baron-Cohen, S., and Staunton, R. (1994) Do children with autism acquire the phonology of their peers? An examination of group identification through the window of bilingualism. *First Language, 14,* 241–8.

Bracken, B.A. (1998) *Bracken Basic Concept Scale – Revised (BBCS-R).* San Antonio, TX: Psychological Corporation.

Brigance, A.H. (1980) *Brigance Diagnostic Inventory of Essential Skills.* North Billerica, MA: Curriculum Associates.

Brown, V.L., Hammill, D.D., and Wiederholt, J.L. (1995) *Test of Reading Comprehension, Third Edition (TORC-3).* Circle Pines, MN: AGS Publishing.

Dawson, J., Stout, C., and Eyer, J. (2003) *Structured Photographic Language Test 3 (SPELT-3).* DeKalb, IL: Janelle Publications.

Dolch, E.W. (1955) *Methods in Reading.* Champaign, IL: Garrard Press.

Dunn, L.M., and Dunn, L.M. (1997) *Peabody Picture Vocabulary Test, Third Edition (PPVT-III).* Circle Pines, MN: AGS Publishing.

Elliott, S.N., and Gresham, F.M. (1991) *Social Skills Intervention Guide: Practical Strategies for Social Skills Training; Grades 3–High School.* Circle Pines, MN: AGS Publishing.

Essential Skills Software (2003a) *Creative Writing.* Toronto, ON: Essential Skills Software. Available at www.essentialskills.net.

Essential Skills Software (2003b) *Reading Comprehension.* Toronto, ON: Essential Skills Software. Available at www.essentialskills.net.

Essential Skills Software (2003c) *Sight Words – Levels 1 and 2.* Toronto, ON: Essential Skills Software. Available at www.essentialskills.net.

Essential Skills Software (2003d) *Spelling Software.* Toronto, ON: Essential Skills Software. Available at www.essentialskills.net.

Essential Skills Software (2003e) *Vocabulary Builder, Grade 3 to 6.* Toronto, ON: Essential Skills Software. Available at: www.essentialskills.net

Essential Skills Software (2003f) *Writing Fundamentals.* Toronto, ON: Essential Skills Software. Available at www.essentialskills.net.

Freeman, S. and Dake, L. (1997) *Teach Me Language: A Language Manual for Children with Autism, Asperger's Syndrome and Related Developmental Disorders.* Langley, BC: SKF Books.

Fry, E.B. (1980) The new instant word list. *The Reading Teacher, 34,* 284–9.

Gajewski, N., Hirn, P., and Mayo, P. (1993) *Social Star: General Interaction Skills (Book 1).* Eau Claire, WI: Thinking Publications.

Gajewski, N., Hirn, P., and Mayo, P. (1994) *Social Star: Peer Interaction Skills (Book 2).* Eau Claire, WI: Thinking Publications.

Gajewski, N., Hirn, P., and Mayo, P. (1996) *Social Star: Conflict Resolution and Community Interaction Skills (Book 3).* Eau Claire, WI: Thinking Publications.

German, D.J. (1989a) *Test of Word Finding 2 (TWF-2).* Circle Pines, MN: AGS Publishing.

German, D.J. (1989b) *Test of Adolescent/Adult Word Finding (TAWF).* Circle Pines, MN: AGS Publishing.

Gray, C. (1994) *Comic Strip Conversations*. Arlington, TX: Future Horizons.

Gray, C., and Garand, J. (1993) Social stories: Improving responses of students with autism with accurate social information. *Focus on Autistic Behavior*, 8, 1–10.

Gresham, F.M., and Elliott, S.N. (1990) *Social Skills Rating Scale*. Circle Pines, MN: AGS Publishing.

Hammill, D.D., and Larsen, S.C. (1995) *Test of Written Language, Third Edition*. Austin, TX: Pro-Ed.

Hammill, D.D., and Newcomer, P. (1997) *Test of Language Development – Intermediate, Third Edition (TOLD-I:3)*. Toronto, ON: Psychological Corporation.

Inspiration Software. Portland, OR: Inspiration Software, Inc. Available at: www.inspiration.com.

Klin, A., Volkmar, F.R., and Sparrow, S.S. (eds) (2000) *Asperger Syndrome*. New York, NY: The Guilford Press.

Masterson, J.J., Apel, K., and Wasowicz, J. (2002) *Spelling Performance Evaluation for Language and Literacy*. Evanston, IL: Learning By Design, Inc.

McAfee, J. (2001) *Navigating the Social World: A Curriculum for Individuals with Asperger's Syndrome, High Functioning Autism and Related Disorders*. Arlington, TX: Future Horizons.

Morrison, J.C., and McCall, W.A. (1951) *Morrison–McCall Spelling Scale for Grades 2 to 8*. Phoenix, Arizona: Spalding Education International.

National Research Council (2001) *Educating Children with Autism*. Washington, DC: National Academy Press.

Newcomer, P., and Hammill, D.D. (1997) *Test of Language Development – Primary, Third Edition (TOLD-P:3)*. Toronto, ON: Psychological Corporation.

Phelps-Terasaki, D., and Phelps-Gunn, T. (1992) *Test of Pragmatic Language (TOPL)*. Toronto, ON: Psychological Corporation.

Robertson, C., and Salter, W. (1997) *The Phonological Awareness Test*. East Moline, IL: LinguiSystems Inc.

Rosner, J. (1979) *Test of Auditory Analysis Skills*. Novato, CA: Academic Therapy Publications.

Semel, E., Wiig, E.H., and Secord, W.A. (2003) *Clinical Evaluation of Language Fundamentals, Fourth Edition (CELF-4)*. Toronto, ON: Psychological Corporation.

Smith, K. (2000) *DT Trainer*. Columbia, SC: Accelerations Educational Software.

Szatmari, P., Bryson, S.E., Boyle, M.H., Streiner, D.L., and Duku, E. (2003) Predictors of outcome among high functioning children with autism and Asperger syndrome. *Journal of Child Psychology and Psychiatry, 44*, 4, 520–8.

Wiig, E.H., and Secord, W.A. (1989) *Test of Language Competence, Expanded Edition (TLC-Expanded)*. Toronto, ON: Psychological Corporation.

Williams, K.T. (1997) *Expressive Vocabulary Test (EVT)*. Circle Pines, MN: AGS Publishing.

Zachman, L., Barrett, M., and Huisingh, R. (1984) *Test of Problem Solving – Elementary (TOPS-Elementary)*. East Moline, IL: LinguiSystems Inc.

Zachman, L., Barrett, M., Huisingh, R., Orman, J., and Blagden, C. (1991) *Test of Problem Solving – Adolescent (TOPS-Adolescent)*. San Antonio, TX: Psychological Corporation.

CHAPTER 9

Integrating paediatrics and child development: Asperger Syndrome and the role of the developmental paediatrician

S. Wendy Roberts and Tamarah Kagan-Kushnir

The last twenty years of the twentieth century saw a huge shift in awareness and understanding of Asperger Syndrome (AS), named after the paediatrician Dr. Hans Asperger. The same two decades has also seen a major change in the role of the paediatrician in identifying and helping manage all developmental disorders, and in particular, AS.

Parents often remark that their paediatrician failed to recognize the early or milder signs of an autistic spectrum disorder (ASD). In AS, when early signs are quite varied, delay in recognition can cause great anguish for parents, children, and teachers, who may perceive differences but do not understand the basis of difficult or unusual behaviour. Many have felt the paediatrician's minimizing of the problem has resulted in unnecessary waits for intervention. Paediatricians, on the other hand, have not felt that their paediatric training has enabled them to identify and manage developmental disorders in the way that community consumers have recently been demanding. Many attend update courses and work to learn about the disorders that regularly present in their offices.

Because of parental demand and paediatricians' increasing awareness of needs, the academic sub-specialty of developmental paediatrics has emerged to meet the educational, clinical and research needs within child development. In 2003, the Royal College of Physicians and Surgeons of Canada declared developmental paediatrics a sub-specialty area within paediatrics. Developmental paediatricians (DPs) in paediatric training programs across Canada now form the core of faculty who teach medical students and residents about developmental disorders including ASDs. DPs spend at least two years after finishing core training in paediatrics studying child development, normal and abnormal. They learn from professionals from various disciplines including psychologists, speech and language pathologists, social workers, occupational therapists, and nurses, as well as medical specialists such as neurologists, psychiatrists, geneticists, and pharmacologists.

As a professional who will take time to study a child's behaviour and learning through talking to the parents and involved community, the DP is in a unique position to do two things. The first is to understand the child's developmental, medical, and family history, both strengths and vulnerabilities. The second is to help in the diagnostic process as well as in planning and monitoring interventions. In this chapter, we will describe the role of the DP in the diagnosis, medical evaluation, and ongoing management of children with AS, and the role in sharing their understanding, as the DP works with the entire team of parents and professionals who assist in the "coaching for life" process.

Understanding through assessment

The DP working in an academic centre or in the community has been able to study the natural history of AS in a unique way. As a person consulted when concerns first appear, the DP identifies that some neurological "wiring" differences exist. In following the child and family through various stages of maturation, new symptoms are seen emerging with nervous system development; new experiences are requiring skill sets that cannot automatically expand to meet the new demands. School provokes reactions that were never dreamt possible. Social skills, which may have allowed reasonable interaction with peers in a small playgroup, may dissolve in the overwhelming flood of challenges and sensory experiences in the playground. The DP may be the person called when an aggressive outburst leads to school suspension, when a narrow diet becomes a nutritional concern, or when anxiety prevents a family from getting onto an airplane to visit grandparents. Because of the many encounters along the pathways of childhood and adolescence, DPs are allowed extraordinary glimpses of the many faces of AS. "Hard wiring" differences interact with unique temperaments, varying levels of anxiety, obsession, reasoning and language ability, as well as different family constellations, to create the heterogeneity familiar in AS.

In the initial assessment process, parents' recollection of the child's history is the most valuable asset for the clinician in understanding presenting symptoms. As in all areas of paediatrics, history taking is the most effective tool in establishing a diagnosis. Walking through the experiences of the parents from prenatal to current events, allows reflection regarding how this child was similar or different from siblings or friends' babies.

The familiar regression or plateau in social communication, seen between one and two years of age in at least 30% of children on the autism spectrum, may or may not have happened to children with AS (Goldberg *et al.* 2003; Lord 2003). Some children appear more irritable and others more passive in the first two years. Unusual hand movements as well as intense interest in letters and numbers may be seen as early as 15 months of age. Reduced eye gaze and social smiling, delayed imitation and unusual degrees of difficulty with change are all familiar early signs of AS (Zwaigenbaum *et al.* in press). The more refined the knowledge of typical child development possessed by the DP, the more able she is to identify when the pathway of development has taken a slightly different turn. She may see social development improve with peer interaction and language development or, to the contrary, take a downturn as the child becomes more "sticky" and averse to change when going into kindergarten.

Understanding the first few years, the response to experience and therapy, and alterations in behaviour, particularly in imaginative and social play, are critical parts of appreciating the basis of parents' concern that something is different about their child. Appreciating the range of normal allows the unusual to be identified. Input from teachers, grandparents, and others who know the child is also helpful. Particularly in less clear presentations, the use of a semi-structured interview such as the Autism Diagnostic Interview (ADI) can be very useful (Lord, Rutter, and LeCouteur 1994) and many DPs now use this tool routinely in clinical assessments. Although designed for autism rather than AS, the ADI allows careful analysis by the parents and clinician of the child's symptoms in retrospect and at present.

The DP's interaction with the child is a unique extension of the typical paediatric physical examination intended to cover the area of social communication, much as the extended physical exam of the musculoskeletal system is for a rheumatologist interested in the exploration of signs of arthritis. Parents are reassured that we are assessing, in a comprehensive way, their child's interaction with an unfamiliar person. Parents often need reassurance that behaviour in this clinical situation is expected to be different from the child's interaction with a parent or familiar teacher. Nonetheless, observing how the child warms up to an unfamiliar person, shares information, asks questions, and shows social interest can be done in a semi-structured way that is standardized and can be reliably assessed using an interview such as the Autism Diagnostic Observation Schedule (ADOS) (Lord *et al.* 2000). This instrument has led to a profound difference in appreciating the features of AS within a one-hour clinical interaction. The "friendly social world" of the ADOS is quite different from the usual clinical assessment. Expectations are based on the child's language level and move from play to conversation regarding perceptions of peers, and insight and curiosity about typical social situations. Anxiety and humour as well as topics of interest, unusual mannerisms or routines are documented. Observations are integrated with the history obtained from parents and others.

Understanding through medical evaluation

Physical examination

The physical examination is a key component of a full developmental assessment and is an important opportunity for a child's medical needs to be viewed holistically in the broader context of his/her developmental, behavioural, and psychosocial needs.

The DP's first role in examining a patient is to ensure there are no underlying, untreated health concerns. This process, started during the detailed medical history, continues with the physical examination. At times, anxiety or behavioural difficulties make it difficult for some children with AS to co-operate with physical examinations. As such, they do not always undergo routine health maintenance assessments or even proper examinations for specific health concerns. The DP can often overcome these barriers because of his/her knowledge of AS, and thus is a key person in ensuring appropriate basic health care.

The neurological examination is an integral part of the general physical examination. Besides ruling out a serious neurological disorder, the examination identifies so-called "soft neurological signs" or findings that are not clearly indicative of underlying structural lesions but rather indicate immaturity of the central nervous system. These are commonly found in individuals with AS and generally include signs of motor overflow and incoordination, as well as problems with motor planning. Identifying these signs can often help to explain a child's motor difficulties and may point to the need for further evaluation or suggest programming strategies (Tupper 1987).

While in most cases AS and other ASDs are not associated with any underlying syndromes or genetic disorders, there are conditions that carry a higher risk of developing ASDs including Fragile X, neurofibromatosis, microdeletion 22, and tuberous sclerosis, amongst others. The physical examination helps the DP assess the probability of these disorders. Larger than expected head circumference may be seen in some children with AS. Recent suggestions of increasing head circumference in the first 14 months after birth is now being followed up in a North American study through programs funded by the National Institutes for Health (Courchesne, Carper and Akshoomoff 2003). Signs of Fragile X, which may co-exist with AS, include specific facial features such as a long face, prominent jaw, and large prominent ears (Rogers, Wehner and Hagerman 2001). Characteristics of female carriers and of patients with smaller

DNA repeat sizes are subtler; therefore, screening for Fragile X should be considered even in the absence of classic facial features or cognitive impairment, and always when there is a family history of developmental disability. Identifying any underlying organic aetiologies is not simply an academic exercise; it may have implications for identifying associated medical problems and determining recurrence risk. Genetic counselling may also be helpful.

On a more subtle level, the physical examination is important for furthering research and understanding of AS. Careful attention to differences on physical examination may help to suggest lines of investigation with respect to the underlying pathogenesis of AS. For example, epidemiological studies have found that many individuals with ASDs have subtle ear anomalies, suggesting possible insults to the developing foetal brain at the time when the ear is developing (around 24 days' gestation: Rodier 2002).

Laboratory investigation

The need for laboratory investigations, if any, follows from the discussion above. If any unaddressed health concerns are identified, further laboratory investigations may be necessary and may also be used to rule out underlying genetic or metabolic disorders. The history and physical examination may point to specific tests. However, even without specific concerns, it may still be helpful to study chromosomes (karyotype through cytogenetics) and DNA for Fragile X assessment since research has suggested that these investigations have the highest aetiological yield. Metabolic screens and neuroimaging (CT, MRI) may be done on a case-by-case basis (Filipek *et al.* 2000).

Sharing the diagnosis: Sharing understanding

We have much to learn about the process of sharing a new diagnosis with parents and with children and youth. Each situation is different. Each parent is at a different stage of understanding his or her child's problems, as well as in his or her knowledge of AS and other ASDs. Worries are different depending on family history or experience with the disorder. Reading has varied and, with the advent of the Internet, both benefits and very negative effects have resulted from exposure to more or less credible sources. Some parents have been told their child's behaviour is due to poor parenting. Some may be confused by different labels and differing interpretations offered by various clinicians. The DP can often help to clarify overlapping terminology and assist parents to integrate various assessment results in order to obtain a unified view of their child.

The goal in giving a diagnosis or applying a label is to facilitate parents' ongoing understanding of their child. Labels can direct parents to suitable literature, allow sharing with other parents, provide access to necessary resources, and support day-to-day problem solving at home or in the school around the basis of their child's behaviour.

The first steps in giving a meaningful diagnosis are demonstrating thorough knowledge of parents' concerns and sharing first-hand experience about what comprises their child's unique characteristics. A review of identified concerns, including developmental areas that are seen to be different or potentially causing problems, is a helpful beginning. Making sure that parents understand and agree with observations at each stage ensures that conclusions and recommendations will be understood and acted upon.

Parents have reported benefits from discussion of typical social communication skills at the age and language level of their child. They can then appreciate more easily the differences in their child, including strengths and challenges, how development has affected specific characteristics, and how a unique way of processing may have affected typical development.

Discussion of the spectrum or continuum of manifestations of certain skills such as social interactions or communication, as well as various presentations of anxiety or obsessions, may help with ongoing problem solving around certain behaviours as they occur. Personality characteristics or temperamental traits can be understood in the context of typical features of AS. Medical, nutritional, sleep, and genetic factors may affect behaviour and have an impact on family functioning.

Learning that AS is a genetic disorder with many different modes of expression, and thus that another family member may have characteristics of an ASD, can be either helpful or distressing to parents struggling with a diagnosis. Feelings of blame or guilt, or resistance to accepting a diagnosis of AS, are common reactions. This is particularly the case when parents know a child who has the AS label, but feel that their own child is very different.

Another ongoing role of the DP is identifying emerging symptoms. Helping parents to understand if new behaviours are consistent with the diagnosis and whether they relate to the next developmental growth spurt may be beneficial. Symptoms changing over time can be confusing, most notably when different clinicians seeing the child at different ages use different diagnostic terms. A child with AS may initially receive a diagnosis of ASD but improve, particularly in language skills, to the point where AS is a more appropriate label. Others may start with the label of communication disorder, but signs of "sticky" behaviour, unusual interests, and distress about change may become more notable over time despite improved language skills, thus moving into the diagnostic category of AS.

Prognosis

After hearing the diagnosis of AS, most parents ask first what needs to be done, and then what it means for the future. For younger children, it is often not possible to give accurate predictions regarding the developmental trajectory that an individual child will follow. At school entry, different challenges emerge. Language ability, intelligence, temperament, ability to generalize the use of strategies, and levels of anxiety and obsession will all play a part in how symptoms are expressed over time. Prognosis is difficult given the dearth of natural history studies in AS. It is frustrating for parents not to know reasonable expectations for the future.

Sharing the diagnosis with the child or youth

Talking to children and adolescents about their "label" can be a challenging task and one that many clinicians avoid and leave to parents. Many children have told us: "All the kids in my school are different"; some say they have a social learning disability (LD). Others say a child in their school has AS but "I am not like that!"

For others it may be a big relief to know there are factors influencing their abilities that are not totally within their control ("You mean it is not my fault?!"). This is similar to many people with LD, who report a huge relief from self-blame when they learn they have an LD instead of just "being lazy" or "stupid", beliefs easily derived from others' careless comments.

Careful discussion of the strengths and unique characteristics shared by individuals with AS can assist in improving self-esteem and a sense of unique competence, which can then protect from anxiety and self-doubt. Books such as *Amazingly...Alfie* (Espin 2003) are available and can be very helpful. Parents often choose to talk about the label with their child alone first and then book an appointment for further discussion with the paediatrician or DP.

Understanding through genetics

At the visit after the diagnosis is shared for the first time, questions are often raised about the recurrence of AS in future pregnancies or features of the disorder noted in a sibling. Genetic research studies can provide detailed assessment of siblings so that their profiles can be assessed in depth and understood by parents.

As outlined above, there are certain genetic syndromes that carry a higher risk of developing ASDs. The reason behind these associations is the focus of investigations in various laboratories around the world and this is helping to identify "candidate genes"; that is, genes that may be involved in the development of ASDs.

Research has demonstrated that AS is a neurobiological disorder that has genetic underpinnings, whether or not a specific genetic syndrome is identified. Evidence for this comes from family and twin studies (Zwaigenbaum *et al.* in press).

As with diabetes and many other disorders currently under investigation, it is apparent that the genetics behind AS are complex. This is different from disorders such as Down Syndrome or muscular dystrophy, where a difference in one specific chromosome or gene is the cause of the disorder. It is currently believed that changes to several genes on different chromosomes are required together, and perhaps in combination with environmental factors, in order for the neurobiological changes that reflect AS to occur. Candidate genes are being investigated on several chromosomes, including chromosomes 1, 2, 7, 15, and 16, with the strongest associations being on chromosomes 7 and 16 (IMGSAC 2001). It is theorized that different individuals may have different combinations of genes affected, and that a certain "threshold" must be reached for the combination of changes to result in AS. This view helps to explain the spectrum of severity and range of symptoms seen across AS. It also helps explain the "broader spectrum" of related disorders, such as obsessive-compulsive and language disorders, that are seen more frequently in families of patients with AS (Rutter 2003).

In terms of recurrence risk, in the absence of a comorbid genetic disorder most studies have suggested that a sibling of a child with AS has a 5–7% risk of developing an ASD. This is higher than the general population risk of approximately 6 per 1000 for all ASDs combined. If these numbers are true, this would suggest that the risk of having a second child on the autism spectrum is greater than 6% (Rutter 2003). If two children are affected in one family, the risk to subsequent children increases to 25%. These estimates come from retrospective studies as well as emerging prospective evidence from evaluations of infant siblings of children with ASDs (Zwaigenbaum *et al.* in press).

Understanding over time: Behaviour and development

One of the privileges and responsibilities of a DP is to follow children with AS in the long term. This is important for continuity of care as well as for establishing trust and a therapeutic relationship. It also helps the DP learn about the natural history of AS and the impact of interventions in the longer term. If a diagnosis is not clear early on, eclectic intervention can be planned with careful monitoring to see if a diagnostic label is warranted and useful.

The DP is often the professional whom parents approach for help when new challenges or concerns arise. Behavioural difficulties are a frequent presenting concern and are often the source of significant distress and impairment for individuals, their families, and their caregivers. The DP can help to problem solve around difficult behaviours, identify contributing factors, suggest interventions, and follow up to evaluate efficacy and suggest next steps.

Anxiety and mood disorders are common in individuals with AS (Smalley, McCracken, and Tanguay 1995). The presentation varies depending on a child's age and developmental level, but it is commonly when the child is around eight or nine years, as his or her insight into reality-based fears increases. Another common peak is in adolescence as societal expectations about independence and the future become more apparent. Both anxiety and mood disorders can affect behaviour, making early identification an important part of planning intervention, including possible pharmacotherapy.

Inattention can be a complex problem to assess and treat in children with AS. While some children have primary problems with sustaining attention, other difficulties can masquerade as inattention, including language and learning problems, anxiety, obsessions, and behavioural rigidity. Research has shown that children with ASDs have difficulty disengaging attention, and this is felt to be a core deficit (Bryson *et al.* 2004). Obsessions can masquerade as inattention to the task at hand. A child who is having difficulty transitioning from the last activity, is anxious because a new teacher is in the class, or is focussed on his current obsession, may appear every bit as inattentive as a child with severe primary inattention. However, stimulant medication could be inappropriate in these situations and, in fact, might exacerbate the problem.

In the situation where primary inattention is felt to be the underlying problem, in whole or in part, stimulant medication can be helpful. However, care needs to be taken in its administration as children with AS seem to be at higher risk of developing side effects, including increases in anxiety, obsessions, and behavioural rigidity. Often, doses much lower than would be used in children with ADHD can be effective for children with AS (Aman and Langworthy 2000).

Initiating and monitoring medication management is often a key role for the DP. At this time, there are no medications that have been shown to have an impact on the core symptoms of AS. However, medications are often useful to help treat symptoms and comorbid problems including anxiety, mood problems, attention problems, aggression, and explosive outbursts. In most situations, medication should be viewed as an adjunct to other interventions, with its primary role being to help alleviate symptoms and "take the edge off" behaviour which may be interfering with academic and social learning. A detailed discussion of pharmacotherapy is outlined in Chapter 11 of this book.

Understanding through possible medical pathology

The frequency of comorbid medical problems in individuals with AS has forced researchers to think beyond traditional neurological and psychological boundaries. Exciting research is occurring around the world, exploring the effects and interactions of various body systems and the brain. This will, it is hoped, lead to new insights into AS and other disorders.

Gastrointestinal symptoms and diet

Gastrointestinal (GI) symptoms, particularly diarrhoea, are common in children with AS. Some experience a recurrent cycle from diarrhoea to severe constipation although this is not documented specifically in AS. There are published reports of various GI symptoms, malabsorption, and enteropathy on biopsy examinations as well as laboratory abnormalities in ASD children. In recent years, there has been increasing interest in the concept and potential importance of a brain–gut axis in ASDs. This theory has suggested lines of investigation into the pathogenesis and treatment of ASDs, although much currently remains at the conceptual level (White 2003).

The high prevalence of diarrhoea in ASD individuals has suggested to some investigators that there may be parallels between ASDs and GI disorders such as coeliac disease. Some authors postulate an opioid theory of ASDs; this suggests that individuals with ASDs have leaky gut epithelium, which allows absorption of opioid-like proteins that then have an effect on the developing brain. These theories have led to the idea that dietary interventions, and in particular gluten- and casein-free diets, might be helpful in improving the core symptoms and behaviour in ASDs (Knivsberg *et al.* 1990; Lucarelli *et al.* 1995; Whiteley *et al.* 1999).

To date, there is no rigorous evidence for or against dietary intervention. Perhaps because of its relative simplicity, the idea is compelling to many parents, and dietary intervention has been tried in up to one-third of patients with ASDs. Unfortunately, this treatment is not without risks, including the creation of iron deficiency or serious protein deficiency; there is also a potential increase in irritability. Careful research (i.e. a randomized controlled trial) is urgently needed in this area but will be difficult and expensive to carry out rigorously.

In the interim, the role of the DP is to evaluate the nutritional status of children with AS and refer them for further investigations of GI symptoms if necessary. In addition, the DP plays a key role in educating patients and their families about dietary interventions, and providing them with support that will minimize potential nutritional consequences should they choose to pursue such interventions (Kagan-Kushnir, Griffiths, and Roberts 2002).

Iron

There is emerging evidence that it is important to check both haemoglobin and ferritin levels in individuals with AS. Iron deficiency is a common and frequently undiagnosed problem that does not seem to be related to dietary factors alone (Roberts *et al.* 2004). The reasons for this association, the degree to which it is related to the increased incidence of GI dysfunction, and the implications it has for pathogenesis and treatment of AS, are not yet clear.

Seizure disorders and anticonvulsant medications

Seizure disorders are common in children on the autism spectrum, occurring in approximately one-third of individuals across the lifespan (Tuchman and Rapin 2002). Some studies have suggested that cognitive impairment is a risk factor for seizures (Tuchman, Rapin, and Shinnar 1991), raising the question as to whether the incidence is lower in children with AS. However, other studies have found no effect of IQ (Elia *et al.* 1995; Kurita 1997), and further research is necessary to clarify this point. So far, there have been a few studies looking at seizures in higher-functioning autism and/or AS which have also documented higher incidence of seizures (7–25%) (Gillberg and Steffenburg 1987; Kurita 1997).

The explanation for this high incidence of seizures is currently part of an active debate and controversy surrounding the effect of seizures on the developing brain. There are many questions about the extent to which seizure activity, clinical or present on EEG only (sub-clinical), causes and/or reflects cognitive and behavioural changes (Tuchman 1994; Deonna 1995).

These hypotheses have important implications for understanding the pathogenesis of AS and the factors contributing to behavioural and cognitive differences in children with AS. In addition, they create questions as to whether treating seizures, clinical or sub-clinical, will have an impact on the core deficits in AS (Tuchman and Rapin 2002). There have been case series and case reports suggesting improvements in children with ASDs treated with anticonvulsants (Plioplys 1994; Childs and Blair 1997; Burd *et al.* 1998; Belsito *et al.* 2001; Hollander *et al.* 2001). However, these reports are anecdotal only, and rigorous evidence in this area is lacking.

Regardless of these factors, the increased incidence of seizures in children with ASDs makes it prudent to maintain a high level of vigilance when doing a medical history and physical examination, as well as when assessing specific concerns such as staring spells, developmental regression, and sleep problems. It may be necessary to conduct an overnight EEG to identify epileptiform abnormalities, as the aetiological yield is generally higher with more prolonged monitoring and, in particular, monitoring that includes a long duration of natural sleep.

All types of seizures have been described in individuals with AS. Although literature on the subject remains limited, there has been no suggestion to date that seizures are more difficult to treat in children with AS than in other children. Therefore, seizure management strategies and anticonvulsant choice would not be different in children with AS, with initial medication choice being determined by seizure type (Tuchman and Rapin 2002). Additionally, anticonvulsants may also be useful in managing behaviour, aggression, and mood instability because of their affect-regulating properties (Di Martino and Tuchman 2001).

Sleep

Sleep difficulties are common in AS. They include problems falling asleep as well as night awakenings. Several factors may be contributory, including anxiety and, especially in younger children, poor sleep hygiene (i.e. the behaviours and environment surrounding bedtime). Seizures can also disrupt sleep and lead to night awakenings. The DP can assess these various factors and offer investigations and treatment recommendations, including education around sleep hygiene, as appropriate.

For some individuals who are having difficulty with sleep onset, melatonin might be helpful. Melatonin is a hormone produced by the pineal gland that regulates sleep–wake cycles. There is emerging evidence that melatonin is beneficial in treating sleep disturbances with secondary improvements in behaviour in children with AS (Paavonen et al. 2003). If melatonin is given, it is necessary to address concomitantly any contributing factors, particularly sleep hygiene, since it will not be efficacious on its own in these situations.

Alternative treatments

Alternative treatments have been gaining prominence in all areas of medicine, in particular in developmental paediatrics. With the popularity and accessibility of the Internet, general knowledge about the large number of alternative treatments available has blossomed, with new ones constantly being promoted. The reasons patients and parents seek out alternative remedies are complex but likely to include the fact that so far there are no identified medications or traditional interventions that affect the core symptoms of AS.

It is important to keep an open mind about all possible avenues of treatment. However, it is also important to approach alternative treatments with the same degree of caution and scepticism that is applied to remedies that are more traditional. "Natural" does not mean safe or free from side effects. Similarly, understanding the evidence for or against a specific treatment, traditional or alternative, is part of making an informed decision. Rigorous research should be demanded of all treatments that make claims of improvement. This is important given the high placebo effect that has been noted in treating ASDs (Belsito *et al.* 2001).

Vaccinations

Possible connections between immunization and developmental disorders, most notably ASDs, have been the subject of much debate and have caused much concern for parents who want to make the safest choices for their children. Anxiety has risen steadily since the mid-1990s, when a medical investigative team led by Wakefield postulated that the measles-mumps-rubella (MMR) vaccine might be a causative factor in the development of ASDs (Wakefield *et al.* 1998). Since this initial publication, immunization has remained controversial for some parents. The uptake of the MMR vaccine has fallen in some countries despite much discussion regarding the safety of MMR, a lack of evidence for an association between MMR and autism, and the risks to children of insufficient protection against wild measles virus infection. This issue has been reviewed in detail by the Canadian Paediatric Society and the American Academy of Pediatrics. Both organizations have published position statements emphasizing the lack of evidence that the MMR vaccine plays any role in the development of ASDs (Halsey and Hyman 2001; Madsen *et al.* 2002; Roberts and Harford 2002). Similarly, no evidence exists regarding an association between autism and the thimerosal preservative used in some vaccines in certain countries: it is not found in common Canadian childhood vaccines (Ball, Ball and Pratt 2001).

Conclusion

As our understanding of AS has drastically changed over the last two decades, so has the field of paediatrics. The existence of developmental paediatrics as a sub-specialty is acknowledgment of the role paediatricians play in the diagnosis and management of children with developmental disorders. Concurrently, important discoveries have been made relating not only to brain development and brain–behaviour relationships, but also to medical factors which need to be considered in the diagnosis and management in AS and ASDs. Much work remains to be done as we move forward with colleagues in many disciplines in our quest to understand this remarkable disorder. More DPs are being trained, further research is being conducted, and clinical knowledge is accumulating. As political advocacy also progresses to improve recognition and resources for intervention and support, the future should indeed be brighter for families of individuals with AS.

References

Aman, M.G., and Langworthy, K.S. (2000) Pharmacotherapy for hyperactivity in children with autism and other pervasive developmental disorders. *Journal of Autism and Developmental Disorders, 30*, 5, 451–9.

Ball, L.K., Ball, R., and Pratt, R.D. (2001) An assessment of thimerosal use in childhood vaccines. *Pediatrics, 107*, 5, 1147–54.

Belsito, K.M., Law, P.A., Kirk, K.S., Landa, R.J., and Zimmerman, A.W. (2001) Lamotrigine therapy for autistic disorder: A randomized, double-blind, placebo-controlled trial. *Journal of Autism and Developmental Disorders, 31*, 2, 175–81.

Bryson, S., Czapinski, P., Landry, R., McConnell, B., Rombough, V., and Wainwright, A. (2004) Autistic spectrum disorders: Causal mechanisms and recent findings on attention and emotion. *International Journal of Special Education, 19*, 1, 14–22.

Burd, L., Ivey, M., Barth, A., and Kerbeshian, J. (1998) Two males with childhood disintegrative disorder: A prospective 14-year outcome study. *Developmental Medicine and Child Neurology, 40*, 10, 702–707.

Childs, J.A., and Blair, J.L. (1997) Valproic acid treatment of epilepsy in autistic twins. *Journal of Neuroscience Nursing, 29*, 4, 244–8.

Courchesne, E., Carper, R., and Akshoomoff, N. (2003) Evidence of brain overgrowth in the first year of life in autism. *Journal of American Medical Association, 290*, 3, 337–44.

Deonna, T. (1995) Cognitive and behavioral disturbances as epileptic manifestations in children: An overview. *Seminars in Pediatric Neurology, 2*, 4, 254–60.

Di Martino, A., and Tuchman, R.F. (2001) Antiepileptic drugs: Affective use in autism spectrum disorders. *Pediatric Neurology, 25*, 3, 199–207.

Elia, M., Musumeci, S.A., Ferri, R., and Bergonzi, P. (1995) Clinical and neurophysiological aspects of epilepsy in subjects with autism and mental retardation. *American Journal of Mental Retardation, 100*, 1, 6–16.

Espin, R. (2003) *Amazingly…Alfie. Understanding and Accepting Different Ways of Being.* Shawnee Mission, KS: Autism Asperger Publishing.

Filipek, P.A., Accardo, P.J., Ashwal, S., Baranek, G.T., Cook, E.H., Jr., Dawson, G., *et al.* (2000) Practice parameter: Screening and diagnosis of autism. Report of the Quality Standards Subcommittee of the American Academy of Neurology and the Child Neurology Society. *Neurology, 55*, 4, 468–79.

Gillberg, C., and Steffenburg, S. (1987) Outcome and prognostic factors in infantile autism and similar conditions: A population-based study of 46 cases followed through puberty. *Journal of Autism and Developmental Disorders, 17*, 2, 273–87.

Goldberg, W.A., Osann, K., Filipek, P.A., Laulhere, T., Jarvis, K., Modahl, C., Flodman, P., and Spence, M.A. (2003) Language and other regression: Assessment and timing. *Journal of Autism and Developmental Disorders, 33*, 6, 607–616.

Halsey, N.A., and Hyman, S.L. (2001) Measles-mumps-rubella vaccine and autistic spectrum disorder. Report from the New Challenges in Childhood Immunizations Conference convened in Oak Brook Illinois, June 12–13, 2000. *Pediatrics, 107*, 5, E84.

Hollander, E., Dolgoff-Kaspar, R., Cartwright, C., Rawitt, R., and Novotny, S. (2001) An open trial of divalproex sodium in autism spectrum disorders. *Journal of Clinical Psychiatry, 62*, 7, 530–4.

IMGSAC (International Molecular Genetic Study of Autism Consortium) (2001) A genome wide screen for autism: Strong evidence for linkage to chromosomes 2q, 7q, and 16p. *American Journal of Human Genetics, 69*, 3, 570–81.

Kagan-Kushnir, T., Griffiths, A., and Roberts, W. (2002) Gastrointestinal symptoms in autism spectrum disorders. Abstract presented at Canadian Paediatric Society Conference, Vancouver, June.

Knivsberg, A.M., Wiig, K., Lind, G., Nodland, M., and Reichelt, K.L. (1990) Dietary intervention in autistic syndromes. *Brain Dysfunction, 3*, 5/6, 315–27.

Kurita, H. (1997) A comparative study of Asperger Syndrome with high-functioning atypical autism. *Psychiatry and Clinical Neurosciences, 51*, 2, 67–70.

Lord, C. (2003) Final discussion: Autism – the challenges ahead. In G. Bock and J. Goode (eds) *Symposium on Autism: Neural Basis and Treatment Possibilities.* Chichester, UK: Wiley.

Lord, C., Risi, S., Lambrecht, L., Cook, E. H., Jr., Leventhal, B. L., DiLavore, P. C., *et al.* (2000) The Autism Diagnostic Observation Schedule – Generic: A standard measure of social and communication deficits associated with the spectrum of autism. *Journal of Autism and Developmental Disorders, 30,* 3, 205–23.

Lord, C., Rutter, M., and LeCouteur, A. (1994) Autism Diagnostic Interview – Revised: A revised version of a diagnostic interview for caregivers of individuals with possible pervasive developmental disorders. *Journal of Autism and Developmental Disorders, 22,* 563–81.

Lucarelli, S., Frediani, T., Zingoni, A.M., Ferruzzi, F., Giardini, O., Quintieri, F., *et al.* (1995) Food allergy and infantile autism. *Panminerva Medica, 37,* 3, 137–41.

Madsen, K.M., Hviid, A., Vestergaard, M., Schendel, D., Wohlfahrt, J., Thorsen, P., *et al.* (2002) A population-based study of measles, mumps, and rubella vaccination and autism. *New England Journal of Medicine, 347,* 19, 1477–82.

Paavonen, E.J., Nieminen-von Wendt, T., Vanhala, R., Aronen, E.T., and von Wendt, L. (2003) Effectiveness of melatonin in the treatment of sleep disturbances in children with Asperger disorder. *Journal of Child and Adolescent Psychopharmacology, 13,* 1, 83–95.

Plioplys, A.V. (1994) Autism: Electroencephalogram abnormalities and clinical improvement with valproic acid. *Archives of Pediatrics and Adolescent Medicine, 148,* 2, 220–2.

Roberts, W., Dosman, C., Drmic, I., Harford, M., Sharieff, W., Smith, R., *et al.* (2004) Serum ferritin and response to iron supplementation in autism. Abstract presented at Society for Pediatric Research, San Francisco, CA, May.

Roberts, W., and Harford, M. (2002) Immunization and children at risk for autism. *Paediatrics and Child Health, 7,* 9, 623–32.

Rodier, P.M. (2002) Converging evidence for brain stem injury in autism. *Development and Psychopathology, 14,* 3, 537–57.

Rogers, S.J., Wehner, D.E., and Hagerman, R. (2001) The behavioral phenotype in fragile X: Symptoms of autism in very young children with Fragile X syndrome, idiopathic autism, and other developmental disorders. *Journal of Developmental and Behavioural Pediatrics, 22,* 6, 409–17.

Rutter, M. (2003) Autism – the challenges ahead. In G. Bock and J. Goode (eds) *Symposium on Autism: Neural Basis and Treatment Possibilities.* Chichester, UK: Wiley.

Smalley, S.L., McCracken, J., and Tanguay, P. (1995) Autism, affective disorders, and social phobia. *American Journal of Medical Genetics, 60,* 1, 19–26.

Tuchman, R.F. (1994) Epilepsy, language, and behavior: Clinical models in childhood. *Journal of Child Neurology, 9,* 1, 95–102.

Tuchman, R.F., and Rapin, I. (2002) Epilepsy in autism. *Lancet Neurology, 1,* 6, 352–8.

Tuchman, R.F., Rapin, I., and Shinnar, S. (1991) Autistic and dysphasic children. II: Epilepsy. *Pediatrics, 88,* 6, 1219–25.

Tupper, D.E. (ed.) (1987) *Soft Neurological Signs.* Orlando, FL: Grune and Stratton.

Wakefield, A.J., Murch, S.H., Anthony, A., Linnell, J. Casson, D.M., Malik, M., *et al.* (1998) Ileal-lymphoid nodular hyperplasia, non-specific colitis, and pervasive developmental disorder in children. *Lancet, 351,* 637–41.

White, J.F. (2003) Intestinal pathophysiology in autism. *Experimental Biology and Medicine, 228,* 6, 639–49.

Whiteley, P., Rodgers, J., Savery, D., and Shattock, P. (1999) A gluten-free diet as an intervention for autism and associated spectrum disorders: Preliminary findings. *Autism: The International Journal of Research and Practice, 3,* 1, 45–65.

Zwaigenbaum, L., Bryson, S., Rogers, T., Roberts, W., Brian, J., and Szatmari, P. (in press) Behavioral manifestations of autism in the first year of life. *International Journal of Developmental Neuroscience.*

CHAPTER 10

Children and adolescents with Asperger Syndrome: Social work assessment and intervention

Kevin P. Stoddart, Barbara Muskat, and Faye Mishna

There is a considerable paucity of literature on social work interventions with respect to autism spectrum disorders (ASDs), and specifically Asperger Syndrome (AS). An ecological systems approach to assessment and intervention, the most widely used approach in social work, has much to offer in the work with this population of children, adolescents, and their families. Moreover, social work's commitment to groups who are marginalized, including the profession's attention to stigma, is salient.

The purpose of this chapter is to demonstrate the relevance of social work assessment and intervention to children and adolescents with AS and their families. The psychosocial issues of children and youth with AS and their parents will be reviewed. Following this, theoretical considerations for social work assessment and intervention are highlighted. We then discuss five social work service areas that are applicable to this population. These consist of case management, parent therapy, family therapy, individual therapy for the child or adolescent, and group work. This discussion is based on the emerging literature on AS and on our clinical experience in the field of AS, ASDs, and learning disabilities.

Children with Asperger Syndrome: Psychosocial issues

In their groundbreaking article on the clinical features of AS, Szatmari, Bremner, and Nagy (1989) noted, "The predicament of these children [with AS] is especially poignant as they try to grapple with a world that is essentially social.

These impairments in socialization, communication, and imagination strike at the very nature of childhood" (p.559). Both in the literature and in practice, the enormous psychosocial difficulties faced by children and adolescents with AS are being increasingly recognized. Despite a desire for friends, many children and adolescents with AS are isolated from their peers because of their difficulty initiating and sustaining social interaction and their poor understanding of social cues (Mishna and Muskat 1998; Marks *et al.* 2000). Their highly individual and sometimes unusual interests may be unappealing to peers and may exacerbate their isolation. Peers frequently bully this population of children and youth (Little 2002a) and they can experience depression or anxiety (Stoddart 1999; Attwood 2003). Difficulties in processing, organizing, and retrieving information pose academic problems (Myles and Simpson 1998). Although educational supports are critical for addressing their academic difficulties, labels reflecting special education designations and segregated school placements often reinforce negative self-perceptions. Their marginalization may unfortunately have long-term negative implications for later social adjustment and mental health (Attwood 2003). Many children and adolescents with AS are painfully aware that they are, in some ways, different from their peers. This realization may be exacerbated by the lack of a helpful framework with which to understand their differences in cases of a late diagnosis (Stoddart 1999).

Parents of children with Asperger Syndrome: Psychosocial issues

Hans Asperger observed that the parents of the boys whom he was studying presented with characteristics similar to their children (Asperger 1944). Significant in Asperger's observation was his assumption that the traits observed in these children were genetic in nature. Gillberg (1989) discovered that a significantly higher number of parents of children with AS had problems with social interaction and displayed more restricted range of interests than parents of children who were lower functioning. DeLong and Dwyer (1988) suggested that many high-functioning individuals with autism have a positive family history of ASDs.

Empirical and clinical evidence indicates that raising a child with autism heightens levels of parental stress (Bristol 1987). While the stress associated with parenting children with autism has been examined for many years (e.g. Holroyd and McArthur 1976), studies that aim to understand stress reactions in parents of children with other Pervasive Developmental Disorders (PDDs) and AS are more recent. For example, Weiss (1991) examined the stressors of 20 parents with children diagnosed with either autism or PDD. She identified the major stressors in these families: arranging for support services and collaborating with the professions who provide them; stress within the family resulting from addressing the child's needs; feelings of stigmatization due to perceptions of the child's condition; dealing with the child's behaviour; and parents' own mental health issues and fears about their child's future. Little (2002b) found that mothers of children with AS and Nonverbal Learning Disabilities (NVLD) reported significantly higher levels of stress than did their partners, and therefore utilized more professional supports.

Although research on the mental health of parents of children with AS is sparse, there is evidence that parents of children with autism frequently display symptoms of anxiety and depression. The frequency of such symptoms is greater for parents of children with autism compared to parents of children with other developmental disabilities, and they may not be entirely related to parenting a child with autism. In comparing parents of autistic children with parents of children with Down Syndrome, Piven and his colleagues (1991) found that anxiety disorder was greater among parents of children with autism. A high percentage of the parents had a depressive episode or anxiety disorder before the birth of their child. In a similar vein, Bolton *et al.* (1998) compared the family histories of children with autism to children with Down Syndrome. Affective disorder was greater in relatives of the children with autism. Mothers were more likely to suffer depression.

Theoretical considerations

There are several key theoretical underpinnings in our work with children and youth with disabilities, which are informed by social work literature. There has been considerable research that substantiates the impact that negative peer attitudes have on children with disabilities (Waddell 1984; Rose and Smith 1993). This is a common clinical concern for children with AS (Marks *et al.* 2000). In the field of child psychopathology, the typical view of disability has been to consider it as an individual deficit whereby the goal is to assess and treat the child who has the defect (Marks 1997; Barnes, Mercer, and Shakespeare 1999). However, the emerging field of disability studies locates the source of the problem in society (Molloy and Vasil 2002). External deterrents of growth and acceptance of the child with AS (such as a lack of understanding of the needs of the child with AS) thus becomes an important focus of social work assessment and intervention.

A major theoretical paradigm used in social work is the ecological systems approach, which is based on the assumption that, since people are embedded in social and environmental contexts, multiple factors interact and contribute to social and behavioural patterns (Barnes 1985; Germain and Bloom 1999). Such factors include individual characteristics, social interactions, and ecological and cultural conditions. Therefore, in working with children and adolescents, attention is given to the functioning within the various relevant systems, for instance the parental sub-system.

Morgan (1988) was one of the first in the field of autism to introduce a systems approach to understanding families of children with autism: "The child is embedded within multiple systems which interact in direct and indirect ways to influence behaviour" (p.264). He also pointed out, "behaviour occurs within relationships that are characterized by reciprocal and bi-directional relationships and that as a system, it functions as a whole with interdependency of the parts" (p.265). Morgan noted that just as a child with autism affects the family, it is also true that the family functioning affects the child with autism. Sloman and Konstantareas (1990) also emphasized a systems approach with children who have biological deficits such as autism and stress the effect of external systems upon the family: "Quantity and quality of community resources and family supports have been shown to have a major impact on the family's ability to cope… The exosystem, including mass media, health, social welfare, and education among other factors, certainly has an impact on the family system" (p.419).

Social work services

Case management

The expertise of many disciplines is required to devise a comprehensive service plan for children with AS. Because services for children and youth with AS are sometimes not well established in the community, the task of advocating for the development and delivery of suitable services is often a priority. Case management tasks for children with AS and their families may include advocating for services, establishing a multidisciplinary team, sharing knowledge and expertise, determining roles, avoiding duplication of services, and organizing and managing the treatment plan.

Consistent with the ecological systems perspective, a case manager advocates for services at a community level to meet the needs of children with AS. This may entail seeking professionals and services with expertise in related fields such as children's mental health, child psychiatry, or special education, and assisting them in tailoring their services to meet this population's needs. Case managers can emphasize to service providers that families of children with AS frequently have considerable knowledge and expertise about AS on which to draw. Educating community professionals about the special needs of children and adolescents with AS is an effective way for case managers to build collaborative relationships for future work involving other families entering the service system.

The service needs of children with AS change throughout their development. During the preschool years, comprehensive assessments and support with inclusion in preschool programs may be needed, as may the services of a speech-language pathologist, occupational therapist, and behaviour therapist. During early school years, there may be a need to aid schools in understanding the specific academic strengths and difficulties of children with AS through the support of a psychologist within the school setting. Assistance in transitioning to adult support services, such as vocational or academic counselling, may be required in late adolescence.

Other professionals will likely need to be involved at various points through the child's development. For instance, psychiatrists would be consulted to consider medication for anxiety, depression, attentional problems, or severe behaviours. Because of the scarcity of child psychiatrists with experience in AS, assessing medication needs often becomes the responsibility of the paediatrician or family doctor. Also required throughout childhood and adolescence are community recreational programs that are sensitive to children with special needs, promote social interaction and modelling of social skills.

The team approach to assessment and intervention is critical for children with AS. For example, a psychiatrist might recommend that a child's anxiety be addressed through pharmacology, the occupational therapist might identify that the child is experiencing sensory overload, and the teacher might observe that the child has problems during transitions and unstructured times. The child's parents and the child himself may have insights into situations that cause anxiety and might identify useful strategies. To be successful, it is necessary to have open communication among professionals, parents, and the child or youth when appropriate. Good case management ensures there is a proper forum for communication and that it occurs as needed.

Parent therapy

Parents require support even before a child's diagnosis with AS. During this time, parents often struggle to understand the meaning of their child's unusual patterns of behaviour and skills. They may question their ability to parent their child or bond with him, even if they were successful in employing similar strategies and approaches with their other children. Mothers often recognize problems earlier than other family members and professionals (Stoddart 1998).

After receiving a diagnosis of AS for their child, parents have reported feeling grief and sadness, although these are often moderated with relief, knowing the problems "have a name" (Stoddart 1998). Parents differ in the extent to which they accept the label and find it useful. Given the previously reviewed literature on the high prevalence of depression and anxiety in parents, professionals must be mindful of stress reactions or depression that may occur beyond the effects of having a child with a disability. Although grief reactions are often unavoidable for parents of a child who has received a diagnosis of a disability, it is important not to assume that the reaction or any subsequent depression is exclusively related to the diagnosis. Social work assessment should include exploring the emotional and social functioning of both parents before the birth of the child with AS, as well as those of other family members; this may offer clues about predisposing factors related to current mental health problems. Counselling may incorporate various models such as the normalizing of the parents' grief response and cognitive behavioural therapy. Pharmacologic interventions for parents are common, and social workers must be aware of when to direct parents to a psychiatrist or family physician (Little 2002a).

It is important that parents receive education about AS (Marcus, Kunce, and Schopler 1997). As information about AS has just begun to be disseminated to the public, many parents know little about AS and its implications. Information can help parents understand the typical problems associated with AS. It is important that parents have access to information specific to AS, as the autism spectrum is broad and functioning levels and characteristics of children on the spectrum vary widely.

Education may occur through parent workshops, conferences, and support groups. The Internet now provides parents of children with AS the opportunity to view websites, participate in bulletin boards, and join listserves related to AS. The quality of this information must be critically examined. Bibliotherapy is another way in which parents receive information about others' experiences and can learn introductory information. Parents may benefit from reading the published accounts of adults with AS such as Willey (1999) and of parents who have children with AS (Fling 2000). Many books address specific issues such as educational needs (Myles and Simpson 1998), sensory differences (Myles *et al.* 2000), adolescence (Bolick 2001), and rage behaviours (Myles and Southwick 1999).

Family therapy

Family therapy is grounded in the assumption that primary interactions in the life of the child are located in the family. Thus, family therapy is the practice of choice when there is a need to change the organization of the family for the benefit of both the family as a whole and its members (Nichols and Schwartz 1998). Family therapy offers the opportunity to negotiate boundaries and roles. For example, adolescents with AS often argue that parents do not give them enough control in matters. Family therapy can assist in establishing appropriate roles and responsibilities. It also gives the social worker an opportunity to view the interactions of family members, which assists in the assessment of boundaries, alliances, and communication between members.

Stoddart (1999) has discussed how meetings of the entire family can provide an opportunity to address conflict, communication problems, perceptions of situations, and behavioural difficulties. In addition, family meetings can provide family members with the chance to discuss their feelings about having a close relative with special needs. Mothers, who are often the main caregivers in families, may become physically and psychologically exhausted and need respite provided by other family members. Siblings may often be in a position of assuming caregiver or protector roles for their brother or sister with AS. The siblings might benefit from a forum in which to voice their feelings. The child with AS may not feel heard in the family and may require help to get others to listen. The therapist can work with the child or adolescent with AS to help her articulate feelings, negotiate with others, and develop empathy. A therapist might explore with the child or adolescent with AS what she wants to say to her family, develop and rehearse responses and help the child bring this into a family session.

Individual therapy for the child or adolescent

Stoddart (1999) makes the case for individual therapy with adolescents who have AS, since they struggle with various issues that can be addressed in this forum. Difficulties at school are often the first concern raised by youth with AS in therapy sessions. Discussion tends to focus on the immense academic and social demands on these young people. Their anxiety may escalate so much that they refuse to attend school. These situations require immediate attention, as the inability to attend is generally labelled as truancy. Not attending school can lead to a host of related problems such as social isolation and missed instruction, which often results in increased school anxiety and avoidance. Individual therapy sessions offer these children and adolescents the opportunity to discuss their subjective experiences of school. For some, the simple act of an adult listening to and validating their concerns about school is immensely therapeutic.

Difficulty with friendships and social relationships is another focus of individual therapy. Children with AS are often described as naïve in their understanding of friendships. Thus, assessment of their friendship skills is an important antecedent to intervention (Attwood 2003). Children with AS often require social skills to be broken down into component parts and taught directly (Attwood 2003). These skills can be reinforced in individual sessions through the discussion of examples from books or movies that are related to their particular interest. Therapy can provide an opportunity to practise and generalize social skills that are also monitored by parents and teachers. It is essential that adults ensure that these children or youth are not being taken advantage of or bullied

(Little 2002a). The increasingly prevalent use of the Internet to meet and socialize with others warrants careful supervision because of their vulnerability (Attwood 2003).

As the adolescent matures, an interest in sex will emerge (Chapter 7, this volume). Specific beliefs or misconceptions about sexual relations and sexuality can be addressed in individual counselling. For example, adolescents might wish to discuss their disappointment that they have not yet had a date, especially if they believe that all their other classmates have had one! Social *faux pas* can be frequent occurrences, which can be sensitively examined in individual counselling. Obsessive thinking about those they want to date may also appear in this age group and may translate into relentless pursuit, which can also have problematic consequences (Marks *et al.* 2000).

As children and adolescents with AS might have difficulty identifying anxiety and depression, an important therapeutic task is to help the individuals with AS identify and voice their emotions. They respond well to visual depictions of anxiety or depression (e.g. scales, thermometers, faces) or can rate their feelings using numeric rating scales (Attwood 2003). The tendency for children and adolescents with AS to perceive or express feelings in extremes may require attention. Teaching relaxation strategies may be helpful and should be developed in consultation with the child. Other interventions for anxiety and depression, such as cognitive behavioural therapy and medication, can be discussed in individual therapy.

Children and adolescents with AS vary in their responses to the diagnostic label of AS. Some embrace the label while others deny that they have AS. It is important not to try to convince the latter group that they have AS. Rather, the therapist must listen to the individual's explanation of his struggles. He may have misconceptions about AS, and whereas some individuals may take comfort in knowing the therapist sees others with AS, others see it as further stigmatization. Those who want to learn more about their symptoms can do so with age-appropriate books, such as the book by Jackson (2002). Ultimately, it is most important that the individual with AS has a forum in which to discuss her problems, regardless of whether a formal diagnostic label is a part of that discussion.

Group work

Because of the wide range of group work, groups may be used as psychotherapy, for mutual aid, for socialization or as a vehicle for psychoeducation. As with any intervention, group work may not be fitting for all children or youth with AS and some may refuse or be reluctant to have such involvement (Mishna and Muskat 1998; Chapter 17, this volume). For instance, the degree of social anxiety, susceptibility to over-stimulation, and disruptive behaviours must be explored to decide their suitability for group involvement. There are several aims of group work with this population. The emphasis has typically been on social skills development. However, generalization of social skills from the group to other environments has been shown to be problematic for this population (e.g. Marriage, Gordon, and Brand 1995). Groups for adolescents often aim to provide support and problem solving. Other benefits include addressing isolation, providing the adolescents with an opportunity to experience social success, and enabling them to feel that they belong to a peer group (Mishna and Muskat 1998).

Groups for parents can be invaluable and address many issues. For example, Sofronoff and Farbotko (2002) described a child management training program, delivered in group format, which led to increased self-efficacy in parents and a reduction of reported behaviour problems in their children. The benefits of parent support groups include helping to reduce parental isolation and increasing awareness that other families face similar challenges. In our experience, the parents of children with AS report that they feel that they have little in common with either parents of "normal children" or with parents of lower-functioning children on the autism spectrum. In the latter case, parents of children with AS may feel guilty for expressing concern about their children's seemingly less severe problems. Sharing experiences with others who have similar concerns can assist parents to view their own situations differently. Besides the emotional support offered by parent groups, parent support groups provide parents the opportunity to share information about helpful community resources.

Case example: John

John is the 16-year-old son of Susan and Frank. He has a 12-year-old brother named Mike. Susan is college educated, works part-time and is outgoing and devoted to her family. Frank has a doctorate and teaches at the local university.

While John achieved most developmental milestones within the normal range, his difficulties with fine and gross motor control, pragmatic language skills, and reciprocal social interaction were evident as early as preschool. His parents consulted his paediatrician, who recommended occupational therapy and enrollment in a specialized preschool program. By Grade 2, John's motor skills and ability to interact with peers were viewed as severely delayed. He was identified as having special needs and placed in a special education classroom. John was often anxious, overwhelmed, and over-stimulated at school, which resulted in him displaying odd behaviours and emotional "meltdowns". He experienced chronic victimization by his peers. Because of these concerns, Susan contacted a local children's social service agency.

In the family assessment conducted by the agency's social worker, Susan described a history of anxiety and depression in her family. Frank described his father as strict yet aloof. He described himself as a loner and immersed in his work at the university. He was irritated with John's constant need for help. John's brother, Mike, was doing well but complained about having to defend his brother on the schoolyard and about being asked by his parents to walk John to and from school. He resented not being able to walk with his own friends, who found John "weird". The social worker referred John for further assessment to a developmental paediatrician and a child psychiatrist. Both concurred that he met the diagnostic criteria for AS, and that he had concurrent learning disabilities, anxiety, and attentional problems. The two physicians prescribed and monitored medication related to his anxiety and distractibility.

Various interventions consistent with an ecological systems approach were offered. The first intervention was psychoeducational, consisting of information on AS being provided to the family. They were encouraged to discuss the meaning and effect of John's AS on their family. The parents enrolled in a support group for parents of children with AS, where others struggled with similar issues and shared ideas for parenting and community resources. Susan met individually with the social worker to address stress related to parenting John and her worry that his need for her care would be endless. With the social worker's support, Susan explored her sense of loss at not having a "normal" child.

Following the social worker's recommendation to address John's social isolation, Susan invited other children to their home and monitored their interaction. Since John was willing to meet other boys, he joined a socialization group in the children's centre for children with symptoms of ASDs. Some of the other members behaved similarly to John and shared interests with him, which allowed him to relax. After group ended, several boys continued their relationships. On the social worker's recommendation, John was enrolled in an overnight camp for children with special needs, which was also attended by two boys from the group. John's ability to attend camp provided him with a sense of accomplishment and offered his parents a much-needed respite.

When John started Grade 5 his behaviour became increasingly challenging for the school. His anxiety caused him to perseverate on issues. This frustrated his teacher, which further exacerbated his anxiety. Susan was frequently called to take John home and to deal with him, which made her feel chastized. The social worker arranged a case conference. School personnel felt their concerns were heard. At the same time, school staff gained greater understanding of AS and a more positive perspective on

John's difficulties. The school implemented plans to stop victimization by peers, which decreased John's anxiety.

As John entered adolescence, Susan noticed that he seemed lonely, sad and confused about his difficulties. In addition, Grade 9 was rapidly approaching, which meant changing schools. John attended individual sessions to discuss his struggle with being different and his awareness that others did not welcome his offers of friendship. The social worker and John discussed the ways he approached others, which often involved talking loudly, standing too close, asking too many questions, and discussing only his areas of interest. They identified strategies to help John become more self-aware. In addition, with John's permission, Susan helped John become aware of his communication style at home and John's special education teacher helped him to communicate with peers. As John's depression did not abate, he was directed to his psychiatrist, to assess a need for a change in his medication. Susan and the social worker worked together to find a high school with a compassionate special education department.

For a period, problems in family dynamics surfaced, which led to the couple meeting with the social worker about their relationship; in particular, Frank's relative unavailability and lack of awareness of Susan's stress. As well, some sessions focussed on parenting issues related to Mike, who was presenting with typical pre-adolescent rebellion. Frank began to explore his characteristics that were similar to John's, specifically those that were suggestive of mild AS.

John is now comfortable in school and with the help of special education staff has found peers to have lunch with. He is uncertain about his academic and vocational future and will need considerable guidance and suitable resources. Frank is now more aware of John's difficulties. Susan has returned to full-time work and enjoys relationships outside the family. She is aware that she needs the support of others to help her cope with the stress she experiences as the mother of a child with AS.

Conclusion

Considering the profession's major theoretical paradigms and approach to assessment and treatment, social work has a significant role to play in the provision of services to families affected by ASDs, and in particular AS. In the future, it is hoped that social work practitioners working with this group will continue to discuss their practice approaches and the theoretical models that guide their practice. Ultimately, well-delineated interventions will require careful evaluation in elucidating those variables that promote good outcomes. Given the central role of feedback from families and youth in refining our practice approaches, so too will the design of an agenda for outcome research benefit greatly from the contribution of families of children and youth with AS.

References

Asperger, H. (1944) Die "autistischen psychopathen" im kindeslater. *Archive für Psychiatrie un Nervenkrankheiten, 117*, 76–136.

Attwood, T. (2003) Frameworks for behavioural interventions. *Child and Adolescent Psychiatric Clinics of North America, 12*, 65–86.

Barnes, C., Mercer, G., and Shakespeare, T. (1999) *Exploring Disability: A Sociological Introduction.* Malden, MA: Polity Press.

Barnes, G.G. (1985) Systems theory and family theory. In M. Rutter and L. Hersov (eds) *Child and Adolescent Psychiatry: Modern Approaches.* Oxford, UK: Blackwell Scientific.

Bolick, T. (2001) *Asperger Syndrome and Adolescence.* Glouchester, MA: Four Winds.

Bolton, P.F., Pickles, A., Murphy, M., and Rutter, M. (1998) Autism, affective and other psychiatric disorders: Patterns of familial aggregation. *Psychological Medicine, 28*, 2, 385–95.

Bristol, M.M. (1987) Mothers of children with autism or communication disorders: Successful adaptation and the double ABCX model. *Journal of Autism and Developmental Disorders, 1*, 4, 469–86.

DeLong, G.R., and Dwyer, J.T. (1988) Correlation of family history with specific autistic subgroups: Asperger's syndrome and bipolar affective disorder. *Journal of Autism and Developmental Disorders, 18*, 4, 593–600.

Fling, E. (2000) *Eating an Artichoke: A Mother's Perspective on Asperger Syndrome.* London, UK: Jessica Kingsley Publishers.

Germain, C.B., and Bloom, M. (1999) *Human Behavior in the Social Environment: An Ecological View, Second Edition.* New York: Columbia University Press.

Gillberg, C. (1989) Asperger Syndrome in 23 Swedish children. *Developmental Medicine and Child Neurology, 31*, 520–31.

Holroyd, J., and McArthur, D. (1976) Mental retardation and stress on the parents: A contrast between Down's syndrome and childhood autism. *American Journal of Mental Deficiency, 80*, 4, 431–6.

Jackson, L. (2002) *Freaks, Geeks and Asperger Syndrome: A User Guide to Adolescence.* London, UK: Jessica Kingsley Publishers.

Little, L. (2002a) Middle-class mothers' perceptions of peer and sibling victimization among children with Asperger's syndrome and nonverbal learning disorders. *Issues in Comprehensive Pediatric Nursing, 25*, 43–57.

Little, L. (2002b) Differences in stress and coping for mothers and fathers of children with Asperger's syndrome and nonverbal learning disorders. *Pediatric Nursing, 28*, 6, 565–70.

Marcus, L.M., Kunce, L.J., and Schopler, E. (1997) Working with families. In D.J. Cohen and F.R. Volkmar (eds) *Handbook of Autism and Pervasive Developmental Disorders.* New York: John Wiley and Sons.

Marks, D. (1997) Models of disability. *Disability and Rehabilitation: An International Multidisciplinary Journal, 19*, 3, 85–91.

Marks, S.U., Schrader, C., Longaker, T., and Levine, M. (2000) Portraits of three adolescent students with Asperger's syndrome: Personal stories and how they can inform practice. *Journal of the Association for Persons with Severe Handicaps (JASH), 25*, 1, 3–17.

Marriage, K.J., Gordon, V., and Brand, L. (1995) A social skills group for boys with Asperger's syndrome. *Australian and New Zealand Journal of Psychiatry, 29*, 58–62.

Mishna, F., and Muskat, B. (1998) Group therapy for boys with features of Asperger syndrome and concurrent learning disabilities: Finding a peer group. *Journal of Child and Adolescent Group Therapy, 8*, 3, 97–114.

Molloy, H., and Vasil, L. (2002) The social construction of Asperger Syndrome: The pathologising of difference? *Disability and Society, 17*, 6, 659–69.

Morgan, S.B. (1988) The autistic child and family functioning: A developmental-family systems perspective. *Journal of Autism and Developmental Disorders, 18*, 2, 263–80.

Myles, B.S., and Simpson, R.L. (1998) *Asperger Syndrome: A Guide for Educators and Parents.* Austin, TX: Pro-Ed.

Myles, B.S., and Southwick, J. (1999) *Asperger Syndrome and Difficult Moments: Practical Solutions for Tantrums, Rage, and Meltdowns.* Shawnee Mission, KS: Autism Asperger Publishing.

Myles, B.S., Tapscott-Cook, K., Miller, N.E., Rinner, L., and Robbins, L.A. (2000) *Asperger Syndrome and Sensory Issues: Practical Solutions for Making Sense of the World.* Shawnee Mission, KS: Autism Asperger Publishing.

Nichols, M.P., and Schwartz, R.C. (1998) *Family Therapy, Concepts and Methods.* Boston, MA: Allyn and Bacon.

Piven, J., Chase, G. A., Landa, R., Wzorek, M., Gayle, J., Cloud, D., and Folstein, S. (1991) Psychiatric disorders in the parents of autistic individuals. *Journal of the American Academy of Child and Adolescent Psychiatry, 30*, 3, 471–8.

Rose, D.F., and Smith, B.J. (1993) Preschool mainstreaming: Attitude barriers and strategies for addressing them. *Young Children, 48*, 59–62.

Sloman, L., and Konstantareas, M.M. (1990) Why families of children with biological deficits require a systems approach. *Family Process, 29*, 417–29.

Sofronoff, K., and Farbotko, M. (2002) The effectiveness of parent management training to increase self-efficacy in parents of children with Asperger syndrome. *Autism: The International Journal of Research and Practice, 6*, 3, 271–86.

Stoddart, K.P. (1998) The treatment of high-functioning Pervasive Developmental Disorder and Asperger's Disorder: Defining the social work role. *Focus on Autism and Other Developmental Disabilities, 13*, 1, 45–52.

Stoddart, K.P. (1999) Adolescents with Asperger syndrome: Three case studies of individual and family therapy. *Autism: The International Journal of Research and Practice, 3*, 3, 255–71.

Szatmari, P., Bremner, R., and Nagy, J. (1989) Asperger's syndrome: A review of clinical features. *Canadian Journal of Psychiatry, 34*, 554–60.

Waddell, K.J. (1984) The self-concept and social adaptation of hyperactive children in adolescence. *Journal of Clinical Child Psychology, 13*, 50–5.

Weiss, S.J. (1991) Stressors experienced by family caregivers of children with pervasive developmental disorders. *Child Psychiatry and Human Development, 21*, 3, 203–15.

Willey, L.H. (1999) *Pretending to be Normal: Living with Asperger's Syndrome.* London, UK: Jessica Kingsley Publishers.

CHAPTER 11

Medication use in children with high-functioning Pervasive Developmental Disorder and Asperger Syndrome

Leon Sloman[1]

There is no specific pharmacological treatment for the Pervasive Developmental Disorders (PDDs). However, psychosocial treatments and appropriate medication can reduce many common maladaptive behaviours. We do not treat PDDs, but rather target symptoms. Medication does not ameliorate the basic deficits in social interaction and communication seen in the children with PDDs. However, it can be considered for use with other measures, when the child seems anxious or depressed, has stereotypies, or is inattentive, hyperactive, and aggressive to self or others.

In this chapter, I will describe medications most commonly used in populations with PDDs and principles that govern their use. Although efforts have been made to distinguish Asperger Syndrome (AS) from high-functioning autism (HFA), it is premature to be certain about this differentiation (Mayes, Calhoun, and Crites 2001). There is also no evidence of any difference in medication response in those with HFA compared with those with AS. As there are no indications that children with AS respond differently to medication from children with other forms of PDD, what will be discussed in this chapter relates to PDDs generally.

---

1   My appreciation goes to Ms Wende Wood, Centre for Addiction and Mental Health, for her helpful suggestions.

The organization of this chapter is derived from intriguing research findings on the relationship between neurotransmitters and clinical features of PDDs. After discussing the role of medication in overall planning, I will review serotonin function studies, dopamine blocking agents, and drugs with multiple neurotransmitter functions. I will discuss managing the side effects of different medications and will briefly discuss the use of medications in sleep problems. Finally, I will summarize the issue of drug interactions.

Consideration of medication as part of a treatment plan

When medication is used for a child with PDD, behavioural and pharmacological approaches should both be part of an overall comprehensive plan. If the physician moves in with medication too quickly, all involved with the child may attribute any subsequent progress or setbacks the child experiences to the medication. For example, parents and teachers may focus on whether the child is taking too little or too much medication, or whether the child requires a change of medication. In so doing, they may overlook other important factors that are affecting the child's behaviour. The calming effect of medication may take the pressure off the school to implement some badly needed changes in the child's program. On the other hand, there are situations where one may wish to use medication to enable the child to continue in a program that is well suited to his or her needs.

Because parents do not wish to expose their child to unnecessary risk, they are understandably reluctant to give their child psychotropic medication, unless they feel stressed by the child's maladaptive behaviours. However, sometimes they resist giving medication because they have reacted to the diagnosis of PDD with defensive denial. Giving medication for them represents an acknowledgment of the severity of their child's condition. Conversely, parents may react to the diagnosis by developing magical expectations and look to medication to "cure" their child. It is therefore important to establish realistic expectations about the effect of medication as well as other treatments.

Over-enthusiastic adherence to a particular philosophically driven position about the merits or dangers of psychotropic medication is both unscientific and unlikely to lead to appropriate advances in care. For example, a blanket perspective that suggests that psychotropic drugs may have a damaging effect on the developing brain is untrue and contrary to the available evidence (Kutcher 2000). The long-term effects of untreated anxiety or depression in a child with PDD may be more damaging than medication. Serotonin not only acts as a neurotransmitter and a neuromodulator, but also plays an important role in neurogenesis. Emerging data suggest that antidepressants, if taken for the recommended duration (in depressed individuals), will reverse hippocampal atrophy and induce neurogenesis. Medication is then protective of the brain. Alternatively, overly enthusiastic embracing of an untested medication may prevent one from having a balanced view of the cost to benefit ratio of this intervention *versus* other possibilities. The doctor must help parents make a balanced decision about the use of medication.

Administration of psychotropic drugs to children should be a collaborative venture with the parents and, when feasible, with the older child. Therefore, it is important to assess the parents' and the child's attitudes to the use of medication before making any recommendations. For the parents to make an informed decision, they need to have adequate information about the possible benefits and negative side effects, as well as information about alternative treatments that may be available.

No medications are specifically marketed to treat PDD and most of the psychotropic medications we use in children have not yet gone through the sophisticated evaluation necessary to establish their efficacy, tolerability, and safety (Kutcher 2000). There is an absence of high-quality studies of the efficacy of different medications for specific symptoms in the PDD population. Most of the studies are case reports or small-scale open trials (Towbin 2003). Because most of the drugs used in PDD, such as the Selective Serotonin Reuptake Inhibitors (SSRIs) and the novel antipsychotics, have been in existence for a brief period, we do not have information about their long-term effects. Without child-specific data, clinicians often employ psychopharmacological strategies based on data extrapolated from adults, which can be misleading. One must also be cautious in applying findings from other conditions to PDD. For example, one cannot assume the responses to a mood stabilizer for HFA/AS and bipolar disorder will be identical (Towbin 2003).

General principles of medication use in Pervasive Developmental Disorders

Parents and teachers play a crucial role in systematically noting behavioural and emotional effects and monitoring for any side effects to a new medication, or a medication change. The use of an individually designed chart may be helpful for this purpose. One can list the target symptoms with perhaps a five-point scale to assess severity. It is generally advisable to make only one medication change at a time to obtain a clear picture of how the child has reacted to the change. An adequate period of time should elapse before any further changes are made.

When prescribing medication to children with AS, it is usually fitting to start with a very low dose (using one-quarter or one-eighth of the dose that is used in other conditions) and, if necessary, to raise the dose slowly. Although this may delay the child's response, this might be preferable to having to stop the medication because of side effects. One reason for starting low is that, when one treats symptoms like depression in a child with PDD, there is no reason to believe that this is equal to treating depression in someone who doesn't have PDD. For that reason, it could be misleading to use dosage guidelines based on the latter group. Another reason for starting with a low dose is that children with PDD often respond to low doses. In addition, with some medications such as the SSRIs, raising the dose may trigger serotonergic side effects (e.g. agitation). In general, the higher the dose the greater the risk of side effects and the greater the risk of withdrawal effects when the medication is stopped.

The two most important categories of medications used in PDD are those that affect serotonin function (the SSRIs) and those that affect dopamine function (dopamine blocking agents or neuroleptics). In general, SSRIs are effective in alleviating depressed mood, anxiety, panic attacks, and obsessive-compulsive symptoms including ritualistic behaviours. However, newer neuroleptics, also called the atypical antipsychotics, affect both the dopamine and serotonin systems. They may lessen aggression, anxiety, and depression, and promote frustration tolerance, social interaction, and calmness.

SSRIs are often preferred over neuroleptics in the belief that they are safer. Because neuroleptics are used in schizophrenia, it is sometimes assumed that they must be more powerful and therefore use is more risky. Though this is true for the older neuroleptics, the newer atypical antipsychotics have fewer side effects. Therefore, the assumption that they are less safe than the SSRIs is debatable. For example, in the study by Remington *et al.* (2001) clomipramine proved to have more adverse effects than haloperidol, an antipsychotic. Other advantages of risperidone over SSRIs are that it acts more quickly (days *versus* weeks), it has been better researched, and it targets a wider range of symptoms (Fisman 2002). For that reason, this clinician usually feels more comfortable giving risperidone than SSRIs to younger children (under seven years of age). Furthermore, as SSRIs become more widely used, they are found to cause a greater number of side effects. On the other hand, risperidone is more prone to cause weight gain and drowsiness and one cannot exclude the possibility of Parkinsonian side effects. Nevertheless, it is logical to first try an SSRI when one is targeting anxiety, panic, and depression and to start with risperidone when one is targeting aggression and hyperactivity (Aman and Langworthy 2000). Sometimes SSRIs may reduce aggression, while risperidone often elevates mood.

While monotherapy is ideal in that it facilitates the task of evaluating the effect of medication, a combination of drugs may be necessary to optimize response, but this demands awareness of potential drug interactions. Finally, it is important to inform the treating physician if the child happens to be taking any herbal products, because of the potential for interaction. For example, St John's Wort may bind to Monoamine Oxidase Inhibitors (MAO) receptors making interaction with antidepressants unpredictable.

Medications that affect serotonin function

All SSRIs achieve their antidepressant effect by blocking the re-uptake of serotonin at the presynaptic serotonin 5-HT receptor sites in the brain. There is evidence that SSRIs may reduce repetitive thoughts, compulsions, and stereotypies (Gordon 2000; McDougle, Kresch, and Posey 2000). Though many selective 5-HT uptake inhibitors have been used in treating symptoms of children with PDD, there are few scientific studies of their relative efficacy. Unfortunately, the earlier SSRI drugs, as well as blocking the re-uptake of serotonin, also secondarily and concurrently block a wide range of important neuroreceptors and cytochrome P450 isoenzymes, making way for many side effects and adverse drug interactions.

Citalopram

Citalopram is one of the newer SSRIs. Open studies support a possible efficacy of citalopram. Namerow *et al.* (2003), in a retrospective study, found that anxiety symptoms improved in two-thirds of subjects and a mood score improved in just under half the subjects. The final dose was 16.9 +/- 12.1 mg/day. Courturier and Nicholson (2002) treated 17 patients with PDD, ages ranging from four to 15 years, for two months or more. Target behaviours included aggression, anxiety, stereotypies, and preoccupations. They started with 5 mg and the final dose range was 5 mg to 40 mg. Ten patients were judged improved and adverse effects were reported in four patients, two of whom had increased agitation, one insomnia and one possible tics. Although it is too early to know, citalopram, the most specific of the SSRIs, appears to be associated with the lowest incidence of side effects among SSRIs, though it tends to be activating early in treatment. One can start with a dose of five mg a.m. (10 mg in an older adolescent) and rarely over 20 mg.

Fluoxetine

As for fluoxetine, in an open study over five to 76 months, DeLong, Ritch, and Burch (2002) found that over half of 129 children aged two to eight years showed a positive response to it. Response to fluoxetine correlated with unusual intellectual achievement. Five children developed bipolar disorder during follow-up. Fatemi *et al.* (1998) found evidence of symptomatic relief, though hyperactivity seemed to be increased. Alcami, Peralg, and Gilaberte (2000) treated 12 autistic children (aged three to 13 years) with fluoxetine (5 to 20 mg/day) in an open study. They found an improvement in communication and attention skills and a decrease in rituals and stereotypical behaviours, but there were increases in impulsiveness, restlessness, sleep disturbance and loss of appetite. Gordon (2000) recommends a very low dose (1–2 mg/day). It has been reported that cyproheptadine may block the action of fluoxetine (Boon 1999).

Fluvoxamine

Fluvoxamine has been utilized in the PDDs. Although McDougle *et al.* (1996) reported an increased irritability, agitation, and aggression while treating with fluvoxamine, a recent "low dose study" (1.5 mg/kg/day) by Martin and colleagues (2003) suggested it could reduce obsessive-compulsive-like behaviour in some children. In a double-blind crossover study, Fukuda's group (2001) found improved eye contact and language use. Gordon (2000) recommends a very low dose (4–8 mg/day) reporting that hyperactivity/ agitation and insomnia are likely to occur at the usual dose for treating depression. It may be necessary to use a specialized pharmacy to obtain such a low dose.

Other medications

Venlafaxine, sertraline, paroxetine, and trazadone have also been used in treating PDDs. Hollander *et al.* (2000), in a small open study, found that venlafaxine in low doses (6.25–50.00 mg/day) could be helpful to children, adolescents, and young adults with PDD. Sertraline has been used in PDD with apparent success (Ozbayrak 1997; Steingard, Zimnitzky, and DeMaso 1997; Scahill and Koenig 1999). Paroxetine has been used but little is published (Snead, Boon, and Presburg 1994; Awad 1996). Some responders reacted negatively to an increase in dose to above 7.5 mg/day. As the same cytochrome enzyme breaks them down, concurrent use of risperidone and paroxetine may lead to an elevation of the blood level of both drugs. Finally, trazadone is highly sedating as well as being antidepressant and can be given at night to promote sleep.

Side effects of SSRIs and management strategies

One must be aware of the various side effects of SSRIs and suitable management strategies for these. If insomnia is a side effect, it may improve as tolerance develops. However, if the medication is being given at night, one can give it in the morning. One may also try lowering the dose or switching medications. For hypersomnia and fatigue, one may wait for tolerance to develop, or give the medication at bedtime instead of in the morning. For nausea, one can wait for tolerance to occur, lower the dose, take the medication with food, or switch medications. To address weight gain, the child should exercise and reduce calories.

Serotonin Syndrome has been reported with high doses, generally with a combination of serotonergic medications. Agitation possibly accompanied by confusion, tremor, myoclonus, and hyperthermia may occur. This is best avoided by dose regulation. Garland and Baerg (2001) described five cases of apathy and lack of motivation in a child and four adolescents. Symptoms were dose related and reversible. Two children were on paroxetine and three were on fluoxetine. Discontinuation Syndrome is more likely after the abrupt cessation of an SSRI. It is associated with flu-like symptoms such as insomnia, nausea, imbalance, sensory disturbances, and hyperarousal. One can try to avoid it by tapering the dose more slowly. Paroxetine and venlafaxine pose a high risk of Discontinuation Syndrome, and citalopram, fluoxetine, and sertraline, a low risk.

Paroxetine appears to have the greatest and fluvoxamine and venlafaxine the least potential for interaction with CYP2D6-dependent drugs. The drugs metabolized by CYP2D6 include antipsychotics (e.g. phenothiazines and risperidone), codeine, trycyclic antidepressants, and beta-blockers (Oesterheld and Shader 1998). Erythromycin, which has an inhibitory effect on CYP3 isoenzymes, elevates the blood level of SSRIs.

A dopaminergic blocking agent

Haloperidol, a potent post-synaptic dopamine-receptor antagonistic, has been shown to be effective in treating severe behavioural problems in this population (Remington *et al.* 2001). In children, at doses ranging from 0.25 mg to 4.0 mg per day, it reduced stereotypies, withdrawal, hyperactivity, fidgeting, and tantrums and increased social relatedness. Perry and colleagues (1989) showed that episodic administration (five days on and two days off medication) might be effective.

Today, most clinicians avoid using this medication because of concerns about its short- and long-term side effects. It has largely been replaced by the atypical antipsychotics, which are less likely to cause the Parkinsonian side effects commonly associated with it. However, at times, children who are unresponsive to the atypical antipsychotics are responsive to haloperidol.

Acute extrapyramidal side effects have been described particularly with rapid dose escalation and a relatively high starting dose. Withdrawal dyskinesia (Perry *et al.* 1997) and tardive dyskinesia (Feeney and Klykylo 1996) have also been described. For acute dyskinesia, diphenhydramine has been found effective (Anderson *et al.* 1984). Campbell *et al.* (1988) conducted a study of tardive dyskinesia and withdrawal dyskinesia in a group of 82 autistic children who were treated with haloperidol for periods ranging from two to 60 months. Although 24 developed dyskinesias, all the dyskinesias were reversible with medication discontinuation. Keeping the dose low, increasing the dose gradually, and an anticholinergic agent such as benztropine (when giving a higher dose), reduces the risk of Parkinsonian side effects.

Drugs with multiple neurotransmitter functions

Risperidone

Risperidone is a new antipsychotic agent. It is a potent dopamine Type 2 (D2) and serotonin Type 2 (5-HT2) receptor antagonist. In a randomized, multisite, double-blind, placebo-controlled eight-week study of 101 children with autism aged five to 17 years (McCracken *et al.* 2002) it was well tolerated and effective for treating tantrums, aggressions, or self-injurious behaviour. Dose range was 0.5 to 3.5 mg/day. In two-thirds of those with a positive response to risperidone at eight weeks, the improvement was maintained at six months. Increased appetite, fatigue, drowsiness, dizziness, and drooling were more common in the risperidone group than in the placebo group. Risperidone seems effective in reducing hyperactivity (Aman and Langworthy 2000) and reducing the frequency and intensity of temper outbursts and aggression. Improvements were also noted in stereotypic behaviour and hyperactivity and in symptoms of most concern to parents (McDougle, Kresch, and Posey 2000; Arnold *et al.* 2003). Risperidone appears to be more effective than olanzapine in reducing repetitive behaviours (McDougle, Kresch, and Posey 2000).

Masi *et al.* (2001) examined the tolerability and efficacy of risperidone in a six-week open trial in 24 children aged 3.6 to 6.6 years. The optimal dose was 0.5 mg/day. Eight subjects showed appreciable improvement in items relating to behavioural control and affect regulation. Only three subjects had a weight gain of more than 10%. Nicholson, Awad, and Sloman (1998) described a prospective 12-week open-label study of risperidone (mean dose 1.3 mg/day) in young autistic children aged 4.5 to 10.8 years. Of the ten children who completed the study, eight were considered responders. Transient sedation was common and the children gained an average of 3.5 kg. Based on clinical experience, I usually start with a dose of 0.125 mg for a child under seven years, and 0.25 mg for older children who weigh more, and increase gradually if necessary. For children over ten years, my average dose of risperidone is about 0.5 mg/day and I do not usually go over 1.5 mg/day.

Weight gain has been one of the most troublesome side effects observed in patients treated with risperidone. That is why the child's weight should be monitored regularly using a pretreatment baseline and, when suitable, a low calorie diet and exercise should be prescribed for the child.

When long-term administration of risperidone causes fatty infiltration of the liver, this can affect liver functioning. Kumra, Herion, and Jacobsen (1997) reported on two boys with psychotic disorders who had fatty infiltration of the liver and abnormal liver function tests that were reversible when the risperidone was discontinued. Although other medications probably contributed, it seems prudent to monitor liver function tests every six to nine months, particularly regarding obese children or those who are rapidly gaining weight.

Risperidone often leads to a rise in serum prolactin level, which should therefore be monitored. Masi *et al.* (2001) found no significant correlations between hyperprolactinemia and age, weight, or risperidone dosage, nor did any of 25 autistic children aged seven years and younger show any clinical signs of hyperprolactinemia. A reduction of risperidone resulted in a decrease of prolactin levels. Although this rise may not necessarily be harmful, gynecomastia, galactorrhoea, amenorrhoea, and sexual dysfunction may result. Valiquette (2002) has raised the spectre of possible hypogonadism and osteoporosis after a prolonged elevation of serum prolactin. However, many of these ill effects were associated with polypharmacy with anticonvulsants, antipsychotics, and SSRIs. Still, lowering the dose of risperidone or changing to another medication is generally the most appropriate course of action.

Extrapyramidal effects are occasionally seen with risperidone but, in the unlikely event that a child on a low dose of risperidone developed a dyskinesia, it is likely to disappear if the medication is discontinued (McDougle, Scahill *et al.* 2000). When the child develops symptoms while on risperidone, dose reduction is the preferred course of action, though an anticholinergic medication like benztropine may be helpful.

Other possible side effects of risperidone include elevated serum cholesterol (particularly when obesity develops), priapism, and withdrawal reaction. The presence of obesity merits a serum cholesterol HDL and LDL. There have been a couple of case reports of priapism when risperidone was combined with other medications (Owley, Leventhal, and Cook 2001; Freudenreich 2002). Withdrawal symptoms such as tics may occur, especially with rapid withdrawal (Rowan and Malone 1997).

Olanzapine

Olanzapine has also been tested in PDD in open-label studies. It is one of the newer atypical antipsychotics, with a similar side-effect profile to risperidone, though it has been less well studied. However, it appears to be more prone to cause weight gain. There is a potential for glucose dysregulation and diabetes. It may be effective in PDD (Malek-Ahmadi and Simonds 1998; Potenza *et al.* 1999; Van Engeland 2000). Malone's group (2001) studied the safety and effectiveness of olanzapine in children with PDD aged 7.8 +/- 2.1 years, using doses of 7.9 +/- 2.5 mg/day, and concluded it was promising. Side effects were weight gain and drowsiness. A comprehensive study by Kemner *et al.* (2002) showed an improvement in irritability and hyperactivity, but also weight gain and loss of strength. The authors conclude that, while it was relatively safe, its clinical relevance in children with PDD may be limited. There have been reports of mania (London 1998) and priapism (Deirmenjian *et al.* 1998).

Quietapine

Martin *et al.* (1999) conducted an open-label study of quietapine in children and adolescents with autistic disorder and found no significant group improvement.

Ziprasidone

McDougle, Kem, and Posey (2002) conducted an open study on 12 children, adolescents, and young adults and described six as responders. They saw ziprasidone as having the potential to improve aggression, agitation, and irritability. Significant weight gain was not observed. However, taking it may affect cardiac conduction by prolonging the QT interval, so caution is required.

Stimulants

Methylphenidate and dextroamphetamine may enhance norepinephrine and dopamine release from sympathetic nerve terminals and inhibit re-uptake in the caudate nucleus. It is now generally accepted that stimulants are effective in decreasing restless, impulsive behaviour and in improving the attention span of children with Attention Deficit Hyperactivity Disorder (ADHD). Some children with PDD have the classical features of ADHD, but are not diagnosed with ADHD because the diagnosis of PDD takes precedence (APA 1994). Although Aman (1982) concluded there was no role for stimulants in the autistic population, a more recent report suggests that stimulants can be helpful, particularly in those with HFA (Quintana *et al.* 1995). Ishizaki and Sugama (2001), in a one-to-five-year follow-up, found methylphenidate effective in the majority of children, but more so in those whose IQ was over 80, than in those whose IQ was under 80. The average dose was 0.3 mg/kg once every morning. Handen, Johnson, and Lubetsky (2000) found a small majority of autistic children showed a moderate decrease in the Conners Hyperactivity Index (Conners 1997), but there were no changes on the Childhood Autism Rating Scale (Schopler *et al.*

1980; Schopler, Reichler, and Renner 1988). They found significant adverse effects, including social withdrawal and irritability, in some children, especially when the dose was raised from 0.3 mg/kg to 0.6 mg/kg.

Dextroamphetamine and methylphenidate have equivalent efficacy, though some children respond better to one than the other. Both have slow release versions. In addition, there is a new combination of rapid and very slow release methylphenidate. Methylphenidate OROS (Concerta), given once a day, works well for some children but is more likely to cause loss of appetite and insomnia. Stimulants have been extensively studied over the long term in children and appear to be relatively safe.

Alpha2-adrenergic agonists

Clonidine can be used for aggressiveness, irritability, and hyperactivity. It must be given in divided doses and the dose must be increased and decreased very gradually. An ECG must be done before starting medication. Jaselskis *et al.* (1992) conducted a double-blind placebo-controlled crossover study of clonidine in eight children with autistic disorder with a dose of 4–10 ug/kg/day. Improvement was seen in hyperactivity, irritability, stereotypies, inappropriate speech, and oppositional behaviour. Adverse effects included hypotension, sedation, and irritability.

Anticonvulsants – mood stabilizers

Hollander *et al.* (2001), in a small retrospective study, concluded that divalproex sodium might be useful to patients with PDD with affective instability, impulsivity, and aggression as well as those with a history of seizures. The disadvantage is the necessity of regular venipunctures to assess blood level and liver functions.

Drugs for sleep

Many medications may lead to insomnia and sometimes administering these earlier in the day may restore normal sleep rhythm. This may hold true for stimulants, SSRIs, and sometimes neuroleptics like risperidone. On the other hand, if the child is on a neuroleptic, one may sometimes improve sleep by giving it at night. For safety reasons, it is preferable first to start with a milder medication, namely an antihistamine such as cyproheptadine HCL or diphenhydramine HCL, even though they usually lose their effectiveness after about a week.

Melatonin is a pineal hormone that plays a central role in regulating bodily rhythms. Melatonin is available in health food stores in the United States. Because of claims of a therapeutic effect, it was reclassified as a drug and is awaiting approval by Health Canada. There is hope that its approval is forthcoming. Melatonin has been found to promote sleep in children (Smits, van Stel, and van der Heijden 2003) and many children with PDD use melatonin with apparent benefit. Clonidine is also sometimes given at night for insomnia.

Drug interactions with the central nervous system

Cytochromes (CYPs) are key enzymes that enable us to metabolize both endogenous and exogenous substances. CYPs in children may have greater metabolic capacity than in adults, which may explain why prepubertal children may require higher doses of psychotropics metabolized by the liver than do adults (Oesterheld and Shader 1998). Drugs that interact with CYPs may inhibit, induce, or have no effect on the activity of the CYP. If a CYP is inhibited, substrates of the CYP will be metabolized less rapidly and more unmetabolized drug will enter the circulation. Conversely, if a CYP is induced, additional CYP enzyme is available for metabolism leading to lower levels in the blood. Many CYPs have been identified as involved in human metabolism. One CYP may handle low concentrations of a drug while another may kick in when higher concentrations are present. When two drugs compete for the same cytochrome isoenzyme, the one with the greater affinity will be metabolized at near the projected rate, whereas the one with the lesser affinity will not and the blood level could become very toxic.

As potent inhibitors of CYP2D6, both paroxetine and fluoxetine have the potential to increase the plasma concentrations of antipsychotic medications metabolized through this enzyme, including haloperidol and risperidone. Even foods can act as inhibitors and inducers of CYPs. Broccoli and cabbage induce the metabolism of CYP1A1/2. Theoretically, broccoli could lower levels of clomipramine, while a glass of grapefruit juice can double or triple clomipramine levels through its inhibition of CYP 3A4/5 (Oesterheld and Shader 1998). A single glass of grapefruit juice has a high potential for adverse drug interactions with respect to the number of drugs involved and the magnitude of the response. Polypharmacy makes psychotropic drugs more risky so one must be aware of possible drug interactions.

Case example: Larry

Larry, age nine, presented as hyperactive, anxious, and was afraid to go anywhere unaccompanied, even in his own home. He also feared constantly that he would be late or had not done his homework properly. At 4½ years old, two years after the diagnosis of AS was made, he was started on methylphenidate 5 mg three times a day. This reduced his hyperactivity but he appeared "dazed". After 18 months, he was started on Concerta (18 mg a.m.), which did not have this side effect. Later, the Concerta was supplemented by sertraline 12.5 mg and, when this was ineffective, it was raised to 25 mg, still without effect. The sertraline was then discontinued. The Concerta suddenly lost its effectiveness and it was replaced by risperidone 0.25 mg a.m., which had a calming effect. After six weeks, it was raised to 0.25 mg twice a day and subsequently to 0.5 mg a.m. and 0.25 mg at night. Because the second increase did not result in an apparent difference, the risperidone was reduced to 0.25 mg twice a day, which is the current dosage. While on the risperidone he gained 20 pounds. After six months, when Larry was starting school, it was decided to recommence the Concerta. A double-blind trial was conducted comparing placebo with Concerta 18 mg and Concerta 27 mg. The Concerta 27 mg was found to be most effective and he is still on this dose as well as risperidone 0.25 mg twice a day. Since the Concerta was added, Larry has lost ten pounds.

This case illustrates how the search for optimal medication is a matter of trial and error and how risperidone increases appetite and stimulants reduce appetite. Raising the risperidone above 0.5 mg/day did not have a positive effect. Because both hyperactivity and short attention span present more of a problem in the school setting, the maximum impact of stimulants may only be apparent at school. Therefore, if the child is coping reasonably well during the day and presenting problems after school, one can give the stimulant in the morning and at noon and the risperidone around 4 p.m. when the stimulant is wearing off.

Conclusion

The dearth of evidence-based studies on the use of pharmacotropic medication in children with PDD means that one has to observe carefully how the child reacts and keep doses low. Prescribing medication should be a collaborative venture between the clinician and the family. At present, antipsychotics and SSRIs are the most heavily used medications. While there are some children who benefit from stimulants, others react negatively to them. The task of research has been complicated by the diversity of syndrome expression and the relatively short duration of most medication studies. Much more research is needed.

References

Alcami, P.M., Peralg, M., and Gilaberte, I. (2000) An open study of fluoxetine in children with autism. *Actas Espanolas de Psiquiatria, 28*, 353–6.

Aman, M.G. (1982) Stimulant drug effects in developmental disorders and hyperactivity – toward a resolution of disparate findings. *Journal of Autism and Developmental Disorders, 12*, 385–98.

Aman, M.G., and Langworthy, K.S. (2000) Pharmacotherapy for hyperactivity in children with autism and other Pervasive Developmental Disorders. *Journal of Autism and Developmental Disorders, 30*, 451–9.

Anderson, L.T., Campbell, M., Grega, D.M., Perry, R., Small, A.M., and Green, W.H. (1984) Haloperidol in the treatment of infantile autism: Effects on learning and behavioral symptoms. *American Journal of Psychiatry, 141*, 1195–202.

APA (American Psychiatric Association) (1994) *Diagnostic and Statistical Manual of Mental Disorders, Fourth Edition.* Washington DC: APA.

Arnold, L.E., Vitiello, B., McDougle, C., Scahill, L., Shah, B., Gonzalez, N.M., *et al.* (2003) Parent-defined target symptoms respond to risperidone in RUPP autism study: Customer approach to clinical trials. *Journal of the American Academy of Child and Adolescent Psychiatry, 42*, 1443–50.

Awad, G.A. (1996) The use of selective serotonin reuptake inhibitors in young children with pervasive developmental disorders: Some clinical observations. *Canadian Journal of Psychiatry, 41*, 361–6.

Boon, F. (1999) Cyproheptadine and SSRI's. *Journal of the American Academy of Child and Adolescent Psychiatry, 38*, 112.

Campbell, M., Adams, P., Perry, R., Spencer, E.K., and Overall, J.E. (1988) Tardive and withdrawal dyskinesia in autistic children: a prospective study. *Psychopharmacology Bulletin, 24*, 251–5.

Conners, C.K. (1997) *Conners' Rating Scales – Revised.* Toronto, ON: Multi-Health Systems Inc.

Courturier, J.L., and Nicholson, R. (2002) A retrospective assessment of citalopram in children and adolescents with pervasive developmental disorders. *Journal of Child and Adolescent Psychopharmacology, 12*, 243–8.

Deirmenjian, J.M., Erhart, S.M., Wirshing, D.A., Spellberg, D.J., and Wirshing, W.C. (1998) Olanzapine-induced reversible priapism: A case report. *Journal of Clinical Psychopharmacology, 18*, 351–3.

DeLong, G.R., Ritch, C.R., and Burch, S. (2002) Fluoxetine response in children with autistic spectrum disorders: Correlation with familial major affective disorder and intellectual achievement. *Developmental Medicine and Child Neurology, 44*, 652–9.

Fatemi, S.H., Realmuto, G.M., Khan, L., and Thurns, P. (1998) Fluoxetine treatment of adolescent patients with autism: A longitudinal open trial. *Journal of Autism and Developmental Disorders, 28*, 303–307.

Feeney, D.J., and Klykylo, W. (1996) Risperidone and tardive dyskinesia. *Journal of the American Academy of Child and Adolescent Psychiatry, 35*, 1421–22.

Fisman, S. (2002) Pervasive Developmental Disorder. In S. Kutcher (ed.) *Practical Child and Adolescent Psychopharmacology.* New York, NY: Cambridge University Press.

Freudenreich, O. (2002) Exacerbation of idiopathic priapism with risperidone citalopram combination. *Journal of Clinical Psychiatry, 63*, 249–50.

Fukuda, T., Sugie, H., Ito, M., and Sugie, Y. (2001) Clinical evaluation of children with fluvoxamine, a selective serotonin reuptake inhibitor in children with autistic disorder. *No to Hattatsu, 33*, 314–18.

Garland, E.J., and Baerg, E.A. (2001) Amotivational syndrome associated with selective serotonin reuptake inhibitors in children and adolescents. *Journal of Child and Adolescent Psychopharmacology, 11*, 181–6.

Gordon, C.T. (2000) Commentary: Considerations on the pharmacological treatment of compulsions and stereotypies with serotonin reuptake inhibitors in Pervasive Developmental Disorders. *Journal of Autism and Developmental Disorders, 30*, 437–8.

Handen, B.J., Johnson, C.R., and Lubetsky, M. (2000) Efficacy of methylphenidate among children with autism and symptoms of attention deficit hyperactivity disorder. *Journal of Autism and Developmental Disorders, 30,* 245–55.

Hollander, E., Kaplin, A., Cartwright, C., and Reichman, D. (2000) Venlafaxine in children, adolescents, and young adults with autism spectrum disorders: An open retrospective clinical report. *Journal of Child Neurology, 15,* 132–5.

Hollander, E., Dolgoff-Kaspar, R., Cartwright, C., Rawitt, R., and Novotny, S. (2001) An open trial of divalproex sodium in autism spectrum disorders. *Journal of Clinical Psychiatry, 62,* 530–4.

Ishizaki, A., and Sugama, M. (2001) Methylphenidate therapy in 141 patients with hyperkinetic disorder or with Pervasive Developmental Disorder and hyperkinesias. *No to Hattatsu, 33,* 323–8.

Jaselskis, C.A., Cook, E.H.Jr., Fletcher, K.E., and Leventhal, B.L. (1992) Clonidine treatment of hyperactive and impulsive children with autistic disorder. *Journal of Clinical Psychopharmacology, 12,* 322–7.

Kemner, C., Willemsen-Swinkels, S.H., de Jonge, M., Tuynman-Qua, H., and Van Engeland, H. (2002) Open-label study of olanzapine in children with pervasive developmental disorder. *Journal of Clinical Psychopharmacology, 22,* 455–60.

Kumra, S., Herion, D., and Jacobsen, L.K. (1997) Case study: Risperidone-induced hepatotoxicity in pediatric patients. *Journal of the American Academy of Child and Adolescent Psychiatry, 35,* 701–5.

Kutcher, S. (2000) Practical and clinical issues regarding child and adolescent psycho- pharmacology. *Child and Adolescent Psychiatric Clinics of North America, 9,* 245–60.

London, J.A. (1998) Mania associated with olanzapine. *Journal of the American Academy of Child and Adolescent Psychiatry, 37,* 135–6.

Malek-Ahmadi, P., and Simonds, J.F. (1998) Olanzapine for autistic disorder with hyperactivity. *Journal of the American Academy of Child and Adolescent Psychiatry, 37,* 902.

Malone, R.P., Cater, J., Sheikh, R.M., Choudhury, M.S., and Delaney, M.A. (2001) Olanzapine versus haloperidol in children with autistic disorder: An open pilot study. *Journal of the American Academy of Child and Adolescent Psychiatry, 40,* 887–94.

Martin, A., Koenig, K., Anderson, G.M., and Scahill, L. (2003) Low-dose fluvoxamine treatment of children and adolescents with Pervasive Developmental Disorders: A prospective open-label study. *Journal of Autism and Developmental Disorders, 33,* 77–85.

Martin, A., Koenig, K., Scahill, L., and Bregman, J. (1999) Open-label quietapine in the treatment of children and adolescents with autistic disorder. *Journal of Child and Adolescent Psychopharmacology, 9,* 99–107.

Masi, G., Cosenza, G., Mucci, M., and Brovedani, P. (2001) Open trial of risperidone in 24 young children with Pervasive Developmental Disorders. *Journal of the American Academy Child and Adolescent Psychiatry, 40,* 1206–14.

Mayes, S.D., Calhoun, S.L., and Crites, D.L. (2001) Does DSM-IV Asperger's exist? *Journal of Abnormal Child Psychology, 29,* 263–71.

McCracken, J.T., McGough, J., Shah, B., Cronin, P., Hong, D., Aman, M.G., *et al.* (2002) Risperidone in children with autism and serious behavioral problems. *The New England Journal of Medicine, 347,* 314–21.

McDougle, C.J., Kem, D.L., and Posey, D.J. (2002) Case series: Use of ziprasidone for maladaptive symptoms for youths with autism. *Journal of the American Academy of Child and Adolescent Psychiatry, 41,* 921–7.

McDougle, C.J., Kresch, L.E., and Posey, D.J. (2000) Repetitive thoughts and behavior in pervasive developmental disorders: Treatment with serotonin reuptake inhibitors. *Journal of Autism and Developmental Disorders, 30,* 427–35.

McDougle, C.D., Naylor, S.T., Cohen, D.J., Volkmar, F.R., Heninger, G.R., and Price, L.H. (1996) A double-blind, placebo-controlled study of fluvoxamine in adults with autistic disorder. *Archives of General Psychiatry, 53,* 1001–1008.

McDougle, C.D., Scahill, L., McCracken, J.T., Aman, M.G., Tierney, E., Arnold, L.E., et al. (2000) Research units on pediatric psychopharmacology (RUPP) autism network: Background and rationale for an initial controlled study of risperidone. Adolescent and Child Psychiatric Clinics of North America, 9, 201–23.

Namerow, L.B., Thomas, P., Bostic, J.Q., Prince, J., and Monuteaux, M.C. (2003) Use of citalopram in pervasive developmental disorders. Journal of Developmental and Behavioral Pediatrics, 24, 104–108.

Nicholson, R., Awad, G., and Sloman, L. (1998) An open trial of risperidone in young autistic children. Journal of the American Academy Child and Adolescent Psychiatry, 37, 372–6.

Oesterheld, J.R., and Shader, R.I. (1998) Cytochromes: A primer for child and adolescent psychiatrists. Journal of the American Academy of Child and Adolescent Psychiatry, 37, 447–50.

Owley, T., Leventhal, B., and Cook, E.H. (2001) Risperidone-induced prolonged erections following the addition of lithium. Journal of Child and Adolescent Psychopharmacology, 11, 441–2.

Ozbayrak, K.R. (1997) Sertraline in PDD. Journal of the American Academy of Child and Adolescent Psychiatry, 36, 7–8.

Perry, R., Campbell, M., Adams, P., Lynch, N., Spencer, E.K., Curren, E.L., and Overall, J.E. (1989) Long-term efficacy of haloperidol in autistic children: Continuous versus discontinuous drug administration. Journal of the American Academy of Child and Adolescent Psychiatry, 28, 87–92.

Perry, R., Pataki, C., Munoz-Silva, D.M., Armenteros, T., and Silva, R.R. (1997) Risperidone in children and adolescents with Pervasive Developmental Disorder: Pilot trial and follow-up. Journal of Child and Adolescent Psychopharmacology, 7, 167–79.

Potenza, M.N., Holmes, J.P., Kanes, S.J., and McDougle, C.J. (1999) Olanzapine treatment of children, adolescents, and adults with Pervasive Developmental Disorders: An open-label study. Journal of Clinical Psychopharmacology, 19, 37–44.

Quintana, H., Birmaher, B., Stedge, D., Lennon, S., Freed, J., Bridge, J., and Greenhill, L. (1995) Use of methylphenidate in the treatment of children with autistic disorder. Journal of Autism and Developmental Disorders, 25, 283–94.

Remington, G., Sloman, L., Konstantareas, M., Parker, K., and Gow, R. (2001) Clomipramine versus haloperidol in the treatment of autistic disorder: A double-blind, placebo controlled, crossover study. Journal of Clinical Psychopharmacology, 21, 440–4.

Rowan, A.B., and Malone, R.P. (1997) Tics with risperidone withdrawal. Journal of the American Academy of Child Adolescent Psychiatry, 36, 162–3.

Scahill, L., and Koenig, K. (1999) Pharmacotherapy in children with Pervasive Developmental Disorders. Journal of Child and Adolescent Psychiatric Nursing, 12, 41–3.

Smits, M.G., van Stel, H.F., and van der Heijden, K. (2003) Melatonin improves health status and sleep in children with idiopathic chronic sleep-onset insomnia: A randomized placebo-controlled trial. Journal of the American Academy of Child and Adolescent Psychiatry, 42, 1286–93.

Snead, R.W., Boon, F., and Presburg, J. (1994) Paroxetine for self-injurious behavior. Journal of the American Academy of Child and Adolescent Psychiatry, 33, 909–910.

Steingard, R.J., Zimnitzky, B., and DeMaso, D.R. (1997) Sertraline treatment of transition-associated anxiety and agitation in children with autistic disorder. Journal of Child and Adolescent Psychopharmacology, 7, 9–15.

Towbin, K.E. (2003) Strategies for pharmacologic treatment of high functioning autism and Asperger syndrome. Child and Adolescent Psychiatric Clinics of North America, 12, 23–45.

Valiquette, G. (2002) Risperidone in children with autism and serious behavioral problems: Comment. New England Journal of Medicine, 347, 1890–1.

Van Engeland, H. (2000) Atypical neuroleptics and autism. European Neuropsychopharmacology, 10, Supl 3, 151–2.

CHAPTER 12

Meeting the educational needs of the student with Asperger Syndrome through assessment, advocacy, and accommodations

Georgina Rayner

Case example: Ben

Ben is a six-year-old boy with Asperger Syndrome. His mother received a call one day from his school warning that Ben was going to be expelled as he was "willfully not paying attention nor following instructions".

Ben presented as having a nasal speech quality along with other speech problems. He had an advanced vocabulary and was found to be gifted by a psychologist. He displayed poor graphomotor skills and was obsessed with toy transformers. He had tics and unusual behaviours that the teacher found difficult to manage. The parents took Ben to his paediatrician on the school's suggestion and Ben was medicated with stimulants. There was no change in his behaviour. Ben spent a great deal of his day sitting in the principal's office on the bench crying, and insisting that he was "not a bad boy".

Ben was sent for an auditory processing test. It was subsequently recommended that tubes be inserted immediately as he had so much fluid in his middle ears, he could hear very little. It was found that he had a central auditory processing disorder and was highly sensitive to sound. On questioning the school, it was noted that Ben was most unsettled at recess, lunch, music, gym, and in the hallways, as well as during reading groups in the classroom.

Ben used an FM system for three months and subsequently a sound field system was put in the class. Ben calmed down almost immediately as the sound system reduced the white noise of the class by 50%. To prevent the over-stimulation of people touching him in the hall, he and another boy now come in five minutes before the bell to hold the doors for the other students. In the gym and music classes, he is using a pair of earplugs. Ben is now being taught how to type on a computer and his written output has increased significantly. In the future, Ben may need to be in a small communication class where he will have fewer stimuli to disturb him. Fortunately, he is now being seen for his strengths instead of his weaknesses.

Introduction

Families with a child with Aspergers Syndrome (AS) experience frustration, anxiety, and challenges in their quest for a normal educational, social, and emotional life for their child. Parents face various challenges as they deal with symptoms, assessments, diagnosis, and social service, medical, and educational systems. Similarly, the school experience can be a difficult one for children with AS since they struggle with academic, social, and emotional demands (Marks *et al.* 2000). School personnel may be unfamiliar with AS or the resulting needs of the student with AS. Often, parents must become case managers and educational advocates for their child.

This chapter will review some of the issues which children and youth with AS face in educational settings. The process of assessment and diagnosis will be reviewed, followed by a discussion of parents' rights and roles. Placement issues specific to the child with AS will be addressed, as will possible accommodations that are relevant to these students. Finally, the role of the advocate is summarized and followed by a case illustrating the complexity of accommodating the unique needs of students with AS. This discussion is based on the author's experience as an educational advocate for students with special needs, including those with AS, and as a member of special education committees. Discussion of the assessment of the unique cognitive profile, and the specific teaching approaches required in light of this, is beyond the scope of this chapter. Detailed discussion of assessment and academic approaches can be found in the books by Cumine, Leach, and Stevenson (1998), Myles and Simpson (1998), and Myles and Adreon (2001).

Assessments and diagnosis

For a student with AS, success in school will be dependent on the proper assessments and diagnosis. Unless the student receives the appropriate identification, placement, and individualized program, her chances for success will be significantly compromised. Most school systems deliver special education using the deficit-based model. The needs of students are met by judging what they cannot do and where they are failing, be it in the social, emotional, academic or psychological areas. All too often, students with AS are judged by their symptoms and placed inappropriately, sometimes in a behaviour class.

Symptoms may vary and change in students with AS depending on the stimuli of the day. Inappropriate behaviours are often the result of a need not being met in the educational setting. Because these students are usually very verbally adept, there is a presumption of competence. This makes the proper identification for educational purposes problematic as teachers feel these students with high intelligence can behave, but choose not to comply. This leads to frustration for the student, parent, and teacher. Therefore, a careful investigation of the student's strengths and areas of weakness, leading to the appropriate accommodations, needs to occur.

It is critical that parents and teachers recognize that AS is a diagnosis delineated in the *DSM-IV* (APA 1994) and that the school team, psychologist or family doctor may not have the necessary training or experience with AS to make a diagnosis. Although teachers or other educational personnel may assist by recognizing traits of AS in an undiagnosed student, the official diagnosis must be made by a psychiatrist, psychologist, or medical doctor trained in this field.

Before the diagnostic assessment the following assessments should be considered: (1) a medical examination to ensure there are no physiological problems; (2) a vision examination; (3) an auditory examination including a central auditory processing test and a sound sensitivity test; (4) an occupational therapy assessment to look at fine and gross motor skills; and (5) a multisensory assessment to determine levels of sensitivity. Armed with the results of this battery of tests, the parent can then make an appointment with a psychiatrist or a registered psychologist.

The results of this testing will be essential for a diagnostician determining the psychological profile of the student. For instance, a student with a central auditory processing problem will have difficulty with a great number of the psychological test instruments, as they are auditory-based and timed. A student who has a slow processing speed or hears sound differently may not do well on the test. If the student does in fact have auditory issues, the parent should ask what test instruments will be used, and how they will reflect their child's true abilities. The same problem will arise with tests requiring fine and gross motor skills. If the occupational therapy assessment report indicates a fine motor skill problem and printing or writing output is significantly impaired, the test instruments used by the psychologist may have a negative effect on the evaluation of the student's abilities.

Parent rights and roles

It is imperative for parents to realize their expertise in understanding their child. Parents often know long before their child starts school that something is amiss. They should keep a journal on their child. Information about the onset of speech, milestones, and early behaviours are important for the diagnostician in evaluating the child. Parents are often frustrated just coping from day to day but it is important to document such information, as it will help in developing the child's profile and diagnosis.

The following are some of the warning signs that parents may see at home and school that will help in profiling their child for professional assessment (Koculym and Rayner 2003). The child:

- displays unusual or no response to emotional situations
- dislikes loud noises and crowded places
- shows signs of stress including crying and temper tantrums
- is unusually clumsy
- tells parents he or she feels "dumb" or "stupid"
- is excessively fearful of being the focus of everyone's attention
- is reluctant to go to school
- appears to have no friends
- has difficulty completing homework and assignments.

Parents have an important role in dealing with all the professionals assessing their child. They must constantly remind them to look at the *whole* child. To look at each aspect of the child's profile in isolation may result in an incorrect diagnosis. Professionals need to compile all the reports and share them with the other appropriate professionals. It is vital to ensure that each assessment report contains a set of proactive recommendations, which can be used to improve the life of the student. A resource such as *The Advocate's Journal* (Koculym and Rayner 2003) is an equalization tool, which helps parents to be proactive, organized, and informed.

Parents need to be cautious with respect to their privacy. They should be careful about signing release-of-information forms for schools to speak to their doctors. Parents may, instead, ask the school what reports they wish and obtain them from the professionals themselves. This is an opportunity to make sure the parent knows what is being shared and with whom. Parents need to be in control of their information so they remain active participants in the process instead of passive observers. There is information that is disclosed during psychiatric consultations that does not need to be shared with schools. If parents sign a release-of-information form, they should ask: (1) why the school needs to speak to their doctor, (2) what information the school wishes to know, (3) who will have access to this information, (4) for how long the consent will be in effect, (5) where the information will be housed, and (6) what the procedures are for removing the information from the school file. Guarding their privacy and that of their child can be stressful for parents of a child with AS.

The author has been involved in circumstances in which information about the child and family was shared that did not need to be. For example, one boy seen for a psychiatric consultation had been conceived by artificial insemination. This was written in the psychiatric notes and should not have been shared with the school. In this case, the mother had signed a release-of-information form and the doctor, by law, had to send a copy of the child's file. In another case, a teacher said to the parents at a school special education meeting that it was not surprising that their children had problems since they were both adopted. The parents had never shared the information about their children's adoption with the school, but the school requested the parents sign a release form to obtain information from a preschool treatment centre they had attended with the children.

Parents of children with AS usually act as their child's case manager. However, they may consider taking an advocate with them to their meetings, especially if they feel that the meeting will be excessively stressful. The advocate, or third party, assists the parents with organization, understanding the "system", listening, translating, mediation, and communication.

Issues specific to Asperger Syndrome and classroom placement

Parents seeking assistance in the school system need to be prepared to present their child's case so the child is placed in the most enabling environment. Sadly, one of the most difficult jobs a parent has is to try to protect their child from bullying. Children can be cruel and AS children attract more than their share of bullying as they are socially different. They strive to be like everyone else and are emotionally devastated when they are rejected. They are seldom picked to be on teams or included in group play.

The most difficult times of the day for many AS students are unstructured times such as recess, lunch, gym class, music, lining up, or a noisy time in the classroom. Here, the child's sensitivity to over-stimulation or multiple stimuli causes behaviours that he may be unable to control. Instead of looking at the cause of the breakdown, the child may be disciplined by loss of recess or time-out in the principal's office. The self-esteem of the child suffers even more as he may not understand what he did that was inappropriate. The school staff may feel that they can change the behaviours by deprivation or behaviour modification techniques. The caring teacher who can include the student, despite difficulties, is therefore paramount to the student's academic and behavioural success.

Parents can be proactive in planning for their children at school. First, they can make a list of what works for the child at home. They may also report things that their child does well and what they think the child needs to be successful. Then, they need to share their lists with the school staff and work on a collaborative plan. It is important to focus on the positive to try to change the negative, and to remember the "whole child".

When parents attend the meeting for special education at the school, they should share copies of all reports available. They should also listen to the school staff give their reports. The school staff will create a dot-to-dot portrait of their child. It is up to the parent to colour the picture by sharing information about the child at home and during play. The school has the child for five hours a day and parents have them for 19. Parents often need to remind the school that their child is sensitive and has emotions that need to be addressed. The placement committee may need reminders of what the child can do. In turn they can use the child's strengths to build an educational plan for success. Sometimes school personnel need to be reminded that the child with AS is not misbehaving "on purpose", and that it is part of her diagnostic profile.

Attending school is a right guaranteed by the UN Rights of the Child. In Canada, the child has this right and must attend school at the age of six. If the child has a special need, identification and placement meetings can be held as soon as the child is on the school registry. For some students, it could mean identification as early as the age of four. Early intervention with support and services then become a right for the student. Parents are often counselled not to label their children. However, a label is often required in order to qualify for supports and services. It should be noted that labels can be changed or removed through annual reviews.

It is essential to understand that AS is a social and communication disorder, and not something that can be changed solely by behaviour modification approaches. In some jurisdictions, if the diagnostician provides a diagnosis of AS with a Nonverbal Learning Disability (NVLD), schools will treat the student differently. Schools will then place the student in programming designed to help the learning disabled instead of focussing on problematic behaviours. Students with AS need to be with others where they see models of appropriate behaviours, not in a classroom where they tend to learn maladaptive ones.

When a child is identified as exceptional, it becomes mandatory for the school board to prepare an Individual Education Plan (IEP). There have been many cases brought before the Canadian Human Rights Commission by parents who feel their children are not receiving the proper accommodations and modifications as outlined in the Education Act. The Canadian Human Rights Commission ruled in 2002 that an IEP is a legal binding document and the child then has the right to expect and secure services. Accommodations are rights and not privileges. Governments enact legislation and expect the boards to comply and carry out the legislative mandates. Unfortunately, this is not always the case, especially where boards choose to embrace the philosophy of total integration and ignore the requirements to maintain a range of placements. In most legislation, the government requires boards to provide placements across the spectrum from the least intrusive – a regular class – to the most restrictive – a small class. The availability of various levels of academic supports, as illustrated in the cascading model (Figure 12.1), allows for the right fit to meet the child's changing needs. Inclusion, one of the options in the range of placements, without suitable supports is inappropriate and leads to further frustration for the child and parents. Enforcement of these mandates has become problematic. Fortunately, parents are becoming better educated about their rights and those of their child and are demanding more accountability from school boards. All children have the right to an education, including those with special needs.

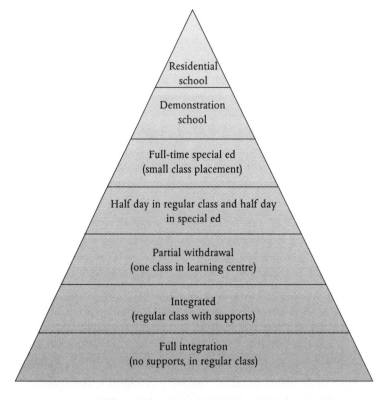

Figure 12.1 The cascading model. Adapted from Webber and Bennett (1999)

Placement should always be based on the child's needs, not the school board's philosophical leaning or perceived financial constraints. Some AS children will do fine in a regular class while others need the security of a small communication class. In a smaller class, there will be fewer external stimuli. AS students do not do well in open concept schools as the noise is too overwhelming for their sensitivities. Another important factor in the placement of the child is the skill and competence of the teacher.

Parents of children with AS are often encouraged to lobby for an educational assistant to be assigned to their child. For some children, working with a teaching assistant is the only way to survive school and they work well with this support; for others, it is perceived as stigmatizing. Few jurisdictions require educational assistants to have any formal education or training in special education. To have an "unqualified baby-sitter" connected to the child for classroom management is counter-productive to the development of the child. It is important to remember that wherever a student with AS is placed, she needs a good teacher who is trained in special education and AS. This person will be crucial if the child is to thrive in school.

Accommodations for students with Asperger Syndrome

There are many ways to accommodate a student with AS in the school setting. Some accommodations come with no expenses, requiring only goodwill, while others may have considerable costs associated with them.

Students with AS often interpret communication literally, and have difficulty with metaphors and "reading between the lines". They need direct instruction that is clear and concise. This tendency may get them into trouble and they may not understand why. Take the case of Stan who, after receiving a test paper, got up from his seat and went to the corner of the room. When the teacher asked what he was doing, he explained he was doing what she asked: writing his name in the right corner. When he was told he would have to pull up his socks, he showed the teacher he did not have socks on that day. His responses reflected his very literal understanding and did not please the teacher!

Technological advances have been advantageous for students with AS. Their poor graphomotor skills and executive function disorders can be addressed with computers that have voice-to-text, writing, and text-to-voice software. Some examples of useful software include *Dragon Naturally Speaking* (21st Century Eloquence 2004), *Inspiration* (Inspiration Software 2004), and *Kurzweil 3000* (Kurzweil Educational Systems 2004). Technological interventions allow the student to produce work at a much higher level, closer to her high verbal skills. Output can also be enhanced in mathematics by the use of a calculator. Educators and parents need to remember that rote memory work does not make a student competent in mathematics. For example, students may have all the multiplication tables memorized and yet not be able to apply them to a particular problem. It is much more important that the student understand the mathematical concepts and how to apply them, and uses a calculator for the mechanics.

Careful attention needs to be given to sensory stimuli. A child's hyper-sensitivities to some stimuli may lead to unusual and unwanted behaviours. This is where the results and recommendations of the occupational therapy and sensory tests can be implemented. There are specific desensitizing activities that will reduce the child's sensitivities. For instance, music therapy has had some success with some children as it allows them to focus on tasks presented. Some children have extreme tactile sensitivities. They may need all the tags removed from clothing. Some boys may need to wear boxer shorts to alleviate the stress caused by the snugness of their jockey briefs. Myles and Simpson (1998) report that some children are bothered by the noise from fluorescent lights. The use of desk lamps has been attempted in some schools.

Snoezelen rooms are now being added to many schools where children with AS and autism spectrum disorders with extreme sensitivities are enrolled. The Snoezelen room is intended to be a safe and non-threatening environment where students can enjoy multisensory stimulation (FlagHouse Canada 2004). Reports of the use of Snoezelen rooms with these students are encouraging and more children with AS need to experience this therapy.

The recommendations of an audiologist after sound sensitivity testing may bring relief to the over-stimulated child. For example, auditory sensitivities can be addressed with the use of FM systems or surround-sound field systems. Often, the child with AS functions better in a quiet classroom. For example, there are some schools where tennis balls have been placed on the ends of all chair and table legs to prevent noises when moving them. Sometimes, children with hypersensitivities to sound are assumed to have Attention Deficit Hyperactivity Disorder (ADHD). As a result, some schools have encouraged parents to visit their family doctor and have the child put on stimulants. Parents need to ensure that their child does indeed have ADHD and that a specialist medical doctor makes the diagnosis of ADHD before the child commences any form of treatment.

Homework can be very problematic for students with AS. Tutors, carefully selected, can alleviate familial stress and bring a fresh perspective to remediate and reinforce the curriculum gaps as identified on the IEP. Positive communication between home, school, and the tutor can lead to better success for the child. Parents should attend to the following issues when considering a tutor: the tutor's educational qualifications and background (knowledge of AS), references, accessibility, and willingness to collaborate with school, parents, and other professionals; tools and techniques used by the tutor; how the tutor relates to special needs children; the reporting process; and cost (Koculym and Rayner 2003).

It is crucial that home and school work as a team in preparing, delivering and evaluating the program and its accommodations for a student with AS. The same consistency experienced at home should be experienced at school and *vice versa*. Success for the AS student will depend on how well the team works.

The following is a general list of accommodations which may help the child with AS (Cumine, Leach, and Stevenson 1998; Myles and Simpson 1998; Ontario Ministry of Education 2001; Tourette Syndrome Foundation of Canada 2001; Safran 2002; Stewart 2002; Koculym and Rayner 2003):

Instructional accommodations

The following are helpful:

- a quiet and well-structured classroom with direct instruction
- preferential seating away from fans, air-conditioning, bells, speakers, pencil sharpeners
- selective grouping of students for projects requiring co-operation between children
- consistent daily routines with limited transitions and surprises
- a non-rotary program to limit changes and number of school personnel
- prompting and preparation for transitions
- a daily schedule posted in the classroom, and taped to the top of the student's desk
- technological aids: computer, FM or surround-sound system, tape recorder, calculator
- models of assignments and behaviours
- breaking assignments down into parts
- extended time for projects, tests, and quizzes
- alternative formats for assessment such as oral or computer assisted
- testing in a quiet area free of noises and distractions
- use of a scribe
- copies of teacher's notes or peer note sharing
- books on tape
- use of graph paper for mathematics

- reduced handwriting expectations
- help with executive functioning
- assistance in organizing notes
- colour-coded subjects
- storing of finished work in a safe place
- teaching of time management skills
- specialized physical education program to address motor deficits.

Social, emotional, and behavioural accommodations

The following are helpful:

- recess with support to promote social competence with peers
- predictable and safe environment
- protection from teasing and bullying
- regular and positive communication with home and professionals
- a prearranged cue for the student to request a break
- a record of triggers that set off unwanted behaviours
- repetition and review to solidify concepts, behaviour, and expectations
- anxiety dealt with proactively
- support provided around social disappointments
- use of a mirror for learning facial expressions
- education on bullying and teaching of coping strategies
- clear and predictable rules and consequences.

Case example: Rachel

Rachel is a ten-year-old girl with AS who has extreme sensory sensitivities. She constantly pulled at clothing in her genital area. The school felt she was being sexually deviant and masturbating and that perhaps this was a symptom of sexual abuse. The family was reported to the local child protection agency, which conducted a thorough investigation of the family. The parents were devastated. No child abuse was found and consequently all trust in the school was lost. The school then ordered the parents to clothe Rachel in shirts that buttoned in the crotch and overalls so she would be unable to remove her underwear. Unfortunately, nobody realized that the texture of the tight-fitting clothing was bothering her.

Rachel was removed from the regular classroom and placed with an educational assistant in the photocopy storeroom to prevent her from displaying her "antisocial" behaviours to her classmates. She did not go out for recess unless accompanied by the educational assistant who did not let her associate with other children. She ate her lunch in the storeroom with the educational assistant. Suggested therapies from the occupational therapist to desensitize her were ignored as the educational assistant was not trained and did not know how to implement them. She was not allowed to go on any school field trips unless a parent took time off work to go along. Rachel stayed secluded from the regular class for the whole school year. Her abilities to communicate and socialize with other students deteriorated. She only related to the educational assistant and became dependent on her. Because Rachel experienced low self-esteem and no self-worth, this was interpreted as her being incapable of benefiting from a regular class. The school felt Rachel was functioning at a kindergarten level, instead of a Grade 5 level.

Her parents took their daughter to a psychiatrist and psychologist not associated with the school system. Her diagnosis of AS was confirmed as well as her severe sensory problems. She tested gifted in some areas and functioning at grade level even though she had not had any formal teaching from a qualified teacher in over a year. It was determined that she was behind in mathematics. A meeting at the school has now placed Rachel in a regular Grade 6 classroom, with the help of an assistant. A mini Snoezelen room has been added to the school where she can go to calm down when she becomes too over-stimulated. She is receiving remedial help in mathematics and doing grade-level work in all other areas of the curriculum. There are still many gaps in her IEP that need to be addressed. The parents have filed a human rights complaint on behalf of their daughter for the treatment she received at school.

References

APA (American Psychiatric Association) (1994) *Diagnostic and Statistical Manual of Mental Disorders, Fourth Edition.* Washington, DC: APA.

Cumine, V., Leach, J., and Stevenson, G. (1998) *Asperger Syndrome: A Practical Guide for Teachers.* London, UK: David Fulton Publishers.

FlagHouse Canada (2004) *Snoezelen® Sensory World™.* North York, ON: FlagHouse. (www.flaghouse.com)

Inspiration Software (2004) *Inspiration.* Bend, OR: Inspiration Software Inc. (www.engaging minds.com/inspiration)

Koculym, C., and Rayner, G. (2003) *The Advocate's Journal.* Kenora, ON: CSP Print and Marketing.

Kurzweil Educational Systems (2004) *Kurzweil 3000.* Bedford, MA: Kurzweil Educational Systems, Inc. (www.kurzweiledu.com)

Marks, S.U., Schrader, C., Longaker, T., and Levine, M. (2000) Portraits of three adolescent students with Asperger's syndrome: Personal stories and how they can inform practice. *Journal of the Association for Persons with Severe Handicaps, 25*, 1, 3–17.

Myles, B.S., and Adreon, D. (2001) *Asperger Syndrome and Adolescence: Practical Solutions for School Success.* Shawnee Mission, KS: Autism Asperger Publishing Co.

Myles, B.S., and Simpson, R. (1998) *Aspergers Syndrome: A Guide for Educators and Parents.* Austin, Texas: Pro-Ed.

Ontario Ministry of Education (2001) *Special Education: A Guide for Educators.* Toronto, ON: Government of Ontario Publishers.

Safran, J. (2002) Supporting students with Aspergers Syndrome in general education. *Teaching Exceptional Children, 34*, 5, 60–6.

Stewart, K. (2002) *Helping a Child with Nonverbal Learning Disorder or Aspergers Syndrome.* Oakland, CA: New Harbinger.

Tourette Syndrome Foundation of Canada (2001) *Understanding Tourette Syndrome: A Guide for Educators.* Toronto, ON: Tourette Syndrome Foundation of Canada.

21st Century Eloquence (voice recognition specialists) (2004) *Dragon Naturally Speaking.* (www.voicerecognition.com)

Weber, K., and Bennett, S. (1999) *Special Education in Ontario Schools, Fourth Edition.* Palgrave, ON: Highland Press.

CHAPTER 13

Sensory and motor differences for individuals with Asperger Syndrome: Occupational therapy assessment and intervention

Paula Aquilla, Ellen Yack, and Shirley Sutton

Case example: Jim

Jim's alarm clock rings at 7 a.m. to ensure that he is not late for work. The sound of the buzzer startles him and he remains startled as he heads for the shower. The water spraying on his body hurts, so Jim stands back against the shower wall. Although he has been told about the importance of hygiene, he does not like the feel of the washcloth and quickly soaps and washes off. Jim dresses in the uniform that he is required to wear at work but immediately becomes irritated by the stiff collar around his neck. He goes into the kitchen to make breakfast. His roommates are in the kitchen and he becomes distracted by their conversation and spills coffee on the counter. Jim takes the bus to work and must stand as there are no seats. He has poor balance and hangs tightly on to the pole, as he is fearful he may fall. The bus is crowded and he cannot see where his hands are on the pole. As his body awareness is poor, Jim becomes anxious because he is uncertain about how to reposition his hand on the pole whenever he is jostled. He starts to become nauseous from the various smells. He hums and rocks to make himself feel better but people start to stare at him, making him feel more nervous. Jim finally arrives at work in a distressed and anxious state. He has difficulty concentrating on his work and yells at a co-worker who brushes by him. Once again, Jim needs to meet with his supervisor to talk about how he can control his temper better.

Introduction

It is critical for Jim's supervisor, as well as other significant people in his life, to be aware of how his sensory processing and motor differences influence his behaviour and ability to perform everyday activities. The theory of sensory integration helps provide this awareness and is a fundamental frame of reference utilized by occupational therapists (OTs).

When Hans Asperger (1944) first described AS, the children in his study exhibited hypersensitivities as well as hyposensitivities to different types of tactile, auditory, and gustatory stimuli. The four children in Asperger's original paper were all described as having awkward movement patterns. When Lorna Wing (1981) used Asperger's criteria to diagnose 34 children presenting with related characteristics, 90% demonstrated impaired motor skills related to performance of gross motor games and penmanship. A growing body of literature addresses the sensory and motor differences that many individuals with AS experience. Entire books are devoted to this topic (Myles *et al.* 2000; Bogdashina 2003). Although the sensory and motor challenges experienced by individuals with AS are not currently reflected in diagnostic criteria (APA 1994), management of these challenges needs to be an integral part of clinical and educational programs.

This chapter will explore the range of sensory and motor differences experienced by individuals with Asperger Syndrome (AS). The theory of sensory integration will be discussed as it facilitates understanding of sensory and motor challenges and guides assessment and intervention practices (Baranek 2002). With their knowledge of the theory and practice of sensory integration, OTs are important members of the multidisciplinary teams that provide services to individuals with AS (Yack, Sutton, and Aquilla 1998; Murray-Slutsky and Paris 2000; Miller-Kuhaneck 2001). Their role in assessment and treatment will be reviewed and specific strategies will be provided.

Sensory differences in autism spectrum disorders and Asperger Syndrome

Baranek (2002) provides an informative review of the literature within the last 30 years that addresses the sensory differences experienced by individuals with autism spectrum disorders (ASDs). Based on this review, the literature suggests that 42% to 88% of children with an ASD show some levels of hypo- or hyper-responsivity to sensory input, display a preoccupation with sensory aspects of objects, and/or have distorted perceptions. The atypical responses to sensory input were associated with both social and non-social input and strengths were reported in visual processing and visual-spatial skills.

Bettison (1994) reported that 65% of parents of children with autism noted that their children displayed mild to severe distress in response to various types of auditory input. In one study, the files of 200 children with autistic disorder were reviewed and it was found that 39% were under-reactive, 19% were over-sensitive, 36% displayed mixed sensitivities, and 100% had auditory processing dysfunction (Greenspan and Wieder 1998). Kientz and Dunn (1997) used a standardized assessment tool (The Sensory Profile: Dunn 1999) and reported significant differences between typical children and children with autism in the areas of auditory and tactile responses. Others recognized that 30 young children with autism showed significant differences compared with a control group in responses to auditory, tactile, visual, gustatory, and vestibular sensory stimuli (Talay-Ongan and Wood 2000).

Autobiographical reports most commonly note hyper-reactivity to sensory input (Grandin and Scariano 1986; Cesaroni and Garber 1991; Stelhi 1991; Williams 1992, 1994; Grandin 1995). Cesaroni and Garber (1991) also note hypo-reactivity and mixed sensory perception.

Some studies are specific to sensory differences in AS. For instance, Dunn, Myles, and Orr (2002) conducted a study on 42 children with AS which provided empirical evidence about the atypical sensory processing patterns of this population. The Sensory Profile (Dunn 1999), which is a 125-item question-naire, was used to compare parental descriptions of the responses of children with AS to sensory input with those of a group of typically developing children. The children with AS displayed significantly different patterns of sensory processing when compared with their peers. Both hyper-responsiveness and hypo-respon-siveness were noted in reaction to auditory and tactile input. The authors postulated that this variability reflects faulty or poor sensory modulation.

Many authors have hypothesized that impaired sensory processing contrib-utes to some of the atypical behaviours used to diagnose AS (Gillberg 1992; Attwood 1998; Myles *et al.* 2000; Huebner 2001; Dunn, Saiter, and Rinner 2002). These behaviours include restricted patterns of interest, inflexible adherence to routines or rituals, stereotypic movement patterns, and preoccupa-tion with objects. Temple Grandin (1995; Grandin and Scariano 1986) reports that many of her stereotypic behaviours were strategies she developed to cope with her hyper-reactivity to auditory and tactile input. Bogdashina (2003) relates unusual sensory processing to the different perceptual and cognitive styles dem-onstrated by individuals with AS.

For any individual with impaired sensory processing, many aspects of daily living can be affected (Ayres 1972, 1979; Bundy, Lane, and Murray 2002). The challenges faced by children and adults with AS are exacerbated when impaired sensory processing patterns are present. Anxiety and arousal levels can be heightened and emotional and general self-regulation can be seriously disrupted. Execution of self-care routines, socialization with peers, and general quality of life can be affected. Furthermore, roles as student, employee, or member of the community can be compromised. Social skills programs can be effective in helping individuals with AS to integrate successfully into educational and vocational settings. However, if the preschooler screams and hides under the table when "Happy Birthday" is sung, or the young adult begins to rock and loudly hum in a crowded cafeteria, acceptance from peers and successful inclusion can be hindered.

Motor differences in autism spectrum disorders and Asperger Syndrome

Both Kanner (1943) and Asperger (1944) included descriptions of motor awkwardness in their accounts of the children they studied, but only recently has there been an increased focus on the motor differences experienced by these groups. Damasio and Maurer (1978) and Maurer and Damasio (1982) formulated neurological models of autism, which identified disturbances in gait patterns as well as other motor impairments. Hill and Leary (1993) and Donnellan and Leary (1995) reviewed movement disturbances common in developmental disorders and compared these disturbances with those found in adult neurology. They reported many similarities between autism and Parkinson's disease and proposed strategies designed to accommodate for these motor disturbances. Manjiviona and Prior (1995) proposed that most children with high-functioning autism (HFA) and AS have motor impairments.

Stone and colleagues (1990) found that motor imitation was the most important characteristic that differentiated children with autism from typically developing children and groups with intellectual disability, hearing impairments, and language impairments. Children with autism had more difficulty imitating facial expressions than a matched group of children with Down Syndrome in the research by Loveland et al. (1994). Hughs (1996) reported that children with autism had greater difficulty completing motor planning tasks compared with a matched group with cognitive delays. Others have noted that, of 200 children diagnosed with autistic disorder, all exhibited motor planning problems and 48% were identified as having severe motor planning dysfunction (Greenspan and Wieder 1998). They also reported that 17% of these children exhibited low muscle tone. Dawson et al. (1998) reported on motor planning difficulties in children with autism who displayed greater difficulty on tasks, requiring imitation with objects and hand imitation and facial imitation, compared with typically developing as well as cognitively delayed children. Problems were noted with both immediate as well as delayed imitation.

In the literature on AS there is debate about the usefulness in using different motor characteristics to differentiate the various sub-types of ASDs (Smith and Bryson 1994). There is also literature that discusses the possibility that motor differences can also be used to distinguish individuals with AS from those with HFA. Ghaziuddin and colleagues (1994) studied nine children with HFA and 11 children with AS. They found no significant difference between performances on fine and gross motor testing but noted that both groups performed well below average. Scores were not related to cognitive abilities. They speculated that their motor delays were related to impaired motor co-ordination and planning, problems with information processing, visual-spatial perception, and sensory processing. Rogers's group (1996) studied adolescents with HFA and found significant differences in performance of single and sequential hand tasks and sequential facial imitation when compared to typically developing adolescents. Charman *et al.* (1997) compared ten children with HFA at the age of 20 months and found significantly reduced ability to imitate simple actions with four novel objects when compared to typically developing toddlers. A study of 20 children with HFA found significant differences in performance of single hand postures compared to matched controls (Smith and Bryson 1998). It has also been noted that 19 adolescents with HFA had more difficulty on imitation tasks than a matched group with dyslexia and specific problems have been identified with kinesthetic aspects of postures and movements (Bennetto, Pennington, and Rogers 1999).

One of the most frequently cited motor disturbances in the literature appears to be impaired praxis or motor planning difficulties with specific problems noted with imitation. "Praxis" involves the ability to form an idea about an action (ideation), plan an action (motor planning) and execute the planned action (Ayres 1979). Difficulties with ideation can be observed when a child is presented with a toy and cannot conceive of the actions required to activate or manipulate the toy. Impaired sensory integration can result in praxis difficulties (Bundy *et al.* 2002). If the brain receives inaccurate information from the tactile, proprioceptive, and vestibular systems, inadequate body awareness can result. An efficient body scheme is needed to plan and sequence actions accurately. Impaired ideation and motor planning contributes to delays and inconsistencies in all areas of motor development. The theory of sensory integration contributes to our understanding of the motor impairments as well as the sensory differences experienced by many individuals with AS.

The theory of sensory integration

The theory of sensory integration is an indispensable framework when working with individuals with AS. The theory was first postulated by occupational therapist Jean Ayres (1972, 1979) and continues to evolve (Fisher, Murray, and Bundy 1991; Bundy *et al.* 2002). The theory relates the neurological process of sensory integration to sensory motor development and behaviour. This framework can assist with understanding sensory and motor differences in AS, provide insight into behaviour and social-emotional development, and optimize assessment and intervention procedures. Sensory integration is a term used to describe the ability of the nervous system to receive and use sensory information. The process of sensory integration involves five interrelated components: (1) sensory registration, (2) orientation to sensory events, (3) interpretation of sensory events, (4) organization of responses, and (5) execution of responses (Williamson and Anzalone 1997).

First, sensory registration provides awareness that a sensory event has occurred. Specialized sensory receptors provide information about touch, sound, smell, taste, sight, body position (proprioceptive awareness), movement, and gravitational changes (vestibular awareness). Proprioceptive receptors are in the muscles, ligaments, and joints, and provide information about body position and changes in body movement. Vestibular receptors are located in the inner ear and provide information about lateral, vertical, and rotary movement, relation to gravity, and head position. A sensory event is not registered until a certain level of intensity or threshold is reached. Individuals have different threshold levels. When an individual has a low threshold for sensory input, minimal input is required in order to be registered. When one has a high threshold, more intense input is required to register a sensory event. In practical terms, the differences in thresholds can be observed when one individual will register the feel of small fibres found on wool clothing while another is oblivious to how wool feels on the skin.

Sensory thresholds vary throughout the day and can change according to previous sensory or emotional experiences, levels of stress, states of wakefulness, and expectations in certain situations. Dunn (1999) and Huebner (2001) offer excellent discussions of sensory thresholds. Characteristics of hyper-registration/low threshold may include concern with insignificant sounds, distress with certain sounds, sensitivity to bright sunlight, sensitivity to glare from television and/or computer screens, discomfort with certain textures, aversion to certain smells and tastes, discomfort with movement (e.g. elevators, escalators, car rides) or avoidance of sensory input. Characteristics of hypo-registration/high threshold might include disregard of certain sounds; lack of awareness of bumping into furniture or people; absence of startle reactions; self-absorption;

lack of attention to environment, persons or things; delayed responses to sensory input; seeking sensory input to meet thresholds; and impaired motor planning because of a lack of body awareness.

The second component of sensory integration, the orientation component, allows attention to specific sensory events and requires efficient sensory modulation. Sensory modulation allows for suppression of irrelevant input to allow attention to relevant information. Sensory modulation is like volume control and allows the brain to disregard irrelevant sensory information while highlighting the important sensory events. Sensory modulation allows a person to become accustomed to and disregard the feel of a bracelet around the wrist while at the same time she is aware that a bug has started to crawl up her arm. When sensory modulation is not intact, a person can be hypo-responsive to important sensory information or hyper-reactive to irrelevant sensory information or alternate between the two extremes. Impaired sensory modulation affects behaviour as it makes it difficult to maintain appropriate levels of arousal and can lead to sensory seeking for the hypo-responsive person and sensory avoidance for the hyper-responsive person. Dunn, Myles, and Orr (2002) identified that children with AS register sensory information differently and suggested problems with sensory modulation.

Third, the interpretation of sensory events determines if sensory input is familiar or unfamiliar, if it is safe or dangerous, if it is pleasurable or unpleasant. Sensory input can alert the body to dangerous situations that require immediate action. The "fright, flight, fight" reaction may occur when sensory input signals possible danger. Individuals who frequently interpret harmless sensory input as being dangerous are described as "sensory defensive". Sensory defensiveness is a type of sensory modulation disorder.

Following the registration, orientation, and interpretation phases, responses to sensory information need to be organized and executed. The child's responses to sensory input often provide insight into the efficiency of the registration, orientation and interpretation phases.

The occupational therapy assessment

OTs focus on the promotion, restoration, and maintenance of productivity in people with a wide range of abilities and disabilities. An occupational therapy assessment can help reveal many of the factors that can interfere with an individual's ability to function in different settings and perform various activities of daily living. The assessment includes evaluation of an individual's underlying abilities including balance and postural reactions, muscle tone and strength, fine/gross/ oral motor planning, visual perception and visual motor integration, attending behaviours, and sensory integration. The individual's ability to perform self-care, community living, pre-academic, play, social, pre-vocational, and vocational, skills are explored. A review of the physical environment, family situation, and community supports is an important part of the assessment process. Occupational therapy assessments are often conducted within multidisciplinary teams and provide other professionals with unique information about occupational performance or an individual's ability to engage in functional activities.

Stuhec and Gisel (2003) note there is a lack of appropriate assessment tools for children with ASDs and state that OTs must either modify standardized test procedures or use non-standardized methods to assess these children. Clinical observations of the quality of motor performance are always conducted by OTs and include observations of muscle tone and strength, body awareness, motor planning abilities, bilateral co-ordination, hand preference, and in-hand manipulation skills. The evaluation may also analyse an individual's ability to complete specific self-care or vocational tasks to determine if any motor impairment is interfering with successful completion of these activities.

OTs analyse whether impaired sensory integration is influencing motor function, perceptual abilities, behaviour, communication or performance of functional activities. The evaluation of sensory integration is quite complex and can include use of standardized assessments as well as a lot of informal "detective work". An excellent standardized assessment is The Sensory Profile (Dunn 1999), which is a questionnaire that can be completed by parents, educators or other caregivers. Another standardized assessment is the Sensory Integration and Praxis Test (SIPT: Ayres 1989). Generally, OTs who have received certification in using this test administer the SIPT. The test evaluates responses to tactile input as well as balance reactions, motor planning abilities, and visual perceptual skills. However, as this test requires a high degree of receptive language, attention, and compliance, it can be difficult to use with this population. There are also non-standardized evaluations of sensory processing that are in questionnaire format and include the Sensory Integration Inventory – Revised for Individuals with Developmental Disabilities (Reisman and Hanschu 1992) and The Sensory Profile Checklist – Revised (Bogdashina 2003).

Responses to sensory input and related behaviours vary across different environments. Arousal and anxiety levels significantly affect sensory processing and atypical behaviours can contribute to unusual responses to sensory input. Fatigue, diet, communication ability, allergies and side effects from medications can also affect responses to sensory input. The Durand Motivation Assessment Scale (Durand and Crimmins 1992) is a useful questionnaire that helps determine if a specific behaviour is motivated by tangible reasons: sensory seeking, escape/avoidance or attention seeking. For example, biting of the hand may reflect an individual's attempt to provide proprioceptive or deep pressure input to help calm an agitated nervous system. However, if the biting only occurs when the individual is presented with a non-preferred activity, it may then represent escape or avoidance behaviours.

An interview with parents, caregivers, educators, and employers is always an integral part of the assessment process as it provides greater insight into the challenges presented by impaired sensory processing and allows for comparison of behaviours across environments. Analysing information documented in questionnaires and discussed in interviews represents the "detective work". As obsessive-like ritualized behaviours are often associated with AS, it is important to analyse whether atypical responses to sensory input represent impaired sensory processing or atypical behavioural patterns. For example, a possible reason for an individual having a restricted diet could be sensitivity to different tastes, smells, and textures. Another possible reason could be that the individual has developed certain rituals around eating and will only ingest foods that are specific colours.

An analysis of home, school or work environments is an important part of an occupational therapy evaluation. Specific environmental factors can facilitate or inhibit an individual's ability to function. The layout of the physical setting, the level of sensory stimulation, the use of visual aids, the amount of structure, the availability of supportive caregivers, educators, supervisors or colleagues, and the nature of required roles and tasks are all examples of factors that can be considered.

Occupational therapy intervention

The OT's role in intervention can take many forms. The intervention provided will naturally depend on assessment results and prioritization of treatment goals, but will also be guided by the nature of the service delivery model under which the OT is employed. OTs provide intervention to individuals with AS through their work in infant and early intervention services, in the school system, in hospital- and clinic-based programs, in private practices, and in vocational settings. Intervention may take the form of direct one-on-one treatment, consultation regarding environmental and equipment adaptation, programming, and education of caregivers, peers, and colleagues.

Anzalone and Williamson (2000) suggest that when children with ASD have associated problems with sensory integration, occupational therapy intervention should focus on increasing parents' or other caregivers' understanding of behaviour, modifying environments according to sensory needs, and providing specific strategies to remediate identified problems. Providing information on sensory processing offers a different perspective on some of the puzzling behaviours exhibited by individuals with AS. Enhanced understanding of the behaviours can lead to more effective and creative solutions as well as increased patience and support.

As consultants, OTs help to create environments, approaches, and activity demands that support the individual with AS in participating optimally in any setting (Anderson 1998; Dunn, Saiter, and Rinner 2002). Questions that can be answered by an OT consultant include: How should the space be organized? What equipment does this person need? How can we get this person to pay attention? What are the right noise and light levels? How can this task be taught?

A "sensory diet" is an intervention strategy that is frequently recommended by OTs. Sensory diets describe combinations of activities and strategies that have been individually designed to provide various types and levels of sensory input (Wilbarger 1995). A sensory diet can improve quality of life as it assists the individual to feel more comfortable and organized throughout the day. It aids with self-regulation and allows for optimum levels of alertness or arousal necessary for participation in and completion of specific activities. A secondary benefit of a sensory diet is that it can help develop trusting relationships as sensory needs become respected and suitable accommodations are made available. Individuals may therefore become more comfortable taking the risks necessary for social interaction and learning. A sensory diet can include a formal schedule of activities offered at specific times throughout the day, activities embedded into daily routines, leisure activities, accommodations to the environment, equipment adaptations, and adjustment of interaction styles according to sensory needs.

Examples of activities to help calm and organize an over-aroused nervous system may include wearing a weighted vest in class, walking to school wearing a heavy weighted knapsack, sucking on a spouted water bottle throughout the day and sitting in a bean bag chair for circle time. Activities to stimulate an under-aroused nervous system may include sucking sour Popsicles, eating spicy foods, quick start and stop movement, and use of a feather for tickling. The sensory diet can be a powerful tool, but it must be dynamic, highly individualized, constantly evaluated, and modified. *The Alert Program for Self-Regulation* (Williams and Shellenberger 1994) and *Sensory Integration Tools for Teens* (Henry, Wheeler, and Sava 2004) are excellent resources for activities that can be included in sensory diets.

Occupational therapy treatment may be recommended when it is determined that hands-on intervention is required to enhance sensory integration, improve praxis or motor planning abilities or develop functional skills. When the goal of treatment is enhancing the process of sensory integration, intervention is characterized by the provision of graded sensory experiences that have been selected to help the child acquire more adaptive behaviours (Ayres 1972, 1979; Fisher *et al.* 1991; Bundy *et al.* 2002). There are other types of sensorimotor approaches used by OTs but they are not as highly individualized. They may include passive sensory stimulation, can be conducted within group situations, and focus on skill development rather than on efficiency of the nervous system.

OTs may work from various frames of reference when treating children with motor planning impairment. The theory of sensory integration may be useful when praxis problems appear related to impaired sensory processing. Cognitive approaches are also used to aid with teaching specific skills and use self-directed verbal guidance to help with the initiation, sequencing, and actual execution of specific skills. When treatment sessions focus on skill development and strength training, home programs are routinely provided.

There is a lack of studies evaluating the efficacy of occupational therapy intervention, but a research base has been developing. One recent study looked at occupational therapy treatment and consultation with five autistic preschoolers and significant improvements in play and social interaction were reported (Case-Smith and Bryan 1999). Another study evaluated the use of weighted vests with preschoolers who had diagnoses of Pervasive Developmental Disorder (Fertel-Daly, Bedell, and Hinojosa 2001). Although the sample size was small, increased attention to tasks and decreased self-stimulatory behaviour were noted as a result of wearing the vests.

Conclusions

OTs need to conduct more research evaluating the efficacy of their interventions and more studies are also necessary to support hypotheses about the relationship between impaired sensory integration and behaviour. However, the demand for occupational therapy services by parents, educators, and other professionals continues to grow as the positive impact of services on quality of life are observed daily. The sensory and motor challenges experienced by individuals with AS need to be explored further by many disciplines. With their understanding of these challenges, OTs can offer the necessary interventions and environmental accommodations that promote active and comfortable participation in an individual's community.

References

Anderson, J. (1998) *Sensory Motor Issues in Autism.* San Antonio, TX: Therapy Skill Builders.

Anzalone, M. and Williamson, G. (2000) Sensory processing and motor performance. In B. Prizant and A. Wetherby (eds) *Autism Spectrum Disorders: A Transactional Perspective.* Baltimore, MD: Paul. H. Brookes.

APA (American Psychiatric Association) (1994) *Diagnostic and Statistical Manual of Mental Disorders, Fourth Edition.* Washington, DC: APA.

Asperger, H. (1944) Die "Autistichen Pyschopathen" im Kindesalter. *Archiv für Psychiatrie und Nervenkrankheiten, 117,* 76–136.

Attwood, T. (1998) *Asperger's Syndrome: A Guide for Parents and Professionals.* London, UK: Jessica Kingsley Publishers.

Ayres, A.J. (1972) *Sensory Integration and Learning Disabilities.* Los Angeles, CA: Western Psychological Services.

Ayres, A.J. (1979) *Sensory Integration and the Child.* Los Angeles, CA: Western Psychological Services.

Ayres, A.J. (1989) *Sensory Integration and Praxis Tests.* Los Angeles, CA: Western Psychological Services.

Baranek, G. (2002) Efficacy of sensory and motor interventions for children with autism. *Journal of Autism and Developmental Disorders, 32,* 5, 397–422.

Bennetto, L., Pennington, B., and Rogers, S. (1999) A componential approach to imitation movement deficits in autism. Manuscript submitted for publication.

Bettison, S. (1994) "Auditory training" as a treatment for sound sensitivity in autism: Preliminary results. *Special Education Perspectives, 3,* 1.

Bogdashina, O. (2003) *Sensory Perceptual Issues in Autism and Asperger Syndrome.* London, UK: Jessica Kingsley Publishers.

Bundy, A., Lane, S., and Murray, E. (eds) (2002) *Sensory Integration Theory and Practice.* Philadelphia, PA: FA Davis Company.

Case-Smith, J., and Bryan, T. (1999) The effects of occupational therapy with sensory integration emphasis on preschool-age children. *American Journal of Occupational Therapy, 53,* 5, 489–97.

Cesaroni, L., and Garber, M. (1991) Exploring the experience of autism through firsthand accounts. *Journal of Autism and Developmental Disorders, 21,* 303–13.

Charman, T., Swittenhan, J., Baron-Cohen, S., Cox, A., Baird, G., and Drew, A. (1997) Infants with autism: An investigation of empathy, pretend play, joint attention and imitation. *Developmental Psychology, 33,* 5, 781–9.

Damasio, A., and Maurer, R. (1978) A neurological model for childhood autism. *Archives of Neurology, 35,* 777–86.

Dawson, G., Meltzoff, A., Osterling, J., and Rinaldi, J. (1998) Neuropsychological correlates of early symptoms of autism. *Child Development, 69,* 5, 1276–85.

Donnellan, A., and Leary, M. (1995) *Movement and Diversity in Autism/Mental Retardation.* Madison, WI: DRI Press.

Dunn, W. (1999) *The Sensory Profile.* San Antonio, TX: Psychological Corp.

Dunn, W., Myles, B.S., and Orr, W. (2002) Sensory processing issues associated with Asperger Syndrome: A preliminary investigation. *American Journal of Occupational Therapy, 56,* 1, 97–102.

Dunn, W., Saiter, J., and Rinner, L. (2002) Asperger Syndrome and sensory processing: A conceptual model and guidance for intervention planning. *Focus on Autism and Other Developmental Disabilities, 17,* 3, 172–85.

Durand, D., and Crimmins, D. (1992) *Motivation Assessment Scale.* Topeka, KS: Monaco and Associates.

Fertel-Daly, D., Bedell, G., and Hinojosa, J. (2001) Effects of a weighted vest on attention to task and self-stimulatory behaviours in preschoolers with pervasive developmental disorders. *American Journal of Occupational Therapy, 55,* 620–40.

Fisher, A., Murray, E., and Bundy, A. (1991) *Sensory Integration Theory and Practice.* Philadelphia, PA: FA Davis Company.

Ghaziuddin, M., Butler, E., Tsai, L., and Ghaziuddin, N. (1994) Is clumsiness a marker for Asperger syndrome? *Journal of Intellectual Disability Research, 38,* 519–27.

Gillberg, C. (1992) Autism and autistic-like conditions: Subclasses among disorders of empathy. *Journal of Child Psychology and Psychiatry, 33,* 813–42.

Grandin, T. (1995) *Thinking in Pictures and Other Reports from My Life with Autism.* New York, NY: Doubleday.

Grandin, T., and Scariano, M. (1986) *Emergence: Labeled Autistic.* Novato, CA: Arena Press.

Greenspan, S., and Wieder, S. (1998) *The Child with Special Needs: Encouraging Intellectual and Emotional Growth.* Reading, MA: Addison-Wesley.

Henry, D., Wheeler, T., and Sava, D. (2004) *Sensory Integration Tools for Teens.* Youngstown, AZ: Henry OT Services.

Hill, D., and Leary, M. (1993) *Movement Disturbance: A Clue to Hidden Competencies in Persons Diagnosed with Autism and Other Developmental Disabilities.* Madison, WI: DRI.

Huebner, R. (2001) *Autism: A Sensorimotor Approach to Management.* Frederick, MD: Aspen Publishing.

Hughs, C. (1996) Control of action and thought: Normal development and dysfunction in autism: A research note. *Journal of Child Psychology and Psychiatry and Allied Disciplines, 37,* 229–36.

Kanner, L. (1943) Autistic disturbances of affective contact. *Nervous Child, 2,* 217–50.

Kientz, M., and Dunn, W. (1997) A comparison of children with autism and typical children using the Sensory Profile. *American Journal of Occupational Therapy, 51,* 530–7.

Loveland, K., Tunali-Kotoski, B., Pearson, D., Brelsford, K., Ortegon, J., and Chen, R. (1994) Imitation and expression of facial affect in autism. *Development and Psychopathology, 6,* 433–44.

Manjiviona, J., and Prior, M. (1995) Comparison of Asperger syndrome and high-functioning autistic children on a test of motor impairments, *Journal of Autism and Developmental Disorders, 25,* 1, 23–39.

Maurer, R., and Damasio, A. (1982) Childhood autism from the point of view of behavioral neurology. *Journal of Autism and Developmental Disorders, 12,* 195–205.

Miller-Kuhaneck, H. (ed.) (2001) *Autism: A Comprehensive Occupational Therapy Approach.* Baltimore, MD: AOTA.

Murray-Slutsky, C., and Paris, B. (2000) *Exploring the Spectrum of Autism and Pervasive Developmental Disorders.* San Antonio, TX: Therapy Skill Builders.

Myles, B.S., Tapscott-Cook, K., Miller, N., Rinner, L., and Robbins, L. (2000) *Asperger Syndrome and Sensory Issues: Practical Solutions for Making Sense of the World.* Shawnee Mission, KS: Autism Asperger Publishing.

Reisman, J., and Hanschu, B. (1992) *Sensory Integration Inventory – Revised for Individuals with Developmental Disabilities: User's Guide.* Hugo, MN: PDP Press.

Rogers, S., Bennetto, L., McEvoy, R., and Pennington, B. (1996) Imitation and pantomime in high functioning adolescents with autism spectrum disorders. *Child Development, 67,* 2060–73.

Smith, I., and Bryson, S. (1994) Imitation and action in autism: A critical review. *Psychological Bulletin, 116,* 259–73.

Smith, I. and Bryson, S. (1998) Gestures imitation in autism: Nonsymbolic postures and sequences. *Cognitive Neuropsychology, 15,* 6, 747–70.

Stelhi, A. (1991) *The Sound of a Miracle: A Child's Triumph Over Autism.* New York, NY: Doubleday Inc.

Stone, W., Lemanek, K., Fishel, P., Fernandez, M., and Altemeier, W. (1990) Play and imitation skills in the diagnosis of autism in young children. *Pediatrics, 86,* 267–72.

Stuhec, V., and Gisel, E. (2003) Compliance with administration procedures of tests for children with pervasive developmental disorders: Does it exist? *Canadian Journal of Occupational Therapy, 70,* 1, 33–41.

Talay-Ongan, A., and Wood, K. (2000) Unusual sensitivities in autism: A possible crossroads. *International Journal of Disability, Development and Education, 47,* 2, 201–211.

Wilbarger, P. (1995) The Sensory Diet: Activity programs based on sensory processing theory. *Sensory Integration Special Interest Section Newsletter, 18,* 2.

Williams, D. (1992) *Nobody Nowhere.* New York, NY: Times Books.

Williams, D. (1994) *Somebody Somewhere*. New York, NY: Times Books.

Williams, M., and Shellenberger, S. (1994) *How does your Engine Run? The Alert Program For Self-Regulation.* Albuquerque, NM: Therapy Works.

Williamson, G.G., and Anzalone, M.E. (1997) Sensory integration: A key component to the evaluation and treatment of young children with severe difficulties in relating and communicating. *Zero to Three, 17*, 29–36.

Wing, L. (1981) Asperger's syndrome: A clinical account. *Psychological Medicine, 11*, 115–29.

Yack, E., Sutton, S., and Aquilla, P. (1998) *Building Bridges through Sensory Integration: Occupational Therapy for Children with Autism and Other Pervasive Developmental Disorders.* Toronto, ON: Print Three.

CHAPTER 14

Psychological assessment of more able adults with autism spectrum disorders

Lillian Burke

Adults with autism spectrum disorders (ASDs) have been identified as some of our "most vulnerable citizens" (Bryson and Autism Society of Ontario 1991, p.5). It is clear from epidemiological studies that the number of children identified with an ASD has increased in the past two decades (Tidmarsh and Volkmar 2003). However, few of these studies refer to the potential increase in the number of adults being identified. From clinical experience, it is clear that more adults are being referred for assessment and many of them are "more able" (Stoddart, Burke, and Temple 2002). A survey from the UK indicates diagnosis after the age of 16 occurred in 18% of those with autism who were "lower functioning", 29% who were "higher functioning", and 46% of those with Asperger Syndrome (AS) (Barnard *et al.* 2001).

Adults who are "more able" are the focus of this chapter. That is, those with AS, and individuals with autism or Pervasive Developmental Disorder – Not Otherwise Specified (PDD-NOS), who have mild or no intellectual disabilities (i.e. a full-scale IQ greater than 70). These individuals have problems in socialization, in communication, and in using knowledge and skills in a functional way. They may also suffer from emotional or psychological difficulties relating to their symptoms and the impact of the symptoms on their lives. This chapter will include a discussion of the reasons adults are seen for assessment, the process and product of an assessment, characteristics of importance in the assessment, and ways to examine these characteristics.

There is currently little consistency in the assessment and diagnosis of more able adults with ASDs. Therefore, while general information is drawn from the literature, much information comes from this clinician's experience in working with adults who have ASDs, both with and without intellectual disabilities. This experience was gained during assessment, therapy, consultation, and research and in various settings including facilities serving those with intellectual disabilities and/or mental health disorders, community treatment teams, and in private practice.

Diagnosis and services in adulthood

Supports and resources are imperative for adults who have an ASD. It is believed that only 3% of those with AS are able to manage without some support (Powell 2002). Assessment and diagnosis are therefore important on two levels. First, identification of adults with ASDs helps service delivery systems determine what services are needed and the number of people who may need them. Second, at the individual level, diagnosis helps a person understand his specific challenges, provides access to funding and services where they exist, and offers hope for an improved quality of life. As greater numbers of adults present for assessment and diagnosis, it is important that we offer consistency in our assessments, make relevant information available to them, and are able to refer them to appropriate services (Powell 2002).

Referrals for assessment of adults come from many sources: physicians, student support offices, community workers, family, and friends. Referrals may be made because of behavioural difficulties, emotional or psychiatric symptoms, inability to obtain work or disability funding, ongoing difficulties in relation-ships, or changes in the family (e.g. a person living with ageing parents who can no longer provide support). Many individuals referred as adults have never been identified as having an ASD. Sometimes symptoms suggesting an autistic disorder were noted in childhood, but a formal diagnosis was not given or, over time, the information was lost. Others who seek assessments were diagnosed with autism/PDD in childhood and received services. As adults, however, they may have had difficulty accessing supports. Some individuals refer themselves for assessment. This may occur after they have seen a television program, found information on the Internet, or met someone else with an ASD. They may bring lists of symptoms, Internet questionnaires, and other materials to the appoint-ment to support their self-diagnosis.

Stoddart, Burke, and Temple (2002) systematically examined 100 cases of adults with ASDs who had been referred to Surrey Place Centre in Toronto for clinical services. Those who were referred presented with a broader range of skills than had been seen previously, including a greater number who were "higher functioning". They had increasingly complex needs, requiring multidisciplinary assessment and treatment plans. Some individuals had been identified as having "autistic traits" in childhood, but had not met diagnostic criteria for autism. Many in the study lived in settings such as group homes, but had little access to clinical or counselling support. Others lived with ageing parents who did not understand the current service system. Some of those referred had immigrated with their families from less developed countries and needed assistance in finding services.

The setting in which this study was carried out had a mandate to provide services to those with intellectual disabilities. It was felt those with AS may not be served appropriately in that setting, but it was recognized that they could not access suitable services elsewhere in the community. It was also unclear whether they were served better in the adult mental health sector. Many of those referred were (sometimes inappropriately) being treated for diagnoses other than an ASD, including Obsessive Compulsive Disorder, Anxiety Disorder, Schizophrenia, Psychotic Disorder, Personality Disorder, Depression or Mood Disorder, Oppositional Disorder, and Impulse Control Disorder.

The assessment process may be difficult for the person who has an ASD. While referring to community assessments, Powell (2002, p.25) identifies problems that are also relevant when doing a diagnostic assessment. The person may:

- wish to avoid any new social situation due to anxiety
- wish to "fit in" and not want others to know about their difficulties or be "labelled"
- have limited insight and understanding of their own emotional needs
- have sensory/perceptual processing or concentration difficulties impairing their ability to attend to questions
- be unable to process too much verbal information
- suffer from depression
- have a propensity to be "inflexible" or use "black or white thinking"
- not understand what assessment means
- attempt to say the "right thing" and so minimize their difficulties
- not understand choices.

Presentation and assessment of autistic spectrum traits in adulthood

Adults with ASDs do not act the same in an assessment, and will not present with all possible characteristics. They may meet criteria for a diagnosis, but have symptoms that cluster in a manner different to someone else with an ASD.

Individuals may have some behaviours or interests that seem normal on the surface but, when explored, are found to be problematic. For example, a person may say she collects an item as a hobby, which is not unusual. However, if one does this to the exclusion of any other activity, spends all one's money on these items, neglects basic needs, or allows the collection to overtake one's living space, this would suggest an excessive or compulsive interest.

It is helpful for the clinician to observe and interact with an individual in more than one context. Structured situations may elicit a different group of abilities and behaviours to unstructured ones. Some people act differently with a stranger to how they act with a familiar person. The way others interact with a person may also provide important information. It is therefore useful to see the person both alone and with others. Family members or friends may attempt to answer questions directed at their loved one, or the person may defer to them. Family may be accustomed to his behaviour, and no longer take any notice or may rationalize a symptom.

The assessment of a more able person suspected of having an ASD should include information from the person specific to his symptoms or difficulties: interviews with family or friends, observations, historical information, and objective measures (Burke 2001). The combination of tools one uses for assessment will vary according to the estimate of the person's intellectual ability, communication skills, social and pragmatic skills, adaptive abilities, and emotional status, and the reason for the assessment. Supportive documents are useful, such as school records, past assessments, and medical reports.

Clinicians experienced in assessing the more able with ASDs use preferred measures and methods to identify relevant features. Those learning to assess may benefit from using a list of characteristics to watch for during the assessment. One may also benefit from videotaping the sessions. Review of the tape with the supervising clinician allows one to note features that were previously missed.

When children are assessed for ASDs, it is standard to have a team of professionals from various disciplines (e.g. psychiatry, speech and language pathology, occupational therapy, optometry, audiology, genetic counselling). This occurs less frequently with adults because resources are not available. The clinician may decide to request another professional be involved in the assessment or may suggest the individual be referred for services as part of her recommendations.

Characteristics identified in assessments

The specific diagnostic criteria for the diagnosis of each ASD are contained in the *Diagnostic and Statistical Manual* (*DSM-IV*: APA 1994) or in *The International Statistical Classification of Diseases and Related Health Problems* (*ICD-10*: WHO 1992).

Symptoms of ASDs are related to communication and pragmatics, social knowledge/skills, and interests and behaviours. Besides the diagnostic criteria, many non-diagnostic characteristics of ASDs have been reported consistently in the literature, and are important to watch for during assessment. These provide a broader view of the person, assist in differentiating between disorders, and reflect areas of difficulty for which the person may wish intervention.

Scales used to identify symptoms

Instruments have been developed for use in the diagnosis of autism (e.g. the Autism Diagnostic Observation Schedule: Lord 1989). However, no comparable instrument is available for AS. Screening tools, such as the Asperger Screening Questionnaire for Adults (ASQ-A: Stoddart and Burke 2002) and the Gilliam Asperger's Disorder Scale (GADS: Gilliam 2001) are used to identify symptoms of specific ASDs. The person (in the case of the use of ASQ-A) or others who know the person (in the case of the use of GADS) rate the frequency of the occurence of each symptom. This leads to a determination of the likelihood that the individual has ASD. While these instruments are helpful in identifying whether the general symptoms of an ASD are present, and to what extent, they may not include all relevant symptoms, and do not distinguish between different specific ASDs. They are useful, however, to supplement clinical information.

Developmental and family history

For developmental history, it is important to identify the onset of symptoms (the age when they were first noted), nature and course of symptoms (type, intensity, frequency, changes), possible effect of symptoms (isolation), and previous interventions (medication, behaviour therapy). This information is needed to make a differential diagnosis both between ASDs and between an ASD and another disorder (e.g. some disorders not in the autism spectrum would not have childhood onset). Family history is also important to elicit because of the increasing research evidence that there is a genetic aetiology of ASDs (Holden 2003) and that an ASD or traits of an ASD often occur in more than one family member (Volkmar and Klin 2000).

Speech, communication, and pragmatics

"Speech" and "language" refer to knowledge and use of words; "communication" implies a social function in the use of speech and language. Individuals with AS are by definition not delayed in speech development. However, they still may experience communication problems and exhibit unusual speech (Volkmar and Klin 2000). Other more able persons with ASDs may have had delays in speech development and will have ongoing speech and communication difficulties. Atypical features of speech include poor modulation, stilted and literal speech, unusual tone, repetition, idiosyncratic words use, difficulty with novel speech, word-finding problems, difficulty initiating and maintaining conversation, delays in answering, out-of-context speech, preoccupation with certain topics, and extremes in amount of speech (i.e. excessive speech or little speech).

"Pragmatics" refers to functional language and occurs in the social context (Landa 2000). Features of pragmatics include: signalling intent (e.g. looking at others, interrupting a task to converse), ensuring understanding (e.g. gesturing to an object so that both speakers understand what is referred to), function of speech (e.g. asking or answering a question), awareness of the social and environmental context (e.g. where one should not yell), and features of the exchange (e.g. turn taking and initiating) (Burke 1992). Because of pragmatic difficulties, one may have problems conversing, only talk about preferred topics, have problems in turn taking, make inappropriate statements, and not understand the concept of "small talk".

Naturally occurring nonverbal communication may also be difficult for someone with an ASD to either perform or understand. For example, facial expressions may be hard to read. In addition, a person may communicate through behaviours such as angry outbursts, which may reflect difficulty finding suitable words to express himself, inability to relate to emotions, or a habitual or automatic response.

Characteristics of communication and pragmatics can be noted in the clinical interview, supported by questions to others and historical reports. Standard tests are available for a wide range of speech and language functions, including some specific to pragmatics such as the Test of Pragmatic Language (Phelps-Terasaki and Phelps-Gunn 1992). While some of these have been developed for school-aged individuals and are not marketed for adults, they can still provide useful information for adults with ASDs. Because of the impact of communication and pragmatic difficulties on people with ASDs, their referral to a speech and language pathologist is suggested where it is possible.

Social awareness and skills

Those with an ASD may attend to different stimuli in the social environment and thus derive a different meaning to it from that ascribed by others. They may react to a social setting based on their own perception of it, or on what they have been taught. They may not understand commonly accepted social rules. For example, the idea of boundaries may be difficult, so a person with an ASD may present as intrusive. Problems understanding and engaging in the social world make "communication" as opposed to "speech" difficult. A person with an ASD may be labelled a "loner" because sharing information is not natural to him. He may have difficulty discriminating between contexts and may have to learn what to say in specific situations. These learned actions will then be more automatic than meaningful. Some people seen by this clinician have developed a strong interest in theatre and act well using not only memorized words, but also memorized inflection and movement. They have frequently been observed to use memorized lines in social interactions.

Issues of social awareness and skill can be assessed through varying the interview context. Casual conversation will more often uncover the issues discussed above than will a structured interview. Exploring the person's relationships will also provide information. For example, they may identify acquaintances as friends, not understanding the difference. Furthermore, those who are married or involved in relationships may not understand the expectations, responsibilities or emotions that are part of such a relationship. Vignettes that present appropriate and inappropriate social responses may be useful in determining social knowledge (Dewey 1991). Similarly, magazines or picture cards that display social situations may act as tools to explore awareness and skill.

Emotional awareness and expression

As with social awareness, the individual with an ASD may react to emotional situations differently than expected. (S)he may laugh or cry out of context but not actually find something funny or sad. This may represent a discharge of emotion without understanding a situation, or a difficulty in interpreting one's own emotions. Those with ASDs may not show a full range of affect and often have difficulty interpreting facial affect and body language. Some report that they cannot understand specific feelings that others describe. Others say they understand emotions but, when asked about their own experiences or how they know how someone else feels, they may intellectualize (i.e. state what one does rather than what one feels). People with ASDs do exhibit physical and verbal emotional reactions (e.g. yelling when angry), but may not recognize they have done so, or may not understand the effect it has on others (Burke 2003). Again, use of vignettes or pictures to elicit information can be helpful if the individual or others are unable to provide adequate information.

Stereotypic and ritualistic behaviours

These include repetitive motor behaviours such as rocking and hand flapping, as well as ritualistic routines (e.g. touching the wall and floor alternately) and repetitive verbal behaviours. These features of the disorder are rarely addressed in the literature on adults who are more able. However, many adults seen by this clinician state they do engage in such behaviours, and they are aware it is seen as odd or unacceptable. Some have learned to contain themselves in public settings, but engage in their specific behaviour in private (e.g. spinning). Others have learned to be less obvious (e.g. subtle rocking). Therefore, to supplement clinical observation, a person and/or her family should be asked about stereotypic/repetitive behaviours.

Restricted range of interests

Some people with ASDs have been described as having no interests. Others engage in specific, intense activities that may appear as fixations (e.g. tying knots, copying pages from books). Individuals may develop interests, which they talk and read about to the exclusion of almost everything else (e.g. cookbooks, schedules, information about religions or cultures). More able people with ASDs may attend college or university, excelling at subjects they can memorize or that reflect their interests. However, they are often unable to apply what they learn or find employment related to their studies. Sometimes interests are considered obsessive; this means that the need for certain activities or routines has become so intense that they interfere with other daily roles.

Transitions and the need for routine

People with ASDs often find transitions difficult. This may relate to difficulties in executive function (perseverating on a task), anxiety (not being able to predict), motor difficulties (problems beginning a motor sequence), sensory difficulties (some negative sensory stimuli in the new environment/activity) or a change in routine.

Those with ASDs need structure and routine in their lives. This becomes particularly evident in vocational contexts. Those who receive no assistance in developing schedules or identifying priorities may fall into their own routine of non-productive activity. Once established, this is difficult to change. Behaviours suggesting need for routine include rigidity about rules, refusing to deviate in routes or order of activities, or being upset by tardiness. Individuals with ASDs also report difficulty with vacations and leisure time. They may pace about or engage in repetitive behaviours to fill "empty" time (Burke 2003). While flexibility and time for relaxation are important, unstructured time can be stressful and lead to entrenched and non-functional activity.

Cognitive functioning

When a comprehensive assessment is requested, tests of cognitive ability are standard. However, this is not always done in the assessment of adults who have an ASD. The assessor must consider if there was a previous assessment, what were the results, how long ago testing was done, what tools were used, how explicit the assessment report was in identifying strengths and difficulties, and why the current assessment is being requested (i.e. confirmation of AS or to qualify for funding).

Individuals with AS by definition do not have an intellectual disability. Those with autism and PDD-NOS may have an intellectual disability, or fall within average ranges (sometimes referred to as high-functioning autism or HFA). Of this latter group, some have been thought to have impairments because symptoms of ASDs masked skills. For them, cognitive testing is done to identify functioning ability. For those who have obvious intellectual strengths, the utility of cognitive testing is to understand specific skills and difficulties. For example, a person may be referred by an employment agency because, although he appears to function with average abilities, he has been unable to hold a job. An assessment might identify poor problem-solving skills, difficulty understanding or remembering instructions, or weak visual-spatial skills.

Attempts have been made to link cognitive profiles to specific ASDs. For example, individuals with autism have better nonverbal than verbal skills, while individuals with AS have better verbal than nonverbal skills (Ozonoff and Griffith 2000). Block design appears to be a strength among individuals with autism while comprehension is a weakness. Those with AS have shown deficits in visual motor integration, visual memory, nonverbal concept formation, and visual spatial perception. This pattern has not been observed in those with HFA (Klin *et al.* 1995). Because these profiles do not occur consistently, there has been disagreement about whether they are valid (Siegel, Minshew, and Goldstein 1996). However, the results of many studies suggest such differences exist (Volkmar and Klin 2000). This clinician has seen these patterns in a substantial number of assessments and finds the information helpful, if not diagnostic.

Cognitive testing also allows observation of behaviours that might not occur in a less structured context. For example, individuals with AS may answer vocabulary questions in an unusually concise manner. Picture completion tasks may elicit responses based on attention to unexpected stimuli. One may also see delayed response, a need to talk through tasks, repetitive touching, stereotypic movements, or a need for frequent breaks. Some individuals are unable to complete tasks in the standard way. One person seen by this assessor was unable to sit and attend to tasks, but was able to work while standing at a wide windowsill. Accommodations must be reported in the assessment document, and this information can be useful to those supporting the individual.

Executive function and theory of mind

It is believed that persons with ASDs are impaired in both executive function and theory of mind. "Executive function" refers to skills used in complex behaviour, such as flexibility, set maintenance, inhibition, planning, organizing, and working memory (Ozonoff and Griffith 2000). Individuals with an ASD may present as rigid, perseverative, and doing best with structure and routine. Those seen clinically have reported difficulty organizing schedules, setting goals, and planning future activities. While knowing what needs to be done, they may not be able to sequence the steps, identify priorities, or project into the future beyond a few days or weeks, or without concrete tools such as a calendar. Tests exist which can assess some aspects of executive function, such as the Wisconsin Card Sorting Test (Heaton *et al.* 1993). However, often difficulties can be observed during interaction, or when administering tests for other characteristics. For example, when using the Thematic Apperception Test (Bellack 1973) as part of a mental health assessment, one may find that the person with an ASD has difficulty projecting backward and forward in time or organizing thoughts, or perseverates on previous answers.

"Theory of mind" (ToM) refers to the ability to understand one's own and others' mental states. Those with AS have been considered as less impaired in ToM than those with other ASDs (Ozonoff and Griffith 2000). Joliffe and Baron-Cohen (1999) used stories by Happé to observe ToM and pragmatic functions in high-functioning adults with autism and AS. They did not find significant differences between the groups. Observation for ToM can be done during conversation, questions can be used to elicit information, and vignettes with accompanying pictures may be helpful. ToM deficits would be seen in an inability to recognize joking, sarcasm, desires, beliefs, innuendo, colloquialisms, lying, coercion or the intent of someone's actions. Impaired ToM also suggests the person may not recognize and therefore cannot modify her behaviour, nor can she understand and/or predict someone else's behaviour.

Motor skills

Children with ASDs are often identified as having poor muscle tone and fine or gross motor difficulties. In adulthood, these problems continue. Smith (2000) reviewed studies on many aspects of motor difficulty associated with ASDs including motor responses, unusual gait and posture, and problems co-ordinating motor functions. Some studies suggested motor difficulties, such as clumsiness in AS, to be diagnostic. While differences in research methods and inconsistent findings make use of motor problems for diagnosis premature, Smith suggests motor functions should be addressed as areas for support and intervention.

Sensory responses

Individuals with ASDs may have unusual sensory experiences, often reflecting extremes (e.g. they may appear unable to hear some sounds and react intensely to others). Such experiences may be observed in any area of sensation: touch, movement, taste, smell, vision, and hearing. A person may connect with the world or calm himself by engaging in sensory stimulation (e.g. rocking, or seeking specific smells). Other experiences may distract the person, cause discomfort, or interfere with adaptive functioning. The organization and processing of sensory experience is referred to as "sensory integration" (Ayers 1979). Tools are available to elicit information about sensory patterns, such as the Adolescent/Adult Sensory Profile (Brown and Dunn 2002). Those experiencing difficulties may benefit from referral to an occupational therapist.

Adaptive functioning

Individuals with ASDs have trouble in adaptive functions such as communication, social skills, and judgement. While most can perform self-care and domestic tasks, they often need reminders. Beginning, completing, or planning tasks may be difficult. Scales are available to rate adaptive skills, but many were written for people who have intellectual disabilities, and may not be suitable for adults that are more able. Scales that allow a person to demonstrate skills are the most useful (e.g. Independent Living Scales: Loeb 1996). While a person with an ASD may feel able to answer questions about adaptive skills, it is helpful to get information from others. The person or his family members may not be cognizant of some areas of adaptive difficulty.

Mental health

Many people with ASDs experience mental health and emotional difficulties. These may reflect a comorbid condition or a reaction to some aspect of the ASD. For instance, individuals may be aware they are not seen as socially competent, or may experience frustration in educational or vocational activities. Their reaction to these events may lead to treatment for anxiety or depression. Some people engage in high levels of activity and appear to be hyperactive, while others may engage in obsessive or compulsive behaviours. Frequently these represent symptoms of the ASD rather than another disorder such as Attention Deficit Hyperactivity Disorder (ADHD) or Obsessive Compulsive Disorder (OCD). Ghaziuddin, Weidmer-Mikhail and Ghaziuddin (1998) found adults with AS often had a comorbid psychiatric condition. The authors stated that adults with AS were less often identified with ADHD when compared with children and proposed that this might be due to misdiagnosis in children. They found depression to be the most frequent comorbid condition and psychotic disorders to be uncommon. Those with AS are reported to experience more severe levels of psychopathology than those with HFA (Tonge *et al.* 1999).

Identification of mental health difficulties is important if a person is to receive fitting intervention (medication or therapy). Many tools are available to support clinical judgement in assessing mental health and emotional difficulties. Both self-report and report-by-other formats are useful, as the individual may not have the same perception of herself as others. The Emotional Problems Scales (Prout and Strohmer 1991) were developed for assessing those with a mild intellectual disability, but are useful for those with ASDs because of the rating-by-others format. When projective measures such as the Thematic Apperception Test (TAT: Bellack 1973) have been used by this clinician, responses are usually inadequate to be scored in a standard way. However, clinical exploration of life difficulties and emotional themes are possible.

Differential diagnosis

When a person is seen for assessment, it is important that the clinician determines if symptoms meet criteria for a diagnosis of an ASD. Sometimes diagnoses such as learning disability or language disorder are given, which reflect some aspect of the person's difficulty. However, these do not take into account other issues such as social problems or restricted range of interests (Filipek *et al.* 1999). If a person is believed to have an ASD, the clinician must decide which diagnosis within the spectrum best fits the person's history and presentation. It is also important to identify if a comorbid condition exists (e.g. anxiety).

When a more able person is determined as having an ASD, the possible diagnoses are AS, autism, or PDD-NOS. While the diagnostic criteria are specific, the literature reports that some clinicians deviate from this when giving a diagnosis. For example, some may call the disorder PDD although the person meets criteria for autism (Buitelaar *et al.* 1999). When an individual presents at a boundary of the disorders, the clinician must evaluate the number, intensity, and quality of the symptoms, and this can be subjective. There is disagreement in the literature whether AS and autism in the more able reflect the same disorder (introduction, this volume). This controversy sometimes influences diagnosis. It is hoped that in the future, more discrete methods of screening will be developed. Until that time, it is important that some consistency be maintained in diagnosis so that adults with an ASD, those supporting them, and those developing and offering services have the same understanding of the person's experiences.

Product of the assessment

An assessment needs to serve a purpose. It should provide: (a) answers to specific questions; (b) information in a clear manner; (c) concrete and realistic recommendations; (d) information about other disorders/difficulties identified; (e) referrals or information about other services (Burke 2003).

When an adult is diagnosed with an ASD after many years of unexplained difficulty, many individuals and families express relief. The diagnosis and related information can present options that did not exist before the assessment. However, the diagnosis may cause distress when it is not expected, when the person has a history of being told there was nothing wrong, or when supporting persons have rationalized behaviours to deny a diagnosis. Clinicians need to be sensitive to these situations. It is helpful to have information available for the person to take with her, to have clinical services to refer to, and to offer follow-up appointments to review the diagnosis, provide additional information, or discuss new issues that may arise.

Conclusion

Psychological assessment of an adult presenting with symptoms of an ASD can help that person by providing a diagnosis, as well as information about the disorder. This can help the person and those supporting him/her to understand personal interests and challenges better, and guide learning, skill development, intervention, and planning better. It is hoped that these will allow the adult with an ASD to find ways to compensate for symptoms, improve quality of life by accessing resources, and allow the person to achieve his or her dreams.

References

APA (American Psychiatric Association) (1994) *Diagnostic and Statistical Manual of Mental Disorders, Fourth Edition.* Washington, DC: APA.

Ayers, A.J. (1979) *Sensory Integration and the Child.* Los Angeles, CA: Western Psychological Services.

Barnard, J., Harvey, V., Porter, D., and Prior, A. (2001) *Ignored or Ineligible? The Reality for Adults with Autism Spectrum Disorders.* London, UK: National Autistic Society.

Bellack, L. (1973) *Thematic Apperception Test, Revised Edition.* San Antonio, TX: The Psychological Corporation.

Brown, C.E., and Dunn, W. (2002) *Adolescent/Adult Sensory Profile.* San Antonio, TX: The Psychological Corporation.

Bryson, S., and Autism Society of Ontario (1991) *Our Most Vulnerable Citizens: Report of the Adult Task Force.* Guelph, ON: Autism Society of Ontario.

Buitelaar, J.K., van der Gaag, R., Klin, A., and Volkmar, F. (1999) Exploring the boundaries of Pervasive Developmental Disorder Not Otherwise Specified: Analysis of data from the DSM-IV Autistic Disorder Field Trial. *Journal of Autism and Developmental Disorders, 29,* 33–43.

Burke, L. (1992) Pragmatic analysis of communicative behaviour in three groups of mentally retarded adults. Doctoral dissertation, York University, Toronto, ON.

Burke, L. (2001) *Assessment of Pervasive Developmental Disorders (PDDs) in Adults*. Prepared for Surrey Place Centre, Toronto, ON, May.

Burke, L. (2003) An overview of psychological assessment of more able youth and adults with autistic spectrum disorders. Paper presented at the Second National Conference on Asperger Syndrome. Toronto, ON, May.

Dewey, M. (1991) Living with Asperger's syndrome. In U. Frith (ed.) *Autism and Asperger Syndrome*. Cambridge, UK: Cambridge University Press.

Filipek, P.A., Accardo, P.J., Baranek, G.T., Cook, E.H., Dawson, G., Garodon, B., *et al.* (1999) The screening and diagnosis of Autistic Spectrum Disorders. *Journal of Autism and Developmental Disorders, 29*, 439–84.

Ghaziuddin, M., Weidmer-Mikhail, E. and Ghaziuddin, N. (1998) Comorbidity of Asperger syndrome: A preliminary report. *Journal of Intellectual Disability Research, 42*, 279–83.

Gilliam, J.E. (2001) *Gilliam Asperger's Disorder Scale*. Austin, TX: Pro-Ed, Inc.

Heaton, R.K., Chelune, G.J., Talley, J.L., Kay, G.G., and Curtiss, G. (1993) *Wisconsin Card Sorting Test Manual, Revised and Expanded*. Odessa, FL: Psychological Assessment Resources.

Holden, J. (2003) Autism and Asperger's: The genetic connection. Paper presented at the Second National Conference on Asperger Syndrome. Toronto, ON, May.

Jolliffe, T., and Baron-Cohen, S. (1999) The Strange Stories Test: A replication with high-functioning adults with autism or Asperger syndrome. *Journal of Autism and Developmental Disorders, 29*, 395–406.

Klin, A., Volkmar, F.R., Sparrow, S.S., Cicchetti, D.V., and Rourke, B.P. (1995) Validity and neuropsychological characterization of Asperger syndrome. *Journal of Child Psychology and Psychiatry, 36*, 1127–140.

Landa, R. (2000) Social language use in Asperger syndrome and high-functioning autism. In A. Klin, F.R. Volkmar, and S.S. Sparrow (eds) *Asperger Syndrome*. New York, NY: The Guilford Press.

Loeb, P.A. (1996) *Independent Living Scales*. San Antonio, TX: The Psychological Corporation.

Lord, C. (1989) *Autism Diagnostic Observation Schedule – Generic*. Los Angeles, CA: Western Psychological Services.

Ozonoff, S., and Griffith, E.M. (2000) Neuropsychological function and the external validity of Asperger Syndrome. In A. Klin, F.R. Volkmar, and S.S. Sparrow (eds) *Asperger Syndrome*. New York, NY: Guilford Press.

Phelps-Terasaki, D., and Phelps-Gunn, T. (1992) *Test of Pragmatic Language*. Austin, TX: Pro-Ed, Inc.

Powell, A. (2002) *Taking Responsibility: Good Practice Guidelines for Services – Adults with Asperger Syndrome*. London, UK: The National Autistic Society.

Prout, H.T., and Strohmer, D.C. (1991) *Emotional Problems Scales*. Lutz, TX: Psychological Assessment Resources.

Siegel, D.J., Minshew, N.J., and Goldstein, G. (1996) Wechsler IQ profiles in diagnosis of high-functioning autism. *Journal of Autism and Developmental Disorders, 26*, 389–406.

Smith, I.M. (2000) Motor functioning in Asperger syndrome. In A. Klin, F.R. Volkmar, and S.S. Sparrow (eds) *Asperger Syndrome*. New York, NY: Guilford Press.

Stoddart, K.P., and Burke, L. (2002) Asperger Screening Questionnaire for Adults (ASQ-A). Unpublished.

Stoddart, K.P., Burke, L., and Temple, V. (2002) A re-examination of the characteristics and clinical needs of adults with Pervasive Developmental Disorders: A summary of 100 cases. Paper presented at State of the HART, sponsored by UBC and BC Association for Mental Health in Developmental Disability, Vancouver, BC, April.

Tidmarsh, L., and Volkmar, F.R. (2003) Diagnosis and epidemiology of Autism Spectrum Disorders. *Canadian Journal of Psychiatry, 48*, 517–25.

Tonge, B.J., Brereton, A.V., Gray, K.M., and Einfeld, S.L. (1999) Behavioural and emotional disturbance in high-functioning autism and Asperger syndrome. *Autism: The International Journal of Research and Practice, 3*, 117–30.

Volkmar, F.R., and Klin, A. (2000) Diagnostic issues in Asperger Syndrome. In A. Klin, F.R. Volkmar, and S.S. Sparrow (eds) *Asperger Syndrome.* New York, NY: The Guilford Press.

WHO (World Health Organization) (1992) *The International Statistical Classification of Diseases and Related Health Problems, Tenth Edition.* Geneva: WHO.

Part III

Theoretical and Research Perspectives

CHAPTER 15

Developing a research agenda in Asperger Syndrome

Peter Szatmari

Children with non-specific social impairments have existed for a long time. For the most part, they do not get into trouble unless there is associated impairment at home, at school, or in the community. The identification by Kanner over 50 years ago of children with impairments characterized by deficits in social reciprocity and joint attention has unleashed an avalanche of papers describing the syndrome, discussing the diagnosis and differential diagnosis, and attempting to find the causes and effective treatments of this condition. Although there is much less research on Asperger Syndrome (AS), the number of papers published each year is growing steadily.

The issue of whether AS "is" or "is not" autism has been extremely controversial, igniting fierce debates in a field known more for its slow and quiet progress (interrupted, it is true, by outlandish claims for "cures"). The objective of this chapter is to stand back and survey the "battlefield". By briefly reviewing the papers that have tried to test for similarities and differences between autism and AS, I also hope to catch a glimpse of the horizon; that is, what lies just beyond our current research endeavours. In that way, a research agenda may be proposed that would settle some of the debates currently occupying the field, and move the science forward to indeed finding the causes and effective treatments for all children with autism spectrum disorders (ASDs).

Two children with social impairments: Same or different?

Consider two children who come to the office on the same day. The first, Johnny, is five years old and has been referred by his kindergarten teacher for speech delay. His parents report that, in addition to his problems in communication, he is

229

also socially isolated, prefers to play by himself, and generally avoids his teachers. He has very little language apart from the scenes from his favourite cartoon videos that he echoes. He spends time lining up toys, playing with bits of string, staring at his fingers, and moving the blinds in the living room. His special educational consultant in school identifies that he has significant receptive and expressive language delays but good visual-spatial skills.

The second boy, Freddie, is eight years old and has been referred because of extreme Attention Deficit Hyperactivity Disorder (ADHD). He, too, is socially isolated but he does interact with his classmates at school. However, all he wants to do is talk about Star Wars. He is always trying to get the other children to play various characters from the movies. He tends to be very bossy and controlling in his interactions with the other children. Freddie is unable to respond to their requests to play something else and he usually walks away if they do not want to engage in a Star Wars activity. His parents report that he started to speak at an appropriate age but it has been very difficult to have much of a conversation with him. He has shown poor eye contact in the past and he rarely smiles, even when he is doing something he really enjoys. His speech is often tangential, he jumps from topic to topic, and recently he rarely talks about anything other than Star Wars. He has never had a best friend over to the house to play and he rarely gets invited to other children's birthday parties. At home, he insists on keeping all the doors on the second floor of the house open, otherwise he becomes quite upset. He is very disorganized at school, is incapable of working independently, and has a short attention span. Psychological testing indicates that his IQ is in the normal range but there is quite a bit of scatter in both the verbal and nonverbal sub-tests. Testing by a speech and language therapist indicates that he has good grammar and vocabulary skills.

Do these children have the *same* disorder or a *different* one? Certainly, at one level, they present with different symptoms and levels of functioning. One has severe speech delay in both expressive and receptive language skills. The other spoke on time and has good basic vocabulary and grammar. One child is very socially isolated and does not interact with either peers or teachers. The other does interact with other children, albeit not always successfully. One does not demonstrate any imaginative play and seems preoccupied with sensory stimuli. The other child does have quite a vivid imagination, but he perseverates on one topic to the exclusion of other imaginary themes. While these differences are obvious, there are similarities too. Both children have impairments in social reci-procity, both children have difficulties in communicating regardless of their variation in language skills, and both children engage in repetitive forms of play even if one is largely sensory and the other more imaginative.

In effect, both children would meet criteria for a Pervasive Developmental Disorder (PDD). One child (Johnny) might meet criteria for autism, and the other (Freddie) for AS. However, a clinician strictly applying the *DSM-IV* criteria (APA 1994) would indicate that even the older boy meets criteria for autism. For example, he presents with difficulties in social responsiveness, the use of nonverbal gestures to communicate, difficulties in peer interactions, difficulties initiating and sustaining a conversation, circumscribed interests and rituals. *DSM-IV* (APA 1994) requires six of twelve symptoms to be present at some point in a child's development and Freddie meets these, even though there has been considerable change in his symptoms over time. These simultaneous similarities in social communication and play between these two "classic" cases have confused parents, clinicians, and policy-makers for years.

Background

Hans Asperger first described AS in 1944 but the clinical presentation and recognition of the disorder did not really come to the attention of the English-speaking world until Lorna Wing's important paper (Wing 1981). It is worth pointing out, however, that such children have been identified for many years. In the classic textbook by Henderson and Gillespie (1947) there is a clear definition of a child with "schizoid disorder" who has a classic presentation of AS. In the even earlier writings of a Russian psychiatrist, there is another classic description quoted (Ssucharewa and Wolff 1996). The confusion about the overlap between AS and autism was underlined by the early Lorna Wing paper (1981). The cases of AS that she identified were all children who originally had a diagnosis of high-functioning autism (HFA) but were now adolescents or young adults with good language skills.

As a consequence, much of the work in the 1980s and 1990s was concerned with establishing the "diagnostic validity" of AS. This meant trying to determine whether AS was *really* HFA, or whether it was a *separate* disorder on the autism "spectrum". Several studies were conducted that compared autism and AS on clinical features to see if they were the same or different. While this research was going on, there was a dramatic increase in the number of children who received a diagnosis of AS and much confusion among diagnosticians, parents, and policy-makers. These groups were not only trying to cope with the increased numbers of cases of autism and AS, but were also trying to make sense of the different diagnoses that these children received from clinicians who were using the diagnostic terms in often idiosyncratic and confusing ways.

The clinical features of Asperger Syndrome

There is in fact, quite a bit of agreement about the clinical features of AS, even if there is little consensus on its diagnostic validity. Almost all writers on the topic agree that children and youth with this diagnosis present with impairments in social reciprocity, especially towards peers; have poor conversation skills; and develop intense and unusual preoccupations (Szatmari, Bremner, and Nagy 1989; Eisenmajer *et al.* 1996; Leekman *et al.* 2000). Usually, these individuals have IQ scores in the normal range and present with an absence of clinically significant language delay. Often, experts remark on poor visual-spatial motor skills, perhaps a later age of onset, and a significant degree of motor clumsiness (Klin *et al.* 1995).

It is instructive to compare this consensus with the diagnostic criteria as outlined in *DSM-IV* (APA 1994) and *ICD-10* (WHO 1992). The official diagnostic manuals of the American Psychiatric Association and the World Health Organization state that, in order to qualify for a diagnosis of AS, a child must meet the same criteria for autism in the social and repetitive domains. There are 12 diagnostic criteria for autism, four in each of the social, communication, and repetitive activity domains. For AS, there must be at least two examples of impairments in social reciprocity and at least one example of a repetitive stereotyped behaviour. Age of onset in social reciprocity, communication or play domains must be less than 36 months. To differentiate these children from those with autism, there must be an "absence of clinically significant cognitive and language delay". Finally, the child cannot also meet criteria for autism. If a child does meet criteria for both autism and AS, he/she is preferentially given a diagnosis of autism. This is based on the assumption that since autism is a much better validated condition, it takes precedence. The appropriateness of this approach has never been addressed however in the empirical literature.

It may well be asked whether these are the "best" criteria for AS. For example, no mention is made of communication impairments even though virtually all commentators remark on the poor conversational skills of these children. The criteria for an "absence" of clinically significant cognitive and language delay is not specified and there is wide variability in the way diagnosticians apply this concept (see Ghaziuddin, Tsai, and Ghaziuddin 1992). Finally, many, if not most, children with AS also meet criteria for autism (Mayes, Calhoun, and Crites 2001). Others and our group have used structured diagnostic interviews that are standard for the diagnosis of autism (Autism Diagnostic Interview: Lord, Rutter, and Le Couteur 1994) and have applied them to children that would meet a best-estimate consensus diagnosis of AS. The vast majority (over 90%) of the AS children also meet criteria for autism. This should not be surprising since the criteria for AS require a similar level of impairment in social reciprocity and repetitive activities. If one were strictly to apply the *DSM-IV* (APA 1994) criteria, the problem of AS disappears. It captures only a very few children and would be an extremely rare disorder (probably less than 10% of all ASD children).

A critical appraisal of research on the diagnostic validity of Asperger Syndrome

The key issue that must be addressed is the identification of the fundamental characteristic that distinguishes children with AS from those with autism and to see whether that distinguishing feature translates into other differences in aetiology, prognosis, and response to treatment. It has been difficult however to isolate that fundamental characteristic. The most common research design is to pick a "candidate" distinguishing feature and see if it makes a difference. If it does not, it should be abandoned and another chosen for testing. Most investigators have chosen the "absence of speech delay" as the candidate criterion. Our research would indicate instead that the fundamental characteristic is "preserved structural language abilities" and that this accounts for differences in presentation and prognosis.

Howlin (2003) has recently completed a systematic review on the studies that have compared AS and autism on a number of features. As mentioned, some papers have suggested that cognitive and language delays are the fundamental characteristics that differentiate children with AS from those with autism. Although there is some variation in how these features are operationalized, the most common approach is to suggest that children with AS have at least a nonverbal or verbal IQ above 70 and are speaking spontaneously in phrases by 36 months of age. Howlin (2003) usefully summarizes cross-sectional and retrospective studies that have looked at the extent to which this differentiation carries implications with respect to differences in other variables. For example, we found that children with AS defined in this way had less social impairment, better language abilities, fewer stereotypies, fewer preoccupations and more imaginative play than children with HFA who also had IQ scores above 70 but were delayed in their phrase speech (Szatmari *et al.* 1995). On the other hand, papers by Mayes and Calhoun (2001), and Ozonoff, Rogers, and Pennington (1991) did not report any significant differences. Similar results have been reported by Kurita (1997), Eisenmajer *et al.* (1998), and Gilchrist *et al.* (2001).

Three separate aspects of aetiology have been studied: obstetric and perinatal events, neuropsychological testing, and family history. No differences between autism and AS have been identified with respect to obstetric complications or perinatal events, but the extent to which this variable is even a marker of aetiology has been questioned (Zwaigenbaum *et al.* 2001). There is greater agreement that individuals with HFA have more impairments in expressive and receptive language abilities on neuropsychological testing than children with AS. This makes sense given that the groups are often differentiated on the basis of speech delay. There are, however, mixed findings on the pattern of cognitive strengths and weaknesses in AS. Klin *et al.* (1995) reported that children with AS more often present with the pattern of low performance IQ and high verbal IQ, suggesting that those with AS suffer from a specific impairment in visual-perceptual functioning. Others have not been able to replicate this finding (Miller and Ozonoff 2000; Szatmari *et al.* 2000). There are also mixed results as to whether those with AS have more motor abnormalities than those with autism, fewer problems in executive function, and better theory of mind. The bottom line is that other than worse language skills in autism, no consistent differences are found on neuropsychological testing.

Another important aetiologic variable studied has been family history. We have collected a large sample of sibling groups in which at least two siblings are affected with an ASD (MacLean *et al.* 1999). We have found there is no familial aggregation on PDD sub-types; there is no evidence that if one member of the sibship has AS, the other member of the sibship is more likely to have AS than autism. In other words, it appears as if the genes that confer susceptibility to an ASD do not necessarily dictate whether the child has AS, autism, or PDD-NOS. That distinction may be dictated by non-genetic factors.

The conclusion of this very brief literature review is clear. If the key differentiating characteristic of HFA and AS is a history of language delay, the only consistent difference found on other variables is that individuals with AS have better expressive and receptive language skills than those with autism. This is hardly surprising and informative given that the groups were differentiated based on the presence or absence of language delay.

There are, however, two fundamental flaws in this research program. As suggested, any differences that have been identified between autism and AS appear almost circular and tautological. The differences depend entirely on the correlation between the variable that distinguishes the groups and the dependent variables being compared. If there is a very high correlation, the difference is circular and does not provide any more information or evidence of validity, above and beyond the distinguishing feature. As has been pointed out, if the correlation between the presence and absence of language delay at 36 months and later language skills is very high, then the added value of the distinction is minimal. The validity of AS needs to be based on differences that are relatively *independent* of the way that the groups were originally defined and language delay does not currently meet that criterion.

The second fatal flaw is that these studies are all based on cross-sectional or retrospective comparisons. Without prospective longitudinal data using an inception cohort, one can never avoid biases associated with sampling a non-representative group. One can never know which PDD individuals have been lost by the time the sample has been ascertained. The average age of diagnosis of autism is between three and five years of age, the average age of diagnosis for AS may be a year or two later, but the difference is not that great. The studies referred to earlier were all based on children who were on average quite a bit older, usually adolescents or young adults. Therefore, we do not know how many, or what kinds of, high-functioning autistic individuals or those with AS have been lost over time. Perhaps some high-functioning autistic individuals at diagnosis have lost cognitive skills over time and would not be sampled later. Perhaps only adolescents with autism who developed fluent language after 36 months are included in the autism group. That might eliminate any differences observed on later comparisons. Perhaps some very high-functioning individuals, who would have met criteria for AS at five and six years of age, might have improved to such an extent that they have moved off the autism spectrum altogether. In other words, a much more valid way to assess the clinical significance of the presence or absence of language delay is to do a prospective study starting out with an inception cohort and following them into at least adolescence. This would allow us to see whether the early differences in language acquisition translate into other differences in, for example, social skills and autistic symptoms over time.

The adolescent outcome of high-functioning autism and Asperger Syndrome

We have published two outcome evaluations of an inception cohort of children with HFA and AS (Szatmari *et al.* 2000; Szatmari *et al.* 2003). The sample was originally ascertained between the ages of four and six years of age. One outcome assessment was conducted two years later, a second one three years after that, and a third one when the children were in adolescence. The sampling strategies and diagnostic procedures used in these outcome evaluations are available in the two publications. The children with autism all had a nonverbal IQ score above 70 (based on the old Leiter Performance IQ test) and all met Autism Diagnostic Interview (ADI) criteria for autism (based on the original ADI: Le Couteur *et al.* 1989). Children with AS also had nonverbal IQ above 70 and many also met ADI criteria for autism. However, the differentiating characteristic was that they were all speaking in phrases by 36 months of age and, in addition, there was no evidence of persistent (that is more than three months) delayed echolalia, pronoun reversal, or use of neologisms. In other words, we relied on the old

DSM-III (APA 1980) criterion of delayed and deviant language development as an important characteristic to differentiate children with autism from those with AS.

Defined in this way, children with AS have higher nonverbal IQ, better social and communication skills, and fewer autistic symptoms at all time points, even into adolescence. The magnitude of the differences is substantial and amounts to almost a full standard deviation. Further, these differences on outcome cannot be accounted for by the original differences on nonverbal IQ or the original differences on their language scores at four to six years of age. The fact that we see differences on variables other than language such as socialization and autistic symptoms (variables independent of the original definition) provides reasonable evidence for the validity of the distinction between autism and AS.

We have also shown that the predictors of outcome in these two groups are slightly different (Szatmari *et al.* 2003). It is well known that both verbal and nonverbal cognitive abilities prior to the age of six are the main predictors of outcome in autism; those who were not speaking fluently by six and those who have poorer nonverbal cognitive abilities have a worse outcome in adolescence and young adulthood. In our data, these findings apply only to children with HFA and not to those with AS. In other words, early language abilities do not predict outcome in children with AS, to the same extent that they do in children with autism. This makes sense, given that children with AS have near-average language abilities and that the predictive ability of this variable on social skills and autistic symptoms is thereby limited. Indeed, the variables that predict outcome among children with AS are not at all clear from our findings.

The importance of Specific Language Impairment

Seen from a longitudinal prospective view then, delays in language acquisition do translate into differences in social skills and autistic symptoms up to ten years later. However, close inspection of these data also indicates there is greater heterogeneity in the outcome of children with autism than there is in that of children with AS. This is especially true in the growth of language skills. A significant proportion of children with HFA develop fluent language after three but before six years of age. These are the high-functioning autistic children who have a good outcome in adolescence. In fact, our data suggest that their outcome is very similar to those with AS. In our study, by definition a child with autism could only develop fluent language after three years of age (for if he or she had fluent language at 36 months the diagnosis would have been AS). If children with autism developed fluent language after 36 months, but before six years of age, they came to resemble more and more the children with AS on their communication, socialization skills, and on the number of autistic symptoms. Once they developed the same level of expressive language skills shown by the children with AS at the beginning of the study, they resembled the AS children in adolescence even more.

Kjelgaard and Tager-Flusberg (2001) have written an important paper looking at the expressive and receptive language abilities of children with autism. They applied the criteria for Specific Language Impairment (SLI) to a group of children with ASDs. They concluded that the majority of children with a high-functioning autism spectrum disorder also have SLI. "SLI" refers to children who have normal nonverbal IQ but specific delays in expressive and receptive language. Kjelgaard and Tager-Flusberg (2001) conclude that children with AS may simply be children with an ASD who do not have SLI.

This would certainly fit with our observations based on the longitudinal study. Instead of differentiating children with autism and AS according to language delay, it may make more sense to distinguish them based on the presence or absence of SLI, and to make this determination not at 36 months of age but, say, at 72 months of age (i.e. six years). Thus, children with "autism" who have normal expressive and receptive language abilities at six years of age would now be classified as having AS, regardless of whether they had speech delay at 36 months. The argument here is that the differentiation of autism and AS cannot be made until six years of age when the presence or absence of SLI becomes much more stable than at three years of age.

This conceptualization supports a model of ASDs that we proposed some years ago (Szatmari 2000). Prior to three years of age, there is an undifferentiated group of children with impairments in social reciprocity and communication and who have a preference for repetitive stereotyped play. While this group is undifferentiated with respect to later PDD sub-types, there is certainly variation within this group on joint attention, imitation, executive function, etc. but these have not yet translated into differences with respect to PDD sub-types. At 36 months of age, some children will be speaking in phrases spontaneously and others will not. Those who are speaking by 36 months are now launched on the developmental pathway called "Asperger Syndrome". Those who do not are on the developmental pathway called "autism". The autism pathway becomes quickly differentiated into those with normal nonverbal skills and those with delayed nonverbal skills (this is the distinction between high- and low-functioning autism). After 36 months, but before six years, some children in the HFA pathway will develop fluent spontaneous speech and on testing will show good expressive and receptive language abilities. These children can be seen as "jumping" to the developmental pathway of the children with AS. Those who do not jump will continue to have significant impairments in language abilities but good nonverbal cognitive skills. Those who are delayed on both will have low-functioning autism and will continue on their pathway at a slow but steady pace. In other words, rather than thinking about specific PDD "sub-types", it may make much more sense to think of different developmental pathways that are parallel but potentially overlapping. There may be critical transition points whereby children on one pathway (say HFA) may jump to another pathway (say, to the pathway of children with AS).

What is the research agenda then?

If this model is credible, the next issue is to identify the empirical research that needs to be conducted to underpin the model. One question is to identify the factors that account for these different developmental pathways. In other words, what are the variables that account for the presence or absence of SLI in some children with an ASD? How do children move from the HFA pathway to that of AS? How can we move the children on the AS pathway off the PDD pathway altogether? What variables prior to 36 months of age predict which developmental pathway a PDD child will follow? All these are research questions that can be addressed in longitudinal prospective studies.

Another research priority becomes identifying the interventions that allow children to jump from one pathway to another. This puts the focus on interventions addressing the speech and language domain. How can ASD children with SLI be treated most effectively? Many interventions have been evaluated and they run the spectrum from discrete trial training and applied behavioural analysis to more naturalistic and incidental teaching focussing on parent–child interaction, synchronicity, and responsiveness. Which intervention is more effective is not known since they have not been tested in head-to-head comparisons. One systematic review points out that the change seen in more naturalistic interventions seems to be greater than that seen in discrete trial training (Delprato 2001). However, this question should be tied to looking at the extent to which interventions can move a PDD child from the HFA pathway to one more like the AS pathway.

Another item on the research agenda would be questions of aetiology. There is now good evidence that SLI is caused by genetic factors (O'Brien *et al.* 2003). A number of different genome scans have been conducted on SLI and, while only one genetic mutation has been identified (FOXP2), other regions that have a high probability of containing susceptibility genes have been identified. It is of considerable interest that the regions identified in genome-wide linkage studies of SLI are very similar to those identified in genome-wide linkage studies of autism (Bartlett *et al.* 2002; O'Brien *et al.* 2003). It may be, in fact, that if these susceptibility genes can be identified, the same gene or gene variant could lead to SLI in one case and to autism in another case, all depending on the genetic background of the child. Investigating the genetic overlap between language and HFA then becomes an important research priority for aetiological studies.

Conclusion

Asperger Syndrome is here to stay. It was introduced into the official classification systems in 1994 and has grown in popularity as a diagnosis, even though its validity has not been clearly established. It is interesting to note that it was introduced not so much as an indication of its status as a "true" disorder, but more to stimulate research. However, "the cat has been set amongst the pigeons" and it seems the diagnosis will remain, at least for the foreseeable future. It must be admitted, though, that its validity is very much in question. The systematic review by Howlin (2003) is fairly convincing in showing that, if the fundamental differentiating characteristic is speech delay at 36 months, then there is little difference between AS and HFA. We would argue that this conclusion is, however, strongly biased by the reliance on cross-sectional and retrospective research designs. These types of design inevitably result in systematic loss of individuals with HFA and AS and tend to bring the groups together. A prospective design that follows all children over time is better able to see whether there are differences in clinical presentation and outcome. Our research would indicate that there are differences between autism and AS on both these parameters when a longitudinal study is used to compare the groups.

In addition, we would argue that speech delay is not the best differentiating characteristic. Rather, our data would suggest that the presence of SLI at six years of age is the most telling characteristic that separates HFA and AS. This fits with other research on aetiology and on SLI as a disorder. In effect, we are saying that *autism is really AS plus SLI!* It is almost as if AS is the fundamental disorder, and if the child also inherits the genes responsible for SLI, he presents with HFA. If he also inherits the genes for intellectual disability, he presents with low-functioning autism. Whether or not the genes for SLI or for intellectual disability in PDD are the same genes for these conditions in children without PDD is a question that will be addressed by current genetic studies.

We hope that this focus on pathways instead of on sub-types will provide a fruitful avenue for further research. In essence, the way ahead lies with longitudinal prospective studies, not with more cross-sectional designs. After all, the PDDs are developmental disorders and need to be studied in a developmental context. If that comes about, the research agenda proposed here will have proven useful and a new agenda will have to be drawn up.

References

APA (American Psychiatric Association) (1980) *Diagnostic and Statistical Manual of Mental Disorders, Third Edition.* Washington, DC: APA.

APA (American Psychiatric Association) (1994) *Diagnostic and Statistical Manual of Mental Disorders, Fourth Edition.* Washington, DC: APA.

Bartlett, C.W., Flax, J.F., Logue, M.W., Vieland, V.J., Bassett, A.S., Tallal, P., and Brzustowicz, L.M. (2002) A major susceptibility locus for specific language impairment is located in 13q21. *American Journal of Human Genetics, 71,* 1, 45–55.

Delprato, D.J. (2001) Comparisons of discrete trial training and normalized behavioural language intervention for young children with autism. *Journal of Autism and Developmental Disorders, 31,* 315–25.

Eisenmajer, R., Prior, M., Leekam, S., Wing, L., Gould, J., Welham, M., and Ong, B. (1996) Comparison of clinical symptoms in autism and Asperger's disorder. *Journal of the American Academy of Child and Adolescent Psychiatry, 35,* 1523–31.

Eisenmajer, R., Prior, M., Leekam, S., Wing, L., Ong, B., Gould, J., and Welham, M. (1998) Delayed language onset as a predictor of clinical symptoms in pervasive developmental disorders. *Journal of Autism and Developmental Disorders, 18,* 6, 527–33.

Ghaziuddin, M., Tsai, L.Y., and Ghaziuddin, N. (1992) Brief report: A comparison of the diagnostic criteria for Asperger syndrome. *Journal of Autism and Developmental Disorders, 22,* 643–9.

Gilchrist, A., Green, J., Cox, A., Burton, D., Rutter, M., and Le Couteur, A. (2001) Development and current functioning in adolescents with Asperger Syndrome: A comparative study. *Journal of Child Psychology and Psychiatry, 42,* 227–40.

Henderson, D.K., and Gillespie, R.D. (1947) *A Textbook of Psychiatry for Students and Practitioners, Sixth Edition.* London, UK: Oxford University Press.

Howlin, P. (2003) Outcome in high-functioning adults with autism with and without early language delays: Implications for the differentiation between autism and Asperger Syndrome. *Journal of Autism and Developmental Disorders, 33,* 2, 3–13.

Kjelgaard, J., and Tager-Flusberg, H (2001) An investigation of language impairment in autism: Implications for genetic subgroups. *Language and Cognitive Processes, 16,* 287–308.

Klin, A., Volkmar, F.R., Sparrow, S.S., Cicchetti, D.V., and Rourke, B.P. (1995) Validity and neuropsychological characterization of Asperger Syndrome: Convergence with nonverbal learning disabilities syndrome. *Journal of Child Psychology and Psychiatry, 36,* 7, 1127–40.

Kurita, H. (1997) A comparative study of Asperger syndrome with high-functioning atypical autism. *Psychiatry and Clinical Neurosciences, 51,* 67–70.

Le Couteur, A., Rutter, M., Lord, C., Rios, P., Robertson, S., Holdgrafer, M., and McLennan, J. (1989) Autism Diagnostic Interview: A standardized investigator-based instrument. *Journal of Autism and Developmental Disorders, 19,* 3, 363–87.

Leekman, S., Libby, S., Wing, L., Gould, J., and Gillberg, C. (2000) Comparison of ICD-10 and Gillberg's criteria for Asperger Syndrome. *Autism: The International Journal of Research and Practice, 4,* 1, 11–28.

Lord, C., Rutter M., and Le Couteur, A. (1994) Autism diagnostic interview – revised: A revised version of a diagnostic interview of caregivers of individuals with possible pervasive developmental disorders. *Journal of Autism and Developmental Disorders, 24,* 659–85.

MacLean, J.E., Szatmari, P., Jones, M.B., Bryson, S.E., Mahoney, W.J., Bartolucci, G., and Tuff, L. (1999) Familial factors influence level of functioning in pervasive developmental disorder. *Journal of the American Academy of Child and Adolescent Psychiatry, 38,* 6, 746–53.

Mayes, S.D., and Calhoun, S.L. (2001) Non-significance of early speech delay in children with autism and normal intelligence and implications for DSM-IV Asperger's disorder. *Autism: The International Journal of Research and Practice, 5,* 81–94.

Mayes, S.D., Calhoun, S.L., and Crites, D.L. (2001) Does DSM-IV Asperger's exist? *Journal of Abnormal Child Psychology, 29,* 263–71.

Miller, J., and Ozonoff, S. (2000) The external validity of Asperger Syndrome: Lack of evidence from the domain of neuropsychology. *Journal of Abnormal Psychology, 109*, 227–38.

O'Brien, E.K., Zhang, X., Nishimura, C., Tomblin, J.B., and Murray, J.C. (2003) Association of specific language impairment (SLI) to the region of 7q31. *American Journal of Human Genetics, 72*, 6, 1536–43.

Ozonoff, S., Rogers, S., and Pennington, B. (1991) Asperger's Syndrome: Evidence of an empirical distinction from high-functioning autism. *Journal of Child Psychology and Psychiatry, 32*, 1107–22.

Ssucharewa, G.E., and Wolff, S. (1996) The first account of the syndrome Asperger described? Translation of a paper entitled "Die schizoiden Psychopathien im Kindesalter". *European Child and Adolescent Psychiatry, 60*, 235–61.

Szatmari, P. (2000) The classification of autism, Asperger's syndrome and pervasive developmental disorder. *Canadian Journal of Psychiatry, 45*, 8, 731–8.

Szatmari, P., Archer, L., Fisman, S., Streiner, D.L., and Wilson, F.J. (1995) Asperger's syndrome and autism: Differences in behavior, cognition and adaptive functioning. *Journal of the American Academy of Child and Adolescent Psychiatry, 34*, 12, 1662–71.

Szatmari, P., Bremner, R., and Nagy, J. (1989) Asperger's syndrome: A review of clinical features. *Canadian Journal of Psychiatry, 34*, 6, 554–60.

Szatmari, P., Bryson, S.E., Boyle, M.H., Streiner, D.L., and Kuku, E. (2003) Predictors of outcome among high-functioning children with autism and Asperger syndrome. *Journal of Child Psychology and Psychiatry, 44*, 4, 520–8.

Szatmari, P., Bryson, S.E., Streiner, D.L., Wilson, F., Archer, L., and Ryerse, C. (2000) Two-year outcome of preschool children with autism or Asperger's syndrome. *American Journal of Psychiatry, 157*, 12, 1980–7.

WHO (World Health Organization) (1992) *The ICD-10 Classification of Mental and Behavioural Disorders – Clinical Descriptions and Diagnostic Guidelines.* Geneva: World Health Organization.

Wing, L. (1981). Asperger's syndrome: A clinical account. *Psychological Medicine, 11*, 115–29.

Zwaigenbaum, L., Szatmari, P., Jones, M.B., Bryson, S.E., MacLean, J.E., Mahoney, W.J., Bartolucci, G., and Tuff, L. (2001) Pregnancy and birth complications in autism and liability to the broader autism phenotype. *Journal of the American Academy of Child and Adolescent Psychiatry, 41*, 5, 572–9.

CHAPTER 16

In search of an Asperger culture

Charmaine C. Williams

Most of us have heard definitions of culture that describe it as a sum of ideas, beliefs, values, and knowledge that belong to a group of people who share a common background. Usually culture is an invisible matrix that aids our interpretation of daily existence, but our awareness of it is heightened when we encounter someone or something that presents experiences and interpretations that make culture, and cultural differences, visible. We are probably most aware of cultures in the moments when they clash; when some conflict or confusion reveals that we are in contact with an unknown people and unknown practices. We evoke culture to explain our perception of the exotic, the unfamiliar and, perhaps, the disturbing elements of other people.

With this in mind, it is intriguing to question if there exists a culture of Asperger Syndrome (AS). People with AS live among us and emerge from within us. What is it about these people that we are experiencing as exotic, unfamiliar, and perhaps disturbing? What do we think we can learn from applying a cultural model to our experience of them? The purpose of this chapter is to explore these questions.

The challenges of evaluating the presence of an Asperger culture are multifold. First, who is in the best position to describe such a culture? I approach the task as an outsider. I have never had a diagnosis of AS applied to me, and I have had limited (known) contact with people who have. My qualifications for the assignment are my experiences as an explorer of cultural difference and its intersection with the experience of mental health problems. I use this peripheral position to enter the world of AS and explore its ways. There was a time when this would not have been an unusual undertaking. Nineteenth-century anthropologists, charged with the same task, would return from distant adventures bearing exotic tales of strange, previously unknown people. However, this is not my situation. I have not travelled to regions unfamiliar to gather my information. Instead, I have relied on the generosity of people who were willing to share their stories and perspectives with me in person, and through their writing.

I am also not describing a strange, exotic people unknown to my audience. The audience for this chapter undoubtedly includes diagnosed individuals, their family members and friends, and professionals who spend much of their lives experiencing AS in a way that I have not. Herein lies a second challenge. What can I tell these people about the culture of AS? There are definite limitations. Yet, I also think there are insights I can contribute from my peripheral vantage point.

I see the purpose of this chapter as delving into the experience of AS to understand what aspects of it could form the foundation of a specific, distinct culture. I am evaluating the validity of a notion that people with AS possess similar traits, share common attitudes and values, negotiate the world using shared strategies, use a common means of communication, and grapple with mutual concerns. Based on these commonalities, they can potentially partake of a group consciousness that can give meaning and assign value to their lives. But first, there are some assumptions that I must make clear.

Basic assumptions

First, I assume the existence of the culture is less important than its utility to individuals with AS and the people that surround them. Ultimately, any culture of AS must be considered and evaluated in the light of how responses to that culture affect perceptions, emotions, behaviours, and experiences of the individuals included in it. In addition, it must be considered and evaluated based on how it directs those who surround the individual to value and support his or her membership in the group. This is knowledge that may be especially relevant to the work of clinicians. They are introduced to people with AS through their affiliation with a world of "experts" who are versed in the nature of disorder. Clinicians have the job of defining, modifying, and equipping individuals with AS in preparation for the challenges of life in a world of neurotypicals. Clinicians, family members, and others also take on the role of educating people about the meaning and implications of the diagnosis. Therefore, we need to be keenly interested in the potential for an AS culture. As neurotypicals our understanding of its potential usefulness to individuals with AS is crucial to our being sensitive, respectful, and helpful to them.

Second, I assume that, although I am engaging in a discussion that positions individuals with AS as different from "the rest of us", I believe that most would agree that our similarities outnumber our differences. This belief makes me feel ambivalent about searching for an AS culture. I realize that some may question whether the greater good is served by contributing to a discourse that emphasizes the differences of people with AS, or by shifting the focus to our mutual participation in an overarching culture that defines us as human. Unfortunately, claiming a universal culture usually serves to obscure pressures to adhere to dominant cultural expectations, and to deny inter-group tensions that stifle the rights and self-expression of people with less power. For example, when we rush toward the comfortable position of embracing a human race over multiple races, or "traditional" family values over multiple family forms, people who do not fit the universalized images are rendered invisible, while oppressive agendas move forward. We can diminish our anxieties about examining difference by pretending that individuals with AS are "just like us", but we would be asking them to exchange marginalization for probable invisibility. Therefore, I proceed assuming that acknowledging the differences associated with AS is preferable to denying the experience of difference that these individuals perceive daily.

Third, I am exploring this question of culture based on the assumption that there is a constellation of traits that we can reliably identify as AS. I am aware there is some controversy about this (Mayes, Calhoun, and Crites 2001). For this discussion, I accept the identity of an individual with AS as it has been defined by the American Psychiatric Association (APA 1994). They have determined that the following characteristics will identify people with AS: qualitative impairments in social interactions; repetitive and restricted activities and interests; significant social, occupational or other impairment; and the absence of other diagnoses or language and cognitive problems. That definition will not be disputed here, but what will be discussed is the potential for developing a sense of meaning and solidarity from taking on this identity. The potential solidarity is of particular interest in this discussion because the identity can exist apart from identification with the culture. Like everyone else, individuals with AS must make their own determinations about what aspects of their identities will determine their cultural identifications and preferences.

I will explore a cultural understanding of AS by laying out the criteria for different iterations of cultural existence, and testing their validity in the professional and personal discourses I have reviewed. My hope is that I can use what I know about culture and mental health to explore the possibilities in a way that will ring true to people who are diagnosed with AS, and will promote new understandings in those who are not.

Is there an Asperger culture?

I propose that the answer to this question is yes, there is the potential for an AS culture. However, this cultural reality can manifest in different ways. There may be a potential AS culture that is available as a resource to individuals diagnosed with AS. Individuals within the group can develop this culture by sharing their stories with others, and self-defining the phenomenology of AS. Alternatively, there may be a potential AS culture that is manifested in the form of a subcultural experience. This subculture can be utilized by others who have constructed a definition of AS and imposed it through the mechanisms of diagnosis and treatment. These two possibilities endorse the presence of an AS culture, but suggest different consequences for the individuals who would be defined by it. Both possibilities will be explored in terms of what is available to substantiate each, and what implications they have for people with AS, their families and friends, professionals, and others who interact with them.

Asperger Syndrome as the basis of a sustaining and valuable culture

Culture is a resource for people, helping individuals to negotiate the world with the support of a group consciousness behind them. Cultures form when individuals in shared circumstances find ways to deal with their common challenges. As individuals become more proficient at addressing these challenges, a pool of knowledge, strategies, and lessons learned accumulate and are available for individuals within the group to discover and use. With time, this storehouse of collective wisdom can be understood as representing group knowledge: values, norms, and skills that are valued for their utility and their capacity to involve individuals in a collective experience of the world. In this way, culture is a legacy that is shared by individuals to aid them in interacting with each other, and in managing the demands of the external environment.

An AS culture could emerge from the accumulated experiences of people living with AS. What we know about the diagnosis suggests there is a set of common challenges to be faced. For example, there are challenges in understanding the rhythms and reciprocations of social interchange with other people. There are challenges in pursuing interests at an intensity that others cannot match. There are challenges in being labelled and mislabelled by others trying to understand how you are different. As individuals face these challenges, they develop strategies and ways of understanding that can be shared to help others in the same situations. This would be one of the benefits of asserting an AS culture: the potential to socialize others into AS experience and save them the pain and confusion of dealing with these challenges alone.

This is a benefit we can understand when we encounter someone for whom the diagnosis of AS provides the answer to a lifetime of questions. When the assessor makes the diagnosis, he or she provides an explanation for why things that seem so simple for others have been so incredibly difficult for this person. The knowledge that others face the same obstacles, and have ways of addressing them, can be a tremendous relief. Waleski describes his experience of this noting, "When I met with this doctor, he confirmed that my characteristics matched those of Asperger Syndrome. Upon knowing this, a heavy weight was lifted from my shoulders... This became the turning point in my life" (Waleski 2002).

Yet there is more that an AS culture can offer. Recognition of this culture could enable individuals to find value and meaning in their experience of AS. The life prospects of individuals with AS would change if we shifted from viewing AS as a set of dysfunctions, to viewing it as a set of differences that have merit. This shift in assumptions has been championed by AS advocates who assert that "Aspies" should embrace their atypical talents and communicative skills (Gray and Attwood 1999; Willey 1999). From their perspective, these individuals should no longer be confined to identification as "disordered", but, instead, should assert a valued identity based on the infrequent occurrence of their unique capabilities. Society values the intellectual, the élite athlete, and the gifted artist and nurtures their uncommon talents. We create space for them to pursue their activities because we recognize them as valuable and useful to the group as a whole. Is it not just as possible that people with AS, with their consistently literal interpretations of social interactions, their unwavering ability to devote themselves passionately to one or a few interests, and their capacity to function outside the distractions of conventional social demands, could be the bearers of valuable and useful traits? If we create the space for people with AS to function without constraint and behavioural modification, we may find that they reveal themselves capable of great things. The diagnosis of AS could be recognized as an invitation to nurture the atypical talents and potential of an individual, rather than correcting those traits out of existence. As one man notes "I want to see people who are proud to have autism and accept themselves for who they are and all that they are" (Hurlbutt and Chalmers 2002, p.106). This is a call for a self-defined affirmative definition of AS existence that offers more than just a secondary space available at the whim and indulgence of others.

Of course, as much as we may wish to nurture the talents of the individual with AS, that individual still has to live in a world with "neurotypicals" who are not necessarily oriented to value and support the talents he or she possesses. Affirming an AS culture does not remove the need to equip individuals to function in an unaccommodating world, but it does shift the way in which individuals can understand the place they occupy in that world. Individuals with AS would need to develop a capacity for a bicultural existence. For some of the time, they could engage in AS culture by participating in activities (e.g. social and recreational groups) with other people with AS. They could benefit from finding venues and relationships within which it is not necessary to modify self-expression in order to connect. They could also benefit from being with people who are aware of AS qualities and can interact based on norms that support and appreciate those qualities. These culture-affirming experiences would confer a sense of meaning and community that would fortify individuals when they needed to negotiate mainstream life. Skills training and behavioural modification would become tools for achieving competence necessary for functioning in that other space.

Of course, this would not eliminate all problems. Outside an AS culture there would still exist a world in which neurotypical people appear to be living easier, richer lives with unlimited possibilities. The desire to sample that richness, even fleetingly, would not necessarily be ameliorated by the company of others who share the same atypical traits. Perhaps this is why depression is an all too common experience for people who are diagnosed with AS (Barnhill 2001). One man describes it by saying, "The first 51 years of my life were absolute misery... I would think that I was a terribly wicked person because I couldn't do many of the achievements that are expected of good people" (Jones, Zahl, and Huws 2001, p.398). The movement between AS and neurotypical cultural venues would need to be eased by helping individuals with AS to perceive themselves as belonging in both worlds. This would be important for family members as well. The apologetic, guilt-ridden posture of family members held accountable for their unsettling relatives (Stoddart 1999) would need to be replaced by a new sense of entitlement to accommodation and respect for the cultural differences of AS. With appropriate psychoeducation, family members could work with clinicians to act as cultural mediators. Their knowledge of both cultures could facilitate smoother, less chaotic interactions with teachers, peers, employers, and others who may not understand and appreciate the unusual talents of the individual with AS. Through a co-ordinated effort of culture promotion, more positive psychological and social spaces could be created to provide options for individuals with AS and their families. The availability of these spaces could provide much-needed shelter from an often unforgiving, overwhelming neurotypical world.

Asperger Syndrome as the basis of an oppressive and controlling subcultural experience

"Subculture" is a designation assigned to an unempowered group by outsiders with the authority to define them as marginal participants in the mainstream culture. The addition of the prefix "sub" to the word culture makes a big difference in what it means to be included. Whereas inclusion in a culture is associated with a sense of value, identity, and community, inclusion in a subculture implies a deviant relationship to a larger, more dominant group (Jenkins 1983). Subculture is created when outsiders want to find an explanation for why a particular group in their midst does not fit into their expectations. The term subculture may still correspond to some understanding of social identity; however, it may also impose rigid boundaries around patterns of association that are less deliberate, and less voluntary, than the label would suggest (Bennett 1999). The subculture is an external invention that functions to categorize people that we do not understand, without obliging us to extend efforts that would further our understanding.

The diagnosis of AS is a process that is led by outsiders. A doctor makes this designation based on the authority to diagnose that has been granted to him by his peers, the state, and the public. There are some people who describe self-identifying themselves as individuals with AS and suggesting the diagnosis to their doctors and families. However, even these individuals do not have the authority to claim AS for themselves. Others must authenticate their judgement. At some point, all individuals with AS must submit to the assessment of professional others who, without ever having lived a moment of their experience, can determine whether they meet diagnostic criteria or not. For people who receive this consultation, the diagnosis may seem like an affirmation of a troubled existence, confirmation of what they have suffered. The process, however, is much more about censure. The doctor confirms your deficiencies. The *DSM* (APA 1994) directs him toward your impairments, your failures, your lacks, your restrictions, your abnormalities and your disturbances. The allusion to near-normalcy that is suggested by the designation of "high-functioning" autism is little compensation for the knowledge that you have been declared not good enough in multiple domains.

Outside the doctor's office, little of the world may know the meaning of the diagnosis of AS, but the message of "not good enough" echoes through the individual's life. In schools and playgrounds, the AS child is bullied and teased by peers, and isolated by teachers attempting to maintain order in their classrooms. At home, AS children frustrate and fight with their parents and siblings, and are sent to their rooms for inappropriate behaviour in front of company. While their peers start dating, marrying, and reproducing, they lag behind, struggling to negotiate the complex, unpredictable dynamics of intimate relationships. When these children, adolescents, and adults seek an explanation for why the world scorns them, we offer them a description of their impairments, their failures, their lacks, their restrictions, their abnormalities, and their disturbances. They are asked to understand themselves as people with neurological problems, behavioural problems, emotional problems, and family problems. With the diagnosis of AS comes the dubious privilege of a double consciousness (DuBois 1969); constantly looking at oneself through the eyes of others who view you with confusion, pity, and disdain.

As outsiders looking in, we see these individuals with AS alone, pursuing their interests in the library or the computer room, or together, in the corners of playgrounds and in the alternative classrooms, or congregated, in quiet, predictable workplaces where they can be shielded from the noise and chaos of an overwhelming world. We see this and, looking in from the outside, we declare "Aha! You see? This is AS culture!" There is something a little absurd about this. Reading of Temple Grandin and her "squeeze machine" (Sacks 1995) we can tell ourselves that she created an artefact that was representative of her culture. However, this would require overlooking that the squeeze machine was probably created to provide something the world would not: solace and comfort without the terror of over-exuberant, injudicious human contact. It takes a willful ignorance to overlook the desperation and pain underlying the survival strategies of individuals with AS in favour of declaring them part of a culture. Through such willful ignorance, we justify our unwillingness to create a space for these people to be part of our world.

It is possible that even a subculture can offer some solace and resource to individuals with AS. In a world where they find few places to belong, even a space on the margins may be better than none at all. Yet AS subculture serves people outside the group better than people within the group. Imposing a subculture provides an unchallenging explanation for why the neurotypical world has little room for people with AS. We could ask ourselves questions about why our world finds it so hard to accommodate a group of people with the normal range of intelligence, and mild communication and physical differences. We could give some thought to how this reveals *our* impairments, *our* failures, *our* lacks, *our* restrictions, *our* abnormalities, and *our* disturbances. This would require a willingness to shed the veil that allows us to pretend that we are not implicated in oppressive social relations. It is a more palatable option to look at the people we have diagnosed away from the mainstream and attribute their separation to forming an alternative culture.

Through the determination that certain groups of people exist on the fringe because they choose to do so, prefer to do so, and have no desire to join the mainstream world, we are able to renounce responsibility for their plight. The symbols and knowledge and norms that individuals with AS are told define and unify the group are easily exposed as the products of a story constructed from the accounts of those that have studied them. Any social capital that can be squeezed from associating with those similarly defined and exiled cannot compensate for what is denied through their exclusion. For individuals with AS, constructing a cultural narrative to overlay the discourse of AS abnormality does not change the negative effects of having others organize their lives around a deviant, pathology-based identity. The most that individuals with AS can gain from a subculture is the ambivalent experience of seeking to fulfill themselves within the psychological and social boundaries the mainstream has erected for them.

Family members and clinicians are inevitably implicated in this process. They are willing to do what it takes to help these individuals enjoy happy, fulfilling lives and they are told that treatment and training are the tools that will achieve this. They support an agenda of identifying these individuals as problematic, rather than finding problems in the world that labels them and pushes them aside. Fear of losing the minimal resources made available to them (e.g. disability benefits) dissuades both individuals with AS and their families from demanding fuller participation in the mainstream. It is safer to follow the program, suppress inconvenient AS qualities, and skill-build toward invisibility. Individuals with AS have a difficult choice: to adopt the subculture in hope of securing the rewards that are allotted for not disturbing the status quo, or to challenge the status quo and risk the little they have in hope of achieving a life based on self-determination. Family members, friends, and clinicians have the uncomfortable role of trying to facilitate a best outcome for the individual, but what is that outcome? They know of the benefits and risks of being obliged to take on the subculture, or daring to reject it and the small aids that are offered to compliant, "insightful" patients. Whether the subculture is taken on or rejected, its existence attaches a meaning to the diagnosis of AS that narrows the psychological and social space that these individuals are allowed to occupy.

Conclusions

I conclude there is the foundation of an AS culture. I would suggest that an AS culture and an AS subculture coexist. However, being the member of the valued cultural group *versus* the devalued subcultural group does seem to have different implications for people with AS, their families, and clinicians. On superficial examination, it may seem the affirmed culture is superior to the imposed subculture. Yet, the subculture may simply represent a more explicit execution of the segregating process. When we speak of cultural differences, there is still a dominant norm being presented as the standard for comparison.

The mainstream world does not allow much flexibility in the manifestation of culture or subculture. I am left wondering if individuals with AS are not amazed that they are the ones who are perceived as rigid and restricted. No one knows better than these people about the stringent etiquette of the neurotypical world. They come to know the inordinate social penalties allotted for an incorrect posture, a flawed interpretation, an uncoordinated gesture, or an ill-timed response. If it is true, as some suggest, that individuals with AS are untroubled by the reverberations that result from their social *faux pas* (Barnhill *et al.* 2000), then they are more fortunate than those of us who react to such missteps with acute anxiety. It seems more likely, however, that they can read some cues, and they acutely sense their blunders, if only some time after the interaction. Unfortunately, we fail to perceive their distress; it does not catch our attention until it erupts in a flood of rage, anguish or self-loathing (Myles and Simpson 2002). A cultural model of AS identifies individuals with AS as people who must define themselves against a pervasive image of "normal" that does not include them. A cultural model suggests that the depression and rage that clinicians currently treat as sequelae of the syndrome need to be understood as sequelae of the exclusion. Under these circumstances, well-intended efforts to skill our clients to withstand the rejection and abuse they receive from the neurotypical world are re-interpreted as assimilative technologies that reinforce the exclusion, and maintain an oppressive status quo. If therapy is to have more than anaesthetic effects, it must create spaces and strategies for individuals to construct a life that is not defined by a world unable to value their existence.

In a postmodern world, we recognize that any cultural identity is changeable and often illusory. It is possible to travel between spaces without seeking group identity, but, instead, seek transient associations to fulfill immediate needs. Those individuals with AS who have found ways to associate with their families, with other "Aspies", with people who share their interests, and with professionals may have discovered that the most tolerable life is one in which expectations of enduring connections are exchanged for expectations of living out selected identities in specific sites. This existence may create a space that, for some individuals, would be a reasonable exchange for the elusive experience of cultural belonging. Alternatively, it may create a means by which individuals can shift their alliances over time, meeting the needs they have in a given moment, and moving on when those needs change. This may be a desirable outcome, but it lets "the rest of us" off the hook too easily. We treat AS as if it is a set of problems that must be dealt with by diagnosed individuals, their relatives, and people in the health care system, but we live in this world together. Those who are not diagnosed, not relatives, and not health professionals have a role to play in determining the latitude that will be given to people who do not conform to what we pretend are fixed rules of social conduct. AS sheds a bright light on the overwhelming, chaotic, unpredictable, and unforgiving aspects of social interaction in the dominant world. The search for AS culture is not just an opportunity to discover the value that lies within it, but also an opportunity to recognize the problems in what lies beyond.

References

APA (American Psychiatric Association) (1994) *Diagnostic and Statistical Manual of Mental Disorders, Fourth Edition.* Washington, DC: APA.

Barnhill, G.P. (2001) Social attribution and depression in adolescents with Asperger syndrome. *Focus on Autism and Other Developmental Disabilities, 16,* 46–53.

Barnhill, G.P., Hagiwara, R., Myles, B.S., Simpson, R.L., Brick, M.L., and Griswold, D.E. (2000) Parent, teacher, and self-report of problem and adaptive behaviors in children and adolescents with Asperger syndrome. *Diagnostique, 25,* 147–67.

Bennett, A. (1999) Subcultures or neotribes? Rethinking the relationship between youth, style and musical taste. *Sociology, 33,* 3, 599–617.

DuBois, W.E.B. (1969) *The Souls of Black Folk.* New York, NY: Signet Classics.

Gray, C., and Attwood, T. (1999) The discovery of "Aspie" criteria. Retrieved from www.tonyattwood.com.au/paper4.htm on January 11, 2004.

Hurlbutt, K., and Chalmers, L. (2002) Adults with autism speak out: Perceptions of their life experiences. *Focus on Autism and Other Developmental Disabilities, 17,* 2, 103–111.

Jenkins, R. (1983) *Lads, Citizens and Ordinary Kids: Working Class Youth Lifestyles in Belfast.* London, UK: Routledge and Kegan Paul.

Jones, R.S.P., Zahl, A., and Huws, J.C. (2001) First hand accounts of emotional experiences in autism: A qualitative analysis. *Disability and Society, 16,* 3, 393–401.

Mayes, S.D., Calhoun, S.L., and Crites, D.L. (2001) Does DSM-IV Asperger's disorder exist? *Journal of Abnormal Child Psychology, 29,* 3, 263–71.

Myles, B.S., and Simpson, R.L. (2002) Asperger syndrome: An overview of characteristics. *Focus on Autism and Other Developmental Disabilities, 17,* 3, 132–7.

Sacks, O. (1995) *An Anthropologist on Mars: Seven Paradoxical Tales.* New York, NY: Alfred A. Knopf.

Stoddart, K.P. (1999) Adolescents with Asperger syndrome: Three case studies of individual and family therapy. *Autism: The International Journal of Research and Practice, 3,* 3, 255–71.

Waleski, G. (2002) Living with Asperger's Syndrome. Retrieved from www.isn.net/~jypsy/gary1.htm on February 27, 2004.

Willey, L.H. (1999) *Pretending to be Normal: Living with Asperger's Syndrome.* London, UK: Jessica Kingsley Publishers.

CHAPTER 17

Child social interaction and parental self-efficacy: Evaluating simultaneous groups for children with Asperger Syndrome and their parents

Leon Sloman and Jonathan Leef [1]

Children with Asperger Syndrome (AS) have difficulty coping with many social aspects of daily life. Although some social skills group interventions have improved the *communication* skills of children and adolescents with AS (Mesibov 1984; Williams 1989; Ozonoff and Miller 1995; Howlin and Yates 1999), the quality of their *social interaction* has not shown significant improvement (Gillberg 1991; Bowler 1992; Greenway 2000; Klin and Volkmar 2000). Recently, Krasny and colleagues (2003) agreed that such interventions fail to significantly improve the social disabilities of children with AS.

We hypothesized that a more effective treatment would comprise concurrent groups for children with AS and their parents, with good two-way communication between the groups. Moreover, we believe that when designing interventions for latency children and young adolescents with AS, it is necessary to consider the defining features of this syndrome, as well as the individual characteristics of each child. Understanding and targeting the child's deficits is essential for designing successful interventions. We use a systems approach (Sloman and Konstantareas

1   We wish to thank Margot Nelles for initiating this program, and the group leaders Carol Nelles, Ian Roth, Elaine Schiller, and Greg Riley, as well as the numerous staff, students, and volunteers who participated in the groups. These groups were a joint venture between the Aspergers Society of Ontario and the Centre for Addiction and Mental Health.

1990). Although AS originates in the biological system, the child's maturation and individuation are reflected in his or her interaction with the family, peer group, and school systems. We therefore held simultaneous peer and parent groups. In the latter, an important agenda item is advocating for the child in the school system.

In this chapter, we describe the social deficits and possible underlying aetiologies seen in children with AS. We then describe our model of child and parent groups, and the methods we used to evaluate outcome, followed by our results and conclusions.

Traits of children with Asperger Syndrome

Problems in social interaction

Difficulty in reciprocal social interaction is a defining feature of AS (APA 1994). This is associated with problems in reading social cues and responding in a socially appropriate manner. As a result, these children are likely to be socially isolated, bullied, and punished. Children with AS may be unable to follow rules because they do not understand the rules, or the reason for the rules' existence (Attwood 1998; Greenway 2000; Klin and Volkmar 2000). Even if a rule is a simple social convention understood by most others, such as standing in a line when waiting, or not speaking while the teacher is talking, it may be difficult for them to follow it. On the other hand, children with AS may follow rules obsessively and often insist that others follow the same rules in a rigid uncompromising fashion, thereby creating difficulties for themselves and others.

Deficit theory of mind (ToM)

A core problem in AS is thought to be a lack, or delay in development of a theory of mind (ToM) (Dewey 1991; Frith 1991; Wing 1991; Bowler 1992; Astington and Jenkins 1995; Happé et al. 1996; Klin and Volkmar 2000). ToM is the cognitive capacity to realize the uniqueness of one's own and others' beliefs, desires, and intentions, and is an essential component of perspective-taking abilities. Empirical evidence suggests that normal ToM is related to typical development of social understanding (Astington 1993; Astington and Jenkins 1995), and that children with AS have more difficulty with ToM tasks than controls (Bowler 1992; Baron-Cohen 2000). Delayed ToM development may contribute to children's difficulties in reading social cues and relating to their peers (Bowler 1992). Neuroimaging studies have found deficits in the left medial prefrontal cortex of AS patients when performing ToM tasks. This is a region usually activated in normal control groups when performing such tasks (Happé et al. 1996). Although these findings support the notion of a ToM deficit in AS, findings are inconsistent. Some individuals with AS succeed in ToM tasks (Bailey, Phillips, and Rutter 1996) while some children with autism have shown a significant developmental improvement in ToM ability over time. This improvement has been shown to be primarily related to the children's language abilities (Steele, Joseph, and Tager-Flusberg 2003). In fact, Astington and Jenkins (1999) have demonstrated a positive correlation between language ability and ToM development in normal child populations.

Poor regulation of affect

Children with AS have difficulty monitoring and regulating their affect. Most children with AS find social interaction threatening, especially with people outside their family. Since they have difficulty regulating their anxiety, as well as problems reading social cues, they often respond to new social situations by acting in a socially inappropriate fashion. Subsequently, many of these children become discouraged and withdrawn. They also experience high anxiety and depression because of the discordance between their strong desire for social contact and inability to perform successfully in social settings (Attwood 1998; Baron-Cohen 2000; Frith 1991; Greenway 2000; Klin and Volkmar 2000). This compromises their ability to function socially and contributes to social withdrawal, which further limits the child's opportunities to practise and acquire new social skills. Nevertheless, the desire for social contact can be a strong motivator and therefore an asset when designing interventions.

Difficulty generalizing knowledge

AS has also been attributed to a difficulty in generalizing knowledge of how to cope in one setting to new social situations (Frith 1991; Bowler 1992; Attwood 1998; Greenway 2000; Klin and Volkmar 2000; Kaland et al. 2002). This difficulty remains a significant obstacle to effective intervention, since skills that are learned in a therapeutic environment may not be transferred to other settings. For example, children with AS may learn rules at home about not speaking too loudly or about the importance of sharing toys, but may not know how to apply that knowledge at school (Greenway 2000).

Rationale for the intervention

Utilizing a group format

Although there are curricula for improving social adaptation in children with AS in a one-to-one setting, few curricula exist for group formats (Krasny et al. 2003). Therefore, we felt it necessary to develop a new approach while still drawing upon the literature on existing formats. Group formats enable the child or adolescent to practise social skills while meeting others with similar challenges and interests (Attwood 1998; Greenway 2000; Klin and Volkmar 2000). Klin and Volkmar maintain that giving the AS child more opportunity to interact socially by joining clubs and community centres should be a therapeutic goal because it provides the child with more opportunity to practise his or her social skills.

A group format has several advantages. First, it enables us directly to address AS children's fundamental difficulty in interacting socially with peers. It represents a setting in which the child's social difficulties are manifested while providing an opportunity to help the child to develop appropriate social skills. Another advantage, we believe, is that the efficacy of the children's groups is enhanced by having simultaneous parent groups and the exchange of information between the children and parent groups. Having these two groups provides an opportunity for both children and parents to forge relationships and have cross-fertilization through an exchange of information between the two groups.

Promoting social skills

The primary aim of our social interaction program was to promote social skills, while addressing the emotional and cognitive difficulties children and adolescents with AS experience. We employed the concept of a "cycle of success" (Sloman and Dunham 2004) that asserts that a child who lacks basic social skills for successful social interaction is likely to be insecure about interacting socially. This insecurity decreases the likelihood the child will engage in social interaction, which will further hamper social skills development. To interrupt this self-defeating cycle, it is necessary to improve social skills and increase the child's confidence in his or her ability to function socially. To achieve this, we believe that parents must be engaged in helping children with AS become more socially competent.

Teaching theory of mind

To promote ToM abilities we discussed how actions affect different people differently. We drew the children's attention to the fact that people have private thoughts and feelings, and suggested steps they can take to learn about them. For example, we might discuss with the children the importance of asking for permission before taking someone else's object.

To underscore perspective taking in social interaction, children shared recent positive or negative experiences with the group. After each child's story, a facilitator asked the group to describe how the experience just described made the storyteller feel. Meta-cognitive and meta-emotional language is purposefully used. For instance, when a boy told the group that he won a basketball tournament that day at school, the facilitator asked the entire group: "How do you think Ed felt today when he won the basketball tournament?" In this manner, children were encouraged to reflect on another participant's thoughts, desires, and emotions. When "reading" another person's emotions was difficult, the facilitator asked the children how they would feel in a similar situation, or told them how the child felt. Then a discussion ensued about why the child felt this way.

We also challenged children's assumptions. For example, when a child initiated a conversation that was incoherent because he assumed the listener's prior knowledge, a facilitator quickly corrected him. Facilitators asked the child to clarify the topic by asking specific questions, and then drew the child's attention to the fact that other people's prior knowledge of the topic could not be assumed.

Facilitating regulation of affect

To reduce the children's anxiety, we made the groups a fun experience, established a supportive and accepting environment in which facilitators discouraged put-downs and teasing, and positively reinforced spontaneous prosocial interactions. Our aim was to enable the children to feel more self-confidant about their ability to interact socially. We permitted open and free discussion about topics the children selected, accepted the idiosyncratic attributes of the participants, and explored and promoted children's common interests. This enabled the children to interact with others who shared their social challenges, as well as their hobbies and interests (Attwood 1998; Klin and Volkmar 2000).

We addressed individual children's difficulty in regulating affect in several ways. In every session, the group leader encouraged the children to notify facilitators when they needed a time-out due to high anxiety and reminded them that this was a fitting request. Because of the high staff-to-child ratio, it was possible for every facilitator to monitor one or two children for evidence of heightened anxiety or any change in mood. We also encouraged the children to incorporate noting their own affect into their individual goals. For example, James decided that he would let the facilitator know when he was becoming angry so he could have a time-out.

Identifying individual goals

As the participants' strengths and weaknesses varied, it was also necessary to develop individual goals for each child. The goals were socially defined and, when possible, positively worded. We used clear language the children could understand. Goals included initiating a conversation with another child during the session, or making eye contact while conversing with facilitators and participants.

To address children's difficulty in comprehending and following rules, some of the children's individual goals were rule based. For example, a child's goal may be not to interrupt for a given amount of time when others are speaking. To implement this, at the beginning of every session, each child negotiated a goal and the reward for successful achievement of that goal with a facilitator. A contract was written, which both the child and facilitator signed. Strategies for successful completion of the goal were written into the contract. For example, if the goal was to initiate a conversation with two children, the strategy involved choosing the children with whom to speak, establishing a suitable time and topic, and calling the other child's name to get his attention. If, during the session, the facilitators observed that a child's goal was too challenging or, conversely, not challenging enough, they modified it accordingly. Some children required direct prompting to remain focussed on their goals. In this manner, the child's individual social deficits were addressed while, at the same time, prosocial interaction between participants was fostered.

Promoting generalization

The collaboration between the child and parent groups enabled us to address the problem of generalization in different ways. First, we incorporated parental goals into the child group. For example, when a mother expressed concern about her son's bullying of others, facilitators repeatedly helped the child to distinguish between bullying and playful teasing. Second, we encouraged parents to follow similar individual goals and suggested strategies they could use at home. Third, we talked to the children about other situations in which they could apply what they learned in the groups. We therefore addressed the problem of generalization by expanding the number of situations where the children could apply what they had learned.

Establishing group goals

We wished to increase the children's awareness of how their behaviours affect others. To achieve this, we established a group reward, which was contingent on all the children attaining their individual goals. For example, in the first session the facilitators suggested four group activities (for the children to enjoy in the last session) from which the children collectively had to choose one activity. This became the group's reward. The group could enjoy this activity, if they accumulated a sufficient number of stickers on a poster board through achieving their individual goals and other prosocial behaviours. Each time a child successfully achieved his goal, he added a sticker to the poster board (on which a mountain was depicted with the goal written at its peak). Furthermore, each time a child spontaneously behaved prosocially, she was awarded a large sticker to add to the "mountain".

Description of the groups

Children's groups

Our groups were composed of children in two age groups: one group for ages between 9 and 12, and another for the ages of 11 to 14. Groups ran for eight to ten weeks. The groups met weekly at the Centre for Addiction and Mental Health for one-and-a-half-hour sessions. Five staff members led the child groups.

The groups began with each child establishing their individual goal for the session with a facilitator. The group then sat down for "circle time" during which the children recounted events from the past week. Children were encouraged to self-disclose. When they did, facilitators reacted in an empathetic and supportive manner, and encouraged the children to empathize and ask questions. We asked the other children what they thought the child felt in his or her situation to promote acceptance and foster ToM development.

Facilitators asked the children to review the purpose of the group and the group rules that were collaboratively established in the first session and were posted in the group's room. They also discussed other topics, such as taking turns and co-operation within the group.

Each week, a specific social communication skill was emphasized through role-play activities. Social conventions, such as eye contact, acknowledging another speaker, and suitable means of getting others' attention were under-scored. Facilitators acted out appropriate and inappropriate ways to practise these skills. Children were then placed in pairs and given a scenario that portrayed the correct use of the particular social skill. They then performed the role play in front of the entire group. Role-play exercises also dealt with ways to cope with teasing and bullying. For instance, children acted out scenarios in which one child was victimizing another. The victim was encouraged to implement coping strategies that were previously discussed in the group.

Recreational activities were sometimes included. For instance, groups played co-operative sports games in the gymnasium and games in which interaction and co-operation with other group members were imperative for success. Other games included charades, in which children were asked to act out a specific emotion through gestures and facial expressions.

The last portion of the session was devoted to snack time and informal social-izing. Children were actively involved in preparing and giving out the snack; they played games of their choice, showed magazines to each other, or simply talked to each other informally. This was a good opportunity for the children to carry out their individual social goals. At the end of the session, facilitators asked the children to share positive social experiences they had had in the group, while rewards for reaching their individual goals were handed out.

Parents' groups

The parent groups, led by a facilitator and overseeing psychiatrist, had several aims. One was to educate the parents about the main features of AS. A second aim was to teach parents about the variety of ways to respond to their child's AS features, especially problems in socializing, anxiety, depression, lack of self-confidence, difficulty in perspective taking and generalizing. When a parent expressed a concern about his or her child's behaviour, we tried to determine whether it was directly due to AS. Parents actively shaped the groups' agenda and initiated free-flowing discussions. When one parent expressed a concern, the group leader often gave each participant a chance to express his or her perspec-tive. They shared ideas about how to manage their child's behaviours and expressed how they felt about being a parent of a child with AS. At times, the psy-chiatrist adopted a more didactic stance, as when the groups were discussing medication or diet.

Outside speakers, including psychiatrists, occupational therapists, behav-ioural therapists, and various advocates for children with special needs in the school system, visited the parent groups. They discussed topics that included medication, the roles of cognitive and sensory integration therapies, anxiety, and depression. In response to the parents' questions about long-term prognosis, we had young adults with AS, as well as their parents and siblings, speak with the groups about their experiences.

To establish two-way communication between the parent and child groups, a facilitator from the children's group asked each parent at the start of their group for salient information about their child's day and whether there were specific issues they wished the children's group to address. To save time at the beginning of the sessions, we devised a form on which parents wrote about the concerns and priorities that they wanted us to address in the children's group. They then emailed the form to the facilitating psychiatrist. A facilitator from the children's group came into the parents' group again near the end of the session to report on the children. He discussed whether each child achieved his or her goal for that session and the reward the child chose. The facilitator provided the parents with specific insights on techniques that might be tried at home. For example, a child facilitator gave parents written descriptions of role-play exercises that we used in the group, and strategies they could practise at home. Through such co-ordination we aimed to promote the children's ability to generalize and the parents' improved understanding of their child.

Method

Subjects

Data were collected for 21 boys and 6 girls between 9 and 14 years of age (Mean = 10.81, SD = 1.70). Participants were referred to the supervising psychiatrist either by the Aspergers Society of Ontario or by other professionals. All participants were screened for AS by a psychiatrist at the Centre for Addiction and Mental Health in Toronto. During the assessment, current problems, a history of previous problems, a developmental history of the child, and family history were recorded. The children were assessed individually and the clinician administered the Questionnaire for Asperger Syndrome and Other High-functioning Autism Spectrum Disorders (Ehlers, Gillberg, and Wing 1999) and the Childhood Autism Rating Scale (Schopler *et al.* 1980; Schopler, Reichler, and Renner 1988). Participants were permitted to join the groups if they met the criteria for AS and were considered as likely to benefit from the group. One child, who was considered too disruptive, was excluded from the program. Another child, who was quiet and withdrawn, reacted so negatively to the first session with a rowdy group of children that it was decided to withdraw him from the group.

Instruments

- *The Childhood Autism Rating Scale (CARS) (Schopler* et al. *1980, 1988)*: The assessing psychiatrist completed the CARS on all children with parents as informants.

- *The Australian Scale for Asperger's Syndrome (ASAS) (Attwood 1998)*: Parents filled out the ASAS before children participated in the groups and immediately after the groups' conclusion. It is comprised of 24 questions; each question has a rating between 0 and 6. A score of 0 expresses the notion that the description in the question rarely occurs, as would be expected from a normal child, while a score of 6 expresses the notion that the symptom occurs frequently. The ASAS is divided into four sections: "Social and Emotional Abilities", "Communication Skills", "Cognitive Skills", and "Specific Interests". A score between 2 and 6 on most questions suggests the probability of AS, and a higher total ASAS score implies a higher probability of AS.

- *ToM tasks*: We used three false-belief tasks and a moral judgement task. The false-belief tasks included the unexpected-contents task based on Perner, Leekam, and Wimmer (1987), in which participants were shown a familiar container (i.e. a box of Smarties) that had unexpected objects inside (i.e. band-aids). A second-order belief attribution task developed by Baron-Cohen (1989), and a task that involved both second-order ignorance and second-order false-belief were used. Second-order belief and ignorance tasks involved stories which were slightly modified to suit our purposes and eliminate cultural biases. The stories emphasized the characters' thoughts about other characters' thoughts. In the third task, children were asked to justify their answers using meta-cognitive language (Sullivan, Zaitchik, and Tager-Flusberg 1994). We used a moral judgement task based on Mant and Perner (1988), reading stories which depicted intentional and unintentional offences. Children were asked to make a moral judgement and justify their answers.

- *Parental Self-efficacy in the Management of Asperger Syndrome (Sofronoff and Farbotko 2002)*: This scale measures the level of parents' confidence in their ability to manage their children when they engage in typical AS behaviours. For example, parents were asked to rate their confidence level, between 0 (no confidence) and 5 (completely confident), when their child "follows routines rigidly", or "does not take turns in conversation".

Results

- *Childhood Autism Rating Scale (CARS)*: Scores ranged from 24 to 35 (Mean = 30.76, SD = 2.83). CARS scores were not correlated with gender or parents' self-efficacy scores, and were almost significantly correlated with pre-group ASAS scores (p = .06).

- *Australian Scale for Asperger's Syndrome (ASAS)*: Mean scores of the 24 ASAS questions were used as pre- and post-treatment indicators of change. The pre-group mean score was 3.9 and the post-group mean was 3.34. A paired-sample *t*-test indicated a significant pre–post difference in ASAS scores (SD = .07, $t(26) = 4.21$, p <.01). Since our groups addressed the social, emotional, and communication deficits in AS, we also analysed changes in the "Social and Emotional Abilities" and "Communication Skills" sub-scales. We found significant pre–post differences in the combined means of these sub-scales (SD = 0.81, $t(26) = 4.29$, p< .01). On a more conservative test, namely the

Wilcoxon signed ranks test, we again found significant pre–post changes for total ASAS scores (p <.01).

- *First-order false belief:* Of the 17 children assessed, 16 correctly answered the two questions about false belief, while one child answered one of the two false-belief questions correctly.

- *Second-order false belief:* Most (11 out of 17) of the children correctly answered questions about the story characters' knowledge and thoughts, but did not use any meta-cognitive language when asked to justify their answers.

- *Second-order ignorance task:* Most of the children (11 out of 13) passed this task. However, the majority only used a small number (two or three) of meta-cognitive statements when justifying their answers.

- *Moral judgement task:* Children were expected to ascribe to the first story, in which the protagonist was not responsible for a negative outcome ("Jeremy didn't go over to Nate's house because the bus broke down"), a more positive moral judgement than to the second story. The second story described the negative outcome as a result of the protagonist's decision ("Jane decided to stay at home and didn't tell Melissa that she wasn't going to meet her. Melissa waited for Jane at the theatre for a long time"). We also evaluated children's justifications of their moral evaluations. Most children (10 out of 13) were not able to make this differentiation and saw both Jeremy's and Jane's behaviour as "bad".

- *Parental Self-Efficacy in the Management of Asperger Syndrome:* We found a significant pre–post difference on the Parental Self-Efficacy in the Management of Asperger Syndrome questionnaire using a paired-sample t-test (n = 15, pre-mean score = 3.2, post-mean score = 3.0, SD = .72, t = -4.43, p <.001).

- *Correlation between Parental Self-efficacy and change in ASAS:* We used a Pearson r correlation to determine whether there was a correlation between pre–post difference scores of the ASAS and the Parental Self-efficacy questionnaire. We wished to discover whether a significant relationship existed between the changes in parents' evaluation of their own parenting abilities (self-efficacy) and the perceived changes in their child's behaviour. We found no significant correlation.

- *Participant feedback and observable progress:* When asked what they most appreciated about the parent groups, parents reported that it was the regular two-way communication between the parent and child groups. Towards the end of the programs, participants forged new friendships.

For instance, some children communicated by email, a few children invited other children to their homes and sometimes parents arranged for their children to meet. This led to ongoing interaction outside the group between children who had been completely socially isolated. Some of these relationships continued long after our groups had terminated. A few children who were initially resistant to coming became more willing, or even enthusiastic about attending the groups. Two children who refused to attend school were willing to come to the groups.

Discussion

The significant difference between pre-group and post-group measures for the ASAS for the sample of 27 subjects is a promising finding. The finding of a change in the sub-sections of the ASAS that tap into the social, emotional, and communication skills suggests that positive changes occurred in the major deficit areas for children with AS. What remains unclear is to what extent the improved social interaction, as the parents noted on the ASAS, can be attributed to the children's acquisition of new social skills or to their decreased anxiety and improved self-esteem. A possibility may be that children did not learn many new social skills, but were better able to interact socially because of their more positive mood and decreased anxiety in social situations.

We have yet to determine which ToM tasks are most fitting for evaluating change in this population. However, we did discover that the children in our groups tended to have difficulty applying meta-cognitive reasoning when analysing situations. Furthermore, when making moral judgements, they evaluated other people's behaviour rigidly without considering moral nuances.

Klin and Volkmar (2000) argued that children with AS must be socially active in order to heighten their social confidence, even though the children themselves may initially refuse this. We found that social activities monitored by trained professionals with a high staff-to-child ratio can lead to increased confidence. The safe, supportive, and fun social environment in our groups made the children feel more accepted and lowered their anxiety, which motivated them to participate in group activities. This fostered more positive social interactions, which, in turn, raised their mood and built their social confidence.

We used concrete rewards to motivate the children to manage their affect and act in socially acceptable ways. Since we used the children's specific interests (such as playing with a Game Boy, or reading a book alone for a given amount of time) as rewards for their successful social interaction, we displayed acceptance of their idiosyncrasies. We thereby linked social success with self-acceptance and positive affect.

The high parental enthusiasm engendered by participation in the parents' and children's groups may have influenced their scoring of the ASAS and the parent self-efficacy scale. Yet, we found no relationship between the way the parents evaluated their child's progress on the ASAS and their evaluation of their own increased self-efficacy. This indicates the parents' evaluation of their child's progress did not directly influence their feeling of self-efficacy. Conversely, it indicates parents' feelings of self-efficacy did not impact the way they evaluated their child.

Since parents reported improved social and communication abilities outside the groups' setting, and several children maintained friendships long after the groups ended, some generalization did occur.

Furthermore, the parents' rise in parental self-efficacy may be because of several factors. First, the program improved parents' understanding of AS. Second, parents acquired new strategies for coping with their children. Third, parents benefited from the support they gave each other: it was reassuring for them to realize they were not alone and that others faced similar challenges. However, the positive results may be a placebo effect fostered by parents' enthusiasm. This may have resulted in their interacting more positively with their child, which, in turn, could have promoted positive interactions between the child and others. It was often reassuring for them to learn that other parents were facing similar dilemmas. The supportive nature of the group made this a positive experience.

Conclusions

The instruments we used to evaluate change, as well as our direct observations, revealed children's improved social interactions and parents' increased confidence in their parenting abilities. These changes were consistent with what we set out to achieve. However, it is not clear whether the children's improved social interactions were because of their participation in the groups, their parents' participation in the parents' groups, or their combined effect. Further research is required to determine the validity and reliability of the ASAS, and to replicate and expand our findings, especially with the use of control groups. New longitudinal measurements should be considered to evaluate changes in children and their parents. We also need better tools to measure anxiety, as well as the generalization and social skills of children with AS. Furthermore, there is a need to discover what aspect of ToM functioning is most relevant to AS. We believe that future research should examine the moral judgements of children with AS. In addition, we require more objective measures to evaluate the effectiveness of parents' groups. Overall, it appears that programs of this kind can benefit children with AS and their parents.

References

APA (American Psychiatric Association) (1994) *Diagnostic and Statistical Manual of Mental Disorders, Fourth Edition.* Washington, DC: APA.

Astington, J.W. (1993) *The Child's Discovery of the Mind.* Cambridge, MA: Harvard University Press.

Astington, J.W., and Jenkins, J.M. (1995) Theory of mind development and social understanding. *Cognition and Emotion, 9,* 151–65.

Astington, J.W., and Jenkins, J.M. (1999) A longitudinal study of the relation between language and theory of mind development. *Developmental Psychology, 35,* 1311–20.

Attwood, T. (1998) *Asperger's Syndrome: A Guide for Parents and Professionals.* London, UK: Jessica Kingsley Publishers.

Bailey, A., Phillips, W., and Rutter, M. (1996) Autism: Toward an integration of clinical, genetic, neuropsychological, and neurobiological perspectives. *Journal of Child Psychology and Psychiatry and Allied Disciplines, 37,* 89–126.

Baron-Cohen, S. (1989) The autistic child's theory of mind: A case of specific developmental delay. *Journal of Child Psychology and Psychiatry, 30,* 285–97.

Baron-Cohen, S. (2000) Is Asperger syndrome/HFA necessarily a disability? *Development and Psychopathology, 12,* 489–500.

Bowler, D.M. (1992) "Theory of mind" in Asperger's syndrome. *Journal of Child Psychology and Psychiatry, 33,* 877–93.

Dewey, M. (1991) Living with Asperger's Syndrome. In U. Frith (ed.) *Autism and Asperger Syndrome.* Cambridge, UK: Cambridge University Press.

Ehlers, S., Gillberg, C., and Wing, L. (1999) A screening questionnaire for Asperger syndrome and other high-functioning autism spectrum disorders in school age children. *Journal of Autism and Developmental Disorders, 29,* 129–41.

Frith, U. (1991) Asperger and his syndrome. In U. Frith (ed.) *Autism and Asperger Syndrome.* Cambridge, UK: Cambridge University Press.

Gillberg, C. (1991) Clinical and neurobiological aspects of Asperger syndrome in six family studies. In U. Frith (ed.) *Autism and Asperger Syndrome.* Cambridge, UK: Cambridge University Press.

Greenway, C. (2000) Autism and Asperger syndrome: Strategies to promote prosocial behaviours. *Educational Psychology in Practice, 16,* 469–86.

Happé, F., Ehlers, S., Fletcher, P., Frith, U., Johansson, M., Gillberg, C., *et al.* (1996) "Theory of mind" in the brain: Evidence from a PET scan study of Asperger syndrome. *Neuroreport, 8,* 197–201.

Howlin, P., and Yates, P. (1999) The potential effectiveness of social skills groups for adults with autism. *Autism: The International Journal of Research and Practice, 3,* 3, 299–307.

Kaland, N., Moller-Nielsen, A., Callesen, K., Mortensen, E.L., Gottlieb, D., and Smith, L. (2002) A new advanced test of theory of mind: Evidence from children and adolescents with Asperger syndrome. *Journal of Child Psychology and Psychiatry, 43,* 517–28.

Klin, A., and Volkmar, F.R. (2000) Treatment and intervention guidelines for individuals with Asperger syndrome. In A. Klin, F.R. Volkmar, and S.S. Sparrow (eds) *Asperger Syndrome.* New York, NY: Guilford Press.

Krasny, L., Williams, B.J., Provencal, S., and Ozonoff, S. (2003) Social skills interventions for the autism spectrum: Essential ingredients and a model curriculum. *Child and Adolescent Psychiatric Clinics of North America, 12,* 107–22.

Mant, C., and Perner, J. (1988) The child's understanding of commitment. *Developmental Psychology, 24,* 343–51.

Mesibov, G.B. (1984) Social skills training with verbal autistic adolescents and adults: A program model. *Journal of Autism and Developmental Disorders, 14*, 4, 395–404.

Ozonoff, S., and Miller, J.N. (1995) Teaching theory of mind: A new approach to social skills training for individuals with autism. *Journal of Autism and Developmental Disorders, 25*, 4, 415–33.

Perner, J., Leekam, S., and Wimmer, H. (1987) Three-year-olds' difficulty with false belief: The case for a conceptual deficit. *British Journal of Developmental Psychology, 5*, 125–37.

Schopler, E., Reichler, R.J., DeVellis, R.F., and Daly, K. (1980) Toward objective classification of childhood autism: The Childhood Autism Rating Scale (CARS). *Journal of Autism and Developmental Disorders, 10*, 91–3.

Schopler, E., Reichler, R.J., and Renner, B.R. (1988) *The Childhood Autism Rating Scale (CARS).* Los Angles, CA: Western Psychological Services.

Sloman, L., and Dunham, D. (2004) The Matthew effect: Evolutionary implications. *Evolutionary Psychology, 2*, 92–104.

Sloman, L., and Konstantareas, M.M. (1990) Why families of children with biological deficits require a systems approach. *Family Process, 29*, 417–29.

Sofronoff, K., and Farbotko, M. (2002) The effectiveness of parent management training to increase self-efficacy in parents of children with Asperger syndrome. *Autism: The International Journal of Research and Practice, 6*, 3, 271–86.

Steele, S., Joseph, R.M., and Tager-Flusberg, H. (2003) Brief report: Developmental change in theory of mind abilities in children with autism. *Journal of Autism and Developmental Disorders, 33*, 4, 461–7.

Sullivan, K., Zaitchik, D., and Tager-Flusberg, H. (1994) Preschoolers can attribute second-order beliefs. *Developmental Psychology, 30*, 395–402.

Williams, T.I. (1989) A social skills group for autistic children. *Journal of Autism and Developmental Disorders, 19*, 1, 143–55.

Wing, L. (1991) The relationship between Asperger's syndrome and Kanner's autism. In U. Frith (ed.) *Autism and Asperger Syndrome.* Cambridge, UK: Cambridge University Press.

CHAPTER 18

The genetics of autism spectrum disorders

Jeanette J.A. Holden and Xudong Liu

It is now widely accepted that Asperger Syndrome (AS) belongs to the group of the autism spectrum disorders (ASDs), which are characterized by a triad of characteristics including problems with reciprocal social interaction and communication impairments, and the presence of restricted, repetitive or stereotyped behaviours. Based on family and twin studies, the spectrum is often perceived as even broader, including individuals with two or even one of these characteristics. The term "broader phenotype" has been used by Bailey and colleagues (Bailey *et al.* 1995; Bailey *et al.* 1998) to describe persons with social and/or language abnormalities, often found in families with a proband with autistic disorder or even in monozygotic co-twins with autism. The results of genetic studies, including genome scans that include the broad spectrum of phenotypes, suggest that at least some of the genes underlying susceptibility to AS are shared by the wider group of persons with autistic disorder and Pervasive Developmental Disorder – Not Otherwise Specified (PDD-NOS). Therefore, this chapter reviews genetic findings on this spectrum of disorders. When available, studies exclusively on individuals with AS are presented, but few such studies have been undertaken to date.

Evidence for the role of genetic factors in susceptibility to autism spectrum disorders

The results of family and twin studies indicate that ASDs are a group of highly genetic disorders, meaning that genes play a significant role in the susceptibility of a person to developing an ASD. Based on the findings from epidemiological studies that indicate a prevalence of ASD of about 3 to 6 per 1000 (Fombonne 2003; Yeargin-Allsopp *et al.* 2003), the recurrence risk to siblings and increased risk for concordance in monozygotic twins, heritability can be estimated as from 0.6 to 0.9 (Constantino and Todd 2003). The co-occurrence of autism with several well-defined genetic conditions suggests that these conditions lower the threshold for autism, perhaps through early developmental differences that occur as a result of the impact of these other genetic disorders. In addition to genetic factors, environmental factors contribute to both the development of autism and the extent of the impairment, as evidenced by the effects of early intensive behavioural intervention in reducing the severity of the condition in a large proportion of children.

Twin studies

There are several studies examining the concordance for autism or the broader phenotype in same-sex twins. In the first such study, Folstein and Rutter (1977) found that 4 of 11 monozygotic twins were concordant for autism. When the spectrum of disabilities was increased to include severe language delay, marked reading disability, articulation problems, and/or mental retardation, the concordance increased to 82%. In a later study, Bailey's group (Bailey *et al.* 1995) found the concordance for monozygotic twins was 60% for autism but 92% when social and/or cognitive disorder in the co-twin was included, compared to 10% in dizygotic twins. The presence of a much higher degree of concordance for autism or the broader spectrum in monozygotic twins, compared to same-sex dizygotic twins, argues for a significant genetic component to the aetiology of ASDs.

Family studies

A second approach to determining the effect of genetic factors on the development of a complex disorder such as autism is to determine the recurrence risk in siblings and other family members. Two different approaches are generally used to examine this: (1) *the family history method*, in which one or more members of a family are interviewed about their family and cases of autism or ASD are identified through the interview, and (2) *the family study method*, in which other cases of ASD are confirmed by direct examination by the investigators. The latter method is more accurate, but is also very costly, and thus most studies rely on asking two or more informants about other family members. Recurrence in siblings is between 2 and 7%, depending on the study (Smalley, Asarnow and Spence 1988). In addition, a further 10–20% of siblings are described as having the broader phenotype, consisting of language, learning, social, and communication impairments (Bolton *et al.* 1994; Piven *et al.* 1997), with parents also showing elevated rates of certain personality traits (aloof, anxious, fewer friendships, communication problems, and cognitive deficits in executive function)

(Murphy *et al.* 2000; Piven 2001). The rapid decrease in the rate of autistic characteristics from identical twins to siblings to more distant relatives suggests that autism results from the epistatic interaction of several genes (i.e. five to ten or more) (Pickles *et al.* 1995).

Co-occurrence with other genetic disorders

Less than 10% of cases of autism co-occur with other well-described genetic disorders, such as tuberous sclerosis complex (TSC), Fragile X Syndrome and PKU (Rutter *et al.* 1990). About 25% of cases of TSC and 30% of individuals with Fragile X syndrome have an ASD. Other genetic disorders associated with autism, but which show much lower rates of co-occurrence, are neurofibromatosis, Prader-Willi Syndrome, Angelman Syndrome, Duchenne muscular dystrophy, Sotos Syndrome, hypomelanososis of Ito, Down Syndrome, and untreated phenylketonuria (Muhle, Trentacoste and Rapin 2004).

Models for the genetics of autism spectrum disorders

Despite many family and epidemiological studies, the mode of inheritance of autistic disorder and the broader group of ASDs remains unclear. There are two different theories about the nature of the variations that contribute to genetic susceptibility to ASD. The first involves mutations in culprit genes, whereas the second suggests that the additive effects of several common variations (called alleles) in particular genes are responsible for conferring vulnerability. Given the high prevalence of ASDs, we favour the common variant – common disorder hypothesis. Since ASDs are quantitative traits, they likely result from an interaction of alleles at several loci, with estimates ranging from five to ten or more. On their own, these alleles may have subtle or no phenotypic effects; but, in combination, they lead to the extreme phenotype of autism. If alleles at, for example, four to five genes are necessary to produce autistic disorder, then the presence of only three to four of the risk-alleles may lead to a milder form of Pervasive Developmental Disorder (see Figure 18.1). If specific alleles at different sets of four to five of ten or more genes results in a general phenotype of autistic disorder, then different combinations might produce different behaviours and physical characteristics and thus different subgroups of ASD. Such a "threshold" model could explain why affected brothers are not always concordant for the sub-type of ASD (Holden *et al.* 1996) and how other forms of ASD are found in families with children with autistic disorder (Bailey *et al.* 1995). This model can also explain comorbidity with known genetic disorders, and may reflect the reduced number of "susceptibility alleles" needed to produce autism in combination with the gene defect causing the syndrome (e.g. Fragile X Syndrome, TSC, PKU, etc.).

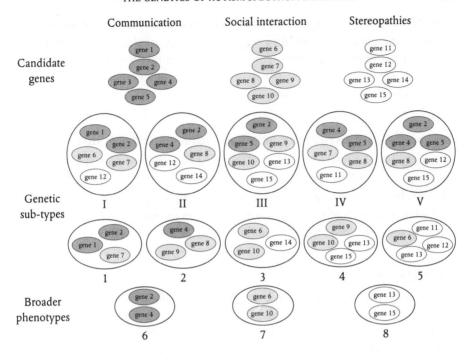

Figure 18.1 Model for the interaction of several genes in the susceptibility for autism spectrum disorders

This model, depicted in Figure 18.1, proposes that there are several genes that have the potential of contributing to the susceptibility of an individual to develop an ASD. Candidate genes may affect communication, social interaction, or behaviours. These genes may be involved in the synthesis, metabolism or functioning of neurotransporters or neuropeptides, or other proteins involved in brain organization or communication among neurons. For each of these "candidate" genes, it is expected that there are two or more alleles (variants) that result in higher or lower relative amounts of the proteins they encode, thereby affecting the function of the biological pathways in which they participate. One can imagine that, for example, low-expressing variations in all of the genes that lead to the production of dopamine or serotonin, together with low-expressing alleles of their respective receptors, would affect the functioning of these systems. In general, most people have a variety of high- and low-expressing alleles in the genes in this system, leading to more-or-less average levels of these neurotransmitters. We propose that persons with ASDs have a disproportionate number of high- or low-expressing alleles in a specific pathway, compromising the function of that pathway. It is further proposed that there are several interacting pathways that can be compromised, and thus several different "autism phenotypes" or different "types of autism". Since the family members share many of these same gene variations, they may display some of the characteristics of ASDs, but not the full syndrome. This is often termed the "broader phenotype" and the characteristics may include socialization problems, communication difficulties, or highly restricted interests.

Approaches for identifying genes for autism spectrum disorders

Various approaches are being applied to identify genes for complex genetic disorders such as ASDs. These include screening the genomes of individuals with ASD for chromosome abnormalities (cytogenetic studies, genomic microarrays), testing large numbers of multiple incidence families for linkage to DNA markers spanning the entire genome, and candidate gene testing.

Cytogenetic studies

Chromosome abnormalities have been used to identify chromosome regions harbouring genes for specific genetic disorders, including the Fragile X chromosome. Here, breakage at Xq27.3 led to the identification of the Fragile X Mental Retardation – 1 (FMR1) gene and translocations involving Xp22 and various autosomes led to the identification of the gene for Duchenne muscular dystrophy. Hence, chromosome studies have been carried out on large numbers of individuals with autism, both with and without dysmorphic features, in the hope that some of these abnormalities might lead to the identification of culprit genes for ASD. Many different chromosome abnormalities have been seen in individuals with autism. Although most chromosome abnormalities (deletions, duplications, rearrangements) are seen in only one or two individuals – and thus their relationship to autism is unknown – there are notable exceptions, including multiple cases with chromosome 15 and chromosome 7 abnormalities.

- *Chromosome 15*: Maternally-derived duplications of a small segment of chromosome 15 (15q11–13) are seen in 1–4% of cases of autistic disorder (Cook *et al.* 1997). These individuals have either an interstitial duplication or a small extra chromosome, resulting in three or four copies of this chromosomal region, respectively. Such individuals have a characteristic but variable phenotype, with ataxia, language delay, epilepsy, intellectual disability, and facial dysmorphology. The 15q11–13 region has both high recombination rates in families with autism, and high rates of breakage. In a study of chromosome fragility, 6 out of 39 children from multiple-incidence families had an isolated cell with a small extra chromosome from chromosome 15p, in contrast to none in a group of 50 children with developmental disability and no autism (Holden, unpublished observation). This chromosomal region contains several genes that are good candidate genes for autism, including genes for three GABAA receptors and the UBE3A gene (the lack of a maternal copy of this gene results in Angelman syndrome). Evidence both for and against a role for GABRB3 in 15q11–13, or a closely linked gene in autism, have been reported. Other genes in this region are currently being pursued as candidate genes, including GABRA5, GABRG3, ATP10C, and OCA2 which show association with autism, and novel genes in this region (Ichikawa *et al.* 2001; Nurmi *et al.* 2001).

- *Chromosome 7*: There have been several reports of translocations and inversions of chromosome 7, with breakpoints in the 7q22–q33 region, in individuals with autism. This finding has been especially exciting, given that several of the genome scans (see below) point to this region of chromosome 7 as harbouring a gene for autism susceptibility. It was hoped that cloning the breakpoints of these rearrangements would lead to the identification of the chromosome 7 autism susceptibility gene(s). Detailed analysis of three translocation breakpoints in 7q led to the identification of the FOXP2 gene (mutations which had previously been found to cause a specific speech and language disorder) (Lai *et al.* 2001) and two new genes (neuronal pentraxin 2 and a noncoding RNA transcript TCAG_4133353), which are being tested as ASD susceptibility loci (Scherer *et al.* 2003). Several other genes on chromosome 7 have been investigated as candidate genes (see candidate gene studies below).

- *Chromosome 17*: Recently, two individuals with AS were found to have different translocations involving the same region of chromosome 17, prompting the investigators to examine expression of candidate genes in the region for altered expression in lymphoblastoid cells. Of 14 genes tested, eight genes showed similar transcription levels in cells from individuals with autism and controls, and no expression of the remaining six genes was detected in the patient or control cell lines (Tentler *et al.* 2003). The findings do, however, suggest a region on chromosome 17 that should be examined more closely using linkage studies in families with AS.

Microdeletions and microduplications

Standard cytogenetic analysis, using G- and/or R-banding techniques, is often not sensitive enough to detect subtle chromosome rearrangements that do not modify the karyotypic banding pattern, or that are too small to be seen micro-scopically. In recent years, the development and application of various subtelomeric probes for fluorescent *in situ* hybridization, led to the awareness that (sub)telomeric regions are often involved in chromosomal rearrangements not visible by routine cytogenetic analysis. Such abnormalities are difficult to detect using conventional methods because the ends of most human chromosomes are morphologically similar. Recent reports have suggested that submicroscopic (cryptic) telomeric rearrangements resulting in gene dosage imbalance might represent a significant cause of idiopathic intellectual disability with or without congenital anomalies, and that they may also be found in a portion of cases of idiopathic autism.

More recently, genomic microarrays have been developed that enable one to examine the entire genome for small duplications and deletions. These microarrays contain 2500 human DNA segments that are 100,000 to 200,000 base pairs (100–200 kb) in length spotted onto a microscope slide. These segments are spaced apart about one to three megabases (million base pairs), and cover the entire genome. The principle is simple: DNA from a control individual is labelled with a fluorochrome (green colour) and DNA from the individual with autism is labelled with another fluorochrome (red colour). The two DNA samples are mixed in a 1:1 ratio, and hybridized to the microscope slide containing the microarrayed chromosome segments. For all chromosome regions that are present in the normal number of copies (two copies of each segment for DNA segments from the autosomes, and for the X chromosome in females), the resulting hybridization of equal amounts of red- and green-labelled DNA leads to a yellow fluorescence. If there is a duplication in the person with autism, the amount of red fluorescence for the segments of DNA that are duplicated will be greater than the amount of green fluorescence for the same segments, and the colour of the spot (or spots) that contain the duplicated DNA will be red. If the person with autism has a small deletion, then the spot containing the region that is deleted in the autistic individual will appear green. This is currently a very expensive technology, but initial studies indicate that this method is very efficient at detecting chromosomal imbalances in persons with autism, particularly those with minor dysmorphic features (Harvard *et al.* 2004).

Genome scans and candidate gene testing

Chromosome and genomic microarray studies are ideal methods for determining whether *individuals* have specific genomic abnormalities. However, these methods cannot identify gene variations or gene mutations that lead to autism suscepti-bility. Thus, these approaches need to be complemented by methods such as genome scans and candidate gene testing. Both of the latter approaches require a large number of families with two or more cases of ASD. For genome scans, many DNA markers (segments of DNA where there are DNA sequence differences among individuals) spanning every chromosome at discrete intervals are tested in parents and affected offspring. Each copy of each marker has a 50% chance of being transmitted to the offspring. If, for example, at a marker called D7S533 (DNA sequence on chromosome 7, called #533), alleles 1 and 2 are present in the mother, then the probability that the same variant is transmitted from the mother to both of her affected offspring is 25%. Increased sharing of alleles by affected offspring suggests that the marker and a gene for autism susceptibility might be closely linked on the chromosome; this linkage is particularly strong if both offspring from a large number of families always share the same allele from a particular parent (or both parents). Thus, if in 100 families with two cases of ASD, the offspring always receive the same allele from one or both parents, then the marker must be so closely linked on the chromosome to the gene for autism that the marker "marks" the place on the chromosome where the gene for autism susceptibility is located. Thus far, no such "autism susceptibility" genes have been located, but promising results where the location of genes can be surmised have been seen, as described below.

A similar approach is used for testing candidate genes for their possible role in autism. In this case, however, one examines markers that are within or very closely juxtaposed to genes of interest – genes which one believes may be involved in the pathophysiology of ASD or genes located in the chromosomal regions that were linked to ASD by genome scans or chromosome studies. These two means for selecting candidate genes are termed the "functional candidate gene" and "positional candidate gene" approaches. Again, the more often that both affected children receive the same variation from a parent, the stronger the evidence the gene in question is involved in susceptibility to ASD. An alternative approach to testing candidate genes is to compare the frequency of a specific variant in a gene in a control population and in a large number of affected individuals. If the frequency of a particular allele is significantly greater in persons with the disorder compared to controls, then it is thought that allele confers vulnerability to developing ASD.

Several genome scans have been performed on families with ASD so far. The first study, published in 1998, identified two chromosomal regions as the most likely ones to contain genes for autism: the long arm of chromosome 7 (7q) and the short arm of chromosome 16 (16p) (IMGSAC 1998). In a follow-up study, with additional markers spanning the regions of interest, as well as more families, these regions remained of great interest, and two other regions showed promise as well (2q and 17q) (IMSAC 2001). Studies by other groups have variously confirmed the 7q (Liu *et al.* 2001) and 2q (Buxbaum *et al.* 2001; Shao *et al.* 2002a) locations, or identified other regions of interest: 1p (Risch *et al.* 1999; Auranen *et al.* 2002), 5q and 19q (Liu *et al.* 2001), 6q (Philippe *et al.* 1999), 13q (Barrett *et al.* 1999), 17q (Auranen *et al.* 2002; Yonan *et al.* 2003), Xq (Liu *et al.* 2001; Shao *et al.* 2002). These differences among studies may be due to differences in the families being studied. Evidence supporting this notion comes from the observation that selecting families based on specific characteristics, such as delayed phrase speech in the children, led to increasing the significance of chromosomes 2q (Shao *et al.* 2002a) and 7q and 13q (Bradford *et al.* 2001) as harbouring genes related to susceptibility for autism. Although both individuals with autistic disorder and those with AS were included in most of these studies, more recently a genome scan was performed on families that had only cases of AS. The findings from that study suggested nine chromosome regions of interest, including regions identified when individuals with the spectrum of autism conditions were included (6q and 13q), as well as novel sites, particularly 1q and 3p (Ylisaukko-Oja *et al.* 2004). These varied findings argue for additional studies, on more well-defined subgroups of families (see below).

The goal of all cytogenetic and genome scanning methods is to identify genes that have an impact on the development of ASD, with the results of these methods providing clues about the chromosomal locations of possible candidate genes (i.e. positional candidate genes). Thus, when a chromosomal region is identified, such as the long arm of chromosome 7, investigators next check the map of human genes, developed as the result of the Human Genome Project, to look for suitable "candidate" genes for further testing. Such testing involves direct assessment of the gene for a role in ASD. This can be done by selecting markers within the gene and testing them as described above, or by sequencing the gene and looking for mutations that are present only in persons with ASD. In general, the best types of markers are those that have some impact on the functioning of the gene. For example, some gene variations alter the amount of the gene product (RNA or protein) made, while other variations alter the action of the protein, or even its stability in the cell. Such variations, called "functional variants", are the ones most likely to play a role in susceptibility to ASD under the hypothesis that common diseases result from the additive effects of common variations within genes. Sometimes, other characteristics are used to select "candidate" genes for study, including biochemical findings (such as increased amounts of serotonin in some individuals with ASD and their family members) or reactions to drugs that target specific neurotransmitter systems.

- *Serotonin system*: The serotonin system appears to be disrupted in about one-third of individuals with autism and their families, and may be involved in some of the behavioural characteristics of autism (including anxiety and repetitive behaviours). As a result, the serotonin transporter gene (5HTTT) has been studied by several research groups. Some groups found the short promoter variant (a smaller size allele) is more prevalent in persons with autism, whereas others found the long promoter allele more prevalent, or there were no differences between cases of autism and controls. Other investigators are studying different serotonin receptor genes, to determine whether different activities of the receptors could account for the hyperserotonemia seen in some families. To date, the reason for this hyperserotonemia is not known.

- *Dopamine system:* Robinson *et al.* (2001) found that a specific variant in the DBH gene, which converts dopamine to norepinephrine, was more frequent in mothers with autistic sons, than in controls. This led to the hypothesis that suboptimal functioning of the dopamine-norepinephrine pathway in the mother could lead to compromised foetal development, particularly in boys. Additional studies on dopamine receptor genes and other genes in the dopamine pathway are under way to test the function of this system in autism.

- *X-linked genes:* Because of the excess of affected males compared to females, and the observation of possible linkage of Xq to autism in at least two genome scans, we and others have tested X-linked genes for linkage in multiple-incidence families with affected boys. The findings have been largely negative so far, for genes such as FMR1, FMR2, and FRAXF (Holden *et al.* 1996). Because of the overlap of clinical findings, the Rett Syndrome gene, MECP2, has also been examined as a candidate gene for autism, with mainly negative findings. More recently, two neuroligin genes have been implicated in autism. Neuroligins are cell-adhesion molecules that are involved in forming synapses between neurons. Initial studies found mutations in two different X-linked neuroligin genes in two families with autistic individuals (Jamain *et al.* 2003).

- *Chromosome 7:* The most consistent finding from genome scans is that specific regions on chromosome 7 are found to be associated with the risk of developing an ASD. Of particular interest is the RELN gene, which codes for a protein that is necessary for proper migration of the cells during the formation of the cortex of the brain. Long variants of a polymorphic triplet repeat in the gene have been found to be associated with autism in some, but not all, studies. A mutation analysis of the RELN gene showed some variants that may be unique to autism, but additional studies are needed to establish the role of this gene in autism. Other genes located in the critical region of chromosome 7 are the

FOXP2 gene (foxhead box P2) which was found to be mutated in a family with specific language impairment (Lai *et al.* 2001); RAY1/ST7, a gene which is disrupted by a translocation in a boy with autism (Vincent *et al.* 2002); and the glutamate receptor GRM8 gene. Again, findings are varied for each of these genes, and thus their roles in autism susceptibility remain possible, but they likely do not play major roles.

Finding genes for susceptibility to autism spectrum disorders: The next steps

It has long been recognized that ASDs are highly variable disorders, with greatly differing behaviours and clinical presentations. It is therefore not too surprising that it is taking time to identify genes that play a significant role in susceptibility to these conditions. The variability in the chromosome findings, as well as in the genome scans and candidate gene results, suggests there is a weakness in the design of these studies. Just as it would not have been possible to identify the gene for Fragile X Syndrome if researchers had combined families with Down Syndrome, Angelman Syndrome, Prader-Willi Syndrome, and Fragile X Syndrome in "genome scans", so it will likely be impossible to identify genes for the different forms of ASD by "lumping" them all together. Thus it is important to subgroup families into groups that are likely to be more homogeneous.

More refined phenotyping of children and families will undoubtedly lead to greater homogeneity among the families, and probably stronger evidence supporting linkage to specific chromosome regions or specific culprit genes. There are obvious phenotypic differences among individuals with ASD – with some having macrocephaly and others microcephaly. Children with autism have various minor malformations including hypertelorism, syndactyly of the toes, anomalies of the mouth and ears, or abnormal ear position. Detailed phenotypic assessments, including anthropometric measurements and 3D photometry, are expected to help to identify some common features and define clinical subgroups for genetic studies. Some individuals have "splinter" skills, such as calculating or artistic skills that are quite remarkable. Still others have very repetitive or stereo-typed behaviours that might be classified as obsessive-compulsive. In still other cases, the family history is remarkable, with either obsessive-compulsive traits or depression in relatives. There are differences in the ability to recognize emotions, and in the use of auditory and visual information when communicating. All of these factors are probably important to consider when subgrouping families for genetic studies, and one or more of them may lead to identifying genes of minor or major impact in the development of ASD.

Once the first gene is discovered that has a major effect on the development of ASD, this will open the way to understanding the pathophysiology of these mysterious and complex conditions. This may then lead to treatments that may be as simple as the removal of specific amino acids from the diet of persons with PKU to prevent the brain damage that leads to intellectual disability, or as complex as teaching infants the intricacies of shared attention and reciprocal communication. But once we find a key that unlocks the barrier to our understanding of autism, we will undoubtedly begin an exciting journey of discovery of the genetic basis for how we, as human beings, relate to one another and how we demonstrate to others our understanding of them.

References

Auranen, M., Vanhala, R., Varilo, T., Ayers, K., Kempas, E., Ylisaukko-Oja, T. *et al.* (2002) A genomewide screen for autism-spectrum disorders: Evidence for a major susceptibility locus on chromosome 3q25–27. *The American Journal of Human Genetics, 71,* 777–90.

Bailey, A., Le Couteur, A., Gottesman, I., Bolton, P., Simonoff, E., Yuzda, E. *et al.* (1995) Autism as a strongly genetic disorder: Evidence from a British twin study. *Psychological Medicine, 25,* 63–77.

Bailey, A., Palferman, S., Heavey, L., and Le Couteur, A. (1998) Autism: The phenotype in relatives. *Journal of Autism and Developmental Disorders, 28,* 369–92.

Barrett, S., Beck, J.C., Bernier, R., Bisson, E., Braun, T.A., Casavant, T.L. *et al.* (1999) An autosomal genomic screen for autism. Collaborative linkage study of autism. *American Journal of Medical Genetics, 88,* 609–615.

Bolton, P., Macdonald, H., Pickles, A., Rios, P., Goode, S., Crowson, M. *et al.* (1994) A case-control family history study of autism. *Journal of Child Psychology and Psychiatry, 35,* 877–900.

Bradford, Y., Haines, J., Hutcheson, H., Gardiner, M., Braun, T., Sheffield, V. *et al.* (2001) Incorporating language phenotypes strengthens evidence of linkage to autism. *American Journal of Medical Genetics, 105,* 539–47.

Buxbaum, J.D., Silverman, J.M., Smith, C.J., Kilifarski, M., Reichert, J., Hollander, E. *et al.* (2001) Evidence for a susceptibility gene for autism on chromosome 2 and for genetic heterogeneity. *American Journal of Human Genetics, 68,* 1514–20.

Constantino, J.N., and Todd, R.D. (2003) Autistic traits in the general population: A twin study. *Archives of General Psychiatry, 60,* 524–30.

Cook, E.H., Jr., Lindgren, V., Leventhal, B.L., Courchesne, R., Lincoln, A., Shulman, C. *et al.* (1997) Autism or atypical autism in maternally but not paternally derived proximal 15q duplication. *American Journal of Human Genetics, 60,* 928–34.

Folstein, S., and Rutter, M. (1977) Infantile autism: A genetic study of 21 twin pairs. *Journal of Child Psychology and Psychiatry, 18,* 297–321.

Fombonne, E. (2003) The prevalence of autism. *Journal of the American Medical Association, 289,* 87–9.

Harvard, C., Malenfant, P., Koochek, M., Holden, J.J., Lewis, S.E., and Rajcan-Separovic, E. (2004) Multiple microdeletions in a patient with intellectual disability and autism detected with a 1Mb array. *Cytogenetic and Genome Research, 106,* 120–41, Abstract #15.

Holden, J.J., Wing, M., Chalifoux, M., Julien-Inalsingh, C., Schutz, C., Robinson, P. *et al.* (1996) Lack of expansion of triplet repeats in the FMR1, FRAXE, and FRAXF loci in male multiplex families with autism and pervasive developmental disorders. *American Journal of Medical Genetics, 64,* 399–403.

Ichikawa, S., Liu, Y., Miles, J.H., Hillman, R.E., and Wang, C.H. (2001) Identification of novel exons and analysis of autism-associated sequence variations within the chromosome 15q11–q13 region. *American Journal of Human Genetics, 69,* 543.

IMGSAC (International Molecular Genetic Study of Autism Consortium) (1998) A full genome screen for autism with evidence for linkage to a region on chromosome 7q. *Human Molecular Genetics, 7,* 571–8.

IMGSAC (International Molecular Genetic Study of Autism Consortium) (2001) Further characterization of the autism susceptibility locus AUTS1 on chromosome 7q. *Human Molecular Genetics, 10,* 973–82.

Jamain, S., Quach, H., Betancur, C., Rastam, M., Colineaux, C., Gillberg, I.C. *et al.* (2003) Mutations of the X-linked genes encoding neuroligins NLGN3 and NLGN4 are associated with autism. *Nature Genetics, 34,* 27–9.

Lai, C.S., Fisher, S.E., Hurst, J.A., Vargha-Khadem, F., and Monaco, A.P. (2001) A forkhead-domain gene is mutated in a severe speech and language disorder. *Nature, 413,* 519–23.

Liu, J., Nyholt, D.R., Magnussen, P., Parano, E., Pavone, P., Geschwind, D. *et al.* (2001) A genomewide screen for autism susceptibility loci. *American Journal of Human Genetics, 69,* 327–40.

Muhle, R., Trentacoste, S.V., and Rapin, I. (2004) The genetics of autism. *Pediatrics, 113,* e472–e486.

Murphy, M., Bolton, P.F., Pickles, A., Fombonne, E., Piven, J., and Rutter, M. (2000) Personality traits of the relatives of autistic probands. *Psychological Medicine, 30,* 1411–24.

Nurmi, E.L., Bradford, Y., Chen, Y., Hall, J., Arnone, B., Gardiner, M.B. *et al.* (2001) Linkage disequilibrium at the Angelman syndrome gene UBE3A in autism families. *Genomics, 77,* 105–113.

Philippe, A., Martinez, M., Guilloud-Bataille, M., Gillberg, C., Rastam, M., Sponheim, E. *et al.* (1999) Genome-wide scan for autism susceptibility genes. Paris Autism Research International Sibpair Study. *Human Molecular Genetics, 8,* 805–812.

Pickles, A., Bolton, P., Macdonald, H., Bailey, A., Le Couteur, A., Sim, C.H. *et al.* (1995) Latent-class analysis of recurrence risks for complex phenotypes with selection and measurement error: A twin and family history study of autism. *American Journal of Human Genetics, 57,* 717–26.

Piven, J. (2001) The broad autism phenotype: a complementary strategy for molecular genetic studies of autism. *American Journal of Medical Genetics, 105,* 34–5.

Piven, J., Palmer, P., Jacobi, D., Childress, D., and Arndt, S. (1997) Broader autism phenotype: Evidence from a family history study of multiple-incidence autism families. *American Journal of Psychiatry, 154,* 185–90.

Risch, N., Spiker, D., Lotspeich, L., Nouri, N., Hinds, D., Hallmayer, J. *et al.* (1999) A genomic screen of autism: Evidence for a multilocus etiology. *American Journal of Human Genetics, 65,* 493–507.

Robinson, P.D., Schutz, C.K., Macciardi, F., White, B.N., and Holden, J.J.A. (2001) Genetically determined low maternal serum dopamine β-hydroxylase levels and the etiology of autism spectrum disorders. *American Journal of Medical Genetics, 100,* 30–36.

Rutter, M., Macdonald, H., Le Couteur, A., Harrington, R., Bolton, P., and Bailey, A. (1990) Genetic factors in child psychiatric disorders: Empirical findings. *Journal of Child Psychology and Psychiatry, 31,* 39–83.

Scherer, S.W., Cheung, J., MacDonald, J.R., Osborne, L.R., Nakabayashi, K., Herbrick, J.A. *et al.* (2003) Human chromosome 7: DNA sequence and biology. *Science, 300,* 767–72.

Shao, Y., Raiford, K.L., Wolpert, C.M., Cope, H.A., Ravan, S.A., Ashley-Koch, A.A. *et al.* (2002a) Phenotypic homogeneity provides increased support for linkage on chromosome 2 in autistic disorder. *American Journal of Human Genetics, 70,* 1058–61.

Shao, Y., Wolpert, C.M., Raiford, K.L., Menold, M.M., Donnelly, S.L., Ravan, S.A. *et al.* (2002b) Genomic screen and follow-up analysis for autistic disorder. *American Journal of Medical Genetics, 114,* 99–105.

Smalley, S.L., Asarnow, R.F., and Spence, M.A. (1988) Autism and genetics. A decade of research. *Archives of General Psychiatry, 45,* 953–61.

Tentler, D., Johannesson, T., Johansson, M., Rastam, M., Gillberg, C., Orsmark, C. *et al.* (2003) A candidate region for Asperger syndrome defined by two 17p breakpoints. *European Journal of Human Genetics, 11,* 189–95.

Vincent, J.B., Petek, E., Thevarkunnel, S., Kolozsvari, D., Cheung, J., Patel, M. *et al.* (2002) The RAY1/ST7 tumor-suppressor locus on chromosome 7q31 represents a complex multi-transcript system. *Genomics, 80,* 283–94.

Yeargin-Allsopp, M., Rice, C., Karapurkar, T., Doernberg, N., Boyle, C., and Murphy, C. (2003) Prevalence of autism in a US metropolitan area. *Journal of American Medical Association, 289,* 49–55.

Ylisaukko-Oja, T., Nieminen-von Wendt, T., Kempas, E., Sarenius, S., Varilo, T., von Wendt, L. *et al.* (2004) Genome-wide scan for loci of Asperger syndrome. *Molecular Psychiatry, 9,* 161–8.

Yonan, A.L., Alarcon, M., Cheng, R., Magnusson, P.K., Spence, S.J., Palmer, A.A. *et al.* (2003) A genomewide screen of 345 families for autism-susceptibility loci. *American Journal of Human Genetics, 73,* 886–97.

CHAPTER 19

Quality of life for children with Asperger Syndrome: Parental perspectives

Ann Fudge Schormans, Rebecca Renwick, Renée Ryan, and HeeSun Lim

Is a good quality of life for children easily achieved? What is required for a "good" quality of life? What if having Asperger Syndrome (AS) complicates a child's quality of life? Until now, there has been no known research specifically examining quality of life issues for children with AS, although issues relevant to "quality of life", but not necessarily conceptualized as such, are found in literature.

Clinical experience and research reveal that children with AS typically experience a vast array of difficulties in their lives that have the potential to affect their quality of life. The social, emotional, behavioural, and cognitive characteristics of AS affect the child's social and academic performance (Myles and Simpson 2002). Being socially isolated, friendless, shunned and victimized by peers (Broderick *et al.* 2002; Little 2002; Foster and King 2003) may result in "emotional stress associated with the basic need to belong" (Carrington and Graham 2001, p.44) and short- and long-term negative health outcomes (Little 2002). Problems with communication, sensory sensitivities, and motor deficits may make this group of children more vulnerable to developing various problems, including low self-esteem and depressive symptomatology (Myles and Simpson 2002; Foster and King 2003). Parents of children with AS cite a lack of social supports, resources, specialized services, and professional training or understanding of AS (Carrington and Graham 2001; Little 2002; Myles and Simpson 2002).

This chapter reports on a qualitative research study examining quality of life for children with AS. Following a brief discussion of how "quality of life" has been conceptualized and the research methodology used in the study, the results of this research will be presented.

Conceptualization of "quality of life"

While quality of life is an important concern for all human beings, there is no one commonly agreed upon approach to understanding this concept and measuring it. Various approaches have been developed for adults, including those with developmental disabilities (Bowling 1991; Renwick, Brown, and Nagler 1996; Schalock 2000). However, relatively few approaches exist for children (Zekovic and Renwick 2003) and fewer still for children with developmental disabilities (Renwick, Fudge Schormans, and Zekovic 2003). There has been no specific approach used to understand quality of life in children with AS.

Two major ways of attempting to understand and measure quality of life are: (1) health-related approaches that are typically associated with a medical orientation (Bowling 1991; Schalock 2000), and (2) holistic approaches, many deriving from the field of developmental disabilities (Renwick, Brown, and Raphael 2000). The former concern issues such as a person's physical comfort or discomfort; emotional functioning; pain; mobility; general and mental health; and self-esteem. Such factors may contribute to a person's quality of life but reveal little about how "good" a life that person experiences (Zekovic and Renwick 2003). However, holistic approaches do address such issues, in that they view complex person–environment relationships as determining the quality a person experiences with respect to important, broad areas of life. Examples of these aspects of life are emotional, material, and physical well-being; interpersonal relations; personal development; self-determination; social inclusion; and individual rights (Schalock 1996).

Several holistic models and measures have been developed for, or are relevant to, adults with developmental disabilities. Less attention has been paid to developing similar approaches for children with developmental disabilities. Interested readers are directed towards two notable models and measures for children and adolescents in general. The "Pediatric Quality of Life Model" and the "Pediatric Quality of Life Inventory" (PedsQL) (Varni, Sied, and Rode 1999), based on this model, represent a health-related functional approach. However, it does not adequately elaborate on how aspects of children's functional abilities enhance or detract from their quality of life.

Lindstrom's (1992, 1994) "Quality of Life Model for Children" integrates micro- and macro-level aspects of quality of life. It considers objective and subjective dimensions of four spheres of human existence: (1) *global*: ecological, societal and political issues; (2) *external*: social and economical resources; (3) *inter-*

personal: relationships, support, family, and friends; and (4) *personal*: physical, mental, and spiritual aspects of the individual. Since it is based on data from Nordic countries, its appropriateness for use in other cultures remains unknown (Zekovic and Renwick 2003).

Renwick, Fudge Schormans, and Zekovic (2003) view quality of life for children with developmental disabilities as a multidimensional and holistic construct; a dynamic process that can change over time and be assessed at any point in a child's life. Based on a grounded theory analysis of data from in-depth interviews with parents of children with a variety of developmental disabilities (including AS), they identify three fundamental, dynamic, continuously inter-relating elements of quality of life: (1) the child, (2) her or his family environment, and (3) the broader environmental influences beyond the family (e.g. neighbour-hood, community, school, government policies). The better the fit among these three elements, the better the child's quality of life will be.

Three major domains of quality of life result from this dynamic relationship: (1) *Being*: refers to whom the child is perceived to be by others, (2) *Belonging*: encompasses the child's connections with people and places, and (3) *Becoming*: refers to the child's nurtured growth and development. Thus, this conceptual framework focusses on the child's life as a whole, including those areas that are strong and those that may need enhancement. It also captures the complex nature of quality of life for this group of children, and reflects the voices of parents who have important insights into what contributes to, and what detracts from, their children's quality of life. Finally, it recognizes the interconnectedness of quality of life for both the child and his or her parents.

Methodology

This study was designed to obtain a more detailed understanding of quality of life for children with AS from their parents' perspective. A purposive convenience sub-sample of eight parents, drawn from 20 parents of children with AS partici-pating in a larger study of quality of life for children with developmental disabili-ties, agreed to a personal interview with a trained interviewer. Audiotaped interviews, lasting from 60 to 120 minutes, were transcribed verbatim and then the content was analysed by the researchers together, as a group. This involved examination of the parents' responses to interview questions to identify major themes expressed by parents. Six mothers and two fathers from the greater Toronto area discussed their children with AS. These children consisted of two girls and six boys ranging in age from eight to 13 years. Both low- and middle-income families were included. Six parents were married, one was separated, and one was widowed. Participants were racially homogeneous but culturally diverse.

Interview questions were based on the three domains of the aforementioned conceptual model developed by Renwick, Fudge Schormans, and Zekovic (2003). Questions concerning *Being* probed how the child is seen and treated by others in her/his family and community (e.g. as a child, as a child with disability, as primarily disabled). Questions about *Belonging* focussed on the nature of the child's relationships with others (e.g. siblings, relatives, friends, community members, teachers, and other professionals); how well home, school, day care, and community environments matched the child's needs (e.g. safety, accessibility, availability of interactions with peers, suitable activities, services, resources, transportation); how well the child was understood by others (e.g. friends, community members, professionals) and how this understanding (or lack thereof) affected the child. Questions associated with *Becoming* centred on how well important others in the child's life (e.g. teachers, professionals, community members, and organizations) recognized, addressed, and met their needs related to ongoing growth and development. These needs are associated with being a child, as well as with the child's disability. Included were opportunities, experiences, resources, programs, supports, and government policies that enabled and fostered the child's nurtured growth and development.

The scope of this chapter permits only an introduction to the major themes and concerns expressed by parents and as much as possible, makes use of the parents' own words.

Being – who the child is perceived to be

Asked to address how their child with AS was seen by others, parents stressed that perceptions varied widely among people having contact with their children. Furthermore, discrepant perceptions could be held by a single individual, in different contexts, at different times in his or her relationship with the child, and even simultaneously. Such ambiguity was not exclusive of parents. While not always satisfied with how other people saw their children, invariably parents believed such perceptions to be very important to their child's quality of life.

The child as a child

For the parents in this study, it was important that their children be seen, first and foremost, as children. Typically, only the child's immediate family members, some extended family members, and a few close family friends shared this view. The manner in which these individuals engaged with the child; their support of, apparent interest in, and acceptance of the child; having "typical" expectations for the child; and, perhaps most important, valuing the child, were interpreted by parents to indicate a perception of the child as being just that – a child.

> I think that they just…are very accepting and it's never occurred to them that…her strange behaviour is anything out of the ordinary.

Characteristically, people at a greater remove from the child, notably peers, failed to share this perception. Parents believed that, while familiarity with the child facilitated a view of the child as a child, familiarity alone was insufficient. Empathy, the ability to "see beyond the disability and see the person" (in the words of one parent), as well as sensitivity to difference were identified as key factors.

The child's intelligence also played a role in others' perception. Parents stressed repeatedly that because their children did not present with an obvious intellectual impairment, people less readily saw them as having a disability. Consequently, it was often easier, at least initially, for other people to see the child "as a child" given the somewhat "hidden" nature of AS. AS is not always immediately apparent, since the child with AS typically does not have any distinctive physical features setting her/him apart.

> You know, to someone who just met him and didn't really know…[and] have any…preconceived notions about him, they would think he's, you know, basically just a bit of an eccentric kid sometimes. So, I think that…he passes for normal most of the time, but there's clearly times where he's not reacting as a kid his age should be reacting.

The oft-reported negative ramifications of a hidden disability, however, generally outweighed this potentially positive outcome. Because the disability is hidden, frequently people did not recognize and/or understand the source of the child's behavioural idiosyncrasies and, instead, formed initial impressions such as the following: "…they don't think that he has a disability…just that he's a bad kid and he needs some discipline".

One notable consequence to the child's quality of life may be ostracization by peers and adults alike. A second is that "[b]ecause they can't see that he's disabled, their expectations, I think, are pretty high". The lack of others' awareness of the existence of a disability precipitates their concomitant lack of awareness as to what are appropriate expectations of the child, and consequently they blame the child who fails to meet these expectations.

The child as a child with a disability

As a group, parents reported that many people in their child's life, both people actively involved and more casual contacts, shared a perception of their child as being a child with a disability. Included in these contacts were immediate and extended family members (inclusive of parents), family friends, school-related individuals (teaching and administrative staff, peers, parents of peers), professionals, community members, and people familiar with AS. Both positive and negative repercussions to quality of life were identified.

> It depends on the people. [S]ome of them seem to be just looking at her faults all the time…always looking for "Is she doing this?" or, "Is she doing that?" Some people react by thinking, "Oh, she's got a disability, that's so romantic, I'm just going to save her", "I'm going to be the best, most helpful person ever", and some people…I mean most reasonable people, just try to make accommodations.

A perception of the child as a child with a disability appeared most pronounced and problematic within the school environment. Here, receipt of the specialized resources this group of children required to function effectively and be successful in the school system was contingent on formal identification as "disabled". Awareness and acknowledgement of the disability often proved positive when they led to the provision of requisite supports and a greater comfort level with the child, thus facilitating more accommodating, gentle, and appropriate interactions and interventions.

> …acknowledging [the disability] in that they understand that this child has real challenges that he has to deal with and he needs their help in order to be successful. That's really what's key with everyone because [he] does need assistance to do a lot of things because he's a product of his environment and if people create the nice, proper type of environment for him, he excels…and a good part of that is understanding what his limitations are and then help him to cope…

However, more than for any other environment in the lives of these children, parents reported that being identified within the school system as having a disability frequently resulted in extremely negative consequences for the child. The label "Asperger Syndrome" typically precipitated negative preconceptions by many people (i.e. educators, professionals, peers, and parents of peers).

> Well, the minute you bring in a label like autism or Asperger's, they've got a preconceived notion that that's going to be a difficult and disruptive child and they can't handle it, so they don't want the child in the classroom. And that happens over and over again.

Repeatedly, parents stressed their belief that the educational system, as a whole, was structured around a "focus on the disability as the thing, as opposed to the child", on the expectation that the child "was going to do something wrong rather than…something right", and to the identification of the child with AS as a problem. Inappropriate supports, services, and interventions; restricted opportunities; poor interactions with others; and "tainting" of how peers perceive the child were commonly cited consequences to the child.

> [The teacher] was so focussed on [my child] having a disability that…it was ridiculous. It was just way overboard and [my child] didn't have a chance to be a kid…

The child as a disability

A tendency to focus so extensively on the disability can extend to the point where the child is lost and all that is seen is the disability. Ironically, some parents suggested that the specialized services geared specifically to children with AS exemplified this tendency. By virtue of the nature and degree of specialization involved in these services, the diagnosis of AS became the child's defining feature. A few parents also reported the child's peers frequently see only the disability. The consequence to the child with AS is that he is shunned, ignored, or even bullied by peers who view the child as "weird".

> Anywhere in society, she's viewed with a label.

Belonging – the child's connections to people and places

Family and adult connections

While many parents wanted to create "a normal family life" for their children with AS and "a normal kind of relationship that you would expect", the expressed reality for these children was a limited number of social relationships, drawn from a restricted pool of contacts. Their primary relationships, even in adolescence, continued to be with their parents. Children typically shared a special relationship with only one or two other extended family members. Identification as a "member of the family" did not guarantee acceptance, inclusion, or love, as typically, "most of the other relatives aren't very comfortable with him". Parents further indicated there were degrees of inclusion:

> …they don't exclude her but they don't actually actively engage her or anything.

Parents identified one or two other non-familial adults in their child's life who were "good" for their child (i.e. supportive, positive, accepting). In each case, these adults were aware the child had AS, were knowledgeable about AS, understanding and sensitive regarding the impact of AS on the child's life, and familiar with the individual child.

Peer connections

For the children in this study, the most glaring deficit was in non-familial peer relationships. Parents identified positive peer relationships as a primary need, stating that their child "really doesn't have any friends". The children were seldom, if ever, invited by non-labelled peers to play, visit their homes, or attend birthday parties:

> ...for example, he has a birthday party like everybody else. The only difference is that he doesn't have any children at it, but we try to find cousins or somebody to come and then do everything the same as they would have done, you know. [W]e have the decorations and the party hats and the whole bit.

Children were included in school activities to varying degrees. While many had interactions with peers, these were rarely true friendships and did not transcend school borders:

> I think they respect his intellect. They can't figure out or understand him sometimes, but they do respect the fact that he's smart... They don't invite him over to play, and he doesn't invite them over, but they're friendly and inclusive of [him] at school.

However, in another case:

> The boys have nothing to do with him...that is actually, in some ways, more difficult for him because he's aware of it, but he's not able to overcome [it].

For those children identified as having positive peer relationships, peers were categorized in two ways. The first group consisted of peers who had long-term, ongoing contact with the child with AS facilitating familiarity and comfort. Distinguishing between "tolerance" and "genuine acceptance", parents again pointed out that familiarity alone was insufficient. As one parent said:

> So they kind of grew up together, kind of, you know, almost like brothers, but they have such distinct differences and interests.

The second group consisted of other socially marginalized and labelled children, primarily those with AS. To some degree, reciprocity existed in these relationships, which seemed to be less evident in their relationships with non-labelled children. As another parent described it:

> ...the kids that she does end up playing with, the other kids with Asperger's or whatever, do share her interests...so she's comfortable with them...because they are both exactly alike.

Obstacles to connections with peers

While the difficulties described in this section can function as impediments to any social relationship, the focus here is on peer relationships which parents perceived as significantly influencing the quality of life experienced by children with AS. Deficits in fine and gross motor skills, co-ordination, and strength meant the child often could not "keep up" with peers and was not "physically able to do it". Along with sensory sensitivities to loud noises and crowds, for example, these difficulties perpetuated social isolation. Other people did not always understand behavioural outbursts or "meltdowns":

> ...but nobody reciprocates any more. It's just like, you know, they remember this crazy kid going off the deep end

and

> ...[we] felt shunned by the school community because of his outrageous behaviour...there's a couple of parents who actually told us they didn't want their children to be near him.

The child's apparent lack of interest in peers and in their activities also posed difficulties:

> [He is] an obstacle to himself...he doesn't necessarily want to do what other people do. He lacks their perspective of wanting to engage in activities that they want him to do.

Further, the child's peers in the wider community typically lack knowledge and understanding of AS. As one parent noted:

> ...it's the exceptional child that is able to understand the needs of this girl... It takes an exceptional adult, never mind a child. So it's even more difficult for a child.

While children with AS often have good expressive language skills, receptive language abilities are more problematic. Consequently, communication strengths may function as deficits when good verbal skills mask underlying comprehension difficulties – as one parent said, "it's a grand illusion". As articulated by another parent:

> Oh, everybody can understand [her communication] on some level…but, you know, what she's actually saying underneath all those words – practically nobody knows that.

Parents suggested that their children seldom understand all that is said to them and may misinterpret or miss critical information. Nor do they necessarily fully comprehend what they, themselves, are saying. It is the immediate family members (parents and siblings) who best understand the child's communication. Also capable are those teachers and/or professionals who have a solid understanding of AS and familiarity with the child. Except for peers sharing long-term relationships with the child, children tended to find communicating with the child with AS difficult. As one parent observed:

> I think that children of her particular age find it difficult to interact with a child with a disability. They are uncomfortable, most kids are uncomfortable in dealing with being able to talk with somebody who has difficulty communicating…

Furthermore, the child's communication difficulties with peers increased as the child reached adolescence:

> [H]e has a lot of difficulty entering conversation…as he's got older and his language has improved…he tries to enter with language. When he was young he would push or shove to get someone's, or grab them to get attention… We have practised social stories, but, you know, by the teen years their social situations are very subtle and complex and he finds it quite difficult…

The consequences of misunderstanding among peers typically involved teasing, bullying, or ostracization. The child with AS often displayed frustration, anger, reactive lashing-out behaviours (often with adjunct outcomes such as school suspensions). However, one parent revealed that her child had become withdrawn and depressed to the point of suicidal ideation:

> Now, as a result of that experience, he often doesn't communicate. If he goes to a group, he just stands on the side. He doesn't talk to anybody because he's afraid it will be a negative experience.

Children with AS habitually lack proper social skills for engagement with peers. As one parent described it:

> …she really just doesn't know how. She would hesitate to invite school
> friends over because she, she really doesn't know what to do with them.

An inability to interpret peers' social behaviour made the child vulnerable to
being misunderstood and misled and also to unintentionally misleading others
(e.g. a child who doesn't understand "flirting" or the related dangers of computer
chat rooms). Parents emphasized the need for more readily available social skills
training that is suitable for the specific needs of this group of children, and
provides them with not only instruction and support, but also with the opportunity to:

> …build relationships, understand that they're not alone, that there are
> other kids out there that are like them, have somebody to talk to that
> knows what they're going through.

Becoming – the child's nurtured growth and development

When asked to identify their child's needs related to being a child, parents
invariably asserted that the needs were "the same as [for] any other kid", that the
child didn't require "anything different…just needs a few things extra". In
contrast, when asked about their child's needs as a child with AS, parents articulated an extensive range of needs, a list that varied according to each child's age,
gender, and current situation. While the scope of this chapter does not permit
elaboration of these needs, what was immediately apparent was the degree to
which parents were responsible for ensuring these needs were met. Whatever the
child had accomplished was primarily a function of what the parents had done.
Several parents spoke about this responsibility:

> I mean, most of the stuff that she has, has been stuff that I've made up or
> done…the obstacle is that what you need you have to create for yourself
> because it basically doesn't exist anywhere.

> The amount of early intervention [my child] got is because I just pounded
> on every door that I could find.

Overwhelming demands are placed on parents. Besides becoming "experts",
about both their child and AS, parents were required to find, or create, the
programs and supports their child needed. Yet parents repeatedly stressed their
own need for education about AS:

> but we had no one telling us…all the things that could go wrong…if I
> knew even 10% of what I know now, probably a lot of things that have
> happened to [my child] wouldn't have happened.

Parents stated that they were frequently responsible for training the numerous support workers, teachers, and educational assistants that pass through their children's lives. They must also identify, co-ordinate, and often manage, teams of professionals, while maintaining the high degree of (pessimistic) vigilance required for ensuring that these teams "don't fall apart". In response to the limited number of social relationships and professional services available to these children, by necessity parents found they must be all things to their child – parent, professional, advocate, and playmate.

> …I used to dread the weekends because…I'm tired of playing and I'm trying to come up with things he likes to do, and he loves to play with other kids. He doesn't want to play with adults…

Emphasizing that their children were more often familiar with failure than with social success, parents strove to create opportunities for success, build on the child's strengths, "feed her interests" (however idiosyncratic), and boost self-esteem.

> I don't think that things are at all tailored for her interests. It's really, really hard when you have kids that are very individual… I mean the school programs and things are tailored for the interests and strengths of the majority of kids and she has very different interests and strengths so she's left out of a lot of stuff…if the community doesn't have what she can do, is interested in, and can excel at available, then she's not having her needs met.

"Typical" parental responsibilities assume a new emphasis when so few people in the lives of these children are knowledgeable about AS, its impact on the child's (and family's) life, or the demands and needs stemming from AS. Despite the impact of this knowledge (or lack of) on quality of life,

> [p]eople with good intentions have done horrible things to these children and they just don't realize, and they're not willing to, and that is a big problem.

Parents documented a dearth of suitable services, long waiting lists, prohibitive costs, restrictive eligibility criteria, insufficient financial and professional supports, resistance, and a lack of acceptance and inclusion. Such criticisms were not restricted to a single service jurisdiction:

> So the whole schooling issue is a big, big gap… [F]or many parents like us it is an endless nightmare and it just puts so much stress on family life… [O]n top of the medical issues that you are already dealing with and the social issues that you're dealing with, having to fight institutions at

the city level who in turn are being under-funded by the province – it's very difficult.

Parents were responsible for providing everything their child required to grow and develop, including those things that other parents take for granted, and to accommodate the child's needs when other services fail to do so. In essence, they provided both typical and specialized childhood opportunities and activities without the benefit of typical or specialized programs and supports. In recognition of this responsibility, parents emphasized the interrelatedness, the "ripple effect", as one parent put it, between their child's quality of life and the quality of their own lives:

> …there needs to be more programs by professionals, the government, and the community that support the entire family because I don't think that focussing on the child with a disability is that productive because the child is only one part of the whole, the whole dynamic, and parents are going to be the people who the child primarily interacts with, so, you've got to support the entire family…

Conclusions

As articulated previously, the quality of life model for children with developmental disabilities developed by Renwick, Fudge Schormans, and Zekovic (2003) identified three fundamental, dynamic, and interrelated elements of quality of life: the child, his or her family environment, and broader environmental influences. Arguably, the perceptions of the parents of children with AS participating in this study support the importance of the fit of these elements. Simultaneously, their perceptions suggested that, at present, this fit is a poor one because the positive aspects of their children's lives rest almost exclusively on the contributions made by the family environment, and particularly by the parents. While this is to be expected in any parent–child relationship, it would appear to be extreme in this instance. Both the child's needs that result from AS, and an insufficient response from important others, necessitate parents assuming almost complete responsibility for ensuring a good quality of life for their children.

Similarly, the concerns expressed in each of the *Being*, *Belonging*, and *Becoming* domains have ramifications for the other domains; no domain exists exclusive of the others. For example, how others perceive a child largely determines the child's opportunities for relationships with others, as well as the services and supports that she or he is provided for growth and development. It is not surprising that parents emphasize the importance of greater individual and community knowledge about AS. They believe that such knowledge can facilitate greater comfort of others with respect to children with AS. Increased comfort can potentially promote greater sensitivity, acceptance, inclusion, valuing, and support of the child with AS, all of which contribute to and enhance the child's quality of life.

References

Bowling, A. (1991) *Measuring Health: A Review of Quality of Life Measurement Scales.* Philadelphia. PA: Open University Press.

Broderick, C., Caswell, R., Gregory, S., Marzolini, S., and Wilson, O. (2002) Can I join the club? *Autism: The International Journal of Research and Practice, 6,* 4, 427–31.

Carrington, S., and Graham, L. (2001) Perceptions of school by two teenage boys with Asperger syndrome and their mothers: A qualitative study. *Autism: The International Journal of Research and Practice, 5,* 1, 37–48.

Foster, B., and King, B.H. (2003) Asperger syndrome: To be or not to be? *Current Opinion in Pediatrics, 15,* 491–4.

Lindstrom, B. (1992) Quality of life: A model for evaluating health for all: Conceptual considerations and policy implications. *Soz Praventivmed, 37,* 301–306.

Lindstrom, B. (1994) *The Essence of Existence: On the Quality of Life of Children in the Nordic Countries.* Göteborg, Sweden: Nordic School of Public Health.

Little, L. (2002) Middle-class mothers' perceptions of peer and sibling victimization among children with Asperger's syndrome and non-verbal learning disorders. *Issues in Comprehensive Pediatric Nursing, 25,* 43–57.

Myles, B.S., and Simpson, R.L. (2002) Asperger syndrome: An overview of characteristics. *Focus on Autism and Other Developmental Disabilities, 17,* 3, 132–7.

Renwick, R., Brown, I., and Nagler, M. (eds) (1996) *Quality of Life in Health Promotion and Rehabilitation: Conceptual Approaches, Issues, and Applications.* Thousand Oaks, CA: Sage.

Renwick, R., Brown, I., and Raphael, D. (2000) Person-centred quality of life: Contributions from Canada to an international understanding. In K.D. Keith and R.L. Schalock (eds) *Cross-Cultural Perspectives on Quality of Life.* Washington, DC: American Association on Mental Retardation.

Renwick, R., Fudge Schormans, A., and Zekovic, B. (2003) Quality of life for children with developmental disabilities: A new conceptual framework. *Journal on Developmental Disabilities, 10,* 104–114.

Schalock, R. (1996) Reconsidering conceptualization and measurement of quality of life. In R.L. Schalock and G.N. Siperstein (eds) *Quality of Life: Conceptualization and Measurement, Volume 1.* Washington, DC: American Association on Mental Retardation.

Schalock, R. (2000) Three decades of quality of life. *Focus on Autism and Other Developmental Disabilities, 15,* 116–27.

Varni, J.W., Sied, M., and Rode, C.A. (1999) The PedsQL: Measurement model for the pediatric quality of life inventory. *Medical Care, 37,* 126–39.

Zekovic, B., and Renwick, R. (2003) Quality of life for children and adolescents with developmental disabilities: Review of conceptual and methodological issues relevant to public policy. *Disability and Society, 18,* 19–34.

CHAPTER 20

Depression and anxiety in parents of children and adolescents with Asperger Syndrome

Kevin P. Stoddart[1]

Researchers and clinicians have long recognized that parenting a child with autism is a significant life stressor (Bristol 1984; Bristol and Schopler 1984). A parent's grief response to a child with a disability may be chronic in nature and may be precipitated by failure of the child to progress typically at periods of developmental transitions (Olshansky 1962; Wikler 1981). Parents of children with autism spectrum disorders (ASDs) experience greater levels of stress than do parents of children with other developmental delays (Donovan 1988; Holroyd and McArthur 1976). Research has also shown that parents of children with ASDs are at greater risk of developing mental health problems such as depression and anxiety when compared to parents of children with other developmental disabilities (e.g. Piven *et al.* 1991; Smalley, McCraken, and Tanguay 1995). Although there has been past examination of variables that may contribute to or ameliorate stress in parents of children with disabilities (e.g. Gallagher, Beckman, and Cross 1983), it is critical to re-examine parent response in the context of current services and parent supports, and because of advances in diagnosis of ASDs.

Few studies examine the mental health profiles of parents of children with Asperger Syndrome (AS) and the contributors to, and moderators of, mental health problems in these parents. Although we have little evidence to believe otherwise, it cannot be assumed that the mental health profiles of parents of children with AS are the same as those for parents of children with other ASDs.

---

1   Appreciation goes to the parents and agencies that participated in this research.

This chapter describes a preliminary study of self-reported depression and anxiety in 60 parents of children and adolescents with AS.

Review of the literature

Parent mental health and relation to the type of disability their child has

One question that has been raised in the literature on parents of children with ASDs is whether they experience mental health problems at rates similar to that of parents of children with other developmental disabilities. Lotter (1966) noted early evidence of increased rates of psychiatric disorders in parents of children with autism when compared with parents of non-autistic disabled children. More recently, Piven and colleagues (Piven *et al.* 1991) compared parents of autistic children with parents of children with Down Syndrome. He found that lifetime rates of anxiety disorder were significantly greater in parents of autistic children than in parents of controls. Out of the 81 parents of children with autism, 12.3% had generalized anxiety disorder, 9.9% had a phobic disorder, and 3.7% had panic disorder. A major depressive disorder was found in 22 parents (27.2%) of the autism group and was more frequently found in the parents of children with autism than in those of children with Down Syndrome, though this difference was not statistically significant.

Results were similar for Shu, Lung, and Chang (2000), who compared mothers of intellectually disabled children who had autism aged five to 18 years to mothers of controls (children with Down syndrome and children with no developmental delays). Subjects included 30 mothers of children with autism, 11 mothers of children with Down syndrome, and 56 mothers of children with no developmental disability. They discovered that 11 (37%) of the mothers of children with autism scored at or above the clinical cut-off of the Chinese Health Questionnaire for depression, compared with only 12 (18%) in the control group. The mothers of children with autism who scored greater or equal to the cut-off score were further assessed. Of these 11 subjects, five (45.5%) were formally diagnosed with an anxiety disorder, four (36.4%) with depression, and one (9.1%) with both depression and anxiety. The researchers note that these mothers had not previously sought professional support for their mental health issues.

Research by Olsson and Hwang (2001) supported the notion that mothers of children with autism are at higher risk of depression compared with other mothers of children with other intellectual disabilities. Using the Swedish version of the Beck Depression Inventory (BDI), mothers of children with autism and intellectual disability reported higher depression scores than mothers of children with developmental disabilities without autism. Of the mothers of children with autism, 50% had elevated scores on the BDI compared with 21% of the fathers.

Parent mental health and parent gender

It is clear that many of the studies cited address the mental health of mothers of children with autism exclusively, or mothers compose the majority of subjects. Mothers may be generally more interested in participating in such studies, in part, since they have traditionally been responsible for the bulk of care of the child with an ASD (Holmes and Carr 1991; Wolf *et al.* 1989), although this trend seems to be changing. It is not clear if stress levels and the resulting psychological symptoms are a result of this "burden of care". Further data on the first onset of symptoms, however, would address this issue, at least in part. Findings about the influence of gender on mental health in these parents are mixed. A logistic regression analysis for presence of an anxiety disorder by Piven and colleagues (1991) showed no significant effects for subject gender. In contrast, Bolton's 1998 study revealed that mothers of children with autism were more likely to suffer from depression than their male counterparts, as did the study by Olsson and Hwang (2001).

Parent mental health and the onset of their symptoms

If parents of children with ASDs experience more mental health problems than parents of children with other disabilities, this could be accounted for by the unique needs of children with ASDs, the complexity of their developmental profile, and the lack of services for children with ASDs. Any onset of mental health symptoms would be expected to occur after the birth of the child with the disability as a reaction to constant stress or concerns about the child's development. However, research suggests there is more than just the unique need of children with ASDs accounting for mental health problems. These supporting data are found in studies examining the onset of symptoms.

Data from Piven *et al.* (1991) on the onset of first symptoms suggests that psychiatric features did not appear to be entirely related to the strains of raising a child with autism. As many as 12 parents (63%) with an anxiety disorder and seven (70%) with generalized anxiety disorder in this study reported that they had at least one episode before the birth of the child with autism. Of the parents of autistic probands who had recurring major depressive disorder episodes, ten (77%) had at least one episode before the birth of the proband. In Smalley's 1995 study, the onset of a major mood disturbance was before the birth of the proband with autism in 64% of the cases, as opposed to 20% in controls. Others have found the rates of depression onset were evenly divided before and after the birth of the proband with autism (Bolton *et al.* 1998).

Parent mental health and family history

Bolton's group (1998) examined the family histories of 99 subjects with autism and 36 subjects with Down Syndrome. Information was gathered about first-, second-, and third-degree relatives. There was a substantial difference between the groups in that affective disorder was much greater in relatives of the autistic probands. Here, affective disorder was defined as anxiety, depression, phobia, or mixed anxiety and depression. Attempted suicides and completed suicides were more common in the relatives in the autism group. Major depression was significantly more frequent in the autism group as was a more broadly defined affective disorder (defined as any combination of major depression, minor depression, and bipolar disorder).

The purpose of the investigation by Smalley et al. (1995) was to compare the rates of affective and anxiety disorders of first-degree relatives of probands with autism to that of controls with tuberous sclerosis complex or seizure disorder. Of the 36 families who had a child with autism, 23 (64%) had at least one relative with major depression which was a significantly greater number than in the controls. As well, 14 (39%) of these 36 families had at least one relative with social phobia, which again was significantly greater than in controls.

Parent mental health and autism spectrum disorder sub-type

There is some discussion by researchers that the significance of family psychiatric disorders may be greater for some types of ASDs than for others. DeLong and Nohria (1994) examined the family history of 40 probands, composed of 20 subjects with a neurological disorder (including rubella, Fragile X, tuberous sclerosis, post-encephalitic epilepsy, ring chromosome, cerebral cortical dysgenesis, brain malformation with hydrocephalus, and undiagnosed encephalopathy with epilepsy) and 20 subjects without a neurological disorder. Of the 20 with neurological disorders, only two had a family history of major affective disorder. In contrast, significantly more probands (14 out of 20) without a neurological disorder had a family history of affective disorder. The families in which affective disorders appeared tended to be those of higher-functioning individuals, whether their diagnosis was Pervasive Developmental Disorder (PDD), autism, or AS. In the study by Smalley's group (1995) a significantly greater number of families of children with autism and no intellectual disability had at least one relative with social phobia, when compared to the families of those children with autism and intellectual disability.

There is little literature specifically addressing the mental health of parents of children with AS. In part, this may be because of continuing diagnostic controversies about the criteria for AS and the relatively recent inclusion of the diagnosis of AS in the *DSM-IV* (APA 1994). There has been mention of severe and recurrent depression in first- or second-degree relatives in case studies of AS, such as those by Gillberg (1991) and Rhodes (2003). One report of mental health problems in parents of children with AS comes from Little (2002), who surveyed 103 mothers and fathers of children with AS and Non-verbal Learning Disorders (NVLD). She found 45% of mothers had taken medication for depression as opposed to 26% of fathers.

Study questions

Four questions were explored in this study: (1) What is the reported mental heath history of the mothers and fathers? (2) What are the levels of depression and anxiety of mothers and fathers? (3) What is the association of the following variables with parental depression (a) parent gender, (b) social support, (c) mental health history, (d) child symptom severity? (4) What is the association of the following variables with parental anxiety (a) parent gender, (b) social support, (c) mental health history, (d) child symptom severity?

Method

Subjects

The investigator contacted local organizations in Ontario that provide services only to children with PDD and their families to determine their interest in this study. There were five sources of subjects: (1) the investigator's private practice, (2) Autism Society Ontario, (3) Geneva Centre for Autism, (4) Kerry's Place Autism Services, and (5) The Aspergers Society of Ontario. An acceptable number of parents (N = 250) expressed initial interest in participating. All participants in this study had a biological and school-aged (six to 18 years old) child clearly diagnosed with PDD by a qualified diagnostician and currently living at home. The criteria for these diagnoses were based on the *DSM-IV* (APA 1994).

Procedure

All organizations requested the involvement of their clients and members through newsletters, the agency website, direct letter mailing, or direct emailing. Parents were asked to contact the investigator by phone or email if they were interested in taking part. If parents agreed to take part after this contact, they were mailed the questionnaires, a letter explaining the study, the procedure in completing the measures, a consent form, and a postage-paid return self-addressed envelope. In total, 167 parents from across Ontario responded to the invitation to participate and completed the package of questionnaires. Data returned from parents over a one year period were entered into a spreadsheet, scored according to the procedure recommended for each measure, and analysed using the Statistical Package for the Social Sciences, Version 12 (SPSS Inc. 2003). In this chapter, only data relating to 60 parents of children with AS will be reviewed.

Measures

- *Hamilton Depression Inventory (Reynolds and Kobak 1995)*: This measure was used to assess symptoms of depression in the parents. The HDI is a contemporary self-report format of the clinician-administered Hamilton Depression Rating Scale. Because the measure assesses both frequency and severity of symptoms, and uses multiple questions for many of the items, it is highly precise. The construct measured is consistent with the *DSM-IV* (APA 1994) definition of depression. The measure has 23 items (consisting of 40 questions) that have been extensively tested, and multiple types of validity have been demonstrated.

- *Multidimensional Anxiety Questionnaire (Reynolds 1999)*: This questionnaire provided the primary source of data for assessing anxiety in the parents. The MAQ is a 40-item, self-report, four-point response format measure that evaluates symptoms of anxiety according to *DSM-IV* (APA 1994) criteria in four domains: (1) *Physiological-Panic* captures physiological symptoms of anxiety such as breathing problems, heart palpitations, dizziness, perspiration, jumpiness, shaky hands and feeling flushed. (2) *Social Phobia* addresses worry about what others think, worry about being anxious in front of other people, performance anxiety in work or school, avoidance of people, difficulty talking with people, and fears of evaluation or negative evaluation by others. (3) *Worry-Fears* address the cognitive component of anxiety such as worries about the future or about being alone, thoughts of harm or bad things occurring, and worries about one's health. (4) *Negative Affectivity* relates to symptoms such as general distress, sleep problems, irritability, and difficulty concentrating.

- *Dyadic Adjustment Scale (Spanier 1976, 1979)*: The Dyadic Adjustment Scale provided a total score of marital/relationship adjustment. Scores for separated and divorced parents were excluded for this analysis. There are four factors of relationship measured in this 32-item instrument: (1) *Dyadic Satisfaction* examines the degree to which the couple agrees on matters of importance to the relationship; (2) *Dyadic Cohesion* measures the degree to which the couple engages in activities together; (3) *Dyadic Consensus* addresses the degree to which the couple is satisfied with the present state of the relationship and is committed to continuing it; (4) *Affectional Expression* assesses the degree to which the couple is satisfied with the expression of sex and affection in the relationship.

- *Gilliam Autism Rating Scale (Gilliam 1995)*: The Gilliam Autism Rating Scale provided a measure of the severity of the child's symptoms. The GARS is a suitable parent-report measure for individuals with ASDs between three and 22 years. The items in the scale, which are based on the current *DSM-IV* (APA 1994) definition of autism, are grouped into four sub-scales of 14 items each: (1) Stereotyped Behaviours, (2) Communication, (3) Social Interaction, and (4) Developmental Disturbances.

- *The Clarke Modification of the Questionnaire on Resources and Stress (Konstantareas, Homatidis, and Plowright 1992)*: This questionnaire was the primary measure of the stress experienced by parents. The Clarke QRS was developed as a short form of the 285-item QRS (Holroyd 1974). The measure has 78 items, uses Likert-type responses, and contains nine scales: (1) Child Characteristics, (2) Community Reaction, (3) Time Demands, (4) Family Sharing, (5) Presenting Symptoms, (6) Sacrifice/Martyrdom, (7) Supports, (8) Family Enrichment, and (9) Existential Issues.

- *Demographic, child, and mental health information*: This questionnaire, developed by the investigator, asked for information on: (1) parent demographics, (2) child demographics, (3) parent/family mental health history.

Results

Description of parents

A total of 60 parents in the study identified that their children had AS; 24 (40%) were fathers and 36 (60%) were mothers. Parents ranged in age from 32 to 55 and their mean age was 44.6 (SD = 5.0). In terms of marital status, 55 (91.7%) were married or in a common-law relationship and the remainder were separated or divorced. The sample was well educated with 15% completing high school, 71.7% completing college or receiving a bachelor's degree, and 13.3% completing graduate education. Of the 47 parents who had a personal income, personal income for 12 (25.5%) of the subjects was under $24,999, for 17 (36.2%) of the subjects it was between $25,000 and $54,999, and the remainder of the parents (18 or 38.3%) had a personal income over $55,000. The average personal income in the province of Ontario at the time of the study was approximately $35,000 (Statistics Canada 2001).

The parents completing the study had 52 (86.7%) sons and eight (13.3%) daughters diagnosed with AS. Children of the parents ranged in age from six to 19 years, with an average age of 12.3 years (SD = 3.74). Their average age of first ASD diagnosis was nine years (SD = 3.68) with six (10%) diagnosed by the age of five, 37 (61.7%) between the ages of six and ten, and 11 (18.3%) between the ages of 11 and 15 years. The balance of the children (6 or 10%), were diagnosed between the ages of 16 and 18.

History of depression and anxiety in the parents

Parents reported on their mental health history and that of their extended family members. Of the 60 parents, 22 (37.7%) indicated that a medical doctor or a mental health professional had diagnosed them in the past. Of these 22, 13 had been diagnosed with depression, five with anxiety, two with depression and anxiety, one with depression and ADD, and one with AS. Of the 22 diagnosed, seven (31.8%) had been diagnosed before the birth of the child with AS. The remaining 15 (68.2%) had been diagnosed after the birth of the child (seven parents between years one and five, four parents between years six and ten, three parents between years 11 and 15, and one parent when the child was 16 years old). Of this group of 22 parents, 18 had been prescribed medication to address their symptoms. Breakdown by gender showed that 33.3% of the mothers and 25% of the fathers in the study were prescribed medication. A total of ten subjects said that they felt they suffered with undiagnosed mental health symptoms; the most common were depression, anxiety, and AS traits. Of the entire group of 60 subjects, 35 (58.3%) reported that at least one relative of the child with AS had a mental health problem, attentional problem, or developmental disability. The most common diagnoses of family members in order of frequency were depression, anxiety, manic depression, ASD/traits, learning disability, ADD, and schizophrenia.

Reported depression and anxiety on the Hamilton Depressive Inventory and the Multidimensional Anxiety Questionnaire

Mean scores were calculated for the parents for the HDI and the MAQ. For the HDI, the subjects' raw scores ranged from 0 to 40 with a mean score of 12.42 (SD = 8.54). This placed the subjects at the 83rd percentile rank when compared to the total community sample. For the MAQ, subjects' raw scores ranged from 41 to 117 with a mean score of 63.93 (SD = 14.74), which placed them at the 78th percentile rank when compared to the total community standardization sample. When scores were considered separately for males and females on the depression measure, females (mean = 14.42, SD = 9.6; percentile rank = 86) scored significantly higher (p <.01) than males (mean = 9.3, SD = 5.5; percentile rank = 76). The latter comparison to the standardization sample to obtain percentile ranks used the gender-matched community sample. There was a similar disparity between males and females for the anxiety measure. The mean score for males was 59.71 (SD = 11.00; percentile rank = 74) and for the females was 66.75 (SD = 9.6; percentile rank = 78). This difference was almost statistically significant (p = .05)

Results for females and males were compared using the chi-square statistic and the clinical cut-off scores for both scales. A significantly greater number of females reported clinical levels of depression according to the HDI (p <0.01). There was less of a difference between the numbers of males and females reporting clinical levels of anxiety, but the difference in the groups continued to be significant (p <.05). Figure 20.1 depicts the differences between the fathers and mothers relative to the cut-off scores for the HDI and MAQ.

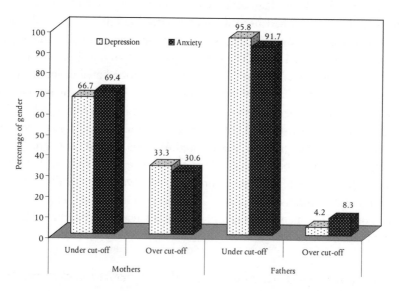

Figure 20.1 Percentage of parents over the cut-off scores for depression and anxiety

Correlations between measures

To discover the relationship between the key variables, a correlation matrix was developed using the six main variables in the study: (1) Depression, (2) Anxiety, (3) Autism Quotient, (4) Dyadic Adjustment, (5) Resources and Stress, and (6)

Mental Health History. For the latter variable, a rating was devised that included parents' reports of: (a) whether they had been previously diagnosed with a mental health problem, (b) whether they had received medication for the mental health problem, (c) whether they felt that they suffered from any additional undiagnosed mental health problems, and (d) whether they had a biological relative who suffered from a mental health problem. This generated a mental health rating of 0 to 4 for each subject (i.e. 0 = No indicators; 4 = All indicators).

Not surprisingly, depression was highly correlated to anxiety, severity of autism, dyadic adjustment (inversely), and mental health history ($p < .01$). However, it was unexpected that the HDI was not significantly correlated to the resources and stress measure. Anxiety was highly associated with autism severity and inversely related to dyadic adjustment ($p < .01$). Anxiety was associated with mental health history, but less so than depression ($p < .05$). Severity of symptoms in the child was inversely correlated to dyadic adjustment ($p < .01$), as was mental health history of the parents ($p < .05$) (see Table 20.1).

Table 20.1 Correlations between the variables

	Depression score	Anxiety score	Autism quotient	Dyadic adjustment	Resources and stress	MH history
Depression score	1.000					
Anxiety score	0.806**	1.000				
Autism quotient	0.516**	0.349**	1.000			
Dyadic adjustment	-0.501**	-0.453**	-0.490**	1.000		
Resources and stress	0.166	0.246	0.127	-0.042	1.000	
MH history	0.403**	0.304*	0.056	-0.287*	0.062	1.000

** Correlation is significant at the 0.01 level (2-tailed)
* Correlation is significant at the 0.05 level (2-tailed)

Predictors of depression and anxiety

To discover predictors of anxiety and depression, regression equations were created using variables that were most closely correlated to both the dependent variables as seen from the correlation matrix. Anxiety and depression were excluded from each equation as a predictor due to possible collinearity. Parent gender was coded using 0=male and 1=female. Table 20.2 depicts the predictors for depression. It is evident that when entered separately, parent gender, dyadic adjustment, mental health history, and autism quotient all contributed to a significant change in F. Using the adjusted R-squared value, these four factors combined contributed to 48% of the variance in depression (as reported on the HDI) in the sample.

Table 20.2 Model summary for depression

Model	R	R square	Adjusted R square	Std error of the estimate	R square change	F change	Sig. F change
1	0.311(a)	0.097	0.079	8.1952	0.097	5.480	0.023
2	0.555(b)	0.308	0.280	7.2463	0.211	15.232	0.000
3	0.605(c)	0.366	0.327	7.0057	0.058	4.492	0.039
4	0.724(d)	0.524	0.484	6.1335	0.158	15.927	0.000

(a) Predictors: (constant), parent gender
(b) Predictors: (constant), parent gender, dyadic adjustment
(c) Predictors: (constant), parent gender, dyadic adjustment, MH history
(d) Predictors: (constant), parent gender, dyadic adjustment, MH history, autism quotient

Similarly, Table 20.3 describes the predictors for anxiety (as reported on the MAQ). The same predictors were entered in the same order for sake of comparison. In this regression equation, it is of note that the parents' mental health history did not contribute significantly to the overall model. However, parent gender, dyadic adjustment, and autism quotient did, but to a lesser extent than in the model for depression.

Table 20.3 Model summary for anxiety

Model	R	R square	Adjusted R square	Std error of the estimate	R square change	F change	Sig. F change
1	0.280(a)	0.078	0.060	12.582	0.078	4.343	0.042
2	0.501(b)	0.251	0.221	11.458	0.172	11.495	0.001
3	0.521(c)	0.272	0.227	11.412	0.021	1.409	0.241
4	0.605(d)	0.366	0.313	10.759	0.094	7.129	0.010

(a) Predictors: (constant), parent gender
(b) Predictors: (constant), parent gender, dyadic adjustment
(c) Predictors: (constant), parent gender, dyadic adjustment, MH history
(d) Predictors: (constant), parent gender, dyadic adjustment, MH history, autism quotient

Discussion and implications for practice

This is a preliminary study examining depression and anxiety in parents of children with AS in Ontario. This research may have captured issues that are specific to the Canadian service system, although it is potentially applicable to other contexts. Further examination of these issues requires unbiased ascertainment of parent subjects and clinical examination of their symptoms. It cannot be ruled out that a portion of this sample engaged in the study because of their personal experience of mental health issues. The responses of the subjects had to be considered as accurate, as there was no cross-validation of responses through a clinical interview. However, all the measures used were intended for self-report. The major advantage of a mail-out approach was that the investment of time was minimized for the subjects. Parents may have also been more truthful in their responses because of the confidential nature of their involvement and the feeling of privacy associated with a self-report approach.

Gathering data on the mental health history of parents of children and youth with AS was one of the contributions of this study. Of the 60 parents, 36.7% said that they had been previously diagnosed with a mental health problem; 33.3% of the mothers and 25% of the fathers in the study were prescribed medication. This is comparable to the rates of medication use reported by Little (2002), who found that 45% of mothers and 26% of fathers had taken medication for depression. Almost one-third of those with mental health problems had been diagnosed before the birth of the child with AS. This rate is much lower than that reported by Piven and colleagues (1991). This difference may be accounted for by the differences in methods of reporting. Similar methods of subject recruitment and clinical assessment of parents of children with AS are required to find out if this is a true difference. It may also be important to consider the severity of autism in the 1991 sample and their lower IQ. The frequent reports of familial mental health problems were consistent with other research and require closer examination.

The correlation between variables was the second contribution of this study. It was surprising to note there was little relationship between the measure of stress and depression and anxiety. This suggests that, regardless of the pressures of raising a child with AS and lack of supports, depression and anxiety may persist. Dyadic support, however, was closely associated with such symptoms. It is also important to note whether parent appraisal of child symptom severity was affected by depressive or anxious traits in parents. Those who were depressed, for example, may have perceived child symptoms as more severe. As well, it is noteworthy that levels of depression and anxiety were closely related, suggesting comorbidity of the disorders.

The rates of depression and anxiety as reported using these measures was the third key finding of this study. For mothers, 33.3% of the sample were over the cut-off for depression and 30.6% were over the cut-off for anxiety. The rate of depression, derived in a similar manner to the study by Shu, Lung, and Chang (2000), was 37% for mothers; again, it is probable that the children of these mothers were lower functioning than those in the current study. Examining the clinical cut-off scores for fathers revealed a significantly different picture. Only 8.3% of the fathers scored above the cut-off for anxiety, and 4.2% for depression. So, although rates of anxiety and depression are significantly lower for fathers, anxiety appeared to be the more significant concern for them. Future replication of rates of anxiety and depression in parents of children with AS are required. Use of standard measures such as the HDI and the MAQ will allow comparison of results and provide indicators of severity, as opposed to dichotomous findings (i.e. depressed/not depressed).

The attempt to develop a regression equation for depression and anxiety was the fourth contribution of this study. Clearly, mothers were more prone to experience depression and anxiety, and gender was more salient in the regression analysis for depression. Dyadic adjustment was important in ameliorating both depression and anxiety for the parents. It will also be helpful to continue to discover predictors of current mental health using data on parent history and on their family members.

What, then, are the implications of these findings for practice? It may be helpful to remember that a mother coming for counselling about her child with AS, may in part be grieving the loss of the "normal child" and experiencing stresses associated with raising a child with AS; however, she also may have a proclivity to anxiety and/or depression. Given what we know about the gene–environment interactions in depression and anxiety generally, it may be fruitful to consider the probability of a vulnerability model of depression and anxiety in parents of children with AS. If clinicians find that traditional supportive counselling approaches to addressing depression or anxiety in parents of children with AS are not productive or have limited meaning to the parent, another approach to addressing mental health, such as pharmacological or cognitive behaviour interventions (McCullough 2000), can be attempted. Careful exploration of the history of symptoms, their onset, and family history should be included in the process of supporting parents of a child with an ASD. As one mother told the writer:

> I've always been depressed – as long as I can remember. My son having AS has nothing to do with it. In fact, my time with him gives me great enjoyment!

Conclusion

Biopsychosocial explanations of mental health in families affected with AS need further empirical investigation. The internal psychological resources that parents must gather in meeting the challenges of not only raising a child with AS, but also in facilitating his or her treatment, are considerable. This may be impeded by pre-existing mental health problems or the development of these problems – chiefly depression and anxiety.

References

APA (American Psychiatric Association) (1994) *Diagnostic and Statistical Manual of Mental Disorders, Fourth Edition.* Washington, DC: APA.

Bolton, P.F., Pickles, A., Murphy, M., and Rutter, M. (1998) Autism, affective and other psychiatric disorders: Patterns of familial aggregation. *Psychological Medicine, 28,* 2, 385–95.

Bristol, M.M. (1984) Family resources and successful adaptation to autistic children. In E. Schopler and G.B. Mesibov (eds) *The Effects of Autism on the Family.* New York, NY: Plenum Press.

Bristol, M.M., and Schopler, E. (1984) Stress and coping in families of autistic adolescents. In E. Schopler and G.B. Mesibov (eds) *The Effects of Autism on the Family.* New York, NY: Plenum Press.

DeLong, R., and Nohria, C. (1994) Psychiatric family history and neurological disease in autistic spectrum disorders. *Developmental Medicine and Child Neurology, 36,* 5, 441–8.

Donovan, A.M. (1988) Family stress and ways of coping with adolescents who have handicaps: Maternal perceptions. *American Journal of Mental Retardation, 92,* 6, 502–509.

Gallagher, J.J., Beckman, P., and Cross, A.H. (1983) Families of handicapped children: Sources of stress and its amelioration. *Exceptional Child, 50,* 1, 10–19.

Gillberg, C. (1991) Clinical and neurobiological aspects of Asperger syndrome in six family studies. In U. Frith (ed.) *Autism and Asperger Syndrome.* Cambridge, UK: Cambridge University Press.

Gilliam, J.E. (1995) *Gilliam Autism Rating Scale.* Austin, TX: Pro-ed Inc.

Holmes, N., and Carr, J. (1991) The pattern of care in families of adults with a mental handicap: a comparison between families of autistic adults and Down syndrome adults. *Journal of Autism and Developmental Disorders, 21,* 2, 159–76.

Holroyd, J. (1974) The Questionnaire on Resources and Stress: An instrument to measure family response to a handicapped member. *Journal of Community Psychology, 2,* 92–4.

Holroyd, J., and McArthur, D. (1976) Mental retardation and stress on the parents: A contrast between Down's syndrome and childhood autism. *American Journal of Mental Deficiency, 80,* 4, 431–6.

Konstantareas, M. M., Homatidis, S., and Plowright, C. M. (1992) Assessing resources and stress in parents of severely dysfunctional children through the Clarke modification of Holroyd's Questionnaire on Resources and Stress. *Journal of Autism and Developmental Disorders, 22,* 2, 217–24.

Little, L. (2002) Differences in stress and coping for mothers and fathers of children with Asperger's syndrome and Nonverbal Learning Disorders. *Pediatric Nursing, 28,* 6, 565–70.

Lotter, V. (1966) Epidemiology of autistic conditions in young children: I-Prevalence. *Social Psychiatry, 1,* 124–37.

McCullough, J.P. (2000) *Treatment for Chronic Depression: Cognitive Behavioural Analysis System of Psychotherapy.* New York, NY: Guilford Press.

Olshansky, S. (1962) Chronic sorrow: A response to having a mentally defective child. *Social Casework, 43,* 190–3.

Olsson, M.B., and Hwang, C.P. (2001) Depression in mothers and fathers of children with intellectual disability. *Journal of Intellectual Disability Research, 45,* 6, 535–43.

Piven, J., Chase, G.A., Landa, R., Wzorek, M., Gayle, J., Cloud, D., and Folstein, S. (1991) Psychiatric disorders in the parents of autistic individuals. *Journal of the American Academy of Child and Adolescent Psychiatry, 30,* 3, 471–8.

Reynolds, W.M. (1999) *Multidimensional Anxiety Questionnaire.* Odessa, FL: Psychological Assessment Resources.

Reynolds, W.M., and Koback, K.A. (1995) *Hamilton Depression Inventory.* Odessa, FL: Psychological Assessment Resources.

Rhodes, P. (2003) Behavioural and family systems interventions in developmental disability: Towards a contemporary and integrative approach. *Journal of Intellectual and Developmental Disability, 28,* 1, 51–64.

Shu, B.C., Lung, F.W., and Chang, Y.Y. (2000) The mental health in mothers with autistic children: A case-control study in Southern Taiwan. *The Kaohsiung Journal of Medical Sciences, 16,* 6, 308–314.

Smalley, S.L., McCraken, J., and Tanguay, P. (1995) Autism, affective disorders and social phobia. *American Journal of Medical Genetics (Neuropsychiatric Genetics), 60,* 19–26.

Spanier, G.B. (1976) Measuring dyadic adjustment: New scales for assessing the quality of marriage and similar dyads. *Journal of Marriage and the Family, 38,* 15–28.

Spanier, G.B. (1979) The measurement of marital quality. *Journal of Sex and Marital Therapy, 5,* 288–300.

SPSS Inc. (2003) *Statistical Package for the Social Sciences, Version 12.0.* Chicago, IL: SPSS Inc.

Statistics Canada (2001) Average earnings of the population 15 years and over by highest level of schooling, by provinces and territories. Retrieved from www.statcan.ca on August 25 2004.

Wikler, L. (1981) Chronic stresses of families of mentally retarded children. *Family Relations, 30,* 281–8.

Wolf, L.C., Noh, S., Fisman, S.N., and Speechley, M. (1989) Brief report: Psychological effects of parenting stress on parents of autistic children. *Journal of Autism and Developmental Disorders, 19,* 1, 157–66.

Part IV

Parent and Personal Perspectives

CHAPTER 21

Asperger Syndrome: Perceiving normality

Peter Jansen

I am a 24-year old Caucasian male with a mysterious condition called Asperger Syndrome (AS). I was diagnosed at the age of ten. As a child, I saw the world through a distorted lens whose refracted images took turns baffling me. A general understanding of the world and human nature has been afforded to me through the medium of the second-hand: books, TV, and movies. If "Life as a Human Being" were a college credit course, I would probably score higher in the pure than the applied sections. I'm hungry for knowledge because I'm hungry for "knowledge-about-life", but I sense there is a stark threshold where learning about life and actually *living* are forever divided. I wonder how well I have done in this course so far. The world's greatest teachings say that all reading, no matter how comprehensive, is preliminary. At this stage, more than ever, the applied section of the course, the hands-on, touchy-feely part, deserves the most attention. No one will issue a final mark. There is no in-class help, no timelines, guidelines, rules, or rubrics. On no transcript will a record of the grade appear.

The label

A label, depending on one's viewpoint, can be one of the most stigmatizing things a majority can inflict on an individual. It's the power of the majority asserted over the minority. A label, psychiatric or otherwise, is a convenient short-hand symbol for defining you as a person. I personally dislike it because it reduces the human being in all his complexity and layers of ego structure down to a single thought or concept, expressible in a single sentence or a short paragraph. It's a handy short-cut for knowing those whom you have never met. I don't want to have AS *define* me as a human being, partly because I don't think any finite cluster of words and ideas ever could.

313

A diagnosis is an idea, a static, inert framing of words, whereas a human being defies quantification. The human being is dynamic, able to change, grow, and evolve. I stress again that a label is static, no matter how quickly they crank out new editions of the *DSM*. The human being is alive. Someone might be an "alcoholic", another negative label created by society. However, this individual who is suffering, who has an illness, who is still going on being, and still trying, simply cannot be written off. It's not fair. It becomes a black mark, and when someone is given a black mark, it can mean society has given up on her. Once she realizes this, something much worse can happen: she acquires a "learned helplessness" and gives up on herself as well.

In the most dramatic terms, AS is a prison from which I can never escape, no matter where I go, what I do, or whom I become. Even if the label, which throws up a barrier between me and the rest of the world, exists largely in my own head, it's created a great deal of suffering in my life, and continues to do so. Sometimes it is crushing to contemplate how I will never be the same as everybody else, not because of any poverty of character but simply because of this thing they cannot fix – ever. Whether you choose to call it a "syndrome" or a "condition" or a "spectrum", it is still a psychological burden to know you have it, like dragging around an iron ball and chain. Sometimes I perceive it as a limit, one I can never exceed. Anyone researching AS will almost immediately come across the word "autism" and the host of negative connotations it drags along with it.

It has been my experience, however, that an AS diagnosis will remain largely undiscussed, and the only stigma will be self-inflicted. This is because of how little the public knows about AS, how unlikely they are to self-educate, and how scarce information is about it. For most people, I imagine the phrase "Asperger Syndrome" would mean nothing, yet would leave an imprint of vague unease in their minds, precisely because they don't know. This vague "ill-at-ease feeling" in the minds of others can be, and often is, the very cause of the stigmatizing effect felt by those implicated by the label – those so simply and haphazardly "expressed" by it. In some situations, it would be better kept secret than revealed.

When I was first presented with the opportunity of speaking at a conference on AS, my initial response was negative. I resented the notion of it, showcasing my defect for all to see. I felt the idea was demeaning; I was ashamed and wanted to draw no more attention to the issue than necessary. That, however, is one extreme interpretation of what would occur, not necessarily correct or incorrect, but a matter of perspective. A more enlightening and progressive opinion that changed my mind came from my family, where it was suggested that I would be doing professionals in the field and those with the diagnosis a service by appearing at the conference.

The experience of Asperger Syndrome

It is strange because you wouldn't have a clue I had AS if you weren't educated about it and knew exactly what to look for, when to look for it, and where. With me, the clues are subtle, but they are there. With others on the spectrum, the indications are hard to ignore. Qualified people have told me that I am on the high end of the autistic spectrum, which means, in plain English, that I could pass for an NT (neurotypical) more easily than could those lower on the spectrum. It is my understanding that autism is not only a question of degree but also one of quality, proportion, and range. It is amazing in that it manifests differently in different people. I have seen it with my own eyes and I still can't explain it – a sameness of diagnosis with different outward traits, behaviours, and complications. I've talked to and become familiar with other people with AS during my time with the Aspergers Society of Ontario and other groups. I've found there are some individuals with whom I can relate quite well, yet there are those who, for me, are on another page altogether. Naturally, I gravitate more toward those I can find a connection with, and less toward those I cannot. Sometimes the problem is a deficiency of intelligence or ability, a developmental delay; while with others, intelligence is not the problem – they are brilliant! In fact, I find these people often have *too much* intelligence – so much so that it is a constraint in many ways. The absorption of all that marvellous intellect and aptitude takes place within a sphere of human knowledge that leaves little else of the mind untapped. In other words, these individuals with AS have concentrated their augmented intellect in areas so confined that they forfeit their ability to see the bigger picture.

I am no exception to this rule. My area of specialty is creative writing, grammar, spelling and punctuation, words, semantics, semantic arguments, and abstract philosophy. I like to read and write and think; those are the things I do best. I have always had an overdeveloped imagination and a proportionately underdeveloped set of pragmatic faculties. Examples of the latter include basic math, names of cities, names of streets, sense of direction, balance, and motor functioning, both fine and gross. I realize I am better with my brain than I am with my body. I excel as a writer, but my handwriting is poor, and I am even a lousy typist. Picture a sound effects board with several levers representing several separate audio tracks. Normally, they would all have to be adjusted to the same position to produce a coherent piece of music, so the bass line doesn't drown out the vocals, and so the guitar track isn't lost. Now if each audio track represented an area of human aptitude and one was allowed to rise while the others were held down unnaturally, you would get a person with a lop-sided mind, semi-functional, overdeveloped here but underdeveloped there.

AS is a feeling. The quality of its presence is a feeling, a palpable sensation of body and mind, body and mind simultaneously, dynamically. Walking through a crowded bus terminal, there is that physical ungainliness, that awkwardness, that constant awareness that I'm out in the open, exposed. I may not be sitting right, standing right, holding my arms, hands or feet right. This isn't something I can put into words. It's occurred to me that maybe no one can. I do know that I was, for whatever reason, denied a certain crucial point of human development – somewhere between late childhood and early adolescence – which I'll never get back. The more time passes, the more remote that possibility of reclamation becomes. My therapist described this feeling as "displacement", and, although I am not entirely sure what it means, it sounds right. Wherever I go, there is usually this feeling of awkwardness, a physical phenomenon with mental origins. It's not that there's something wrong with the world; rather, there's something wrong with me. Just what, I can't say. I can't put my finger on it. You might assume, from what I've said, that I'm much more comfortable being alone, but that isn't always true. I often have an acute sense of loneliness that magnifies the problem instead of alleviating it. In other words, I am prone to loneliness, both in an empty house and in a room full of people. Both situations bring out the childlike vulnerability – the insecurity – that counts as one of my character flaws.

I have come across people with more serious delays than I have, with considerably fewer cognitive skills, and it may surprise you to know I sometimes envy them. I figure I am smart enough to know what I am missing, where the big gaps of information and experience are, and yet these people may not. They are seemingly without a care in the world, and this, I think, is simply because they seem to have no idea what they are missing. I know precisely what I am missing, because I see it all around me – what I am missing, and what I missed – but not where or how I missed it. I am tempted to think ignorance really *is* bliss. Maybe I would be better off with a subnormal IQ or some other drastic separation from the world. I have an awful sense of this vast, incredibly complex world from which I am cut off. A world I can see, hear, and touch, but never quite comprehend, never quite grasp.

At 24 years of age, I feel I am a foreign element here in the world of adults. I'm never sure if I belong in the category of "adult", "adolescent", or "child". I am caught between the three. I definitely have the thoughts and feelings of a man, the personality of an adolescent, and some of the needs and vulnerabilities of a child. All these are apparent at different times. In terms of development, my therapist asked me where I thought I fell within these three categories. My category does not seem to be static. There are times, situations both social and personal, when I feel in turns like an adult, an adolescent, and a child.

Relationships and depression

One cause of my depression is my need for intimacy – that which I feel I am sorely lacking. I have a deep-rooted need for intimacy, specifically romantic intimacy, that I feel is not being fulfilled in my life. Material (not necessarily materialistic) status would naturally facilitate the arising of these desperately desired conditions. For example, it would be good if I had a car in which to drive my projected girlfriend around town on a date. Other prime examples would be the job to earn the money to buy the car and knowledge of the "hot date" spots of the town. When the average twenty-something guy sees a twenty-something "knockout" in a club, bar, or any other social situation, his instinctive response is to instigate the inchoate levels of contemporary courtship (i.e. "getting her number" and so forth). He feels he is capable of this, because on a superficial level, he has the material resources to "back up" a daring gambit like that. I feel, since I am "poor", I am capable of no such daring gambits. But the supreme irony here is that, although I couldn't drive her anywhere, buy her anything, show her any "cool" things, or introduce her to any "cool" people, I feel in my heart I could nurture a woman's spirit without limit. Why? Because I am a genuine human being, faults and limitations included. I have integrity. I possess innate gentleness and an innate intuition to inform that gentleness, to direct it. In other words, I have a certain knack about knowing how to handle the emotions of a person to whom I have committed myself in that way.

Since I was born with AS, there were certain things I was denied as a child and adolescent. Namely, a genuine sense of commonality with my peers, that I was truly "one of the gang". This carried over into my high school years, where the "culture lag" became even more pronounced. As an Aspie I was naturally withdrawn and awkward, less inclined to participate in school activities or even take note of them, and the lag grew wider. The lag grew as wide as it did because, at that age, school activities were the smithy in which most adolescent relations, both casual and romantic, were forged. This I can comprehend in retrospect. There was no intimacy there. High school, perhaps not incidentally, was when I first fell ill with serious depression, my graduating year of 1997. While all of my peers went on through upper grades and to various universities throughout the country, got jobs, and moved on, I was stuck. I was stuck in the hospital and outpatient programs for three or four times through the next four years, and stuck in depression. This later officially became manic depression or Bipolar Disorder. In the most despairing sense, I was left in the starter's blocks, left in the dust of the other supercharged athletes.

If I had to paint a picture of what happens when I go to pieces over a seemingly trivial event or stimulus, I would liken it to a mountain-climber's convulsive sneeze and the resulting, obliterating avalanche. While the "sneeze" may be as tiny and as silly as a cartoon illustration in a newspaper, the "avalanche" is nothing less than the sum total of all my life-frustrations crashing down on me like tons of crumbling masonry. The depressive trigger is a like a collapsing star, sucking everything into its infinitely powerful field of gravity, sucking thoughts and emotions into its field of gravity and distorting them beyond any semblance of what they were just moments before. In this way, the mind devours itself, and the emotions devour themselves. The depressive ego is a cannibal. Thought distortion is among the hallmark characteristics of clinical depression and mental illnesses in general, as I understand them. The ego is more often than not completely helpless to halt this process of potentially dangerous distortion; it is too weak. The distorted thoughts, fiendishly intelligent unto themselves, wheedle the victimized ego into believing that they are real and the others false. Furthermore, they lead one to believe that the entire world conceptualized by the healthy pre-depression ego is fundamentally false, and has always been fundamentally false. The depressed ego gives in and swallows the lies without hesitation (much as I swallow my medication at certain times of day without hesitation). Thus the self-victimized ego indulges, enters the state of hopelessness, worthlessness, apathy, despair, and becomes the wretched puppet of the illness; it thinks whatever the illness wants it to think; it says whatever the illness wants it to say; it does whatever the illness wants it to do.

I have been told that pills can only take me so far, and for a while I refused to accept that platitude. I interpreted that as an open admission of the prescribed medications' inefficacy and resented it. My childish instinct would have been to resent anyone who tried to "push that on me". However, since then I have discovered that, while certain chemical reactions in the brain produce certain moods or thoughts in the mind, the opposite process can and does occur: conscious neurochemical control. Cheering up, calming down, relaxing, gaining reassurance, and reclaiming a neurochemical homeostasis: all possible by certain cognitive activities and strategies. It is possible, but not always easy – rarely easy in fact. I have realized that much of my illness is non-chemical. "Cognitive habituation patterns", willfully instigated by yours truly, can also upset internal neurochemical balances.

These patterns of cognitive activity enjoy a subtlety that escapes the ego's watchtowers because they have formed a deep groove, and because they have been doing it for a long time. They are ninjas within the mind, operating by stealth. On the one hand, you have the chemical component of the illness, ultimately genetic, which is a non-negotiable factor. On the other, you have the cognitive component, which, extrinsic to the chemical because it is not genetic, because it is the dynamic fabric of the ego, is the pass key to the control room. It is the cognitive component with which we can work more easily and more accommodatingly, I feel. The cognitive is negotiable. Maybe there is a set potential for how much abnormal chemical reactivity can take place in the brain because of the illness. I will wager though there is also a similar, if not equal, amount of counter-acting normal cognitive reactivity that can take place in the ego because of conscious effort. In addition, that is where the psychotherapeutic process comes in, working in tandem with drug therapy.

The phrase "cognitive habituation patterns" is, I will admit, a fancy one, especially for a guy who has never studied psychology or even been to university. A pattern of habituation is anything the mind has become accustomed to doing or experiencing repeatedly, regularly, something that it's come to like so much it becomes part of the way basic cognition occurs. You perform deeply ingrained habits without even realizing what you are doing or why. The processor has become the process. "Abnormal chemical reactivity" is, in this chapter, until I am further enlightened on the topic, neurochemicals fluctuating in relation to each other within the brain to produce an affective disorder (depression). "Normal cognitive reactivity", what I see as the antidote, is cognitive processes working with each other, co-operating, to ameliorate the neurochemical imbalance. Reactivity implies a reaction to something, in this case, the depression, which is itself a process of reactive chemical events.

Perceiving normality

What is "normal"? It is a referent to which we attach persons, places, or things that are unremarkable, exceeding no limits or boundaries. An empty word, empty only until we fill it with our mores, values, likes and dislikes, attractions and repulsions. Meaningless until it contains an entire society, all its idiosyncratic quirks. It is most likely the oldest antipathy amongst human beings: fear and/or hatred of those who are different. The formal name for this is *xenophobia*. The human motives defy analysis and quantification, but the overarching explanation is simple. Difference creates discomfort, discord, friction, and, ultimately, hatred. The high-functioning Aspie, able to perceive that (s)he is different, travels the path of self-consciousness, guilt, shame, awkwardness, which, if allowed to progress, festers like an infected sore to become self-hatred. If it is not self-hate then it becomes hatred of others or of the entire world, which is perceived as a frightening and menacing place. The abstract state of normality, we find, is dependent on its context. In any given context, any given condition can be considered normal, just as the equally arbitrary opposite will be considered deviant. In some cultures, public nudity is the status quo; in others, it's a felony.

The high-functioning Aspie is in a unique quandary. I do not possess a fully vocabularized world, and by that I mean there are certain things I can process visually, yet have no linguistic designation for. Riding in a car, looking out the window at a house with gables and cupolas; this is the moment that I think illustrates what I'm talking about. You could take me out and show me a hundred "gables" and perhaps twice that number of "cupolas" or "cornices" on an old-fashioned house, but I would have no idea what I was looking at. I have no available referent until I go home and look up each of those terms in a modern dictionary. If I did that, however, I would be given a textual description of what a "cupola" or a "cornice" looks like, and likely not an accompanying illustration. In the perceptual world that I as an AS individual inhabit, referents – borrowed second-hand from my exhaustive, lifelong reading – often don't match up with their corresponding sense-objects. These referents stand in not just for words, but also for thought, emotions, and entire experiences. Through entertainment media, I think I vicariously have the life of any "normal" person my age. My mind is riddled with perceptual gaps, too many and too comprehensive to count. There exists a big gap in my memory where this information is supposed to be. I realize that my imaginative abilities far exceed those of the average person, and yet my everyday knowledge of the world, finance, travel, law, and sports is greatly inferior to that of the average person. I deem myself somewhat of an imaginative savant, one whose mind functions primarily in the creative mode, while for others it is the opposite.

From late adolescence to the present, I have observed human behaviour; not in any formal capacity, of course. It was in the process of being buffeted around by the whirlwind of social life, struck on the head by the occasional golf-ball, dodging as many folding aluminum chairs as I could. I think all Aspies are forced to be anthropologists on Mars,[1] whether they want to be or not. AS is not something that just popped up in the early 1990s. Like lactose intolerance and alcoholism, this condition has likely been around since the beginning of recorded history, unrecognized, untreated, unknown for what it is. Worse yet, it has been misunderstood and mistreated. I have heard more than my fair share of horror stories from fellow Aspies, people well into adulthood, whose parents were, regarding their child's condition, indifferent, ignorant, or abusive. The abuse, damage to the mind, body, and spirit, comes from an instinctive fear, deep-seated shame, disappointment, frustration, panic, anger, or a combination of all these emotions. The parent doesn't know what to do with the child, is desperate to eradicate all signs of the diagnosis by a ruthlessly artificial regimen of behaviour modification, or, worse yet, shames the child into thinking he or she

---

1   Phrase coined by Temple Grandin, PhD.

is a burden. Even Aspies reared in supportive environments feel the anxious wound of being what they are, wrestling to define *who* they are.

We understand the basis for AS is genetic. The professionals, the care providers, and some of us, the Aspies ourselves, know this. Since it occurs mainly in boys, on a purely social level, that translates as bad news for guys looking for dates within our own genetic enclave. The ladies, being the minority, have their pick. We do not. Alternatively, should an Aspie pursue an NT romantically? Is this desirable? Possible? For the young adults on the spectrum, dating and sexuality can be extremely sensitive issues. They are ordeals unto themselves. Should we seek companionship strictly within our own demographic, or seek out "normality"?

My Asperger Syndrome philosophy

A person for whom certain doors have closed because of AS, may have had other doors opened to which a non-AS person would never have access, or, more precisely, would never *see*. I can vouch that this condition does entail a different way of seeing the world, other people, and the self. It is another perspective, as if the optical illusion in which you see the two white faces is nothing but a black vase to everyone else, no matter how long they look. To give you an everyday example of this, I was at a pizza party not so long ago with other Asperger's young adults. When we opened the box, there were those little white plastic things that prevent the cheese from sticking to the inside of the box. To a friend, I remarked it looked like a little white patio table, and he got a good laugh out of that. He had never seen them as "little white patio tables", whereas I always have.

The existential struggle, which is excruciating, entails the mental integration of self, others, and the world. That is the biggest hurdle, the realization that these three are out of joint, and then the attempt to correct that imbalance. Again, I have to stress that higher-functioning individuals are not necessarily better off in terms of emotional well-being. When you are not completely aloof and sealed inside your own microcosm, so to speak, you naturally look around and become starkly aware of your differences. It is not a concept that easily lends itself to words. I know something, but what I know I cannot explain.

As I was preparing to write this section of my chapter, a powerful aphorism from my life sprang to mind:

Deficiency is another form of beauty

AS is unarguably a form of deficiency, but it has infinite potential to be transformed into something lovely, something great. Sometimes deficiency, be it mental or physical, is a hidden gateway to great achievement, great realization.

All you have to do is see the gateway. Franklin Roosevelt was crippled by polio at the age of 39. While in therapy for his illness, he had ample time to re-examine his life and destroy himself as an egotist, coming out of the experience as a warmer, more caring, selfless individual. After his inner transformation, he ran for Governor of New York State, won, and eventually became President of the United States for four consecutive terms.

Thomas Edison, deafened by injury as a boy after another boy hit him in the head, did not let himself be consumed by anger. He was instead grateful to be free of all the noise, able to continue his experiments in peace. Years later, a fire destroyed his lab when Edison was in his late 60s. His assistants thought that would be the crushing blow for an old man like him, but instead Edison was merely grateful the fire had destroyed only equipment and not his own life. He said, "All our mistakes are gone, so we'll start again!" Edison's deafness was the catalyst of his achievements and led to the state of the world today. Had he not been struck deaf as a child, he might never have gone on to give the world the light-bulb, the radio, the microphone, the electric motor, and a long a list of other inventions.

Deficiency and disability are more states of mind than anything else. Forgetting compassion, forgetting tolerance, not just with others but more so with yourself, I would propose, is the most limiting defect.

CHAPTER 22

From despair to hope:
A mother's Asperger story

Fern Lee Quint

– In honour of my parents Bess and Hyman Quint –

If I had been told 15 years ago that I would now be living a peaceful life with my family, I never would have believed it. "Ineffective parenting", "poor impulse control", and "unresolved feelings from a divorce" were the three main diagnoses given to my son Nathan over 12 long and draining years. As both a mother and a registered nurse specializing in mental health, I did not understand nor believe these diagnoses. Despite the tortuous years of an ongoing search for help, I am now grateful for my perseverance. Nathan's story was one of despair; now it is one of hope.

Our story

The early years

My pregnancy with Nathan was normal with a respiratory arrest at birth. He was an irritable baby who remained clingy for years. When he was about two years old, I used to attend a program and leave Nathan in the baby-sitting area with all the other little ones. As I walked away, I could hear his screaming over the other children, but hoped he would settle. However, each time I would retrieve him, his screams drowned out all the others. After about three trials, I had to quit my program.

From the time Nathan was 3½ he would only sleep with me. My family doctor told me that he must learn to sleep on his own. For a few months, the night would consist of Nathan waking up and running into my bed, then me putting him back. My mother told me he needed the security of being with me and would grow out of it when he was ready. Oddly enough, after I relaxed and did what was most natural, Nathan came to me some time later and said, "I'm a big boy now. I don't need to sleep with you any more." He happily went back to his own bed. Getting Nathan to sleep has never been a problem, since. Now getting him *out* of his bed in the morning is a chore!

When Nathan was 3½, my marriage dissolved, resulting in Nathan presenting with depressed, regressed, and aggressive behaviours. I used some contacts in the field to get what I thought was the best help. After about a year of play therapy, I asked for a diagnosis and was told that Nathan had developmental delay. When I asked what this meant, the psychiatrist told me that he would always be at least a year or two behind in his development. The appointment was over and it was never again discussed. No mention was made of how we were going to cope. All I can remember thinking was that somehow we were going to conquer this, but I had no idea how.

The grade school years

Nathan was involved in play therapy from age five to age eight. When he was six he was enrolled in a parochial school for children with special needs and remained there for six years. Psychological testing in the early years revealed learning disabilities, high anxiety levels, difficulty with peer relationships, and low self-esteem. When Nathan was eight he was assessed at a children's mental health facility for school and day treatment. The treatment plan suggested an environment with a strong focus on therapy. After observing the recommended class in progress through a one-way mirror, it was obvious to me that this would be an inappropriate placement. I saw a lot of violence in the classroom with few controls in place. When I said that I did not think that this was a suitable placement, I was told that Nathan's problems were a result of poor parenting and unresolved feelings from the marriage break-up. I was working in the field of mental health and providing counselling and insight to others, only to be told that I had none for my own situation. It was only after the principal of the parochial school observed the classroom and agreed with me that the treatment centre backed down. I wondered why my opinion had been devalued. I soon learned that this would be a constant theme.

We did end up at this facility as outpatients, to work on my parenting skills. Therapy consisted of watching me play board games with my children. The length of the game was the measure of success of the session. The next 1½ years consisted of a succession of three therapists. I was strongly encouraged to partici-pate in marital resolution therapy. The frequent changes in therapists resulted in blatant inconsistencies. I was and continue to be amazed at Nathan's resilience and tolerance of a system that failed him in many ways.

The adolescent years

During the therapy, special schooling, and testing, there was never any attempt to diagnose Nathan. All my questions were responded to with references to my lack of parenting skills. I found this frustrating and sometimes even amusing since I also had another child who was happy, easygoing, and successful. I was fortunate to have a wonderful support system of family and friends who constantly gave me the positive feedback and reassurance that I needed to face each day.

When Nathan was 12, we had our first breakthrough from the paternalistic attitudes to which we were subjected by professionals. I obtained an independent, objective psychological assessment by a psychologist whose philosophical and professional approach mirrored my own. The results of his testing addressed the usual impulsivity, high anxiety, unresolved dependency needs. He also identified neuropsychological deficits for the first time and emphatically ruled out a parenting problem.

Shortly afterward, Nathan's behaviour escalated with many obsessions and compulsions, and perseveration of thought, resulting in many episodes of violent behaviour at home and difficulties with peer relationships. There were increasing management problems both at home and at school. We were referred to a pilot program called Family Builders. I believe the worker from Family Builders saved my life and my sanity. When I felt I had no options and hit rock bottom, this program stepped in and helped me regain my emotional strength for the difficult task of parenting. It also gave me back hope, which I so desperately needed. The worker was one of the kindest therapists I had ever met. Unfortunately, the mandate of this program was short and intensive and it was terminated after one month.

The fall of 1992 was a nightmare. I contacted the social worker who was my only professional support at the time. I told him that he had been ineffective and that he had to get us help immediately. I also told him that I would be contacting the board of directors of his agency as well as the media and gave him 24 hours. He called me back 20 minutes later with an appointment for the following day with the psychiatrist who had originally recommended analysis. At that appointment, I brought the psychiatrist up to date and told him that something was definitely wrong and Nathan needed to be diagnosed and treated. He said he was sure things were fine and as a favour to the social worker he would see Nathan the next day. After seeing Nathan for 20 minutes, he told me he was concerned about Nathan and wanted him admitted to a children's hospital on the crisis unit for assessment. He reiterated all my concerns from the previous day as part of his own observations. He was leaving town for a few days and admission was arranged for the following week, or so I thought.

During that week, I travelled to another city with both kids to visit my parents. The trip home required a police escort because of Nathan's behaviour. The following day I called the doctor to arrange admission as planned. He never returned my calls. I called the previous psychologist who called the hospital and directed me to Emergency where Nathan was refused admission since this was a longstanding problem. They said that they had consulted with the psychiatrist by phone who supported their decision. I was stunned! This same man only a week earlier had recommended admission! In the meantime, Nathan's behaviour at home had deteriorated. Increasingly violent behaviour made frequent visits by the police a necessity. I was afraid to be home and not to be home. I functioned by rote and feared for all of us. A couple of friends had keys to my home with instructions to check if there was no answer when we were supposed to be home. This was not supposed to happen to me.

A few more threats on my part resulted in Nathan being admitted to a residential program for 1½ years. The most difficult and heart-wrenching decision I ever made was the one that saved us. The consulting psychiatrist asked me if I had ever noticed the peculiar set of symptoms Nathan was displaying – the same ones that I had been begging the professionals to watch during the previous years. Further consultation led to the diagnosis of Asperger Syndrome (AS). I knew my search for a diagnosis had ended.

What worked for us: A guide for parents

My philosophy

It was important for me first to develop an attitude and philosophy that I could live with. I believe that society will not change to accommodate anybody. We must be prepared to make the changes to fit in. I believe that if we expect change from the outside world, then we waste valuable time that could be used instead to provide role modelling and problem solving for our children. Keep in mind that our children learn from us. The way we deal with problems will influence how they deal with their own.

Although getting the diagnosis was initially a real blow, with perseverance and a determined mindset my family was able to overcome and move forward. Of course, we have struggles – who doesn't? One of the most difficult things I had to do was to learn to stay true to myself and fight for what I believed was right for my son. Positive thinking, combined with a strong will and fierce determination kept me going during the times that my heart was breaking.

I used to daydream about what I wanted to happen; I still do. I am a dreamer by nature. I would watch my son and let my imagination wander. I would rehearse in my head (and with friends) how I wanted to approach a situation and what outcome I wanted. I decided early that I would do my best to overcome the barriers and yet learn to live with the hand we were dealt, while continuing to achieve. I set expectations and goals that I believed were within our reach despite the sometimes dubious reactions of others. It was and is my personal belief that my son would achieve his goals if he were held accountable for his actions and behaviour.

Coping techniques

Some of the coping skills that have worked for me and I recommend are: Take one day at a time. Deal with one task at a time. Celebrate the small successes. Remember that everyone has some challenge to live with. Take time to nurture your relationships: family and friends were a constant support and I asked for help when needed. Time away for me remains important. I kept a busy social life. Having a sense of humour has been invaluable. Nurture yourself. Take as many breaks as you can. Get a baby-sitter or caregiver. Go out. Laugh with friends. See a funny movie. Hire someone to clean the house. Get enough rest. Take a course. Make love. Find something positive and relish each day. Teach your child by taking care of yourself.

Role play

Role play has been my most valuable tool. I used to role play with my son almost every day. We would take turns acting out whatever situation needed to be dealt with or worked on. Role play addresses every possible scenario. Play-acting gives our kids the opportunity to practise and build confidence. You can act as your child did in a specific situation. There is a double benefit to this. Your child sees his own behaviour while also getting a sense of how the recipient feels. This is also a start to helping your child develop the ability to empathize with another person. Talk about how you each felt in the roles you played. Role play how to have a conversation in person and how to call a friend on the phone. Some points to remember about conversational skills are: what to talk about, taking turns with dialogue, small talk, and what words to use. Role play also helps our kids prepare emotionally for whatever they are concerned about. Remember, when used properly, role play is fun!

Friends

Parents must do much of the work to enhance friendships. As long as there is no great objection from your child, I think it is a good idea to have birthday parties. Keep them small and be sure your child has input about who is coming. Plan the party around an activity. Some of the parties that worked well were swimming, bowling, movies, or video arcade parties. On one occasion, I tried an impromptu "roast" of my son. I had each child say what it was that he or she liked about my son. It was fun and started a pattern that continued for many years with both my children.

Invite people to your home. Let your child be around as many people as possible. Remember we are raising them to live in this world. Try not to get frustrated if you have to do the inviting most of the time. In the end, it is not a big deal. I believe that with each interaction our children will learn and be more comfortable with appropriate social skills and start to use them without prompting. With a younger child, plan activities around your child's interests. With teens, discuss what activities they can do when a friend comes over and set up equipment first (e.g. videos). If the kids are going out together, assess how much supervision they need. If teens are going by themselves, plan with them together before they go. Review the rules and make strategies for potential obstacles.

School

Be sure you introduce yourself to your child's teacher at the beginning of the school year and stay in frequent contact. Teach the teachers. Give them printed material. Talk to them. Make them your allies so they become part of the team guiding your child ahead. Praise them for successes and tell their supervisors. Make strategies together. Inform the teacher that our kids are vulnerable and more prone to bullying and teasing. Find out how to ensure that your child will be watched and protected at recess times. Ask for a buddy – a mature kid in the same class who can relate to your child and be a special friend. Ask the teacher to arrange seating and/or groups with others who are more receptive and the least threatening of the children in the class. If you hear about a difficult social situation or altercation with your child in school, get all the facts first. Be sure the teacher uses your child's special interest in a positive way and lets him or her shine. Once, Nathan taught part of a geography class to a higher grade. After, the other kids saw him in a different light as he had earned their respect.

Ask the teacher what the homework and expectations are. Make homework time fun. Give a lot of praise. I think it is important to do homework with your child and work together. My son learned about study habits and my enthusiasm for the material he was learning often became contagious. I made a big deal that I was learning new information too. I would act as if I was having a great time and more often than not, my child would join in. I found that learning came easier this way. I also used tutors. First, I would suggest to the tutor teaching styles that worked with my child. Then, I would putter around out of sight but within hearing range to monitor what was going on until I developed my own trust of the tutor. Although this can be a costly option, it saved me a lot of aggravation! Sometimes getting a high school student to tutor works wonders.

The school system places our children at a predetermined level based on age. To increase our children's self-esteem it is better to start easy and move forward. Our kids experience too much failure and thus think of themselves as never being able to achieve. This then results in lowered self-expectations and even fear of trying. Why should they bother, when we do not expect much from them in the first place?

It was and is my view that our kids need to feel and smell success. If they try the feeling of success on for size, they might even get to feel comfortable with it and move forward. I chose a basic-level high school for my son. Most of the kids in the class could not read nor do math. Although my son's skills were more advanced, I wanted him to know what it felt like for others to ask him for help. Why should our children always be labelled and be at the bottom of the class? I wanted him to be the one that others came to. During the planning session for high school, I was strongly discouraged from placing him in that class because he was too "high functioning". I thought, "So what! Let him feel it for once!" It worked. After 1½ years, during which his confidence soared, he was streamed into a regular high school. Over three years he worked his way out of special education, graduated high school on the honour roll, and completed a program at community college. After a co-op job placement, he was offered the position that he has today.

Anger and violent behaviour

Violent behaviour is one of the most difficult issues that some of us must deal with. I believe that this acting out stems from two sources. First, our children live with intense anxiety. Besides living with this constant anxiety, they also have difficulty processing and resolving anxiety-provoking situations. They may be worried about something, cannot express it, and act out instead of talking about it or working it out. Second, our kids have problems integrating and complying with social norms. Each interaction is a new event. Social subtleties, nuances, and all the steps that we take for granted in a social situation become a maze of confusion, awkwardness, and terror for them.

Watch out for any precipitants or warning signs of violent behaviour. If you see them – address the problem immediately. If your child cannot talk about it at the time – take action. Do something physical. Go for a walk or do something else that will distract him. My son used to love to go for drives. I would run for my car keys and take him out. Once he is settled and the situation is defused you can talk together.

Stop any violent behaviour. If your child gets out of control at home, you feel that you cannot handle him, and danger is a possibility, call the police! Forget about the neighbours. Although many people are reluctant to call the police, your child will remember this experience. It will make him think twice before breaking things or hurting someone next time. We must maintain control of our homes. It is frightening for any child to think that he is in control.

After a violent episode, remember your child feels worse about his behaviour than you do. He probably received all the recriminations and reactions and already feels horrible. Calm down! Take a few deep breaths and plan how you are going to handle it. If possible, try to discover what precipitated the violence. Ask your child what was happening and why he broke the window, hit the person, etc. You may want to say something like, "Let's figure out why you did that so we can find a better way to handle it next time." It is important to find out what he was thinking at the time. Ask open-ended questions (those that cannot be answered with a yes or no) to get more information. Pretend you feel calm!

Restricted interests and rigidity

Turn bizarre interests into strengths. Focussing on restricted interests reduces anxiety. It is a real balancing act for parents. I think we can use our child's restricted interests in a positive way. Rather than try to distract our children it is important to give them time to pursue their interests. We never know if these interests will become the basis of a career in later years with the expertise they will have! Use the interest to expand knowledge in other areas. When my son was in elementary school, his main interest was geography. He could barely read a primary reader but was coming home with new information about geography every day. When I asked him where he had learned the information, he told me he was reading the *World Book Encyclopaedia*. I immediately bought a set of encyclopaedias for our home, which he devoured, and while he read, he would become interested in other subjects. From geography, he expanded to history, politics, religions, and cultures.

Our children's special interests cause others to give them recognition in a positive way. Besides being the easiest people to buy presents for, our kids become known for their expertise. The recognition they get can only increase their self-esteem. Our kids ask questions they already know the answer to but want to hear the answer again and again…and again! Instead of answering questions repeatedly, start to reflect back to them and ask, "What do you think?" Then listen quietly.

Try to adhere to a consistent daily routine. A predictable and structured environment is necessary for younger children to build trust and reduce anxiety. They must know what to expect. Keep visual written timetables that your child can use.

If there is going to be an event that is anxiety provoking for your child, try to have as short a time as possible elapse from telling the child until the event. It saves unnecessary aggravation!

Family

In my family, life revolved around my son with AS. During one period, I was taking him to two or three appointments each week. I was working three or four days a week, taking courses, running a household, and having a busy social life. I also had another son 2½ years younger who was usually content and happy and thus received much less of my time. When my younger son was eight, his signals indicated that I needed to even out things. I scheduled one period per week to be alone with each son who could spend time with me as he chose. Sometimes we would go for dinner, play some board games, or go to a movie and a snack. Time alone with a parent is important for each child. The added benefit is that the child with AS becomes less self-focussed and begins to realize that his brother or sister needs time with parents too. This is another step in building empathy for others.

Advocacy

There were few resources available for anyone with AS at the time Nathan was diagnosed. I became my son's case manager. My 12-year search for help forced me to develop my own coping skills and treatment plan for my son, which contributed to the many successes he enjoys today. The most important part of advocacy is knowing what you want and taking the necessary steps to get there. The system is an intimidating one and we, as parents, have to struggle continually to keep our vision of what we want for our child. Fighting for my child was the second most difficult thing I have ever had to do. (Parenting was the first!)

Get as much information as possible regarding what you want. Speak to anyone and everyone you can. If someone has a friend who experienced something similar, call that person. Find out what worked and what did not. Ask around. Do not be ashamed. If embarrassment gets in the way, remember that every person you are opening up to has some problem of her own and inwardly admires your guts. Make notes. Practise before you go. Try out your approach on anyone who will listen. Ask for and evaluate feedback you get. Be prepared. Have achievable goals and stay focussed. Take notes with you to meetings. Be sure you have the names and phone numbers of all people in the meetings. Know what you want and what compromises you are willing to accept. Keep in mind that you can always go to the next higher level. If you do not reach results acceptable to you, ask for that person's supervisor. Enlist support for yourself when you face the big guns. Bring and pay for whatever professionals you need to support your quest.

Ask friends to come with you. Make everyone in meetings feel like they are a part of your team rooting for your child. Compliments and smiles go a long way. Personalize the meetings so your child is not just another case. Keep up hope. Remember that even if you do not get what you want, nothing is final. There is always tomorrow. As you practise your advocacy skills, you will become better and more successful.

Professional help

Therapy and professional help should be a beneficial experience. Engage in whatever therapy you or your child need – individual, family or group. Every kind has its benefits. Assess what you need. There has to be positive chemistry between the professional and the client and family. If you are not happy with the professional whom you are seeing, first discuss it with him or her. Perhaps there has been a simple misunderstanding that can be resolved. If not, change professionals. You do not owe anybody any explanations. You are choosing treatment that will ultimately affect your entire family. You need to feel supported. Choose a therapist whose philosophical approach resembles your own. Interview therapists before you go. Ask whatever you like. Critically evaluate the responses. It has to feel right.

Find a mentor to spend time with your child. I created an ad, called, and faxed university psychology and social work departments. I would call the schools and chat to the person who answered the phone. While I was chatting, I would also slip my story in – perhaps they knew of a student? When my son was around seven, I spoke to the principal of a high school who told me a new volunteer project was beginning. The co-ordinator of that project called me, and, after a gruelling interview, he became a big brother for my son. Their relationship has been a lasting treasure.

A word to professionals

As professionals, you were all taught communication skills – use them. One must do more than hear. Listen to the person you are trying to help. Parents know their children; we are with them 24 hours a day. Trust what they are saying. The professional has only snapshot glimpses of the child or family. Respect our thoughts and intuitions. Too often, the treatment plan is based on what the professional thinks the problem is. Make your job easier – ask us! The best professionals I ever dealt with, both personally and professionally, were the ones who humbly asked, "How can I help to make your life better?"

Say nice things about our child. Each day brings invasive stares from strangers when our child acts out in public. We accept any invitations with guarded caution. How will my child behave? Will I be embarrassed this time? How will any of us have fun? Each morning we are faced with the worries and the challenges that take every ounce of energy to hold our heads up and walk proudly. We need to hear something positive, as long as it is genuine. We spend therapy sessions focussing on the problems. It makes a world of difference when kind words are spoken.

Help your client to advocate for what he or she wants and needs. I knew the system and had to fight every step of the way. I shudder when I think of parents who, for whatever reason, do not have the confidence or skill to speak up to the authorities. It is a degrading and intimidating process at best and often is a full-time job. You may be the only connection to other supports the parent has.

Nobody ever knows what the future will bring. Help us take one day at a time. Give us hope. We need to believe things will get better. When combined with knowledge, hope can be a real saviour. We need something to hang on to and parents depend on and desperately need the professional to help us with warmth, kindness, and skill to face the adversity in our life with dignity.

Forget the expression "realistic expectations". It really means nothing. When I refused to put Nathan in a program for individuals with severe developmental difficulties, I was told I had to have realistic expectations. I cannot bear to think what would have happened had I listened. I believe the term "realistic expectations" is totally limiting. It ultimately prevents growth and progress.

In closing

Now, aged 26, Nathan has been working in his chosen field for three years. He completed a two-year program in college and takes part-time courses. He has taken trips alone in Europe for periods of three to five weeks, presented at conferences, spoken to parent groups, and mentored boys who have AS.

Parenting is the most challenging job there is. How we handle the obstacles in our lives will influence how our children will handle their own. We must stay optimistic and continually remind ourselves of all we are grateful for in our lives. When we define our core values and live them with courage, determination, and perseverance, we build the confidence of our children and create a new definition of success.

CHAPTER 23

Searching for home in a foreign land: My discovery of Asperger Syndrome

Donna Moon

My journey towards self-discovery and my discovery of Asperger Syndrome (AS) has been a convoluted and unexpected one. It was a journey that was forced on me unwillingly – one that I had to take. My search for answers showed me that I wasn't as alone as I felt; that I was connected to my parents, my brother, and others. I saw how my mannerisms, interests, strengths, and weaknesses were related. Being able to put a name to my difficulties helped me see more clearly who I was and where I fit into the scheme of society. There are times that I would rather not know any of this, but I know that I am more empowered because of it. To know my strengths and weaknesses has given me a sense of purpose and the power to be able to direct my life in the way that I want it to go.

Early childhood

I began to know that I was different when I was four. Before that, I don't remember much of what my personal thoughts or reflections were. Nevertheless, on asking my parents about my infancy and early childhood I can recognize significant differences that suggest to me traits of AS.

My parents describe me as a quiet baby who hardly ever cried and was well behaved. My mom tells of being able to leave me with a baby-sitter and to return to find me sitting on the blanket in the same position she left me. I was also shy and quiet. At the preschool I attended, I was content to be by myself all day constructing structures out of building blocks. This behaviour didn't cause my parents much concern because, when compared with my brother, who had severe autism and was hyperactive, I couldn't have been more different. The main concern was my timidity, which was assumed would go away with time.

I grew up as an only child, with my older brother living in a group home. I had a good relationship with my dad and I enjoyed doing activities with him and learning new things. I was friends with some of the children in my neighbourhood and would spend many afternoons at their houses. These relationships were ones that my parents had made an effort to initiate, and they made sure I maintained them by encouraging me to visit my friends regularly and invite them over. I can remember feeling happy and content with my neighbourhood friendships. However, when new children arrived and started vying for the attention of my friends, I was unable to adjust and I began to feel left out.

My childhood friendships tended to be with people who were more passive than me and would go along with my ideas of what to do. This was perfect for me, and it wasn't until later (in middle school) that I discovered the activities that I liked doing were considered atypical, for my gender and for children in general.

I don't have any negative memories from primary school. I felt accepted within my group of friends, although I remember certain instances of being teased by outsiders. In particular, I can remember being teased for being "spacey" and for staring inappropriately. I often didn't understand jokes and I was gullible to tricks played on me by others. On my report cards, it was often mentioned that I spent too much time daydreaming, and that I needed to participate more. Socially, I tended to have one good friend I played with and I didn't reach out to others. Academically, I had problems with spelling new words, pronunciation of certain sounds, and handwriting. I had a good memory and found I could excel in these areas despite my initial difficulties. My favourite activities at school were creating, directing, and performing in plays. I also enjoyed writing stories and doing handicrafts.

Growing up as an only child, I had lots of time by myself. I developed an active imagination and I would create elaborate story lines, making my stuffed animals "come to life". I developed an intense attachment to stuffed animals and I wouldn't go anywhere without one. In my early childhood, my shyness, lack of social interactions, and overactive fantasy life didn't cause me grief or concern. I felt that since I was young my shyness was accepted, and my parents helped me by initiating social interactions and organizing activities.

With regard to my brother and autism, I didn't think much about either. I remember often feeling alone and desperately wanting another sibling to relate to. I would often fantasize about my brother miraculously becoming healed and coming home to live with us, or even coming home as he was: autistic. I didn't know much about autism, and at that time, no one seemed to know much. My family and I believed that my brother was of low intelligence, would never learn any skills, and didn't know who we were. This seemed a reasonable assumption to me, as his outward behaviour didn't show anything to the contrary. To me it was a bizarre disorder, a random occurrence that had nothing to do with my family, or with me.

Adolescence

Social interactions

During my early teens, I began to find making and maintaining relationships harder than before. I was at an age where I was expected to "get over my shyness". It was no longer socially acceptable to be shy. In addition, relationships and social interactions became more complex, and I discovered that most of my peers were no longer interested in doing the activities I wanted to do. My peers soon berated me for being too shy, too quiet, having nothing interesting to say, and being unaware of what everybody else was interested in. I was also taken advantage of since I was naïve and gullible.

Because of my quietness and passivity, I attracted people who were more dominant, outgoing, and aggressive than myself. Some of these friendships were good for me and others were bad. I usually found myself as somebody's best friend and part of a social group; however, I never felt I belonged. I hardly contributed to the conversation or initiated any activities. Instead, I preferred to follow along.

Over the years, I began to feel increasingly frustrated over my inability to make any meaningful relationships or connections with others. I had trouble engaging in simple social practices, such as carrying on a casual conversation with people, and I rarely felt a part of the group of girls with whom I associated. I often felt clueless, bored, or indifferent to what they were talking about, which usually included make-up, boys, fashion, TV shows, or music. Although I felt out of sync with my peers on all these topics, I tried hard to feign interest and to pretend to know what was going on. I also felt powerless to initiate and maintain any relationship with others apart from responding to their wishes and demands. Eventually I got tired of this charade and tired of trying to belong. I felt it was easier to socially isolate myself from everyone than to continue pretending to be what I wasn't.

During this time, I was also giving some serious thought to what exactly my social problems were. While I had always assumed they were the result of being shy and timid, I began to doubt whether this could explain everything. Since my peers were constantly asking me why I was quiet, I wanted answers. Other shy people I knew were still able to connect emotionally with others, showing affection and concern. Clearly, my shyness wasn't the sole cause of my social problems. Overcoming some of my timidity was one problem; however, overcoming my lack of emotion, affection, and understanding of social dynamics was something I was unsure how to do. To me, it seemed that these traits came naturally to others, and that somehow they weren't innate for me.

Running

Throughout my adolescence, while I felt left out on a social level, I was involved in other activities that gave me enjoyment and helped to boost my self-esteem. I had a curious mind, enjoyed my classes, and looked forward to learning new things. I found it easy to understand concepts and get good grades, which helped me to feel good about myself. My parents actively encouraged me to get involved and to reach out and socialize with my peers. In retrospect, I am appreciative of the effort they made.

During my early adolescence, I discovered that I had a talent for running. Soon I gained the respect of other runners and my peers for my running ability. I felt included as part of the running group at my school. I also enjoyed the social status that my achievements in running brought me. Classmates who normally wouldn't talk to me did, and even though I was still socially awkward, I felt my success in running gave me status and made up for my social deficiencies. In the following years, I became more involved in running until everything revolved around it. My social network, sense of belonging, and my self-esteem were all defined by running. Nothing else mattered to me. Through running, I was going to prove to others and myself that not only was I worthy as a person, but I was capable of success. I could ignore my loneliness and social rejection and focus on achieving success in something I was good at doing. Running was my self-esteem, my identity, and my purpose, and it gave me validity as a person. Without it, my social situation would have been overwhelming and, most likely, would have resulted in me being distressed at an earlier time in my life.

I never fully realized how much running meant to me or how much my identity was dependent on it, until the unthinkable happened: I was injured and had to miss a season of competitions. This seemingly minor occurrence caused me a lot of distress at the time. It is what started me on the path towards self-discovery.

Depression

The loss of my running success resulted in me becoming severely depressed and despondent. I believed God was punishing me for hubris and I began analysing everything that I considered wrong with me. With my achievements in running gone, I no longer had anything to give my self-esteem a boost. Long after my injury had healed, I was still battling depression. I had no motivation or energy to do anything. My marks suffered and I was not able to get back into running. I developed many bad habits that still haunt me to this day. I spent a lot of time trying to determine what my inner motivations were and why I behaved and thought the way I did. I became obsessed with knowing why I was different. Why were social interactions so hard for me? Why could I never think of anything to say, or carry on a simple conversation? Why was I nervous and anxious when meeting people? Why was I so quiet? Why was I always unaware of what the joke was about? Why did I find it hard to join in the conversation with a group of people or to approach someone I knew, and to start and maintain a conversation? No matter how hard I tried to be friendly and participate in group conversation, I always ended up left out, made fun of, and excluded. I didn't know why it was difficult for me to connect with others. All I knew was that social situations caused me stress and anxiety. I was also lonely and I felt that I had no true friend in whom I could confide.

During this period of self-reflection I learned why I behaved the way I did. I felt that I understood myself and my own reactions, motivations, and defences better. I understood what situations caused me anxiety and I tried to devise ways to overcome this. While I wasn't "cured" of my social awkwardness, at least I was able to recognize my motivations for certain behaviours and responses. I felt liberated by this knowledge and I made a concerted effort to confront and conquer my weaknesses, fears, and anxieties. However, these positive experiences were often overshadowed by times of depression and social isolation.

Autism

It was during this time of self-reflection that I started learning more about autism. I was given the book *Nobody Nowhere* written by Donna Williams, which is an autobiographical account of her experience with autism. As I read the book, I found that I could relate personally to many of the things that she said. While I found many of her reactions to situations more extreme than mine, it was her self-analysis and explanations of her behaviour and thoughts to which I could connect. Having previously spent time dissecting the motives and reasons behind my own behaviours, I was surprised and relieved to discover someone who had similar thought processes and responses. It was reading Donna William's book that first led me to believe that I had some form of autism.

This book also led me to view my brother with autism differently. Whereas at first I only saw a stranger, someone foreign to me in his behaviour and thinking, I now saw someone similar, someone to whom I could connect. The more time I spent with my brother and observed his behaviour, the more I realized how similar it was to my own. His fixations, obsessive behaviours, anxious responses to new situations, lack of eye contact, and discomfort with physical affection all seemed eerily similar to my own behaviour.

Around this time, I was also reading articles and books by Temple Grandin, another woman with autism. One issue that caught my attention was her discussion of autism as a continuum and being able to identify "autistic traits" in the extended family of an autistic person. She noted traits such as emotional aloofness, lack of physical affection, tendency towards detailed object-oriented occupations, anxiety and other mood disorders, learning disabilities, social awkwardness, and food sensitivities. Many of these traits were evident in my parents, my extended family, and me.

The excitement I felt over this "discovery" of autism is hard to describe. For me it meant that autism was no longer an unknown, a bizarre disorder that no one knew anything about. It meant that my brother was like the rest of our family and was not some anomaly that no one understood. I felt that this new insight I had into autism and my brother's behaviours meant that I would be better able to relate to him and to form some emotional connection. I was also excited by the possibility that my behaviours, perceptions, and social awkwardness were a part of something bigger than myself and could be related to autism and my whole family.

However, this news wasn't met with the same excitement when I shared it with my parents. They immediately became defensive and were insulted and shocked that I would suggest that they or members of our extended family had anything remotely related to autism. Autism and my brother were a taboo topic in my family, something to be ashamed of and not to be discussed. While their response was disappointing, it didn't alter my new-found beliefs about autism, my brother, and me. I was convinced there was a connection, and that my behaviours, responses, and perceptions were related to autism and the autism spectrum.

Nevertheless, to say that I had autism would seem absurd to most, if not all people, so I kept this thought to myself. It wasn't until a few years later, when I discovered AS, that I began to consider the possibility that I might have that, and I began to seek connections within the AS community.

Early adulthood

Discovery of Asperger Syndrome

I first learned of AS during my first year away at university. Uninterested in my school courses, I spent much of my time reading psychology books and looking for some insight into myself. It was while researching autism on the Internet that I came across AS for the first time. As I read about it there were parts I could relate to and others that seemed foreign. For the most part, I could relate to it. I felt relief that I could finally put a name to my social difficulties. I knew that my social problems were more than just shyness, but for a long time it was hard for me or anyone else to see this. Usually, people saw me as being quiet, reserved, and boring. I suppose some of my quietness was shyness, but I also knew some of it was because I felt what I had to say wasn't appropriate somehow or of any interest to others. The times when I felt most inadequate and uncomfortable were when I was expected to show some emotional response, yet I felt none and I didn't know what to do or say. I found other people's expression of emotion extremely hard and painful to deal with. It was this failure to connect with people on an emotional level which made me realize that my social problems were more than mere shyness.

The Asperger community

Once I had discovered AS, I was eager to find and connect with others with similar experiences. Initially, I was both excited and apprehensive about meeting others with AS. Finally, I would be with a group of people who understood me. I wouldn't have to worry about pretending to be normal and being socially acceptable. There was an opportunity to connect with others who had similar problems and stories to tell. I could find support and acceptance with these people. I was more interested in making individual connections with people and participating in discussion groups rather than in large group social outings.

I did have some positive experiences from the AS social group I joined. I had the opportunity to meet others with AS whom I would not have met otherwise. I felt I could relate to and form a connection with a few people. However, initiating and maintaining a relationship proved to be difficult since we were prone to depressed moods and were used to others taking the initiative.

I also began seeing a therapist who specialized in working with people with AS. Initially my goal for therapy was to express my thoughts regarding AS and its connection to my social difficulties. I was looking for some confirmation that I had AS and a practical plan about what to do next. I feel the largest benefit I gained from regular counselling sessions was the opportunity to express my thoughts, feelings, fears, and desires in an open and caring environment. I felt great relief in being able to share my inner thoughts with another human being whom I trusted. Just the act of communicating these thoughts aloud or on paper helped. Therapy also helped me to gain new insights about myself and explore areas of myself from new and different perspectives.

The army

While I was learning more about AS, I was also struggling with depression and trying to decide what I was going to do in my life. I began considering the army as a possible solution to both my social problems and my depression.

My time in an army training camp provided me with a structured setting where I knew exactly what was expected from me. I had grown up in a structured environment and I find that I tend to be less anxious and accomplish more if my schedule is highly structured. At the time I joined the army, my need for some structure in my life was strong. Because of my prolonged depressed moods I was unable, on my own, to enforce any structure in my life and I felt helpless as a result. The army provided a high level of structure that left no time for self-contemplation or reflection. The army also provided a structured social environment. This was something I craved. I found it easier to relate to others when there was a strict social protocol to follow. I was able to relate to my co-trainee, as a result of shared experiences and discussing practical tasks. I felt a part of the group as we were all going through the same struggle and were working towards the same goal. Over my two months of training, I had formed a bond with a small group of people that I felt accepted me.

This was truly a rare experience for me. I was sad when the training was over and everyone returned to his or her own cities. This illustrates an important point: that my best social relationships with others are when the relationship is based on a common activity that brings us together. Also, in the army environment I had to be a part of a group. Working with others was essential for survival and the only time alone I had was when we were allowed to sleep. Socially, the army helped me in many ways because it forced me to be social, to be assertive, and to take charge even when I didn't want to.

The present

University

Currently, I am studying biochemistry at university. After my bachelor's degree, I plan to go to graduate school with the long-term goal of doing research in the areas of autism and related disorders or mental illnesses. I am interested in looking at autism spectrum disorders and depression from a neurological and genetic perspective.

I had some apprehension about going back to university after being out of school for a while. I had doubts about whether I could still achieve academically as I once had. I worried the depression had permanently altered my brain in some way, and that perhaps my intellect had been altered. I also worried that I wouldn't be able to handle the pressure and stress of school and that I would drop out again.

Fortunately, I discovered that I still had the ability to learn. My moods have been kept relatively stable over the past few years with antidepressant medication. I still am prone to negative thoughts and depressed moods, but they are not as severe and disabling as when I wasn't on medication. I also know that I do not handle stress as well as I used to and I must be careful not to overwhelm myself academically, or socially.

Socializing and Spain

Social situations still cause stress and anxiety for me, and while in school I have been avoiding them. I have done this partly because I feel that attending classes and doing the required schoolwork takes all the mental energy I have to stay focussed, to not get discouraged, and to fight depression. For me, attempting to socialize and be friendly requires a lot of mental energy to both motivate myself and deal with the excess anxiety socializing causes. I am lucky to have a few understanding friends who know what I am like and don't misconstrue my lack of social initiative and contact as rejection.

I still spend a lot of time inside my head, thinking and imagining things. At times, the urge is so strong that it is hard to get me to be social and I'll turn down social engagements with friends, so I can spend time with my own thoughts. I seem to need this time and when I'm forced to be around people with constant interaction and no time for self-reflection, I start to feel really agitated and worn out.

Recently, I spent some time living in Spain. My main reason for going there was to experience the culture and to be involved with the people. The first time I visited Spain I was amazed at how much the people enjoyed each moment of the day and how they made relationships with others a priority. I was also pleasantly surprised at how they welcomed me, a foreigner who spoke no Spanish, and included me as a part of their group. I felt accepted, and surprisingly less anxious and more relaxed in their company. The language and cultural barrier masked my social awkwardness and I felt that many of my social *faux pas* were accepted, since I was a foreigner.

* * * *

Lately I haven't been involved with the AS community or my therapist. I also spend a lot of time alone. I don't find this situation depressing or hopeless. I feel that concentrating on schoolwork and achieving success in this area is important for my self-esteem, since it is something that I have failed at in the past.

Ultimately, though, I would like to have a more balanced life that includes being involved socially. I know that it is possible for me to make social connections and be more involved with others; it takes some effort and dedication on my part. I feel that my life experiences up to this point have shown me that this is possible, and that my future lies in my hands. While I feel I still have a long way to go, I realize that change takes time and recovering and rebuilding my life after living for years with depression and self-doubt is hard and sometimes painful. I am proud of the progress I have made and I am optimistic about my future.

CHAPTER 24

Asperger Syndrome: It's a family matter

Margot Nelles

I am the mother of two boys and a girl. My six-year-old son has been diagnosed with Asperger Syndrome (AS), and my 13-year-old-son with AS and Tourette Syndrome. This chapter will discuss our road to diagnosis for the boys, my family's reactions, and how parents and professionals can work together to create what we know to be the best way to support an individual with AS. My thanks go to the hundreds of families over the past four years to whom I have spoken in my role with the Aspergers Society of Ontario. The insight I have gained comes not only from my children, but also from these families. It is comforting to know that we are not alone in our quest to support our children with AS. My hope is that family members of a child with AS will relate to some of what I have to say, as I find that many family stories are surprisingly similar.

In the beginning

I first became concerned about Zack when he displayed several traits that were unlike those that my older child had experienced during her development. Zack was an odd kid in that he said only three words. Those were "juice", "milk", and "water". All these words were said in Spanish, even though we spoke Spanish at home very little at the time. One day, aged 18 months, he started speaking in sentences, whole phrases, and long descriptive narratives. Needless to say, this took us aback. I started to look at him carefully and noticed that he always seemed to be on the outside looking in on everyone else. He would "play" with his sister, just 18 months older, but always played the same role. He would ride his little bike in circles for hours if I let him, appearing to be in some unending spiral. Zack also obsessed over the vacuum cleaner, floor polisher, and leaf blower. He would take them apart and try to turn everything into one. He had a great desire for sameness and couldn't cope when day-to-day routines changed. Furthermore, he was very shy and didn't like people outside the family.

No one I talked to about my concerns took them seriously. They all said it was merely a matter of discipline. This was extremely frustrating and confusing for me, as there was an essence to Zack that I noticed, but no one else did. Most thought my concerns were related to the loss of my first child a few years earlier at the age of 13 months, and because I had just left a dysfunctional marriage. With time and, more importantly, I was told, with consistent discipline, the situation would improve. It seems odd to me that people saw there were difficulties, but couldn't explain it further than my parenting. My guilt around my so-called lack of parenting skills and coping abilities was enormous. I was sure that if I could just stick with the "Magic 123" program, or if I watched the instructional parenting videotape one more time, I would find the missing piece. That, in turn, would make me a "better parent" and solve the problem.

The gift of a diagnosis

When we finally received the diagnosis of AS, Zack had previously received the diagnoses of Gender Association Disorder, Oppositional Defiance Disorder, Anxiety Disorder, Attention Deficit Hyperactivity Disorder, Giftedness, and Attachment Disorder. When we were given the diagnosis of AS it was like a gift! I had finally found the reasons for so many things that I just could not figure out. There was a name for this and it came with some strategies for effective support. I was not "crazy", "neurotic", or "crisis-seeking".

The hard part was trying to define this new label to others, especially family members. It was particularly difficult to explain it when I told them that AS was related to autism. The public, on hearing the word "autism", conjures up all sorts of myths. However, I was so relieved that I just plugged away regardless of what others said. I felt like a load had been lifted off my shoulders. Now I could get on with finding the most effective ways of helping Zack to manage his challenges while fostering his innate gifts. This was not an easy task, but at least I had a road to travel on, with directional signs pointing the way.

My sons' reactions

One day Zack saw me reading Tony Attwood's book *Asperger's Syndrome* and said, "Is that what I have? Is that what is wrong with me?" I told him we thought that this was finally the answer. I tried to explain to him that it wasn't that anything was "wrong", just unique, and that now that we understood better, things would get easier. He pondered this for a while and said, "I always thought that I was a broken, rotten kid." I was shocked to hear this from an 8½-year-old! He told me that when he was young, he thought all boys were bad. Once he started school, he noticed that other boys did not act the way he did, and that other boys were going to Cubs and soccer. He was sent off to the clinic for more assessments, to see more doctors, and to go to more "stupid groups". He saw that other boys had friends and were invited to parties, and he was not. With these realizations, his self-doubt grew and led him to his heart-breaking conclusion.

Knowing that he wasn't responsible made him feel better. However, he still is often angry about it and asks, "Why me?" His realization that he sees and responds to situations differently, and that this will often get him into trouble, led to a depression and thoughts of suicide last year. He was 11 years old. So, while he embraces our acceptance of him and is thankful, I suppose, for the support offered, it is the rejection of the outside world that weighs heavily on him. This is something that we are still struggling with.

For my younger son, by the time he was diagnosed, we were heavily involved in the AS world. For him, AS is so natural to hear and talk about that he doesn't necessarily associate it with anything other than a way of explaining who he is and his unique ways of doing things. He is brilliant and at six years has a great deal of insight into the issue of acceptance. However, he is also painfully aware of the difference between himself and others. He once said to me that he didn't want to be "smart". Regular kids weren't smart and he wanted to be "regular". His therapist and I often talk about how hard it will be to nurture his intellect and help him to manage his many challenges, while encouraging him to be like any other child.

The family's response to the diagnosis

When one considers the reactions to a diagnosis, whether it is one of grief or acceptance, it is important to remember the process is different for every individual. I have found that, in my own family, each person has reacted differently and has come to accept the diagnosis at different times. My boys' fathers, for instance, have each had a different response. Since Zack's dad hasn't lived with Zack for the past 11 years, it has taken him some time to come to terms with the fact that his son has "differences". It seemed as though a diagnosis for Zack meant some deficiency on his part as a father. In the beginning, his mistrust of the medical profession only served to strengthen his disbelief of anything they had to say, and that led him to distance himself from what we were trying to do to help Zack. Over the years, and with reinforcement of what we as a family were doing for Zack, he has come to terms with Zack's diagnosis. He now can admit that Zack has special needs that are different from our daughter's and is willing to listen to my advice.

Isaac's dad, on the other hand, has had a different experience. He has been a part of our family for many years and was instrumental in my search for answers for Zack. When Zack was diagnosed, Charles helped me to jump full force into the world of AS and has been extremely supportive of my work in the Aspergers Society of Ontario. When our son Isaac was diagnosed we were already aware that he had many of the traits of AS, and pursuing a diagnosis was more of a formality than a search for an answer. I think for Charles there was a glimmer of hope that we were wrong about Isaac. He had seen Zack struggle for so many years that he couldn't imagine Isaac also having to go through those same struggles. I feel that he went through a grieving process after the confirmation of diagnosis and is only now accepting it as a reality.

We still find ourselves "on different pages" when it comes to understanding and supporting our children, but I think that is common for all families no matter the situation, and especially for mothers and fathers. My place as a mother, as far as the boys' fathers are concerned, is to organize appointments, help with school, pick up the pieces after a hard day, and keep the family working in a functional manner. This can be hard as there are not many resources left over to take care of myself and I can become resentful at what is expected of me, which of course leads to discord within my relationships. I think that this too is a common reaction in most families and one that I continue to work on.

For my daughter, it has also been a long road. She has had to take a back seat to her brothers' needs (no matter how hard I try not to have it this way) and she often feels overwhelmed and pushed aside. I do recognize that she has had to make many sacrifices along the way and that she is not yet emotionally mature enough to realize the "whys" involved in those sacrifices. I try to accommodate her and her needs in as many ways as I can. Although it can be hard sometimes, I try to make time to listen to her and help her to feel that she is part of the "team" and can play a role in helping her brothers with their difficulties. However, it can be hard for adults to see past the "typical appearances" of a child with AS to the root of the problem, let alone for a young teenage girl to do so. Generally, her response is to shut herself away in her room. This is a great concern for me, as I fear that because of her vulnerability she will be drawn to those who may claim to understand her and befriend her in a way that may not be suitable. Because of what may seem to her as a lack of fulfillment and acknowledgement from those at home, she may have a greater willingness to stray from those who really love and care for her. The teenage years are hard and emotions run wild at the best of times within any family. Having two siblings with disabilities makes that time more difficult. On the other hand, I feel that it is because of her emerging under-standing of her brothers that she has a compassion for human strife that surpasses that of most children her age. I know this compassion will only grow and serve her well in the future.

My mother has been an amazing participant in the whole process. It took her a while to recognize that the difficulties were not because of my inability to "consistently parent" my children, but due to a real and tangible set of characteristics that made "regular parenting" next to impossible. Once that realization came to her, she jumped in with both feet and is now in charge of the Aspergers Society of Ontario's parent psychoeducational support group. She is a strength that I draw on continually and I would be lost without her support.

As for my siblings and other extended family members, they have been supportive to a certain extent. They do care, but there is still a lack of understanding and acceptance among them. The research suggests that AS may be a genetic disorder. The fear of what that may mean to them and their children is, in my opinion, one of the main reasons they push away the notion that my boys have AS.

For me, genetics simply explains many issues that I had as a child and young adult (and still have) that I couldn't explain without thinking that I was "crazy" or "weird". Some are opposed to a genetic theory of AS since they think it shifts the blame back onto the parents again, when we are barely out of the Bettelheim days. I say, who is to blame for genetics? Would you blame yourself or resent your heritage if the genetics you passed on were the cause of some other medical issue? To me, there is no difference in one of my children getting my wavy hair, or my dislike of loud noises, or any other characteristic that I have. For some, the resistance to embracing the genetic theory and research about it is their fear that eventually families will be able to choose not to have a child that may have an autism spectrum disorder.

It is the general lack of understanding and fear of the word "autism" that is the real culprit for this resistance, not whether traits come from the mom's side of the family or the dad's. That being said, I think there needs to be a lot more research into the area of genetics before any conclusions can be drawn. The reason for that is not to erase AS from society, but, rather, to understand its origins better to provide the most effective support. It is a family matter and needs to be treated as such. I am hopeful that, with an increase in general awareness and acceptance, those who have a difficult time "buying into" the existence of AS will in turn realize that what we are doing to help our children is right.

Finding services

Shortly after Zack's diagnosis, I founded the Aspergers Society of Ontario because I could not find services specific to AS. Those that may have been able to provide something for children with AS, either had years-long waiting lists, or the program was not specific to AS. There needed to be a central place for families to go, somewhere that you did not have to spend the first hour-and-a-half trying to define what you were saying. My road to services was a road that I built with others who felt the same way, and I have been creating the services for my kids as I go along. In my experience, "treatment" has meant a combination of teaching social skills, theory of mind, emotional management skills, and medication.[1] These approaches, with my continued education and research into the best way to support my children with AS, have been key.

The problem with waiting on a list for services, or relying on any one service system to create and implement services, is there are not enough people who have the understanding and knowledge about AS to know that these kids critically need services. The answer is not just to create services, but also to do so with awareness. The bureaucracy involved with attaining services that may be covered by provincial health funding can be overwhelming; parents are burned out. Once families are at that point, their need for services grows to include mental health services for the parents and other family members. When my son was in a depression last year, I spent months looking for someone to help him. Anyone whom I asked either was not taking referrals or was not comfortable enough with AS to see him. I am a parent with connections for heaven's sake! Imagine the parent that does not know the way. It is not the AS that burns families out. For the most part, it is the systemic barriers to services and supports that cause the most stress for families. How can parents pay for the services needed, as most are not available through the public system, if one of them cannot go to work because of the daily calls from schools, the suspensions, and the child's avoidance of school? How many times can you say to an employer, regardless of his or her outward compassion, that you will not be in today? If the supports were readily available within our communities, including in the education system, parents would be able to create a program for their child that fosters success. The lack of under-standing and awareness in society about the nature of AS and how best to support a family member with AS eventually results in isolating the family further and exacerbating the difficulties experienced by the individual diagnosed with AS. We need to solve the problem from the other side, starting with raising awareness. We will *never* get the kinds of services that our children need until there is a general societal understanding and acceptance of AS.

---

1   I am not one who would advocate for medication alone or as a first course of action. However, if my children needed medication for some other medical reason and if that medication, together with a complete plan, would increase their quality of life, I would not hesitate to administer it.

Asperger strengths

What I admire most about my boys, especially Zack, is the courage, strength, and character that they have to keep going back out every day into what can often seem like a war zone; coming home, worn, tired, and stressed at having tried to keep it together for the day, and getting up the next day to do it again. What a load that is for someone of any age to have to carry. My sons' uniqueness and way of looking at things has altered my way of seeing the world. I look at this as their gift to me. To understand why a certain behaviour might be present, one has to understand the essence of AS. My children have given me that insight. I once had a discussion with a friend of mine and I was trying to make her see the "logical" point. Her words to me were "Margot, not *everyone* sees the world from outside the planet!" Well, thanks to my children, *I* do!

My advice to parents

When trying to access assessment and services, my advice to parents is: be the squeaky wheel! Never underestimate your ability to know your child better than anyone does. You know when you are watching your child and you see the difficulties that he or she is encountering. If only someone could put a video camera in your home for a few days. They would get it, wouldn't they? As a parent, you must believe in your instincts and pursue a diagnosis. For families seeking a diagnosis for an individual with AS, there are so many symptoms of AS that are also symptoms of other stand-alone disorders, that it can be hard to obtain a diagnosis that "fits" the whole child. A family may be seeing a clinician that specializes in one particular disorder (i.e. ADHD) and who may miss the more subtle symptoms of AS. If you do not feel like the light-bulb went on or if you don't think, "Ah, so that's it! This explains my child to a tee", perhaps it would be a good idea to keep asking questions and seeking answers until you do.

As I have said to many to whom I have spoken over the last four years, I could write the book on "proven strategies" that don't work with the particular set of difficulties associated with AS. It is only now that I am coming to realize that instinctively I was right. I go forward now with what I know to be the best way of supporting an individual with AS. I don't let the misinformation or lack of understanding of AS from others get in the way any more.

My advice to professionals

It is my feeling that it would be unlikely for a family to come to you, the professional, were there not a reason. Developmental or mental health professionals need to hear what parents are saying. Your role is much like the emergency room doctor when a mother brings her child in and says, "Look at his eyes. He is sick." Take what she says as the truth until otherwise proven, and work *with* the parent to get answers. If you, the clinician, feel that diagnosing a Pervasive Developmental Disorder makes sense, tell the family. They have been searching and need to know how to put into context what they already know, the better to support and understand their child. Clinicians also need to keep in mind the genetic factor. This is a "whole family affair". AS is not just about the individual child. It may be that Mom or Dad shares particular traits and/or difficulties. Giving an accurate and timely diagnosis can be a great stepping-stone for the whole family.

Those in positions to effect change also need to recognize that individuals with AS have real needs that cannot be met through the fractured services offered by one agency or another. We need to create a place where a family or individual can go for support and have a whole plan put in place for that support. This would not be limited to the individual, but open to all who are working at supporting someone with AS. With the increase in identification and diagnosis of AS, professionals need to be willing to learn all that they can. As it is now, just finding a professional who can diagnose AS is a challenge for the parents, never mind finding ongoing support and education. We need to be creating teams that work together in helping a family or individual. It is only then that the outcome will be a successful one.

CHAPTER 25

Life on the outside: A personal perspective of Asperger Syndrome

Chris J. Dakin

I am 33 years old, male, and diagnosed with Asperger Syndrome (AS).[1] I spend much of my life watching other people do things, while I am sitting on the sidelines. Sometimes I want to do what I see, sometimes I don't. Sometimes I don't understand what I see. It is like watching some strange species on National Geographic TV doing their mating dance. While watching "typical people", I have come to realize that how I see the world is not the same as most people see the world. I'll try to explain what "life on the outside" is like for me.

My philosophy

Autism is a different way of being, not an inferior way of being. As a person with AS see the same world, but in a profoundly different way. I have a tendency to "mono-focus". Typical people see a room as if all the lights are on. I see the room as if the lights are off and all you have to see with is a flashlight. You only see a small part of what is in the entire room, the part where the flashlight beam points. The room may have, for example, one piano and 45 desks, but if your flashlight is focussed on the piano, then that is all you can see. You don't see the 45 desks. So you think the room is full of pianos, and no desks. That is autism. I am not seeing different things, I just have a more intense focus on specific parts of the whole. I don't necessarily see things in context or perspective. Classic autistic "stimming"

---

1   I use the terms "Asperger Syndrome" (AS) and "autism" interchangeably as I view AS as a form of autism. "Neurotypical" refers to non-autistic people.

is the ultimate of this – being lost in the focussed world of objects or movement to the exclusion of everything else. People with AS may also do this, but to a degree that is less disconnected from the world.

If people understood and accepted AS, it would be a lot less disabling. The AS mind has its advantages. My AS strengths include: thinking outside the box, innovating, being persistent, having very good orientation to detail, not being swayed by peer or group pressure, and having a knack for original thought, the ability to work long hours, and a tenacity that can get me through difficult tasks that many would have abandoned. My sister says I am the hardest-working person she knows. She knows a lot of people!

Strengths or intelligence does not mean that people do not struggle or fall through the cracks. I believe I am a part of a "lost generation" of people with ASDs who grew up before AS was entered into the *Diagnostic and Statistical Manual*. We were never diagnosed, at least not officially or correctly. Bullies in school labelled us many things, like "loser" or "freak". We may have given ourselves negative labels like "worthless" or "unlovable" because of the constant put-downs from others. Lots of us are probably in the mental health system, criminal justice system, or living on the streets, or enduring some combination of all three. The people who try to help wonder why we fail to "get better" while we are treated for conditions and problems that we either don't have, or which are not our primary disorder. This is a population where anxiety and depression are more the norm than the exception. I hope this will change as young people today are getting diagnosed earlier and getting the supports and services they need to achieve better outcomes.

On this note, as you read my story, please remember that I was not diagnosed until I was 30 years old. I hope that kids today will not have to go through what I did. Also, when I speak about AS, I speak about my own experiences. My own experiences are exactly that: my own. They may apply to other people with autism, but they may not.

My history

As far back as I can remember I have always known I was different. My mother says that my "play patterns were always a little different" and I "seemed to do my own thing more than most". I was taken to a psychologist in preschool because of concerns about my inability to play with others. The psychologist said I was "bright but a little different". As I grew older, my younger sister learned to do many things before me, like whistling, roller-skating, or setting the table correctly. She has often said in many ways she felt like an older sister. In school, I had some academic difficulties and many social problems. I always knew something was wrong, but no one had a name for it. So I believed what other people said: "just not trying", "attitude problem", "not living up to potential", and "brings the bullying on himself". The bullying and constant struggles to do things other people found easy led to chronic depression and low self-esteem. This led to alcohol abuse, which eventually led to drugs, trouble with the law, and suicide attempts.

If it were not for my family, who never stopped loving me, never gave up on me, and never stopped being supportive, I probably would not be here. Plus, there were a few professionals who could see "human being" or "somebody's son" through the labels and stigma of "brought in by police", "heroin overdose" or "mental health issues", and cared enough to get me the help I needed. I am grateful to all of those who were there for me.

At age 28, I was sent for a full neuropsychological examination, which was fascinating for my family and me to read. On the *WISC III* IQ test, I had scores on sub-tests ranging from the first to the 95th percentiles. This psychologist raised AS as a possible diagnosis; something I had never heard of. Shortly after that, I received a formal diagnosis from a psychiatrist who has worked extensively with people on the spectrum. Getting the diagnosis was like someone finally handing me the manual to a difficult appliance I had been trying to fix for years, without success. Having a label did not make the problems go away, but it did help with the self-judgement that has been so devastating in my life. Now I could replace words like "freak" and "weirdo" with "Asperger Syndrome".

Dogs and other interests

Dogs have been a significant part of my life since I was in high school. I spent a lot of time outdoors with dogs. I remember thinking how people ruled the world and functioned better during the day in the city, but in the wilderness or at night my dogs and I were the ones who ruled the world. Someone once said to me, "Don't you feel unsafe being the only one in a remote park at night?" I remember thinking how it was just the opposite for me. People scared me and it was their world I did not understand and feared, not the night or the wilderness.

Understanding people has always been hard for me. A big reason why I like dogs and why I am good with them is that their nonverbal communication is easy for me to read. Dogs don't have the hidden motives that most neurotypical people have. If they are affectionate, it is because they want to be, not because they think they may get a walk later. If they want something, they do not try to disguise it as something else. I feel safe with dogs, something I don't feel with most people. Dogs are based in a world of clear, visible, and direct communication. What you see is what you get. I wish people were more like that.

I also like dogs because I can touch dogs and not get anxious in the way that I do when I touch people. I read about a parent wondering why her autistic child would hug the dog but not her. The answer, suggested by another person with autism, was that dogs don't touch back. This makes a lot of sense to me. I want to touch people I know and care about, but there is touch my body cannot handle receiving.

My house is decorated with a dog theme. One of my special interests that I have had since my early 20s is collecting things from the Disney movie *101 Dalmatians*. I have several hundred items featuring the movie characters. It cannot just be anything from *101 Dalmatians* though; it has to be the original style of animation from the original movie. I am not certain why I like *101 Dalmatians* so much. Perhaps it is partly because I like dogs and partly because the story is simple and the way I wish the world was. The bad characters are clearly bad; the good characters are clearly good. In the end, good wins over bad, and everybody lives happily ever after. Perhaps, on some childlike level, I wish the world was like this and that my life was like this.

Appropriate behaviour

I don't buy into the belief that the interests of people with developmental disabilities must be age appropriate. If someone enjoys something that is typically enjoyed by younger people, but he enjoys it in places or ways that don't make him stand out or get him teased, let him do it. I think there is too much emphasis put on what is age appropriate, on eliminating stims, and other things that bring comfort to some of us on the autism spectrum. There is too much focus on eliminating abnormal behaviour simply because it is abnormal, when it may not be harmful and may serve a purpose or bring pleasure to the person exhibiting it. As a person with AS I tend to find the everyday actions required by the human world draining, so downtime is important. Self-calming behaviours, stimming, and special interests are often needed for recharging the batteries.

As a kid with AS, I was not happy and my self-esteem was not great. Some of this came from frequent, negative comments from my parents, teachers, and other adults in my life. I can now see in hindsight that their intent was to be helpful, as feedback is necessary for kids with AS. Children with AS need to know how to deal with the world, do not know this intuitively, and may not "pick it up along the way". However, teaching appropriate behaviour needs to occur with the least possible harm to self-esteem.

I remember being told as a child "do not be rude". That phrase meant nothing to me. I probably did not know what I did that was rude and, even if I did, the whole idea of not doing something just because it was "rude" was based on the social understanding I lacked. What I needed was to be told clearly what the problem was, how it hurt people, and what I could do instead. For example, when I was a child, I remember telling someone blocking my path, with no smile on my face, to "move". It made sense to me, as that is what I wanted him to do. Telling me "do not be rude" did not tell me what I did wrong, nor did it tell me what to do instead. It just made me feel "bad" and angry. I needed to be told: "When people are in your way and you want them to move, they don't feel good if you just tell them what you need. It would make them happy and they would be more likely to do what you want if you used their names and said please." I would have been more likely to hear the suggestion, and actually to consider doing it!

I wish more people would acknowledge the underlying good intent that people with AS usually have. I often still do things that offend or hurt others, or are seen as rude, when I have every intent to "do good" or at least not do any harm. It is hard to be criticized when all someone sees is the harm I caused, without seeing my good intentions. I wish they would ask some exploratory questions like, "I am wondering what led you to say or do that?" Then they would realize that I at least had good intent and did something that made sense to me, but that because of lack of social knowledge it just came across the wrong way.

Relationships

Relationships have always been hard for me and social isolation has been a constant struggle throughout my adult life. I often open my agenda book for the next few months and see there is nothing other than appointments with people who are paid to spend time with me. The AS makes it hard for me to make the connections where many people find much of the meaning and joy in their lives. My family is great but they have their own busy lives and live in another city. I live on an island and I don't own a car, so we don't see one another much, no matter how much we may care.

All my long-term friends are outsiders in some way; they have a disability themselves or live with family who does, or are gay or lesbian, or are from some other socially marginalized group. I did not try to make it that way, but these people understand me and I can relate to them. My friends are of great importance to me and I am appreciative of their support. All my friends fit this pattern, as they are the people open to knowing someone like me.

I like time to prepare mentally before interacting with people. Even relating to friends can be stressful. My answering machine says: "Please leave a message. I may pick up if I am here." People who know me know I will pick up when I hear who it is, if I am able to deal with a call. It is better for me and the caller that way.

That way I am not overly harsh with people calling because I have not had time emotionally and mentally to get ready to take the call.

Employment and university

Right now, I am on long-term disability benefits but when I did have a paid job, I worked in group homes with people with disabilities. This was one area of human interaction in which I found success. While many staff found the clients (the people who lived in the home) hard to deal with, I found the staff hard to deal with and the clients easy. I felt safe with the clients and they liked me. I did this work for over ten years and have never been able to hold any other type of job long term. Perhaps one reason I was successful working in group homes with people with disabilities was that things that may have been an issue at other places were not an issue there. Most of the people who work in the field are tolerant of people who are different or they would not work there.

Working in group homes was a good fit for me in many ways but I did not find that work environment right away. I had a few years of "job of the month". People who knew me in my early 20s used to ask, "What job are you doing this month?" I had no problem getting jobs, as I am good intellectually and verbally. I was less than successful at keeping them as I kept violating unwritten social rules that I just did not understand. I have had jobs in so many fields that I joke I could pick a job out of the paper blindfolded and still claim some related experience. (References were another story.)

I have a bachelor's degree in social work. University can be an ideal environment for people with AS but not all people on the spectrum can handle the non-academic demands that come as part of the package. When I went to college, and later university, the hardest part for me was not the reading, writing reports or understanding the ideas, but executive functioning tasks such as getting to class on time, arriving there with what I needed, or not losing my belongings.

Not everyone with AS thrives at university. Parents want to believe the best is possible for their children, but this can lead to unrealistic expectations. It is important to focus on strengths but it is also important to see people for who they are, as opposed to who you wish they were.

Finding supports

Life can be a struggle for adults with AS. I have often felt in danger of being too capable for intellectually disabled services but too disabled to compete successfully in the real world, and getting left on the sidelines with nothing. My own life experience and the shared experiences of other adults with AS on the Internet suggest that there are many of us who have university or college degrees but who still have a hard time finding and keeping jobs. Many people have difficulty understanding how someone who seems so intelligent can have so many problems in other areas. A significant number of adults with AS struggle with chronic unemployment and poverty, which only makes living with the disability harder still. Adequate income for those who cannot work (or cannot work consistently) is an issue that needs to be addressed. The constant threat of having my disability income cut off, while knowing my ability to compete successfully in the mainstream workforce is limited, is an ongoing source of stress in my life.

There are not many support services available from autism societies for AS adults. The boards of directors of local autism societies tend to be dominated by parents and professionals and rarely, if ever, include significant numbers of individuals with autism. This leads to the focus of these agencies being primarily on the needs of parents and children. There is nothing intrinsically wrong with this, but the needs of adults may be ignored, as nobody is there to speak on their behalf. Parents need to remember that their children will grow up to become adults. Once you are out of the school system, unless you cannot cope with the most basic activities of life and need to go into a group home, there is no support in most areas. If you were from another planet and went to a meeting of a local autism society, you would think that death at the age of 18 was a side effect of autism as you might hear a lot of talk about kids and services for them and nothing about people over 18. I hope this is slowly changing. Thanks mainly to the Internet, adults with autism are becoming more organized and politicized. A developing autism culture celebrates diversity and emphasizes our strengths, rather than the "victim of autism" mentality. As we become stronger within ourselves and as a group, we will be more able to fight for representation on boards of directors of local autism societies and for services that meet the needs of adults.

Stresses of everyday life

I am still left dealing with everyday life, which translates into a large amount of stress. Once, I lost my car on the street and I got so desperate, I called a cab to help me find it. I gave up after about half an hour in the cab, walked again for a few hours, and then hailed another cab. It was the same guy again. I bet he wondered, "Where did that one escape from?" I still could not find the car and eventually I gave up and reported it stolen to the police. Close to a week later, I passed a car while on my bike and thought "that looks like my car and look at all the parking tickets on it!" Well it was my car! I went to city hall and gave them the police file number for the theft report (without mentioning that it never was stolen) and they let me off the tickets. I then forgot to go to the police and tell them I found it so I was driving around in a car for over a week that was still listed as stolen!

Keys are another struggle for me. Once, I slept through my alarm for the night shift at the group home and was rushing out to my car when I realized I could not get into my car. I had forgotten my car keys in the house. No problem, I had a spare under the car. So I went to work and did my shift then I came home in the morning, went around back to where I hide my spare house key and it was not there. I must have forgotten to put it back last time I used it! Knowing I would have to call a locksmith, I thought I might as well wait until after 9 a.m. so it would cost the regular rate. I went to a local thrift store and went shopping for 40 minutes. When I was done I put some stuff in the trunk and slammed it with a bang, only to realize that I just locked my car keys in the trunk! So, I now had my regular and emergency house keys and my regular car keys locked in the house and my emergency car key locked in the car so I was locked out of both my car and my house! Arrrggghhh!

When I am anxious, my functioning deteriorates significantly, which does not help. What is even more disabling, is that nobody can see the disability. Most people today do not look at someone in a wheelchair and think: "You could walk if you wanted to – if you just tried hard enough." But, as somebody with AS, I get this all the time. People assume that *my* behaviours are within *my* control, because for them that behaviour would be within *their* control.

I was thrilled to hear there is an agency in Ontario (National Service Dogs) that places dogs with children who have ASDs. If a blind person bumped into you, you would notice the white cane or guide dog and think, "Oh she is blind" and not "Oh how rude!" As people with AS generally look outwardly normal and do not have the equivalent of the white cane, we get "Oh how rude!" when we do things because of our AS. If I do not recognize someone because I do not recognize faces, people think I just don't care or I am a snob when this is anything but the case. I wish I could have a service dog or some other way people could know I have a disability so they would perhaps give my behaviour more thought before leaping so quickly to judgement and rejection.

Medication and self-medicating

I was not on meds as a kid as nobody knew about AS then. Either you were "retarded" and they put you in an institution for life or you were "normal" and you got no help. In school, the bullying was constant and nasty. I started to self-medicate with alcohol around Grade 5. My self-medicating continued as an adult with injection drugs (mostly heroin). I have had lengthy hospital stays from drug overdoses and the resulting complications. Suicide attempts have led to some psychiatric ward and hospital stays.

I have been off the drugs for a few years. Alcohol is still a problem if I use it but at least it does not get me hospitalized. I now am on various prescribed meds that help me cope with the world. My point here is not that meds are risk-free or the best solution, but that neither were the other ways I dealt with difficult feelings. If we lived in a just world, schools and police would protect vulnerable individuals. However, we don't live in a just world, and people (kids and adults) prey on the different. That often leads to anxiety and depression that, if not dealt with, can lead to suicide attempts or other serious problems. It is great to say the world just should be more tolerant of difference and the schools should deal with bullies. None of that helps the kid who hates himself because he has no friends and does not understand why people are so mean to him when he does nothing to them.

Spotting abusers

Kids with AS need to be taught about the bad things some people do and how to spot these things. The combination of low self-esteem and social naïveté often found in young people with AS leaves them vulnerable to bullies and predators. Many people tell children with AS that most people are good because that is what they experience or that is what they want to believe. My experience is that most people are uncomfortable around difference and avoid those who are different, and that those who do take an interest (and do not have a professional or family connection) are often predators. What others seem to "just know" I often miss completely. People with AS are predator magnets in my opinion. The predators see our vulnerability and seek us out. Children with AS need to be told that, if in doubt, they should check with a trusted adult. Parents need to tell kids how people really are as opposed to how they wish people were. Otherwise we are left swimming in the shark pond while thinking it is the pool at the YMCA.

I have been used and abused several times by people who I thought were my friends. There was the person who I thought was my friend because he helpfully suggested I lock my wallet in the trunk of my car since we were in a bad part of town. While I hung out with him, his girlfriend took my keys from my coat, went back, and got my wallet, and then they cleaned out a large amount of money from my bank account. He seemed nice. The suggestion made sense. I didn't notice anything wrong.

Then there was the woman with whom I had been friends for a number of months. She waited until I was in hospital from a suicide attempt to go to my house and get my wallet, and headed off to go shopping. When she hit close to

4000 dollars on my credit card, her spending was so unlike my spending, that the credit card company computer alerted them, and she was cut off. I thought she was a good friend because she did not drink excessively nor do drugs and she came from a nice family. Everything seemed fine until this happened.

In conclusion

It is easy to get lost in the struggles and to forget about my strengths. I have had two good long-term relationships – with dogs of course! I have a gift with dogs. Perhaps the brain cells that were supposed to be devoted to understanding the human species were instead given over to understanding the canine species.

Another area of strength is my ability to visualize things, which helps with building and fixing things. I am currently restoring a turn-of-the-century heritage home. Autistic attention to detail translates into slow work but excellent results. When finished, I will have accomplished a job that rivals those done by the local heritage society.

It is my hope that with early identification and intervention there will be more opportunities to prevent bullying and provide appropriate supports to kids and adults with AS. I hope that services have a primary focus on strengths as opposed to solely getting rid of difference. My life has been lived for the most part on the outside. I hope that as society becomes more tolerant of diversity there will be more help for those with AS to find a place where they fit and their contributions are valued. I hope that in my own way, I can be part of making that happen.

Afterword

This collection of papers brings together various perspectives that might initially appear disparate in their views. Nevertheless, my hope is that the reader will also recognize the themes and issues that run throughout this book. Regardless of the "confusions and controversies" (Frith 2003) about AS, we have been able to generate an initial foundation of practice knowledge. It is exciting, and at the same time disconcerting, to realize that this knowledge base is not static. This volume has provided a survey of the current state of practice and research related to AS. First-hand accounts of ASDs have provided, and continue to provide, valuable instruction for the practitioner and researcher. It is hoped that this book will be a catalyst for similar future discussions.

Considering our preoccupation with defining a discrete set of symptoms that characterize "Asperger Syndrome", we find our attempts are often problematic. Ultimately, a true understanding of AS must reach beyond the controversies about diagnosis, and beyond available research. The breadth of human personality, emotion, cognitive characteristics, social relating, sensory processing – in a word, "neurodiversity" (Harmon 2004) – cannot be simply captured, as Peter Jansen has stated, "in a static, inert framing of words". This is not to say there is no utility in such a label; its worth is clear in this volume. However, realization must also occur as to the limits of this enterprise.

In any discussion of a "social disability" we cannot help take note of the various contexts in which such difference is most apparent – in families, schools, workplaces, and the community. The presentation of symptoms related to AS is often dependent on the individual's surroundings. Any consideration of supporting individuals with AS therefore needs to be contextually based.

Many parents I have worked with embrace all the traits of their children with AS, including those related to AS. There is much about individuals with AS to enjoy, not the least of which is their strong appreciation for human diversity. As "neurotypical" as I profess to be, I am always strangely comforted when somebody with AS boasts about their knowledge of a particular subject, their narrow range of interests, or their ability to function without so much human approval. There is always something refreshing about this excitement, and their insights. Luke Jackson (2002), an adolescent with AS insists: "Remember different is cool!" – a refreshing message indeed!

So, what is our role as professionals? I often think of our professional role as analogous to that of a *cultural mediator*. Such an individual, guided by an acute social awareness, is appreciative of diverse peoples. He is versed in the language and traditions of cultures, and, learning about each in the process, facilitates dialogue between them. We mediate when we help an adolescent with AS address the bullying they are subject to at school, when we interpret the behaviour of a young adult with AS, or when we explain the behaviour of a child as relating to sensory sensitivities. The requirement to "adapt" cannot be left to the child, youth, or adult with AS. Our professional undertakings must involve the promotion of systemic change. Supporting and understanding individuals with AS, grounded in our emerging practice knowledge and our appreciation of individual difference, is a complex but satisfying endeavour, and, I would suggest, results in the most lasting outcome.

References

Frith, U. (2004) Emanuel Miller lecture: Confusions and controversies about Asperger syndrome. *Journal of Child Psychology and Psychiatry, 45,* 4, 672–686.

Harmon, A. (May 9 2004). The disability movement turns to brains. *The New York Times, 4,* 1.

Jackson, L. (2002) *Freaks, Geeks and Asperger Syndrome: A User Guide to Adolescence.* London: Jessica Kingsley Publishers.

Contributing authors

Paula Aquilla BSc (OT), Reg (Ont)
Paula Aquilla is an occupational therapist who works with adults and children in clinical, educational, community, and home-based settings in Toronto, Ontario. She has a special interest in sensory integration and is a co-author of *Building Bridges through Sensory Integration*.

Lillian Burke PhD CPsych
Dr Lillian Burke is a psychologist who works in private practice and as a consultant with Regional Support Associates in Ontario. She works with individuals who have ASDs and/or intellectual disabilities, their families, and other care providers, providing assessment, therapy, and consultation. In addition to clinical work, she has carried out research and presented on persons with ASDs.

Chris J. Dakin
Chris Dakin was diagnosed with Asperger Syndrome in his early 30s. He is a participant in the online autism community and has spoken at conferences in Ontario and British Columbia. He has a degree in social work and has worked for over ten years in group homes with people with disabilities. He lives in Victoria, BC and is restoring a turn-of-the-century heritage house.

Trina Epstein PsyD CPsych
Dr Trina Epstein is a clinical psychologist in the Tourette Syndrome Neurodevelopmental Clinic at the Toronto Western Hospital. She provides clinical care for children and adolescents and is involved in research endeavours exploring the comorbidity of Asperger Syndrome and Tourette Syndrome.

Ann Fudge Schormans MSW PhD (Cand) RSW
Ann Fudge Schormans is completing her PHD in social work at the University of Toronto. She has been a practising social worker in the community living and the child welfare sectors. Her research focus is children and young adults with developmental disabilities in child welfare services. She is the Project Co-ordinator for The Children's Quality of Life Project, University of Toronto.

Gail Hawkins
Gail Hawkins is the Founding Executive Director of Mission Possible, an employment service for people with Asperger Syndrome in Toronto, Ontario. She developed an innovative model of teaching vocational skills and has over 15 years' experience in the field of employment counselling for people with ASDs. She is the author of *How to Find Work that Works for People with Asperger Syndrome*, also published by Jessica Kingsley Publishers.

Isabelle Hénault PhD
Dr Isabelle Hénault is a sex therapist and psychologist from the University of Quebec at Montreal, Canada. Her practice and studies have focussed on the education and support of adolescents, adults, and couples with autism and Asperger Syndrome. She offers therapy to couples that aims at elaborating communication strategies and increasing intimacy, and has developed a sex education program.

Jeanette J.A. Holden PhD FCCMG
Dr Jeanette Holden is a professor in the Departments of Psychiatry and Physiology at Queen's University in Kingston, Ontario, and Director of the Cytogenetics and DNA Research Laboratory at Ongwanada. Her research focus is the genetics of ASDs, and she is Program Director for Autism Spectrum Disorders Canadian–American Research Consortium (ASD-CARC) funded by CIHR.

Peter Jansen
Peter Jansen is 25 years old and was diagnosed with Asperger Syndrome at the age of ten. He works part time and attends community college in Toronto. He has spoken at conferences and workshops on Asperger Syndrome in Ontario. He is an avid reader and creative writer and lives in Brampton, Ontario.

Tamarah Kagan-Kushnir MD FRCP(C)
Dr Tamarah Kagan-Kushnir is a developmental paediatrician at Bloorview MacMillan Children's Centre and provides clinical care to children with a range of developmental needs including ASDs. She is currently completing a PHD in clinical epidemiology and is developing a new outcome measure for autism research. Her other research interests include seizures and GI dysfunction in the context of ASDs.

M. Mary Konstantareas PhD CPsych
Dr Mary Konstantareas has been a professor of psychology at the University of Guelph since 1991, and professor of psychiatry since 1988 at the University of Toronto. She worked at the Clarke Institute of Psychiatry from 1974 to 1993 serving as the Head of the Autism Clinic and the Director of Research of the Child and Family Studies Centre. She has published extensively in the field of ASDs.

Jonathan Leef
Jonathan Leef is a graduate student in the Department of Human Development and Applied Psychology at the University of Toronto. He has planned, facilitated, and collected data on the child and adolescent social interaction groups for the Aspergers Society of Ontario in co-operation with the Centre for Addiction and Mental Health since 2000.

HeeSun Lim
Hee Sun Lim is an undergraduate student in the Faculty of Arts and Sciences at the University of Toronto, completing a double major in human biology and psychology. She is planning to pursue a Master's degree in occupational therapy. She is Research Associate with The Children's Quality of Life Project at the University of Toronto.

Tracie Lindblad MSc MEd
Tracie Lindblad is a speech-language pathologist with extensive experience in the assessment, design, and implementation of strategies to address the communication, social skills, and curriculum difficulties of children with ASDs. She is Co-founder and Executive Director of the Child Development Centre of Oakville, and has presented in Canada and the US.

Xudong Liu PhD
Dr Xudong Liu is a molecular geneticist at Queen's University in Kingston, Ontario. He is a senior research associate with Dr Jeanette Holden working on the genetics of autism spectrum disorders. He is also the research manager of the Cytogenetics and DNA Research Laboratory at Ongwanada. His research focus is the identification of genes involved in the development of ASDs through genetic epidemiological and statistical genetics approaches.

Faye Mishna MSW PhD RSW

Dr Faye Mishna is an associate professor of social work at the University of Toronto. She has been a practising social worker in children's mental health for 25 years. Her program of research includes investigating bullying and group work with children and adolescents with learning disabilities. She is a faculty member of the Toronto Child Psychoanalytic Program.

Donna Moon

Donna Moon is currently residing in Toronto where she is studying for a degree in biochemistry at York University, Ontario. She was diagnosed with Asperger Syndrome in her early 20s. She has an interest in the genetics of autism and Asperger Syndrome and has an older brother with autism.

Barbara Muskat MSW PhD (Cand) RSW

Barbara Muskat has been a social worker for over 25 years. She works at Integra, a children's mental health centre in Toronto specializing in learning disabilities. She has worked as a family therapist and is currently Integra's Director of Community Education and Outreach. She is a doctoral student in social work at University of Toronto and is on the Board of the Aspergers Society of Ontario.

Margot Nelles

Margot Nelles is the mother of two school-aged boys with Asperger Syndrome and a teenage daughter. She is the Founding Director of the Aspergers Society of Ontario. She has co-ordinated groups for children and adults with Asperger Syndrome, consulted to families and schools, and responded to requests for information from families and professionals since the founding of the society in 2000.

Fern Lee Quint RN BA

Fern Lee Quint is the single mother of two sons aged 26 and 23. Her older son was diagnosed with Asperger Syndrome at the age of 15. She has been a registered nurse for over 30 years and currently works in a general hospital in Toronto as a psychiatric crisis nurse. She has presented workshops on Asperger Syndrome and has led groups for parents of children and adults with ASDs.

Georgina Rayner BSc BEd

Georgina Rayner is a parent advocate for special learners and instructor at Centennial College, Ontario. She is the Past President of Learning Disabilities Association of Toronto and the former Chair of the Special Education Advisory Committee for the Toronto Board of Education. She is co-author of *The Advocate's Journal, An Interactive Profiling Diary*, and was co-instructor of a course in advocacy at Humber College in Toronto.

Rebecca Renwick PhD

Dr Rebecca Renwick is Director of the Quality of Life Research Unit at the University of Toronto where she is an associate professor in the Graduate Department of Rehabilitation Science and the Department of Occupational Therapy. She is the principal investigator of The Children's Quality of Life Project, a research program on quality of life for children with developmental disabilities.

S. Wendy Roberts MD

Dr Wendy Roberts is a developmental paediatrician, Associate Professor of Paediatrics at the University of Toronto, Director of the Child Development Centre and Co-director of the Autism Research Unit at the Hospital for Sick Children in Toronto. Research and clinical training for all levels of health personnel are provided in the Child Development Centre under her direction.

Renée Ryan BMus BMus Ed

Renée Ryan is completing her MSC in occupational therapy at the Faculty of Medicine, University of Toronto. She is a research associate with The Children's Quality of Life Project, University of Toronto. Her research includes the use of music as an extension of OT for persons with dementia.

Jennifer Saltzman-Benaiah PhD CPsych

Dr Jennifer Saltzman-Benaiah is a clinical neuropsychologist in the Tourette Syndrome Neurodevelopmental Clinic at the Toronto Western Hospital. She provides clinical care for children and adolescents and is involved in research endeavours exploring the comorbidity of Asperger Syndrome and Tourette Syndrome.

Rosina G. Schnurr PhD FACLP (ABPP)

Dr Rosina Schnurr is a clinical psychologist in private practice in Ottawa, Canada, is on the staff of Children's Hospital of Eastern Ontario, and is a clinical assistant professor at the University of Ottawa. She has worked with children for over 30 years and is the author of the book *Asperger's Huh? A Child's Perspective*.

Leon Sloman MRCS LRCP FRCP(C)

Dr Leon Sloman is Honorary Consultant in Psychiatry, Centre for Addiction and Mental Health and Associate Professor, Department of Psychiatry, University of Toronto. He has published extensively in books and journals and co-edited the book *Subordination and Defeat: An Evolutionary Approach to Mood Disorders and their Therapy* (2000). He is Head of a clinic for children with ASDs at the Centre for Addiction and Mental Health.

Shirley Sutton BSc OT OT Reg (Ont)

Shirley Sutton is an occupational therapist with 25 years' experience working with children and young adults with special needs. Her experience ranges from running a clinical private practice to consulting with community agencies to working for the Early Intervention System in Ontario. She is the co-author of *Building Bridges through Sensory Integration*.

Kevin P. Stoddart

Kevin P. Stoddart has worked with people affected by Autism Spectrum Disorders (ASDs), mental health issues and developmental disabilities for over 25 years. For the last 15 years, people with mild ASDs and Asperger Syndrome have been his clinical focus. He received his PhD in Social Work from the University of Toronto. He has carried out research and published on ASDs and other developmental disabilities, focusing on understanding the clinical needs of affected individuals and their families. He is Director of Clinical and Professional Services of the Aspergers Society of Ontario, and is a Consultant in Private Practice in Toronto.

Peter Szatmari MD FRCP(C)

Dr Peter Szatmari is Professor and Vice-chair of Research, Head of the Division of Child Psychiatry, and holder of the Chedoke Health Chair in Child Psychiatry in the Department of Psychiatry and Behavioural Neurosciences, the Offord Centre for Child Studies at McMaster University, Ontario and Hamilton Health Sciences. His research interests include early intervention, the genetics of ASDs, and anxiety and mood disorders in ASDs.

Charmaine C. Williams MSW PhD RSW

Dr Charmaine Williams is an assistant professor at the University of Toronto, Faculty of Social Work, and is the Race Relations and Anti-racism Initiatives Officer, University of Toronto. She has worked in the area of mental health for the past ten years with children, adults, family, and group practice in inpatient and outpatient services. Her practice, research, teaching, and publications address clinical practice, mental illness, diversity, anti-racism, and access to services.

Ellen Yack MEd BSc OT

Ellen Yack has practised as an occupational therapist since 1979. She is the Director of Ellen Yack and Associates Paediatric Occupational Therapy Services and is Consultant to Geneva Centre for Autism. Her expertise includes sensory integration, ASDs, developmental co-ordination disorder, and learning disabilities. She is a co-author of the book *Building Bridges through Sensory Integration*.

Subject Index